W9-BUV-994

BOOKS BY ALEXIS BESPALOFF

The Fireside Book of Wine
Alexis Bespaloff's Guide to Inexpensive Wines
The Signet Book of Wine

The Fireside Book

EDITED BY
Alexis Bespaloff

SIMON AND SCHUSTER | NEW YORK

# of Wine

AN ANTHOLOGY
FOR
WINE DRINKERS

Library of Congress Cataloging in Publication Data

Main entry under title:

The Fireside book of wine

1. Wine—Literary collections. I. Bespaloff, Alexis.
PN6071.W57F5   808.8'0355   77-22497
ISBN 0-671-22466-2

Acknowledgment is made to the following for permission to use material owned by them. Every reasonable effort has been made to clear the use of the material in this volume with copyright owners. If notified of any omissions, the editor and publisher will gladly make the proper corrections in future editions.

The New Yorker: from "A Dreamer of Wine" by Joseph Wechsberg, a Profile of Alexis Lichine in *The New Yorker*. Copyright © 1958 The New Yorker Magazine, Inc. Reprinted by permission.

Pages 435–439 constitute an extension of this copyright page.

My thanks, first, to William Cole for sharing his anthological expertise with me. Benjamin Sonnenberg, Jr., suggested a number of unusual references to wine when I first began this book, as did Michael Train. Cyril Ray, who edited *The Compleat Imbiber* series, generously helped me locate a number of English authors.

I was fortunate in being able to look through the wine books at Château Loudenne in the Médoc, at Elizabeth Woodburn's Booknoll Farm, at The Vintners' Club in San Francisco, and at the general collection of The New York Society Library.

I am grateful to Pat McNees Mancini for her many perceptive observations about the contents of this book. Robert and Susan Lescher gave me, as always, sound advice and affectionate encouragement throughout the compilation of this anthology.

A.B.

For my mother and father

Contents

Introduction

The past few years have seen a great many wine books published, almost all of them designed to inform and instruct. Anyone who enjoys wine must surely welcome the best of these books, and especially those that focus on the wines of a specific country or region. Even those who drink only an occasional glass of wine must find it reassuring that so much information about the proper service of wine, the way it's made, and where it comes from is so readily available. But wine was drunk, enjoyed, and written about long before it finally became popular in this country, and people found ways of expressing their delight with wine long before rules were established for its appreciation.

It occurred to me some time ago that a book that brought together various writings about wine found in literature might be of as much interest to someone who enjoys a carafe of jug wine as to those with elaborate cellars. Here is the result. You will find in this anthology many of the well-known passages about wine—Keats on claret, Falstaff on sack, Chaucer on the wine of Lepe, François Villon on the merchants who water their wine, Stephen Potter on winesmanship, Longfellow on Catawba wine, George Meredith on the virtues of old wines, Art Buchwald on tasting wine in Bordeaux, Robert Louis Stevenson on the Napa Valley, Milton on the evils of wine, and Robert Burton on wine and melancholy. You will also find and, I hope, enjoy passages less frequently quoted, such as Henry James on the similarities between Bordeaux and the French character, C. P. Snow on a university claret party, "Adam Smith" on wine as an investment, A. J. Liebling on tasting in Burgundy, Dorothy L. Sayers on an old port mishandled, Ford Madox Ford on how to order wine, Ernest Hemingway on buying a leather wine-bottle in Pamplona, G. B. Stern on an interminable visit to Sauternes, Michael Flanders' "Have Some Madeira, M'Dear," Cyril Connolly on a visit to the Médoc, Baudelaire on wine and hashish, De Quincey on opium and wine, Vyvyan Holland on vintages in sardines and Sauternes, James Joyce describing his favorite wine, Baron Philippe de Rothschild on his first morning at Mouton, François Mauriac on a hailstorm in the vineyards, Jefferson on 1784 Margaux, Colette on her earliest recollections of wine, Benjamin Franklin on mixing water with wine, Stendhal on a visit to Bordeaux, Montaigne on fastidiousness in wine drinking, James Boswell on drinking with Samuel Johnson, and many more.

Most of the selections are relatively short, but two sections contain longer pieces. One is "In Praise of Older Wines," which contains recollections and tasting notes about old wines, most of them from the nineteenth century. I confess to a weakness for descriptions of such wines, even if it is unlikely that I shall ever be given the chance to taste any of them, and I thought the best of these accounts deserved a place in this book. "Extended Diversions" contains only longer selections—short stories, excerpts from novels, humorous essays, and recollections. Roald Dahl's classic wine story, "Taste," is here, as well as stories by Stanley Ellin, Marcel Aymé, and Bruce Todd. I reluctantly left out J. M. Scott's novella *The Man Who Made Wine* because of its length, as well as E. C. Bentley's "The Unknown Peer," Dorothy Sayers' "The Bibulous Business of a Matter of Taste" and Max Brand's "Wine on the Desert" because they are by now familiar to many readers.

Three writers who were frequently suggested to me—Brillat-Savarin, Dickens, and Proust—had a lot to say about food, but very little about wine. As a matter of fact, Baudelaire became quite incensed about Brillat-Savarin's neglect of wine. After quoting Brillat-Savarin's reference to wine as "an alcoholic beverage made of the fruit of the vine," Baudelaire goes on: "And then? Then, nothing: that is all. In vain you will leaf through the volume, turning it about in all directions, reading it backwards, inside out, from right to left and from left to right; you will find nothing about wine in *La Physiologie du Gout*." Actually, that's not quite true: Brillat-Savarin also says that "tea can very well take the place of wine at breakfast." Dickens did write an appreciative passage about Mr. Tulkinghorn's port in *Bleak House*, which I've quoted, as well as this rather sour comment: "Cloudy fluid, served up by shabby waiters in vinegar cruets to disconsolate bachelors at second rate restaurants and miscalled sherry." As for Proust, one of his rare mentions of a specific wine is Swann's gift of a bottle of Asti Spumante to Céline and Flora. Two characters in contemporary fiction, Georges Simenon's Inspector Maigret and Rex Stout's Nero Wolfe, both enjoy food and wine, but I was unable to find quotable wine passages in which either one figures.

I suppose few lines are more famous than those from *The Rubaiyat of Omar Khayyam* in Edward Fitzgerald's translation:

> A Book of Verses underneath the Bough,
> A Jug of Wine, a Loaf of Bread—and Thou
>   Beside me singing in the Wilderness—
> Oh, Wilderness were Paradise enow! . . .
>
> And much as Wine has play'd the Infidel,
> And robb'd me of my Robe of Honor—Well,
>   I wonder often what the Vintners buy
> One half so precious as the stuff they sell.

Since the entire poem is more or less about the pleasures of wine, it seemed unfair to quote just a few lines out of context, but I thought quoting all 101 verses might tax the patience of even a dedicated enophile. Considering the exaggerated profits that some wine merchants take, I've often thought that Omar's lines about what the vintner buys might make even more sense if you substitute the word "expensive" for "precious." Which reminds me of a friend who refers to a particularly unreliable wine merchant as "the vintner of our discontent."

Several people mentioned Rabelais' bottle-shaped poem toward the end of *Pantagruel*, but it's no longer the right shape in the translations I've seen, and I find John Hollander's bottle-shaped poem more successful. Other familiar poems, such as Maurice Healy's "The Liquor of Bray," seemed dated to me; and as to Hilaire Belloc's "Heroic Poem in Praise of Wine," well, I didn't include it because I was never able to get through it.

I was reluctant to quote lines or repeat anecdotes that I could not trace back to their sources. For example, did Galileo really say "Wine is sunlight, held together by water"? Where did Elmer Rice say, "You can have too much champagne, but you can never have enough"? On what occasion did Jonathan Swift refuse a bottle of old wine with the words "Sir, I drink no memories"? I have read several times that Voltaire served his guests Beaujolais while he himself drank Corton, but I couldn't find any reference to this in his letters.

The Greeks and Romans are not as widely represented as might have been expected, because many of their references to wine are of interest only to the wine historian who wants to know which wines were drunk when. One exception, of course, is Horace, several of whose odes are about Bacchus and the pleasures of wine. Treatises on viticulture and winemaking have been written by poets as well as farmers—the *Georgics* of Virgil is perhaps the most notable example—but technical material seemed out of place in this book. So did historical references, some of which are well known. In 1663, at the Royal Oak Tavern, Samuel Pepys "drank a sort of French wine called Ho Bryan, that hath a good and most particular taste that I never met with." This is considered the first reference in English to a specific Bordeaux vineyard, and in fact, Pepys drank this wine with Alexander Brome, one of whose poems is included here. In his *Journals*, Thomas Jefferson describes visits to the vineyards of France and Germany in 1787 and 1788. He notes, on his visit to Bordeaux, that "there are four vineyards of the first quality," and they are the same four that were later ranked at the top of the 1855 classification. In 1836 Cyrus Redding writes about red and white Chambertin, and goes on to say, "They also make an effervescing Chambertin, a wine only inferior to a very good Champagne." The works of five nineteenth-century wine writers—Alexander Henderson, Robert Druitt, Charles Tovey, Henry Vizetelly, and Cyrus Redding—may be primarily of historical interest, but I found a number of entertaining passages in their works which are quoted in this volume. Such well-known twentieth-century wine writers as George Saintsbury, André Simon, and H. Warner Allen also show up more than once here.

Although I found many references to bad wine or to wine badly served, I didn't come across as many references to wine and murder as I anticipated, even in Renaissance literature. There's the Duke of Clarence drowned in a butt of Malmsey, of course, and in *Hamlet* the Queen drinks a cup of poisoned wine intended for Hamlet. There's an attempted murder by poisoned wine in Arnold Bennett's *The Grand Babylon Hotel,* part of which I've excerpted, and more recently there's an unusual murder in Margaret Millar's *Ask for Me Tomorrow,* a novel set in Mexico. The body of Magistrate Hernandez has been found in his study and there's an open bottle of wine on a table nearby. The police inspector explains, "You see the forced air opener still in the cork of the wine bottle over there? I think before it was inserted in the cork, it was inserted in Hernandez." Murder aside, there's the self-inflicted death of the poet Anacreon, who is said to have died from choking on a grape pit. Abraham Cowley wrote a curious elegy which contains the lines, " 'Tis neither love nor poesy / Can arm against death's smallest dart."

Originally, my idea was to include whatever I could find about wine, but I soon discovered that many of the most famous references to wine are just that—a line or two that may provide a historical perspective or demonstrate the writer's appreciation of wine, but that are not very interesting out of context. For example, St. Paul's advice to Timothy, "Drink no longer water, but use a little wine for thy stomach's sake and thine often infirmities" is of more interest, perhaps, to an anti-prohibitionist than to the casual reader. Byron's "And then there was champagne, with foaming whirls / As white as Cleopatra's melted pearls" is charmingly put, as is George Farquhar's description of champagne in *Love and a Bottle* (1699): ". . . how it puns and quibbles in the glass!" These references to wine, however, cannot stand on their own, nor does it help to establish the context in which these lines appear, as they have nothing to do with wine.

There are, of course, a great many of these odd lines to be found in literature. Ben Jonson often refers in passing to the pleasures of sack, as in these lines from "Inviting a Friend to Supper": "But that which most doth take my muse and me / Is a pure cup of rich Canary-wine." Alexandre Dumas, in his *Dictionary of Cuisine,* wrote that "Wine is the intellectual part of a meal. Meats are merely the material part," and in the seventeenth century Madame de Sevigné predicted that the fad for Bordeaux, Racine, and coffee could not last. And then there's the description of the 1945 vintage in the English translation of J. R. Rogers' book on Bordeaux: "exceptionally great . . . full and round . . . wines to lay down with."

These snippets are fun, and it's a pity to lose others like them, but I decided to restrict my choices to passages and excerpts that are not only entertaining but also self-contained. However, I do quote some of the odd lines and anecdotes in the short introductions that precede each section of this anthology, to which I now invite your attention.

1

The Pleasures of Wine

"Drinking with him, except so far as it cooled a feverish thirst, was not a sensual but an intellectual pleasure; it lighted up his fading fancy, enriched his humor, and impelled the struggling thought or beautiful image into day." So T. N. Talfourd described the effects of wine on Charles Lamb, and judging by the evidence in the pages that follow, many others have found joy and satisfaction in wine.

James Boswell wrote in his journals, after a vinous evening, "I recollect having felt much warmth of heart, fertility of fancy, and joyous complacency mingled in a sort of delirium. Such a state is at least equal to a pleasing dream." Wine and dreams, without Boswell's delirium, also figure in these lines from D. H. Lawrence's poem "Grapes":

> Our pale day is sinking into twilight,
> And if we sip the wine, we find dreams coming upon us
> Out of the imminent night.

James Joyce enjoyed wine and is quoted in Richard Ellmann's biography as having said, "What is better than to sit at the end of the day and drink wine with friends, or substitutes for friends?" We can assume that he did not drink a substitute for wine. The dangers of such a substitution were anticipated by Ned Ward, in "The Delights of the Bottle," published in 1720: "Well may the poet's fancy halt, / That's doomed to rhime o'er muddy malt." This thought was echoed fifty years later by George Crabbe in "Inebriety":

> Lo! the poor toper whose untutor'd sense,
> Sees bliss in ale, and can with wine dispense;
> Whose head proud fancy never taught to steer,
> Beyond the muddy ecstasies of beer.

Today we depend on the corkscrew to open the bottles in our cellars, and so this section closes with two anonymous poems on this device—one a riddle and the other an imaginative account of how it came to be invented. Of course, wine was enjoyed well before the appearance of the corkscrew, as these lines from Proverbs remind us:

Give strong drink unto him that is ready to perish, and wine unto those that be of heavy hearts. Let him drink, and forget his poverty, and remember his misery no more.

A Draught of Vintage

> O, for a draught of vintage! that hath been
>   Cool'd a long age in the deep-delved earth,
> Tasting of Flora and the country green,
>   Dance, and Provençal song, and sunburnt mirth!
> O for a beaker full of the warm South,
>   Full of the true, the blushful Hippocrene,
>   With beaded bubbles winking at the brim,
>   And purple-stained mouth;
> That I might drink, and leave the world unseen,
>   And with thee fade away into the forest dim . . .

JOHN KEATS
"Ode to a Nightingale"

Persuasive

[Wine] awakens and refreshes the lurking passions of the mind, as varnish does the colours which are sunk in a picture, and brings them out in all their natural glowings.

ALEXANDER POPE

Make Merry over Wine

Make merry over wine.
Three cups, and already
The walls of sadness are overthrown.
Alas, no sooner are we sober
Than sadness walls us in again.

CHIN P'ING MEI
16th Century

An Acknowledgment

I have already made mention of the happiness I have derived throughout my life from literature, and I should here, perhaps, acknowledge the consolation I have never failed to find in the fermented juice of the grape. Writing in my sixty-fourth year, I can truthfully say that since I reached the age of discretion I have consistently drunk more than most people would say was good for me. Nor do I regret it. Wine has been to me a firm friend and a wise counsellor. Often, as on the occasion just related, wine has shown me matters in their true perspective, and has, as though by the touch of a magic wand, reduced great disasters to small inconveniences. Wine has lit up for me the pages of literature, and revealed in life romance lurking in the commonplace. Wine has made me bold but not foolish; has induced me to say silly things but not to do them. Under its influence words have often come too easily which had better not have been spoken, and letters have been written which had better not have been sent. But if such small indiscretions standing in the debit column of wine's account were added up, they would amount to nothing in comparison with the vast accumulation on the credit side.

DUFF COOPER
Old Men Forget

Contentment

The man who could sit under the shade of his own vine with his wife and children about him, and the ripe clusters hanging within their reach, and not feel the highest enjoyment is incapable of happiness and does not know what the word means.

JAMES BUSBY

An Explanation

The use of wine in dry and consumed bodies is hurtful; in moist and full bodies it is good. The cause is, for that the spirits of the wine do prey upon the dew, or radical moisture of the body, and so deceive the animal spirits; but where there is moisture enough, or superfluous, there wine helpeth to digest and to dessicate the moisture.

FRANCIS BACON

Pleasure Recalled

It is possible that someone, not a hopeless *bo*bolitionist, may say, 'Mr. Saintsbury appears to have spent a great deal of money on mere luxuries.' If I meet this 'by anticipation' (as some people say when they want to save themselves the trouble of a letter of thanks, having previously tormented others with one of request) it is not out of pusillanimity or a guilty conscience. But I would request readers to observe in the first place that the outlay here implied or acknowledged was spread over rather more than half a century; and secondly, that, as I have more fully explained in the little book itself, I very rarely bought more at a time than a single dozen of each wine named, nay, half a dozen or even odd bottles by way of experiment. In wine, as in books and other things, I have tried to be a (very minor) Ulysses, steering ever from the known to the unknown. Thirdly, for nearly twenty years of the time I was a journalist and in other ways a working man of letters—a state of life to which Thackeray's ejaculation, 'Grudge myself good wine? as soon grudge my horse corn,' doth more particularly and specially apply; while for full another twenty I occupied a position in which, as one received much hospitality, it was not merely a pleasure but a duty to show some. But I offer these as explanations, not excuses.

There is no money, among that which I have spent since I began to earn my living, of the expenditure of which I am less ashamed, or which gave me better value in return, than the price of the liquids chronicled in this booklet. When they were good they pleased my senses, cheered my spirits, improved my moral and intellectual powers, besides enabling me to confer the same benefits on other people. And whether they were bad or good, the grapes that had yielded them were fruits of that Tree of Knowledge which, as theologians too commonly forget to expound, it became not merely lawful but incumbent on us to use, with discernment, when our First Mother had paid the price for it, and handed it on to us to pay for likewise.

GEORGE SAINTSBURY
Notes on a Cellar-Book

The Soul of the Wine

One evening, wine sang out with all its soul:
'I send you, Man, dear disinherited,
From my glass prison with its scarlet seals,
A song of sunshine and of brotherhood!

I know what toil upon the hill aflame,
What sweat and toil and scorching sun it needs
To give me life, give me a soul and name;
I shall not harm you, show ingratitude,

For I feel vast delight when I'm interred
In some deep-throated man, through toil grown old,
His warm breast is a grateful sepulchre
More pleasing, far, to me than cellars cold.

Hear you the echoing songs of holidays,
The hope which murmurs in my quivering breast?
Your sleeves rolled up, at table, at your ease,
You'll glorify me, with contentment blest;

I'll light the eyes of your delighted wife,
And to your son new strength and colour give,
And for this athlete delicate in life
I'll be the oil which makes the wrestler thrive.

I'll fall in you, ambrosia from the sky,
Rare seed by the eternal sower cast,
So that our love creates the poetry
Which like a flower shall praise the Holy Ghost!'

CHARLES BAUDELAIRE

A Good Cellar

Up, and having set my neighbor Mr. Hudson, wine cooper, at work drawing out a tierce of wine for the sending of some of it to my wife—I abroad, only taking notice to what a condition it hath pleased God to bring me, that at this time I have two tierces of claret—two quarter-cask of canary, and a smaller vessel of sack—a vessel of tent, another of Malaga, and another of white wine, all in my wine-cellar together—which I believe none of my friends now alive ever had of his own at one time.

SAMUEL PEPYS
Diary
1665

Sounds Good

[Wine is] a light, clean, beautiful fluid of a fragrant scent and delicious flavour, easy of digestion, and the most homogeneous to the human body of all vegetable production. . . . wine is no temporary or imaginary cordial, whose effects will soon vanish, but one that is true, real and permanent, general, easy and powerful, affording matter for a fresh supply of blood and spirits, at the same time that it solicits the exercise and expense of them. . . . Wine drunk in moderate quantities, or proportionately to the respective constitutions of men, in health, has, as we find from experience, a power to give sudden refreshment, to warm the stomach, gently stimulate its fibres, promote digestion, raise the pulse, rarify the blood, add to its velocity, open all obstructions, forward excretions, greatly promote insensible perspiration, increase the natural strength, and enlarge the faculties both of body and mind. But when used too freely, it carries all these effects to excess, tho' it soon ends in a perfect recovery and an healthful state.

DR. SHAW
"The Juice of the Grape: or,
Wine Preferable to Water"

Pamplona

We stood at the counter. They had Brett seated on a wine-cask. It was dark in the wine-shop and full of men singing, hard-voiced singing. Back of the counter they drew the wine from casks. I put down money for the wine, but one of the men picked it up and put it back in my pocket.

"I want a leather wine-bottle," Bill said.

"There's a place down the street," I said. "I'll go get a couple."

The dancers did not want me to go out. Three of them were sitting on the high wine-cask beside Brett, teaching her to drink out of the wine-skins. They had hung a wreath of garlics around her neck. Someone insisted on giving her a glass. Somebody was teaching Bill a song. Singing it into his ear. Beating time on Bill's back.

I explained to them that I would be back. Outside in the street I went down the street looking for the shop that made leather wine-bottles. The crowd was packed on the sidewalks and many of the shops were shuttered, and I could not find it. I walked as far as the church, looking on both sides of the street. Then I asked a man and he took me by the arm and led me to it. The shutters were up but the door was open.

Inside it smelled of fresh tanned leather and hot tar. A man was stencilling completed wine-skins. They hung from the roof in bunches. He took one down, blew it up, screwed the nozzle tight, and then jumped on it.

"See! It doesn't leak."

"I want another one, too. A big one."

He took down a big one that would hold a gallon or more, from the roof. He blew it up, his cheeks puffing ahead of the wine-skin, and stood on the bota holding on to a chair.

"What are you going to do? Sell them in Bayonne?"

"No. Drink out of them."

He slapped me on the back.

"Good man. Eight pesetas for the two. The lowest price."

The man who was stencilling the new ones and tossing them into a pile stopped.

"It's true," he said. "Eight pesetas is cheap."

I paid and went out and along the street back to the wine-shop. It was darker than ever inside and very crowded. I did not see Brett and Bill, and someone said they were in the back room. At the counter the girl filled the two wine-skins for me. One held two litres. The other held five litres. Filling them both cost three pesetas sixty centimos. Someone at the counter, that I had never seen before, tried to pay for the wine, but I finally paid for it myself. The man who had wanted to pay then bought me a drink. He would not let me buy one in return, but said he would take a rinse of the mouth from the new wine-bag. He tipped the big five-litre bag up and squeezed it so the wine hissed against the back of his throat.

ERNEST HEMINGWAY
The Sun Also Rises

A Lasting Pleasure

Let us return to our bottles. The discomforts of old age, which have need of some support and invigoration, might reasonably create in me a desire for this license, for it is almost the last pleasure that the passage of years steals from us. The natural warmth, say boon companions, is at first in the feet; that belongs to childhood. Thence it ascends to the middle region, where it is fixed for a long time, and where it produces, in my opinion, the only true pleasures of bodily life. All other pleasures are dull in comparison. Finally, like a vapour which keeps ascending and spreading, it reaches the throat, where it makes its last stop. I can not, however, understand how a man can prolong the pleasure of drinking beyond thirst, and forge by his imagination an artificial and unnatural appetite. My stomach would not go so far; it has enough to do to manage what it takes for its need.

MICHEL DE MONTAIGNE
Of Drunkenness

The Best Medicine

"I feel impelled to report to you the effect of the Imperial Tokay which I recently ordered from you for my patient Mrs. ———, of ————. I can honestly say I have never seen so dramatic a recovery in all my experience as resulted from its use in this case. My patient, who is suffering, I fear, from an inoperable and hopeless intestinal cancer, had reached a comatose condition in which death was hourly expected. She had refused all food for ten days, and was practically beyond human help. As a last resource, and mainly to satisfy the relatives' craving to do something, I suggested the use of this wine, which I had recently read of in a brochure of yours. The effect was staggering. After three two-teaspoonful doses, the patient recovered complete consciousness and began demanding food of all kinds. She ate voraciously, and in three or four days was eating bacon and eggs for breakfast, and showing an amazing return of spirits and vitality. She now sits up for all meals and is taking a keen interest in the redecoration of her house. During this time the only alteration in treatment that has been made is the addition of two teaspoonsful of Imperial Tokay two or three times a day. I have reported this result to ———, who saw the case some weeks ago and agreed with me as to the diagnosis; and also to a number of other physicians and surgeons, who are as impressed as I am myself with the phenomenon.

"In view of the nature of the case, I have, of course, no hope of a permanent recovery, but of this I am certain, that my patient would have been dead five weeks ago but for the vitalising effect of this astonishing wine. I feel it is only fair to apprise you of the facts. You can make what use you like of this letter, providing, of course, that you eliminate all names.

"Yours faithfully, . . ."

CHARLES WALTER BERRY
A Miscellany of Wine

Drinking Alone Beneath the Moon

A pot of wine among the flowers:
I drink alone, no kith or kin near.
I raise my cup to invite the moon to join me;
It and my shadow make a party of three.
Alas, the moon is unconcerned about drinking,
And my shadow merely follows me around.
Briefly I cavort with the moon and my shadow:
Pleasure must be sought while it is spring.
I sing and the moon goes back and forth,
I dance and my shadow falls at random.
While sober we seek pleasure in fellowship;
When drunk we go each our own way.
Then let us pledge a friendship without human ties
And meet again at the far end of the Milky Way.

LI PO
8th century

A Very Young Enophile

In this state he lived till he was a year and ten months old, at which time, by the advice of physicians, they began to take him out, and a fine ox-wagon was made for him, to the design of Jean Denyau. In this he travelled around most merrily to one place and another; and they made a great show of him. For he had a fine face and almost eighteen chins; and he cried very seldom. But he shat himself every hour. For he was amazingly phlegmatic in his actions, partly from natural character and partly for accidental reasons connected with over-indulgence in the new wines of September. But he never drank a drop without reason. For if by chance he was vexed, angry, displeased, or peeved, if he stamped, if he wept or if he screamed, they always brought him drink to restore his temper, and immediately he became quiet and happy.

One of his governesses told me, on her Bible oath, that he was so accustomed to this treatment, that at the mere sound of pint-pots and flagons he would fall into an ecstasy, as if tasting the joys of paradise. Taking this divine disposition of his into account, therefore, in order to cheer him up in the mornings they would have glasses chinked for him with a knife, or flagons tapped with their stoppers; and at this sound he would become merry, leap up, and rock himself in his cradle, nodding his head, playing scales with his fingers, and beating slow time with his bottom.

FRANÇOIS RABELAIS
Gargantua and Pantagruel

Ma Vie Avec le Grape Nut

How refreshingly primitive his tastes were when we met. He wanted giant egg creams. No egg, no cream, he explained very patiently, native New Yorker to the aborigine from the Middle West . . . just a dash of milk in the bottom of the cocktail shaker, a big glop of chocolate syrup and seltzer to the top. He wanted orange juice. Fresh squeezed, he said, by my very own left hand pressed against a highly efficient electric juicer, shanghaied from his mother's kitchen. Poor dear. That was her first shattering hint that her precious baby boy might actually Marry That Woman . . . me. Sunning in our penthouse slum, he sipped icy Tuborg beer (he had been until recently engaged to a Danish beauty and an assumed affection for Scandinavian potables had quite naturally developed). When I invited him to dinner he would bring a bottle of whatever the neighborhood liquor store was featuring that week in the $1.19 bin.

Let me say this for the Kultur Maven, longest-running joy of my life, he was always a class guy. Even in those days of blissful solvent poverty. He never even considered the 99-cent specials. He bought $1.19 Chablis and $1.49 Moselle and even Châteauneuf-du-Pape once for $1.99. Even in the glorious green of his innocence, he had an innate sense of where the line falls between *shlock* and *dreck*.

I mean primitive. Refreshingly unmaterialistic. He arrived for the big wedding scene on the lawn in Bloomfield Hills, Michigan, with all his gear in a small canvas gym bag . . . his high school gym bag. What is this wedding twitter? It is a short, predictable story. In the pinch the bride got disgustingly old-fashioned. She put on shoes and got married because she wanted silver that matched and the heirloom Spode. Did I say the groom was primitive? The bride was a simpleton. She'd never heard of the silver auctions at Parke-Bernet.

Never once did I suspect that I had promised to love, honor and humidify the closet of an incipient oenosnob. They'd never heard of the mythic egg cream in St. Clair, Michigan, where we honeymooned on Lake Huron. But he had hidden a bottle of French champagne in his gym bag. We twirled it in a polyurethane bucket, and, being slightly nervous—living together married after the simple sanity of living together single is fraught with anxiety—we ordered five desserts from room service. The potential for a gourmand future was clear. But I did not suspect he had been bitten by The Grape.

Thinking back, I can see the first signs of serious exposure to oenophilic contamination. I began to cook with early haute pretension. And he stopped heading automatically for the $1.19 wine specials and began consulting the assorted thieves, knaves and humanitarian wine vendors in our neighborhood liquor shops. We culled some wine lore from the Frenchman next door. Mme. Rochat was an early organic food cultist and the transplanted Rochats never drank anything stronger than papaya tea. But that didn't stifle their natural arrogance on such pitiful American customs as plastic corks and pasteurized wine. (Amazing how the French forget who invented pasteurization.) Then Jules the Ophthalmologist came home from the European fields. It was the peacetime sixties and Jules' war was the Waterloo of his liver in the gastronomic fleshshops in and about the Army hospitals at La Rochelle, France. Jules' budding winesmanship was contagious and appealing. It seemed like a gift, not a disease. When he did his little lecture on the '59 harvest and sang the magic litany of good years and bad years and little fruity vins du pays, crisp but honest whites, humble but charming reds, we sat rapt and envious of such esoteric wisdom.

When my eager mate brought home a '55 Château Margaux to drink with my Swedish meatballs, I had a feeling we were into something over our heads. Our European odyssey with pilgrimages to varied epicurean shrines fueled the obsession. We discovered little nontransportable oenophilic graces like Epomeo, a pale, dry white of Ischia, and Condrieu, the enchanting white wine of the Rhône valley. And there were many pedantic hours spent in oenophilic discourse with other similarly seized souls.

I bought the blossoming oenophile a magnum of 1947 Lafite-Rothschild and a vineyard guide for Christmas. I had to cook a dinner glorious enough to complement the Lafite. It took four days and cost $130. He began to talk about calcareous sand and marl, *Appellation Contrôlée,* premiers grands crus, upper slopes versus lower slopes, racy wines, flabby wines, the mettlesome wines of Lower Burgundy, the fleshy fat Côte de Nuits . . . what a cast of characters dominated our lives. He began to practice his oenokultur in the neighborhood, terrorizing a teenage waitress at the pizzaria because she had the innocence to serve Chianti from the refrigerator. She offered to put it through a dishwasher cycle to warm it up . . . his scorn was withering. He had amiable waiters in the nearby home-style delicatessen scurrying back and forth to find out the year of a $3 Médoc.

Technique perfected, he took on the pompous *sommeliers* of our town's haughtier French restaurants: sniffing corks, swirling, sniffing, sipping, nibbling, sloshing, chewing, sneering, raising an arrogant eyebrow . . . and, when appropriate, offering a restrained smile of benediction.

He does not speak a word of French. But overnight he graduated from an uncertain "very nice" to a confident "charming," "roguish," "a tannin-wracked little wench," "bien meublé," "puissant," "un peu anémique, non?"

An oenophile's companion must have an unfailing sense of humor.

GAEL GREENE

An Autumn Dinner

Four fresh-opened Oysters,
Soft as grey velvet,
Cold as—deep-sea water;
One long-stemmed glass
Half full of light Rhinewine,
Tasting of fruit-flowers.

Soup from late Peas,
Mint, their faint flavour,
With it a mouthful
Of lightest East India.

Sole, bubbling and brown,
Showing soft white to the fork,
Bone-patterned, roe-inlaid.
Wise, reticent Meursault.

Slices of Saddle
And tiny potatoes,
Cooked soft and succulent.
Beaune, Grèves Enfant-Jésus.

A plump basted Woodcock,
Well done, yet undone,
Cold Celery salad
And then—the great Chambertin.

Here, chilled Mountain Strawberries
Straight from the Vosges,
Kirsch-flavoured cream,
And a glass of Tokay.

Bear in the Stilton
Ripe in its turban!
Now serve Oporto,
Not too light, not too heavy.

End in aromas—
Delicate Cognac,
Scent of fine Coffee,
Blue smoke of Havanas.

Wit, kindness, peace,
Shared between humans
Rise from this culture
Of two glorious senses,
Spurned by the arid
And narrow-soul'd pundit.

TREVOR BLAKEMORE

Tiresias Speaks of Bacchus

   I tell you,
this god whom you ridicule shall someday have
enormous power and prestige throughout Hellas.
Mankind, young man, possesses two supreme blessings.
First of these is the goddess Demeter, or Earth—
whichever name you choose to call her by.
It was she who gave to man his nourishment of grain.
But after her there came the son of Semele,
who matched her present by inventing liquid wine
as his gift to man. For filled with that good gift,
suffering mankind forgets its grief; from it
comes sleep; with it oblivion of the troubles
of the day. There is no other medicine
for misery. And when we pour libations
to the gods, we pour the god of wine himself
that through his intercession man may win
the favor of heaven.

EURIPIDES
The Bacchae

Fastidiousness in Wine

Fastidiousness is to be avoided, and careful selection of the wine. If you base your enjoyment on drinking delicate wines, you oblige yourself to suffer in drinking the other kinds. The taste must be wider and freer; to be a good drinker, the palate must not be so dainty. The Germans drink almost every kind of wine with equal pleasure. Their object is to swallow it rather than to taste it. They have thus the better bargain; their enjoyment is more abundant and nearer at hand. Secondly, to drink in the French fashion at two meals, and moderately, is to restrict too much the favours of this god; more time and persistency are necessary. The ancients used to pass whole nights at this business, and often joined the days to them; and, indeed, we should make our regular allowance more liberal and more fixed. I have seen a great nobleman of my time, a personage of eminent undertakings and famous triumphs, who, without effort and in the course of his regular meals, rarely drank less than five bottles of wine, and afterward appeared only too wise and shrewd, at the expense of our affairs. The pleasure which we wish to count on throughout our life should occupy more space in it. Like shop-boys and workingmen, we should never refuse an opportunity to drink, and should have that desire always in our minds.

MICHEL DE MONTAIGNE
Of Drunkenness

The Second Bottle

Oh! That second bottle is the sincerest, wisest, and most impartial, downright friend we have; tells us truth of ourselves, and forces us to speak truths of others; banishes flattery from our tongues, and distrust from our hearts; sets us above the mean policy of court prudence, which makes us lie to one another all day, for fear of being betrayed by each other at night. And . . . I believe, the errantest villain breathing, is honest as long as that bottle lives.

JOHN WILMOT, Earl of Rochester

Wines and Bullfighting

The comparison with wine drinking is not so far-fetched as it might seem. Wine is one of the most civilized things in the world and one of the natural things of the world that has been brought to the greatest perfection, and it offers a greater range for enjoyment and appreciation than, possibly, any other purely sensory thing which may be purchased. One can learn about wines and pursue the education of one's palate with great enjoyment all of a lifetime, the palate becoming more educated and capable of appreciation and you having constantly increasing enjoyment and appreciation of wine even though the kidneys may weaken, the big toe become painful, the finger joints stiffen, until finally, just when you love it the most you are finally forbidden wine entirely. Just as the eye which is only a good healthy instrument to start with becomes, even though it is no longer so strong and is weakened and worn by excesses, capable of transmitting constantly greater enjoyment to the brain because of the knowledge or ability to see that it has acquired. Our bodies all wear out in some way and we die, and I would rather have a palate that will give me the pleasure of enjoying completely a Château Margaux or a Haut Brion, even though excesses indulged in in the acquiring of it have brought a liver that will not allow me to drink Richebourg, Corton, or Chambertin, than to have the corrugated iron internals of my boyhood when all red wines were bitter except port and drinking was the process of getting down enough of anything to make you feel reckless. The thing, of course, is to avoid having to give up wine entirely just as, with the eye, it is to avoid going blind. But there seems to be much luck in all these things and no man can avoid death by honest effort nor say what use any part of his body will bear until he tries it.

This seems to have gotten away from bullfighting, but the point was that a person with increasing knowledge and sensory education may derive infinite enjoyment from wine, as a man's enjoyment of the bullfight might grow to become one of his greatest minor passions, yet a person drinking, not tasting or savoring but *drinking*, wine for the first time will know, although he may not care to taste or be able to taste, whether he likes the effect or not and whether or not it is good for him. In wine, most people at the start prefer sweet vintages, Sauternes, Graves, Barsac, and sparkling wines, such as not too dry champagne and sparkling Burgundy because of their picturesque quality while later they would trade all these for a light but full and fine example of the grands crus of

Médoc though it may be in a plain bottle without label, dust, or cobwebs, with nothing picturesque, but only its honesty and delicacy and the light body of it on your tongue, cool in your mouth and warm when you have drunk it. So in bullfighting, at the start it is the picturesqueness of the paseo, the color, the scene, the picturesqueness of farols and molinetes, the bullfighter putting his hand on the muzzle of the bull, stroking the horns, and all such useless and romantic things that the spectators like. They are glad to see the horses protected if it saves them from awkward sights and they applaud all such moves. Finally, when they have learned to appreciate values through experience what they seek is honesty and true, not tricked, emotion and always classicism and the purity of execution of all the suertes, and, as in the change in taste for wines, they want no sweetening but prefer to see the horses with no protection worn so that all wounds may be seen and death given rather than suffering caused by something designed to allow the horses to suffer while their suffering is spared the spectator. But, as with wine, you will know when you first try it whether you like it as a thing or not from the effect it will have on you. There are forms of it to appeal to all tastes and if you do not like it, none of it, nor, as a whole, while not caring for details, than it is not for you. It would be pleasant of course for those who do like it if those who do not would not feel that they had to go to war against it or give money to try to suppress it, since it offends them or does not please them, but that is too much to expect and anything capable of arousing passion in its favor will surely raise as much passion against it.

ERNEST HEMINGWAY
Death in the Afternoon

Meursault in the Garden

On Saturday I went down to New York and back on the Merritt Parkway. . . . Since I had a car I brought home a load of mangoes, fresh apricots, the outsized cherries that I like, a little Chablis and a little Meursault, and so on. This last always seems the coldest thing in the world on a hot day in the garden where I like to have lunch occasionally if the neighbors are away as they often are.

WALLACE STEVENS

Just Give me the Bottle

I admit that occasionally an unprofessional enthusiasm seems to seize certain individuals. I have myself heard Dr Eylaud, of the Faculty of Medicine, sustain vigorously the thesis that the best enemas should be compounded with 25 per cent of St Emilion; I find this hard to believe. In any case, that is not the way I prefer to take my St Emilion.

RAYMOND POSTGATE
"Oinoposiai"

Money Well Spent

I think wealth has lost much of its value if it has not wine. I abstain from wine only on account of the expense. When I heard that Mr. Sturgis had given up wine I had the same regret that I had lately in hearing that Mr. Bowditch had broken his hip.

RALPH WALDO EMERSON

Vinous Bookkeeping

My revenues by the miserable oppressions of this kingdom are sunk three hundred pounds a year, for tithes are become a drug, and I have but little rents from the deanery lands, which are my only sure payments. I have here a large convenient house; I live at two-thirds cheaper here than I could there; I drink a bottle of French wine myself every day, though I love it not, but it is the only thing that keeps me out of pain; I ride every fair day a dozen miles, on a large strand or turnpike roads. You in London have no such advantages. I can buy a chicken for a groat, and entertain three or four friends, with as many dishes, and two or three bottles of French wine, for ten shillings. When I dine alone, my pint and chicken with the appendixes cost me about fifteen pence. I am thrifty in everything but wine, of which though I be not a constant housekeeper, I spend between five and six hogshead a year. When I ride to a friend a few miles off, if he be not richer than I, I carry my bottle, my bread and chicken, that he may be no loser.

JONATHAN SWIFT
Letter to John Arbuthnot
1734

Money Helps

As I sat in the Café I said to myself,
They may talk as they please about what they call pelf,
They may sneer as they like about eating and drinking,
But help it I cannot, I cannot help thinking
How pleasant it is to have money, heigh-ho!
How pleasant it is to have money. . . .

After oysters, sauterne; then sherry, champagne,
Ere one bottle goes, comes another again;
Fly up, thou bold cork, to the ceiling above,
And tell to our ears in the sound that they love
How pleasant it is to have money, heigh-ho!
How pleasant it is to have money. . . .

Your Chablis is acid, away with the Hock,
Give me the pure juice of the purple Médoc:
St Peray is exquisite; but, if you please,
Some Burgundy just before tasting the cheese.
So pleasant it is to have money, heigh-ho!
So pleasant it is to have money.

ARTHUR HUGH CLOUGH
"Spectator ab Extra"

The Spirit of Wine

The Spirit of Wine
Sang in my glass, and I listened
With love to his odorous music,
His flushed and magnificent song.

——— 'I am health, I am heart, I am life!
For I give for the asking
The fire of my father, the Sun,
And the strength of my mother, the Earth.
Inspiration in essence,
I am wisdom and wit to the wise,
His visible muse to the poet,
The soul of desire to the lover,
The genius of laughter to all.

'Come, lean on me, ye that are weary!
Rise, ye faint-hearted and doubting!
Haste, ye that lag by the way!
I am Pride, the consoler;
Valour and Hope are my henchmen;
I am the Angel of Rest.

'I am life, I am wealth, I am fame:
For I captain an army
Of shining and generous dreams;
And mine, too, all mine, are the keys
Of that secret spiritual shrine,
Where, his work-a-day soul put by,
Shut in with his saint of saints—
With his radiant and conquering self—
Man worships, and talks, and is glad.

'Come, sit with me, ye that are lonely,
Ye that are paid with disdain,
Ye that are chained and would soar!
I am beauty and love;
I am friendship, the comforter;
I am that which forgives and forgets.'——

The Spirit of Wine
Sang in my heart, and I triumphed
In the savour and scent of his music,
His magnetic and mastering song.

WILLIAM ERNEST HENLEY

Make Mine Wine

Coffee excites the brain, and tea the liver, with an unbalanced action. Hasheesh and opium are liars which cheat the senses with unreal objects, born of the vapors of the brain they disorder. But wine acts honestly on the real, and, while exalting the action of every part within us, and the effect of every object without us, works only with the actual and the true.

WILLIAM J. FLAGG
Three Seasons in European Vineyards
1869

Logic

French wines may be said but to pickle meat in the stomach, but this is the wine that digests, and doth not only breed good blood, but it nutrifieth also, being a glutinous substantial liquor; of this wine, if of any other, may be verified that merry induction: That good wine makes good blood, good blood causeth good humors, good humors cause good thoughts, good thoughts bring forth good works, good works carry a man to heaven, *ergo* good wine carrieth a man to heaven.

JAMES HOWELL
1634

Fellow Bibbers

To all lovers, admirers and doters on claret,
(Who tho' at death's door, yet can hardly forbear it)
Who can miracles credit, and fancy red Port
To be sprightly Pontac, and the best of the sort, . . .

To all lovers of red and white Port, Syracuse,
Barcelona, Navarre, or Canary's sweet juice.
To all drinkers of sherry, old hock, or Moselle,
Or of Tent, which soon teaches the flesh to rebel.
To all Alicant tasters, and Malaga sots.
To all friends to straw bottles, and nicking quart-pots.
To all Bacchus his friends, who have tavern's frequented,
This following poem is humbly presented.

RICHARD AMES
"The Search After Claret"
1691

Enigma on a Corkscrew

Though I, alas! a pris'ner be,
My trade is others to set free:
No slave his lord's behest obeys
With such insinuating ways.
My genius, piercing, sharp, and bright,

Wherein the men of wit delight.
The clergy keep me for their ease,
And turn and wind me as they please.
A new and wondrous art I show,
Of raising spirits from below;
In scarlet some, and some in white,
They rise, walk round, yet ne'er affright.
In at each mouth the spirits pass,
Distinctly seen, as through a glass;
O'er head and body make a rout,
And drive, at last, all secrets out;
And still, the more I show my art,
The more they open every heart.
Although I'm often out of case,
I'm not asham'd to show my face;
And the plain squire, when dinner's done,
Is never pleas'd till I make one.
I twice a day a hunting go.
Nor ever fail to seize my foe;
And, when I have him by the poll,
I drag him upwards from his hole;
Though some are of so stubborn kind,
I'm forc'd to leave a limb behind.
I hourly wait some fatal end,
For I can break, but never bend.

                                        ANON.

The Bottle Scrue

Oh, shame! The Bottle Scrue remains
The Bottle Scrue whose worth, whose use
All men confess, that love the juice:
Forgotten sleeps the man to whom
We owe the invention, in his tomb
No publick honours grace his name
No pious bard records his fame
Elate with pride and joy I see
The deathless task reserved for me. . . .

Wherefore the supper now was over
And Thomas brought up the October.

The hoary bottle seem'd to tell
That all within was ripe and well
When studious to extract the cork
Sir Roger set his teeth to work
This way and that the cork he ply'd
And wrench'd in vain from side to side.
In vain his ivory grinders strain'd
For still unmov'd the cork remained
And as a chieftain stout in fight
Exert his utmost, warlike might
Loth to desert his destin'd post.
So did the Cork maintain the field
And scorned to human force to yield
Still kept the feat each shock repressed
Which in the cellar it possessed
At length enrag'd with foul defeat
The levite burn'd with fiercer heat
Firm on the spungy cork he placed
His doubty thumb and downwards pressed
The yielding wood: —— But oh! dire luck
Fast in its place his own thumb stuck!

*The bottle has to be broken and he goes home
very much vexed; that night he has a dream and
sees in his dream Bacchus himself holding in one
hand a corkscrew and in the other a bottle of
champagne.*
Waking up, Master Roger remembers his dream:

Now to the mighty task he sets
His hands and o'er the anvil sweats
First put the iron in the fire
And hammers out the glowing wire
Then tortures it in curls around
As tendrils on the vine are found
Sharpens the bottom round the top
And finished bears it from the shop
Well pleased a Bottle-scrue he names
And sacred to the god proclaim.

ANON.
1732

2

Knaves and Rascals: Fake Wines

Wherever there is wine there is also fake wine to be found. Every age had its own recipes. One hundred fifty years ago, for example, it was difficult to find an authentic bottle of Bordeaux. Alexander Henderson describes the unflatteringly named *travail à l'Anglaise*, "which consists of adding to each hogshead of Bordeaux wine three of four gallons of Alicant or Benicarlo, half a gallon of stum wine, and sometimes a small quantity of Hermitage. This mixture . . . is exported under the name of claret."

Two hundred years earlier, Richard Lovelace, in the famous poem that contains the lines "Stone walls do not a prison make, / Nor iron bars a cage," refers to the practice then current of diluting wine with water in the lines "When flowing cups run swiftly round / With no allaying Thames." The anonymous poem "Quack Vintners" is mostly doggerel but testifies to the difficulty of finding undoctored wine in London of 1712. The poet praises "honest Folwell" who serves "genuine Claret, undisguis'd by art, / Quick to the taste, and cheerful to the heart." The French town of Cette (now Sète) was notorious for the production of fake wines, as recorded by visitors as different as Jefferson and Stendhal, quoted in this section. The final selection, taken from Richard Condon's novel *Arigato*, concerns, not fake wines, but stolen wines. The discussion is between a top criminal and an English wine merchant who plans to steal the inventory of Cruse, the Bordeaux shippers.

A classic wine story, which I could not trace back to its source, concerns a winemaker dying in whatever country has just experienced the latest wine scandal. Here is a version as told by Hugh Johnson:

. . . a wine grower lay on his death-bed. Even while the priest hovered, he beckoned his son to his side. "Before I go, my boy: the secret of the red wine." And he mumbled it into his son's attentive ear. He lay back. The priest gave him the last rites. And still he lingered.

His son bent over him again. "Father, if you have strength: I beseech you the secret of the white wine." "But my boy," he said, "there is no secret. The white wine is made from grapes."

How to Make Rhenish Wine

Take one Handful of dried Lemon Peels, and put them into ten or twelve Gallons of White-wine, and put into it one Pint of Damask-Rose-water; then rowl it up and down, and lay it upright, and open the Bung of it, and take a little Branch of Clarey, and let it sleep twenty-four Hours; then take it out, and it will taste very well.

The Art and Mystery of Vintners
1750

House Wines

The author, meeting a stranger in a country churchyard, recognises Burley, the late landlord of an inn he used to frequent near Cambridge, but now, it appears, retired to enjoy the fruits of his industry. Falling into a confidential discourse about the way in which this worthy conducted his business, the author receives from him a most luminous and satisfactory account of his wines.

"You can't deny it, Burley; your wines, of all kinds, were detestable—Port, Madeira, Claret, Champagne—"

"There now, sir! to prove how much gentlemen may be mistaken, I assure you, sir, as I'm an honest man, I never had but two sorts of wine in my cellar—Port and Sherry."

"How! when I myself have tried your Claret, your—"

"Yes, sir—*my* Claret, sir. One is obliged to give gentlemen everything they ask for, sir. Gentlemen who pay their money, sir, have a right to be served with whatever they may please to order, sir—especially young gentlemen from Cambridge, sir. I'll tell you how it was, sir. I would never have any wines in my house, sir, but Port and Sherry, because I *knew them* to be wholesome wines, sir; and this I will say, sir, my Port and Sherry were *the—very—best* I could procure in all England."

"How! the *best?*"

"Yes, sir—*at the price I paid for them.* But to explain the thing at once, sir. You must know, sir, that I hadn't been long in business when I discovered that gentlemen know very little about wine; but that if they didn't find some fault or other, they would appear to know much less—always excepting the young gentlemen from Cambridge, sir; *and they are excellent judges!* (And here again Burley's little eyes twinkled a humorous commentary on the concluding words of his sentence.) Well, sir; with respect to my dinner wines I was always tolerably safe; gentlemen seldom find fault at dinner; so whether it might happen to be Madeira, or pale Sherry, or brown, or—"

"Why, just now you told me you had but two sorts of wine in your cellar!"

"Very true, sir; Port *and* Sherry. But this was my plan, sir. If any one ordered Madeira:—From one bottle of Sherry take two glasses of wine, which replace by two glasses of water, and add thereto a slight squeeze of lemon; and this I found to give general satisfaction, especially to the young gentlemen from Cambridge, sir. But, upon the word of an honest man, I could scarcely get a living profit by my Madeira, sir, for I always used the best Brandy. As to the pale and brown Sherry, sir—a couple of glasses of nice pure water, in place of the same quantity of wine, made what I used to call *my delicate pale* (by the by, a squeeze of lemon added to *that* made a very fair Bucellas, sir—a wine not much called for now, sir); and for my old *brown* Sherry, a *leetle* burnt sugar was the thing. It looked very much like Sherry that had been twice to East Indies, sir; and, indeed, to my customers who were *very* particular about their wines I used to serve it as such."

"But, Mr. Burley, wasn't such a proceeding of a character rather—"

"I guess what you would say, sir; but I knew it to be a wholesome wine at bottom, sir. But my Port was the wine which gave me the most trouble. Gentlemen seldom agree about Port, sir. One gentleman would say, 'Burley, I don't like this wine; it is too heavy!' 'Is it, sir? I think I can find you a lighter.' *Out* went a glass of wine, and *in* went a glass of water. 'Well, sir,' I'd say, 'how do you approve of *that?*' 'Why—um—no; I can't say—' 'I understand, sir, you like an *older* wine—*softer*. I think I can please you, sir.' Pump again, sir. 'Now, sir,' says I (wiping the decanter with a napkin, and triumphantly holding it up to the light), 'try this, if you please.' 'That's it, Burley—that's the very wine; bring another bottle of the same.' But one can't please everybody the same way, sir. Some gentlemen would complain of my Port as being poor—without body. In went *one* glass of Brandy. If that didn't answer, 'Ay, gentlemen,' says I, 'I know what will please you; you like a fuller-bodied, rougher wine.' Out went *two* glasses of wine, and in went *two* or *three* glasses of Brandy. This used to be a *very* favorite wine—but *only* with the young gentlemen from Cambridge, sir.''

"And your Claret?"

"My good, wholesome Port, again, sir. Three wines out, three waters in, one pinch of tartaric acid, two ditto orris-powder. For a fuller Claret, a little Brandy; for a lighter Claret, more water."

"But how did you contrive about Burgundy?"

"That was *my Claret*, sir, with from three to six drops of Bergamot, according as gentlemen liked a full flavour or a delicate flavour. As for Champagne, sir, that, *of course*, I made myself."

"How do you mean 'of course,' Burley?"

"Oh, sir," said he, with an innocent yet waggish look, "surely everybody makes his own Champagne—*else what* CAN *become of all the gooseberries?*"

CHARLES TOVEY
Wine and Wine Countries

Château Kelly

Michael Kelly, the once popular singer and composer, was once in business in the Haymarket as a wine merchant, and wrote over his door, 'Michael Kelly, Composer of Music, and Importer of Wine.' Sheridan suggested the following alteration, 'Michael Kelly, Importer of Music and Composer of Wine;' 'for,' said the wit, 'none of his music is original, and all his wine is, since he makes it himself.'

London City Press
1863

Bordeaux '73—A Great Scandal?

Bonjour.

Many people, you know, seem to think that the supply of Bordeaux wines is rather like the world supply of oil—that there is only a limited amount available each year. But there are big differences between the wine situation and the oil crisis. For one thing, new sources of Bordeaux wine are being found every day in countries all over the world. For another, ordinary Bordeaux wine has a slightly fruitier taste than oil.

Wine-growing can briefly be described as "the art of mixing and skilfully labelling fermented grape juice." It is a craft found in many countries, yet sadly has been surrounded with such secrecy and snobbery that many newcomers find themselves confused by the lore attached to it. Will this year's Bordeaux scandal be a great one or just passable? How well has the Italian wine scandal of four years ago lasted? Are the wine labels attached to bottles in England as good as the French ones they have replaced? Where does wine marked "Produce of France" come from? To answer this sort of question is the task of this little guide. When it has been mastered the novice should be in a position to choose for himself, with some confidence, whether he wishes to drink wine or something far safer like stout or mineral water.

Red wine has to be nurtured and constantly looked after if it is to grow from a crude fermentation to a superb beverage. A really good wine can start life as a rough vintage in Morocco or Australia, travel across the sea to France to become a modest local growth and end life as one of the finest clarets money can buy. But it must be carefully guarded during this process in case it is contaminated by the gaze of the tax inspector or in case it accidentally ends up as a Spanish red.

(There is nothing wrong with a good Spanish red, of course, except the profit margin.)

There are three great wine-growing areas in the Bordeaux region:—a huge mixing vat not far from the city, a lorry depot to the south and a vast tanker installation near the coast. (Bordeaux, incidentally, means in French "near water" and has always been applied to wines from this region.) It is here that many of the great Château wines come from.

(Château is the French word for the little drawing of a castle that many firms like to put on the label, to encourage confidence in the wine. Some of these Châteaux are very big and important, which means more money being spent on the ink for the label, which usually means less money spent on the wine. By French law the word Château cannot be put on a wine label unless it is spelled correctly.)

The process of wine-producing starts with the traditional ceremony of treading the invoices. The invoices, import documents and tax returns are all put into a large vat and there trodden by several accountants until the ink has begun to run a juicy blue colour. The documents are then removed and carefully treated so that the wine begins to mature into something much better than the rough Tunisian it may have started as. This is known as the "first labelling," and by the end of the week the wine should have turned into a respectable mixture of Moroccan red and Chablis, somewhat resembling an immature rosé.

Now comes the long process of fermentation and filtering during which all impure elements must be removed from the label it will eventually bear in the shops (the "second labelling"). It is at this point that the wine is awarded its so-called "cru." Cru, in French, means "thought to be," and it is one of the traditional skills of the French wine-grower that he can judge by tasting the wine, mixing it, testing it again and sloshing in some rosé to be on the safe side, just how high a cru he can put on it. "Premier cru" is thought to be first class, "grand cru" is thought to be great, "cru exceptionnel" is supposed to be excellent, and so on. The whole point of the word cru, of course, is that it protects the grower against trades description offences.

MILES KINGTON

A Merry Ballad of Vintners

By dint of dart, by push of sharpened spear,
  By sweep of scythe or thump of spike-set mace,
By poleaxe, steel-tipped arrow-head or shear
  Of double-handed sword or well-ground ace,
  By dig of dirk or tuck with double face,
Let them be done to death; or let them light
On some ill stead, where brigands lurk by night,
  That they the hearts from out their breasts may tear,

Cut off their heads, then drag them by the hair
And cast them on the dunghill to the swine,
   That sows and porkers on their flesh may fare,
The vintners that put water in our wine.

Let Turkish quarrels run them through the rear
   And rapiers keen their guts and vitals lace;
Singe their perukes with Greek fire, ay, and sear
   Their brains with levins; string them brace by brace
   Up to the gibbet; or for greater grace,
Let gout and dropsy slay the knaves outright:
Or else let drive into each felon wight
   Irons red-heated in the furnace-flare:
   Let half a score of hangmen flay them bare;
And on the morrow, seethed in oil or brine,
   Let four great horses rend them then and there,
The vintners that put water in our wine.

Let some great gunshot blow their heads off sheer;
   Let thunders catch them in the market-place;
Let rend their limbs and cast them far and near,
   For dogs to batten on their bodies base;
   Or let the lightning-stroke their sight efface.
Frost, hail and snow let still upon them bite;
Strip off their clothes and leave them naked quite,
   For rain to drench them in the open air;
   Lard them with knives and poniards and then bear
Their carrion forth and soak it in the Rhine;
   Break all their bones with mauls and do not spare
The vintners that put water in our wine.

ENVOI

Prince, may God curse their vitals! is my prayer;
   And may they burst with venom all, in fine,
These traitorous thieves, accursèd and unfair,
   The vintners that put water in our wine.

FRANÇOIS VILLON

Milk or Cream?

The expansion of the company [Harveys of Bristol] was smooth, efficient, and uneventful save for one ludicrous episode of bureaucratic farce just after the last war. It was a period of muddled government and preposterous restrictions, when Mr. John Strachey was enjoying distinguished office as Minister of Food with Dr. Edith Summerskill as his parliamentary secretary. A literal-minded hack in the 'Food Standards and Labelling Division' of this thankless ministry was suddenly inspired with the thought that the name *Bristol Milk* contravened Regulation 1 of the Defence (Sale of Food) Regulations and misled the gullible public 'as to the nature, substance, or quality of a food or in particular as to its nutritional or dietary value,' as it had no connexion whatsoever with a cow, even though, no doubt, it could be used for making a syllabub. But that had not occurred to him. There came into the bureaucratic mind the horrific image of an inept nanny filling her charge's little bottle with an alcholic beverage from distant Spain—not even a decent, British sherry. When, with unkind logic, Harveys suggested that if *Bristol Milk* were illegal, then so, surely, was *Bristol Cream,* and if so there would have to be a general and widespread purge of shaving creams, hair creams, face creams, vanishing creams, boot creams, perhaps even Cream of Magnesia, and certainly all the lesser creams, the literal mind of the ministry could only reply that it was 'discussing regulations pertaining to the sale of food only.' The answer opens up an endless realm of speculation: what, for instance, of the unfortunate child who asks for a taurine optic and is given a mere peppermint confection? Warner Allen was moved to poetry:

> A Book of Verses underneath the Bough,
> A Jug of Wine milk'd from the Sherry Cow—
> And Thou beside me in the Wilderness. . . .

JULIAN JEFFS
Sherry

But Will it Sell?

The English merchants knew that the first-rate wine of the Factory had become excellent; but they wished it to exceed the limits which Nature had assigned to it, and that when drunk, it should feel like liquid fire in the stomach; that it should burn like inflamed gunpowder; that it should have the tint of ink; that it should be like the sugar of Brazil in sweetness, and like the spices of India in aromatic flavour. They began by recommending, by way of secret, that it was proper to dash it with brandy to give it strength; and with elder-berries, or the rind of the ripe grape, to give it colour; and as the persons who used the prescription found the wine increase in price, and the English merchants still complaining of a want of strength, colour and maturity in the article supplied, the recipe was propagated till the wines became a mere confusion of mixtures.*

JOSEPH JAMES FORRESTER
A Word or Two on Port Wine
1844

Port, Anyone?

I remember my grandfather, Lord Pembroke, when he placed wine before his guests, said, 'There, gentlemen, is my champagne, my claret, &c. I am no great judge, and I give you these on the authority of my wine merchant; but I can answer for my port, for *I made it myself.'*

LORD PALMERSTON

Underground Wines

There is in this city a certain fraternity of chemical operators, who work under ground in holes, caverns, and dark retirements, to conceal their mysteries from the eyes and observation of mankind. These subterraneous philosophers are daily employed in the trans-mutation of liquors, and, by the power of magical drugs and incantations, raising under the streets of London the choicest products of the hills and valleys of France. They can squeeze Bordeaux out of the sloe, and draw Champagne from an apple. Virgil, in that remarkable prophecy,
"The ripening grape shall hang on every thorn,"
seems to have hinted at this art, which can turn a plantation of northern hedges into a vineyard. These adepts are known among one another by the name of wine-brewers, and, I am afraid, do

* 1754 letter from Douro agents to Oporto shippers.

great injury, not only to her Majesty's customs, but to the bodies of many of her good subjects.

Having received sundry complaints against these invisible workmen, I ordered the proper officer of my court to ferret them out of their respective caves, and bring them before me, which was yesterday executed accordingly. . . .

The counsel for the brewers had a face so extremely inflamed and illuminated with carbuncles, that I did not wonder to see him an advocate for these sophistications. His rhetoric was likewise such as I should have expected from the common draught, which I found he often drank to great excess. Indeed, I was so surprised at his figure and parts, that I ordered him to give me a taste of his usual liquor; which I had no sooner drank, than I found a pimple rising in my forehead; and felt such a sensible decay in my understanding, that I would not proceed in the trial till the fume of it was entirely dissipated. . . .

When I had sent out my summons to these people, I gave at the same time orders to each of them to bring the several ingredients he made use of in distinct phials, which they had done accordingly, and ranged them into two rows on each side of the court. The workmen were drawn up in ranks behind them. The merchant informed me, that in one row of phials were the several colours they dealt with, and in the other the tastes. He then showed me, on the right hand, one who went by the name of Tom Tintoret, who (as he told me) was the greatest master in his colouring of any vintner in London. To give me proof of his art, he took a glass of fair water, and by the infusion of three drops out of one of his phials, converted it into a most beautiful pale Burgundy. Two more of the same kind heightened it into a perfect Languedoc; from thence it passed into a florid Hermitage; and after having gone through two or three other changes, by the addition of a single drop, ended in a very deep Pontac. This ingenious virtuoso, seeing me very much surprised at his art, told me, that he had not an opportunity of showing it in perfection, having only made use of water for the groundwork of his colouring; but that if I were to see an operation upon liquors of stronger bodies, the art would appear to a much greater advantage. . . .

The artists on my other hand were ordered, in the second place, to make some experiments of their skill before me: upon which the famous Harry Sippet stepped out, and asked me, what I would be pleased to drink? At the same time he filled out three or four white liquors in a glass, and told me, that it should be what I pleased to call for; adding very learnedly, that the liquor before him was as the naked substance or first matter of his compound, to which he and his friend, who stood over against him, could give what accidents or form they pleased. Finding him so great a philospher, I desired that he would convey into it the qualities and essence of right Bordeaux. "Coming, coming, sir," said he, with the air of a drawer; and after having cast his eye on the several tastes and flavours that stood before him, he took up a little cruet that was filled with a kind of inky juice, and pouring some of it out into the glass of white wine, presented it to me, and told me, this was the wine over which most of the business of the last term had been dispatched. I must confess, I looked upon that sooty drug, which he held up in his cruet, as the quintessence of English Bordeaux, and therefore desired him to give me a glass of it by itself, which he did with great unwillingness. My cat at that time sat by me upon the elbow of my chair; and as I did not care for making the experiment upon myself, I reached it to her to sip of it, which had like to have cost her her life; for notwithstanding it flung her at first into freakish tricks, quite contrary to her usual gravity, in less than a quarter of an hour she fell into convulsions; and, had it not been a creature more tenacious of life than any other, would certainly have died under the operation. . . .

For my own part, I have resolved hereafter to be very careful in my liquors; and have agreed with a friend of mine in the army, upon their next march, to secure for me two hogsheads of the best stomach-wine in the cellars of Versailles, for the good of my lucubrations, and the comfort of my old age.

JOSEPH ADDISON
The Tatler
1708

A Word to the Wise

These quantities [of imported wine] amount to a very great value; and, being imported in one year, show us the magnitude of the trade; the quantity too being increased, if common fame may be believed, by some mixtures they receive here, to the scandal of the tradesmen concerned in it: and indeed the charge is made apparent, on the sale of a vintner's stock, when he dies or fails; for none of his brethren will buy it under a deduction too monstrous to be mention'd; knowing, no doubt, how little genuine wine is in the quantity, in proportion thereto.

DANIEL DEFOE
The Complete English Tradesman
1726

Vin du Pays

Today I performed what might be called some tourist chores. I saw a soap factory and a *chai,* or wine factory. Out of wine, sugar, iron filings, and some flower essences, they make the wines of every country. A personage wrapped up in dignity assured me that neither litharge nor any injurious substances were used in the factory. I took that with a grain of salt.

STENDHAL
Memoirs of a Tourist

Cette to Go

The inferior quality is not at all esteemed. It is bought by the merchants of Cette, as is also the wine of Bezieres, and sold by them for Frontignan of the first quality. They sell thirty thousand pieces a year under that name. The town of Frontignan marks its casks with a hot iron: an individual of that place having two casks emptied, was offered forty livres for the empty cask by a merchant of Cette.

THOMAS JEFFERSON
Journals
1787

Choose Your Wine

I said that it was good—good for our stomachs—to see no English bunting at Cette. The reason is, that Cette is a great manufacturing place, and that what they manufacture there is neither cotton nor wool, Perigord pies, nor Rheims biscuits,—but wine. "*Ici,*" will a Cette industrial write with the greatest coolness over his Porte Cochere—"*Ici on fabrique des vins.*" All the wines in the world, indeed, are made in Cette. You have only to give an order for Johannisberg, or Tokay—nay, for all I know, for the Falernian of the Romans, or the Nectar of the gods—and the Cette manufacturers will promptly supply you. They are great chemists, these gentlemen, and have brought the noble art of adulteration to a perfection which would make our own mere logwood and sloe-juice practitioners pale and wan with envy. But the great trade of the place is not so much adulterating as concocting wine. Cette is well-situated for this notable manufacture. The wines of southern Spain are brought by coasters from Barcelona and Valencia. The inferior Bordeaux growths come pouring from the Garonne by the Canal du Midi; and the hot and fiery Rhône wines are floated along the chain of etangs and canals from Beaucaire. With all these raw materials, and, of course, a chemical laboratory to boot, it would be hard if the clever folks of Cette could not turn out a very good imitation of any wine in demand. They will doctor you up bad Bordeaux with violet powders and rough cider—colour it with cochineal and turnsole, and outswear creation that it is precious Château Margaux—vintage of '25. Champagne, of course, they make by hogsheads. Do you wish sweet liqueur wines from Italy and the Levant? The Cette people will mingle old Rhône wines with boiled sweet wines from the neighbourhood of Lunel, and charge you any price per bottle. Do you wish to make new Claret old? A Cette manufacturer will place it in his oven, and, after twenty hours regulated application of heat, return it to you nine years in bottle. Port, Sherry, and Madeira, of course, are fabricated in abundance with any sort of bad, cheap wine and brandy, for a stock, and with half the concoctions in a druggist's shop for seasoning. Cette, in fact, is the very capital and emporium of the tricks and rascalities of the wine-trade; and it supplies almost all the Brazils, and a great proportion of the northern European nations with their after-dinner drinks. To the grateful Yankees it sends out thousands of tons of Ay and Moët, besides no end of Johannisberg, Hermitage, and Château Margaux, the fine qualities and dainty aroma of which are highly prized by the transatlantic amateurs. The Dutch flag fluttered plentifully in the harbour, so that I presume Mynheer is a customer to the Cette industrials—or, at all events, he helps in the distribution of their wares. The old French West Indian colonies also patronise their ingenious countrymen of Cette; and Russian magnates get drunk on Chambertin and Romanée Conti, made of low Rhône, and low Burgundy brewages, eked out by the contents of the graduated phial. I fear, however, that we do come in—in the matter of "fine golden Sherries, at 22s. 9½d. a dozen," or "peculiar old-crusted Port, at 1s. 9d."—for a share of the Cette manufactures; and it is very probable that after the wine is fabricated upon the shores of the Mediterranean, it is still further improved upon the banks of the Thames.

ANGUS B. REACH
Claret and Olives

Decorated Cheats

Dear Mr. Punch:—I trust that, under the circumstances, I may be pardoned for obtruding my own concerns on your attention. It is not to my taste generally to court public attention, but I find that my modesty is really prejudicial to my interests. For instance, on looking over the awards given to wine merchants in the Paris Exposition of this year, I find that a bronze medal has been awarded to a certain firm in Cette for 'imitation wines;' and, in another instance, a gentleman from the same town, engaged in a similar occupation, has been awarded 'an honourable mention.'

I too, sir, am interested in the fabrication of 'imitations,' but my efforts are directed rather to money than to wine; in short, I have a great idea that a good business could be done in imitation bank-notes. I can assure you they can be produced at twopence each in any quantities; but hitherto I have had the fear of the police before my eyes. Hearing, however, that 'imitation wines' have received the favour of the Great National Exposition under Government patronage in France, I am induced to believe that the art of falsification is not by any means criminal. Do you think, Mr. Punch, that if I were to send a few specimens of Bank of England fivers (imitation), that they would be too late to obtain the attention of the jury on specie? I may not aspire to a bronze medal; but perhaps a false bank-note may be as worthy of an 'honourable mention' as an 'imitation' of Port or Sherry.

Your obedient servant,

A FORGER, *(sub rosa)*.

Punch
1867

A Judicious Blend

The first growths of Médoc are never sent to England in a perfect state, but are, when destined for that market, mingled with other wines and with spirit of wine. The taste of the pure wine is not spirituous enough for the English palate, and more body is given these wines by the mixture of Hermitage, of Beni Carlos from Spain, and alcohol, ordinarily to the extent of three or four-twentieths per cent. By this means all the delicate flavour, the delicious and salutary quality of the wine is destroyed, to give it a warmer and more intoxicating effect, without which in England these wines would not find a market. Mixing Hermitage or Beni Carlos alone with the wines of Médoc would not be prejudicial, though it must alter their delicate quality. Beni Carlos is often mixed with Médoc wines, when they are nearly worn out, to restore their body. Natural and healthful wines, the genuine offspring of simple fermentation, are not the fashion in England; hence artificial means must be used to please an artificial taste.

CYRUS REDDING
1836

Wine Merchant to the King

In the royal cellars of Carlton House, there was enshrined, if we may so speak, a small quantity of wine which, like the gems worn by the Irish lady, was both "rich and rare." It was only produced by George IV when he had around him his most select and wittiest friends. The precious deposit gradually diminished; year by year, as in the case of the famous shagreen skin of the French novelist Balzac, it grew less, until, at last, a couple of dozen bottles only were left, gleaming at the bottom of their bins like gems in a mine, and full of liquid promise to those who needed the especial comfort which it was their duty to impart. These, however, were left so long unasked for, that the gentlemen of the King's suite who had the control of the grape department, deemed them forgotten, and at their own mirthful table drank them all but two, with infinite delight to themselves, and to the better health of their master. They soon found, however, that there was "garlic in the flowers," as the Turkish proverb has it; and their embarrassment was not small, when the King, giving his orders for a choice dinner on a certain night, intimated his desire that a good supply of his favourite wine should grace the board. In Courts, "to hear is to obey;" and the officials who had drunk the wine, at once resorted to an eminent firm, well-skilled to give advice in such delicate wine-cases. The physician asked but for a sample bottle, and to be told the exact hour at which the favourite draught would be asked for. This was complied with, and in due time a proper amount of the counterfeit wine was forwarded to Carlton House, and there broached and drunk with such encomiums, that the officers who were in the secret had some difficulty in maintaining an official gravity of countenance. The brewer of the new wine was certainly a first-rate artist; and if he ever achieved knighthood and a coat-of-arms, I would give him a "Bruin" for his crest, and, "The drink! the drink! dear Hamlet!" for his device. This anecdote, I may farther notice, has often been told, and nearly as often been discredited; but I am assured by an officer of the household, who speaks "*avec connaissance de fait*," that it is substantially true.

JOHN DORAN
Table Traits

Call My Lawyer

Once upon a time, a long, long time ago, when I first came to England, there were two bad men in London: one was an Englishman and the other a Frenchman: birds of a feather, they worked together. The Englishman was a banqueting wine waiter, that is a part-time waiter called in on nights when extra staff happened to be wanted for large parties. The Frenchman was a wine 'expert.' They had a cellar under one of the arches below the Adelphi: the Englishman collected empty Champagne bottles and corks, brought them to his partner who filled the bottles with a cheap, sweetish white wine, pumped a dash of gas in it, corked the bottle, wired it, and dressed it with a little gold or silver paper to match the rest of the foil. The Englishman had a wonderful frock coat with six leather inside pockets, three left and three right, and he would go to Hurst Park and other race meetings near London, with a stock of fake Champagne in a cart; he would mix with the crowd and offer 'first-class Champagne' at 5s. per bottle. The price was tempting and out of the six pockets of his frock coat came the bottles of Champagne asked for, just as a conjuror produces a live rabbit out of a top-hat. One Saturday afternoon, at Hurst Park, a clerk from the offices of Messrs. Moët et Chandon's London agents had a win and called for a bottle of his firm's wine: the bottle that was handed to him looked quite right to him, but he happened to look at the cork as it came out with remarkable promptness, and there was no possible doubt about the lettering burnt on the side of the cork: it was POMMERY and not MOËT. This is how the man with the six-pocket frock coat was arrested and charged by the London agents of Moët and Pommery. Robert Billings, for Moët, and I for Pommery, gave evidence in Court, and we agreed that it was possible, even probable, that both firms had bought corks from the same Spanish cork merchants, but that it was quite impossible for Moët to use Pommery corks, as each firm did its own branding of the corks in its cellars; and between the Moët cellars at Epernay, and the Pommery cellars at Reims, there were some miles of hills, woods and vineyards. Eventually the man was found guilty, and fined some ridiculous sum—I forget exactly what it was, but I know that he paid it at once and went home. . . .

The next time I was in the witness box, the case had a far more satisfactory ending. The traveller of a City firm who sold a great deal of the cheaper types of wine in the London East End had called upon one of his regular customers to be told that he, the traveller, need not call any more for orders as his wines were too dear. The traveller swore that there were no cheaper wines than those sold by his firm, and when he was given what his former customer sold as wine, he spat it out and said in the presence of all in the room 'This is not wine; it is poison!' The publican brought an action for slander, demanding damages from the traveller's firm. The head of the firm accused of slander came to see me and asked me to taste a sample of the 'poison' wine, and tell him whether he had better settle the matter out of court, or go to court with a fair chance of winning. There was no need to taste the stuff; its stink was enough. I advised going to Court, and promised to give evidence—which I did. When in the witness box I was given a full glass and asked to say what the wine was. I tasted it and said that it was a cheap but fair enough wine, probably from Algeria. I was then given another full glass and asked the same question. The moment the glass came near my nose I knew what it was and did not taste it. 'This,' I said, 'I can swear is not wine, but I cannot tell you what it is. You had better ask a drain inspector.' The prosecution lost the case and had to pay all costs, but that was not all: the defence made the prosecuting publican admit that he did not buy the stuff; he made it on the premises!

ANDRÉ L. SIMON
In the Twilight

An Instant Wine Cellar

"I put it this way, Monsieur Bonnette. I have need of a number of experienced men in your field to share approximately ten million francs with me."

"A good day's pay."

"For most of us."

"What kind of work? It must be very dangerous work to offer so much."

"I like to think that most of the danger has been foreseen and will have been removed."

"You make it sound as if you are asking me to help you to rob a bank," Bonnette said blandly. "What else could yield ten million francs?"

"Wine."

"The wine is here, Captain Huntington," the sommelier said,

pouring into an empty glass beside the canary Blagny. The Captain regarded the wine, inhaled it, then sipped it. "It is not only noble, it is royal," he said to the wine waiter. "As you commanded, Captain." He poured the red wine into the glasses of both men as the *commis* cleared away the Barquette of Mussels. As Bonnette sipped the Clos du Vougeot '34 he rolled his eyes like an apprentice minstrel man to indicate that he wanted to praise the wine, but first to business.

"What kind of work if not a bank?" he asked.

"Eighteen thousand cases of the finest wine in France. Ten million francs' worth of wine—our share."

Bonnette worked away at the saddle of lamb as he answered. "You will need an army of men just to lift it."

"I will need eighteen unskilled laborers, two skilled technicians, two executives, two trucks, eighteen forklift trucks, three long moving belt mechanisms, four walkie-talkie units, twenty-seven feet of nylon line, two three-inch rolls of adhesive tape, nine telephone numbers, one hypodermic needle, two heavy-duty Mercedes tow trucks, four car mechanics, and certain other things I will provide myself."

"You don't sound like you need help to me," Bonnette said.

"I need people, reliable, experienced people."

"What kind of technicians?"

"An arsonist and an alarms man. The alarms man has to have daring and physical strength."

"All alarms men have to have daring, my friend. They go in first and feed on their own nerves. The job depends on them."

"Indeed."

"What do you pay this daring alarms man out of the ten million francs?"

"Fifty thousand francs."

"Never."

"I won't be making the arrangement with him, you will."

From across the room, they were two businessmen beating the stockholders out of an expensive lunch. Bonnette sipped his wine and rolled his eyes again like a burnt cork darky. "If your job turns up more wine like that, my friend, I'll take a case." He burped discreetly into a napkin. "Is that all you want me to do? Make your deals?"

"Much more. You would be in charge of the entire operation directly under me. You would procure the men and materials. You would be in charge of security."

"For how much of the ten million?"

"One third to you, including your assistant. You pay him whatever you work out with him."

"What does my assistant do?"

"He should steal all necessary transport and equipment for one thing. He should be in charge of loading, we think."

"Who is we?"

"I have a friend who is an IBM computer."

"Why should you get two thirds?"

"I don't actually. I get one third for originating the idea and running the operation, for financing it as well, of course. Only I am qualified to run this operation as it is organized. The other third goes for the manner in which it has been organized—for the foolproof, superdetailed, incredibly complex plan."

"When do I see the plan?"

"Probably never. But if we should decide to reveal it that would happen on the morning of the day we leave."

"How do you dispose of eighteen thousand cases of wine?"

"Well—that would be part of the plan, wouldn't it?"

"I am very sorry, that is something I have to know."

"You will know that part. I did not say you would never know. I will tell you one hour before we make the transfer. Which will be eleven hours after we have the wine."

"Hot wine."

"What?"

"The whole country will be looking for us. It would be like stealing the secret formula for Coca-Cola in the United States. Eleven hours with eighteen thousand cases of classic French wine will be like a lifetime."

RICHARD CONDON
Arigato

3

The Vintage Observed

The harvest and the transformation of grapes into wine is a subject that has often been written about, both technically and romantically, and many writers have recorded their impressions of vineyards and vintages. Some are included in the section "Travelers' Tales," others are collected here, especially those that concern the vintage itself. There is, of course, a certain similarity to such descriptions, and I have chosen just a few, along with several observations about the practice of treading grapes by foot.

A number of Greek and Roman writers turned their attention to the practice of viticulture, and their works are still useful after two thousand years. Although practical manuals are outside the scope of this book, I can't resist quoting a few lines from the *Georgics* of Virgil, in C. Day Lewis' translation:

> Be the first to dig the land, the first to wheel off the
>   prunings
> For the bonfire, the first to bring your vine-poles under
>   cover;
> But the last to gather the vintage. Twice will the vines
>   grow thick
> With shade, and twice will a tangle of brairs overrun the
>   vineyards;
> Each makes for hard work: so admire a large estate if you
>   like,
> But farm a small one.

Although the vintage is picturesque, it is hard work and can also be dangerous, as we learn from Pliny. In his *Natural History* he describes the vineyards of Campania, whose vines are entwined around tall poplar trees, "the height being sometimes so stupendous that the vintager when hired is wont to stipulate for his funeral pile and a grave at the owner's expense."

The Roman poet Ausonius owned a vineyard in Bordeaux, although whether or not it was at the site of the present Château Ausone is not certain. In his long poem "The Moselle," written in the fourth century, the sight of a German vineyard reminds him of his own property, "so do my own vineyards cast their reflection on the yellowing Garonne. For from the topmost ridge to the foot of the slope the river-side is thickly planted with green vines. The people, happy in their toil, and the restless husbandmen are busy, now on the hill-top, now on the slope, exchanging shouts in boisterous rivalry." A few lines later, he describes the vineyards of the Moselle reflected in the river:

What color paints the river shallows, when Hesperus has brought the shades of evening and dyed the Moselle with the green of the hillside! The hill-tops quiver in the ripples, the vine leaves tremble from afar and the grape clusters swell in the crystal stream.

Although I wasn't looking for technical information, I often came across descriptions of winemaking that were charmingly phrased, especially in comparison to the enological tracts of today. For example, a leading enologist recently described fermentation as "essentially a process of reversible inter- and intra-molecular oxidation reductions, phosphorylations and an irreversible decarboxylation."

Here is Alexander Henderson, writing 150 years ago:

. . . small bubbles first collect on the top, and may be seen gradually issuing from the central parts of the liquor, and buoying up the husks, stones, and other grosser matters which it contains: as the disengagement of gas proceeds, a hissing noise is produced by the bursting of bubbles, and a frothy crust, or scum, is formed by the viscid particles which they have carried to the surface. . . . At length, these commotions of the fluid abate spontaneously; and after a few days' and sometimes a few hours' rapid fermentation, the ebullition ceases altogether, the mass subsides to its former bulk, and the crust, and solid particles which disturbed the transparency of the liquor, are precipitated to the bottom of the vessel.

More recently, some sense of the mystery of grapes and wine is conveyed in D. H. Lawrence's poem "Grapes." Writing about "Green, dim, invisible flourishing of vines / Royally gesticulate," Lawrence continues:

Look now even now, how it keeps its power of invisibility!
Look how black, how blue-black, how globed in Egyptian darkness
Dropping among his leaves, hangs the dark grape!
See him there, the swart, so palpably invisible:
Whom shall we ask about him?

In this section you will find such dissimilar writings as Homer's description of Achilles' shield; an excerpt from François Mauriac, who came from Bordeaux and set many of his novels there; part of a report by the philosopher John Locke; and a reflection by Everett Crosby, who for many years owned a vineyard not far from New York City.

I Am the True Vine

I am the true vine, and my Father is the husbandman.
Every branch in me that beareth not fruit he taketh away: and every branch that beareth fruit, he purgeth it, that it may bring forth more fruit.
Now ye are clean through the word which I have spoken unto you.
Abide in me, and I in you. As the branch cannot bear fruit of itself, except it abide in the vine; no more can ye, except ye abide in me.
I am the vine, ye are the branches: He that abideth in me, and I in him, the same bringeth forth much fruit: for without me ye can do nothing.

St. John, Chapter 15

The Vine

I Dream'd this mortal part of mine
Was Metamorphoz'd to a Vine;
Which crawling one and every way,
Enthrall'd my dainty *Lucia*.
Me thought, her long small legs and thighs
I with my *Tendrils* did surprize;
Her Belly, Buttocks, and her Waste
By my soft *Nerv'lits* were embrac'd:
About her head I writhing hung, ⎫
And with rich clusters (hid among ⎬
The leaves) her temples I behung: ⎭
So that my *Lucia* seem'd to me
Young *Bacchus* ravisht by his tree.
My curles about her neck did craule,
And armes and hands they did enthrall:
So that she could not freely stir,
(All parts there made one prisoner.)
But when I crept with leaves to hide
Those parts, which maids keep unespy'd,
Such fleeting pleasures there I took,
That with the fancie I awook;
And found (Ah me!) this flesh of mine
More like a *Stock,* then like a *Vine.*

ROBERT HERRICK

Achilles' Shield

Also he set therein a vineyard teeming plenteously with clusters, wrought fair in gold; black were the grapes, but the vines hung throughout on silver poles. And around it he ran a ditch of cyanus, and round that a fence of tin; and one single pathway led to it, whereby the vintagers might go when they should gather the vintage. And maidens and striplings in childish glee bare the sweet fruit in plaited baskets. And in the midst of them a boy made pleasant music on a clear-toned viol, and sang thereto a sweet Linossong with delicate voice; while the rest with feet falling together kept time with the music and song.

HOMER
The Iliad

A Vineyard Cycle

But wine is a challenge that never ends, because no two wines and no two seasons are ever alike. The leaves fall, the wood grows hard. The snow comes, and the naked vines stand out in the empty night, alone and unprotected. What will happen to them *this* year? What form will the pruning take in the early days of spring? Each vine must be examined and trimmed according to how well it grew the previous summer, and how well it survived the winter. Then the sap runs, the growth starts once again. No two springs proceed in the same way. Maybe it will be cold and wet, or maybe unduly warm, bringing unseasonal growth and the chance of being caught by a late frost. Will June be cool? How many sprays will we have to use to keep at bay the ever lurking bugs and blights that prey upon the vines? Will late summer be hot and dry, bringing the acid down and the sugar up to the peak of perfection? Or will it rain during the ripening period, forcing more liquid into the grape than the ripened skin can hold, causing it to burst and spill the juice on the berries below, which in turn will cause them to rot? Will the birds be kind or will they literally destroy the harvest? And what about the yellowjackets, which in their search for liquid, any liquid, punch holes in the grapes, reducing each bunch to a soggy mess?

Then it is over (generally before one is quite prepared) and the grapes are in and the winemaking has begun. In most other fruit-growing endeavors this is the end of the line, but with wine it is just the beginning. An apple is picked, an apple is shipped, an apple is eaten, period. But to the winemaker the crucial time is at hand. No two fermentations ever go exactly alike, and the young wine must be watched as an infant is watched. Will it turn moodily sick, or will it bound exuberantly upward into excellence? And even as the winemaker ponders these matters the leaves are falling, the wood is growing hard, the snow falls and the vines renew their never ending battle with the cold. The whole cycle is beginning again, and it is a challenge not only to the vines but also to the winemaker. One must be an optimist, I think, to be a successful vineyardist, and if I am nothing else I am that. The challenge must be confidently met as we met it for more than twenty years, and if one does not have complete faith in the ultimate outcome then the challenge is not worth facing. I have enjoyed this challenge and though unhorsed in many a joust I have ridden out each spring with the sure conviction that nothing can possibly go wrong this time.

It is this inevitability, this being at the beck and call of a gigantic force too complex to understand, that the neophyte winemaker finds so hard to fathom. There can be no long-range planning during the growing season for the simple reason that there can be no long-range planning of the weather. In the winter, with snow on the ground and the vines asleep, the work of bottling, labeling, racking, evaluating can proceed on a more or less preplanned schedule. But in the summer everything must hang loose. No fine, quiet, clear and cool day can be squandered on inside work, for this is a luxury that may cost the winemaker dearly. It makes no difference that he has made plans to bottle on Tuesday and Wednesday. If a spraying is coming up, and the vines need tying before the sprayer can run the rows, the bottling must wait if Tuesday dawns fair. The orders? The orders can wait. The grapes cannot.

EVERETT CROSBY
The Vintage Years

A Hailstorm

Tonight I woke, fighting for breath. I felt a compulsion to get up. I dragged myself to my chair, and sat, reading over, to the accompaniment of a howling wind, the last few pages I had written. I was appalled by the light they shed on my deepest self. Before settling down to go on with them, I leaned for a while at the window. The gale had dropped. Calèse was wrapped in sleep. There was not so much as a breeze, and the sky was full of stars. Suddenly, about three o'clock, there was another squall. The sky rumbled, and heavy, icy drops began to fall. They rattled on the tiles so loudly that I feared they might be hail. I thought that my heart had stopped beating.

The grapes have barely "set." Next year's harvest covers all the slopes. But it seems that it may be with it as it is with those young animals which the hunter tethers and then leaves in darkness to attract the prowling beasts of prey. Clouds, heavy with thunder, are snuffling round the proffered vines. . . .

A hiss like that of a wild beast, then a deafening din and a great glare filling all the sky. In the panic silence that followed, I heard the sound of fireworks on the hills, set off by the vine-growers to scatter the clouds or resolve the hail to water. Rockets were leaping into the air from the darkness where shrouded Barsac and Sauternes were waiting in terror for the coming of the scourge. The bell of St. Vincent's, which keeps the hail away, has been ringing with might and main. The sound of it is like that of someone singing in the night because he is afraid. Suddenly, from the roof there came that noise as of a handful of flung pebbles . . . hailstones! Time was when I should have rushed to the window. I could hear the sound of shutters flung back, and your voice crying down to a man who was hurrying across the yard: "Is it serious?" . . . " 'Tis all mixed with rain," he replied; "and that be lucky: but 'tis coming down proper hard." A frightened child has just run barefoot down the passage. I find myself, from force of habit, reckoning: "A hundred thousand francs gone west . . ."—but I have not stirred. Nothing, in the old days, could have kept me from rushing downstairs—one night they found me out among the vines, wearing my slippers, holding a candle, and bare-headed under the hail. Some profound peasant instinct had driven me out as though to fling myself upon the ground and cover the beaten vines with my body. But tonight I have become a stranger to all that was once best in me. Those restricting bonds have, at last, been loosened, by what or by whom I do not know. The cables have been cut, Isa, and I am adrift. What power is leading me on? Is it blind—or is it love? Perhaps it may be love.

FRANÇOIS MAURIAC
The Knot of Vipers

Consolation

An English autumn, though it hath no vines,
　　Blushing with Bacchant coronals along
The paths, o'er which the far festoon entwines
　　The red grape in the sunny lands of song,
Hath yet a purchased choice of choicest wines;
　　The claret light, and the Madeira strong.
If Britain mourn her bleakness, we can tell her,
The very best of vineyards is the cellar.

LORD BYRON
Don Juan

For a Wine Festival

Now the late fruits are in.
Now moves the leaf-starred year
Down, in the sun's decline.
Stoop. Have no fear.
Glance at the burdened tree:
Dark is the grape's wild skin.
Dance, limbs, be free.
Bring the bright clusters here
And crush them into wine.

Acorns from yellow boughs
Drop to the listening ground.
Spirits who never tire,
Dance, dance your round.
Old roots, old thoughts and dry,
Catch, as your footprints rouse
Flames where they fly,
Knowing the year has found
Its own more secret fire.

Nothing supreme shall pass.
Earth to an ember gone
Wears but the death it feigns
And still burns on.
One note more true than time
And shattered falls his glass.
Steal, steal from rhyme:
Take from the glass that shone
The vintage that remains.

VERNON WATKINS

A Happy Scene

In some parts of the country, through which we passed, they were
getting in the vintage [of 1822], which will be a memorable one.
Men, women, and children, were busy in the vineyards on the side
of the hills; the road was alive with peasants laden with baskets of
fruit, or tubs in which the grapes were pressed. Some were pressing the grapes in great tubs or vats, on the roadside. In the after-

noon there was continual firing of guns, and shouting of the peasants on the vine hills, making merry after their labor, for the vintage is the season when labor and jollity go hand in hand. We bought clusters of delicious grapes for almost nothing, as we travelled along, and I drank of the newly pressed wine, which has the sweetness of new cider. The farther we advanced into the Duchy of Baden, the richer the scenery became; for this is a most fertile territory, and one where the peasantry are remarkably well off. The comfortable villages are buried in orchards and surrounded by vineyards, and the country people are healthy, well clad, good-looking and cheerful.

WASHINGTON IRVING

Vintage Memories

Only Giorgio, sitting far up in the pergola, saw him weave through the tracts of dark purple and sunlight to the basin, then the splash into the water. Tall, box-sided wagons on the far road were trailing amid dust to the wineries. Crickets twanged in the vine-shaded pergola; now and then a grape plopped on the hot tiles; wasps and enamelled blue flies poured up and down in the heady sunlight; behind him was the golden march of the hills towering over all. Giorgio was aware of a benign continuity of life. Something about the slope, when he first saw it, reminded him of an Alpine valley where he had lived as a child. Vineyards were the same everywhere, and so were the vignerons, bound to the earth and their plants by a feeling deep, subtle and reciprocal; their affections

74   THE FIRESIDE BOOK OF WINE

reaching out, the vine tendrils holding upon them; the rhythms and tensions of the seasons answering in the depths of their being. He found solace in the recollection of his early past, and the tie with it visible in the life on the fields of Montino below him. There were even harvest melodies: Flores singing at the wine-press, and the pickers, led by Wing, chanting the Watermelon Seed lullaby.

IDWAL JONES
The Vineyard

It's Not Cider

September 23d [1858]—The vintage has been going on in our *podere* for about a week, and I saw a part of the process of making wine, under one of our back windows. It was on a very small scale, the grapes being thrown into a barrel, and crushed with a sort of pestle; and as each estate seems to make its own wine, there are probably no very extensive and elaborate appliances in general use for the manufacture. The cider-making of New England is far more picturesque; the great heap of golden or rosy apples under the trees, and the cider-mill worked by a circumgyratory horse, and all agush with sweet juice. Indeed, nothing connected with the grape-culture and the vintage here has been picturesque, except the large inverted pyramids in which the clusters hang; those great bunches, white or purple, really satisfy my idea both as to aspect and taste. We can buy a large basketful for less than a paul; and they are the only things that one can never devour too much of—and there is no enough short of a little too much—without subsequent repentance. It is a shame to turn such delicious juice into such sour wine as they make in Tuscany. I tasted a sip or two of a flask which the contadini sent us for trial,—the rich result of the process I had witnessed in the barrel. It took me altogether by surprise; for I remembered the nectareousness of the new cider, which I used to sip through a straw in my boyhood, and I never doubted that this would be as dulcet, but finer and more ethereal; as much more delectable, in short, as these grapes are better than puckery cider apples. Positively, I never tasted anything so detestable, such a sour and bitter juice, still lukewarm with fermentation: it was a wail of woe, squeezed out of the wine-press of tribulation, and the more a man drinks of such, the sorrier he will be.

NATHANIEL HAWTHORNE
French and Italian Notebooks

Leave It to Nature

Often have we ridden through villages redolent with vinous aroma, and inundated with the blood of the berry, until the very mud was encarnadined; what a busy scene! Donkeys laden with panniers of the ripe fruit, damsels bending under heavy baskets, men with reddened legs and arms, joyous and jovial as satyrs, hurry jostling on to the rude and dirty vat, into which the fruit is thrown indiscriminately, the black-coloured with the white ones, the ripe bunches with the sour, the sound berries with those decayed; no pains are taken, no selection is made; the filth and negligence are commensurate with this carelessness; the husks are either trampled under naked feet or pressed out under a rude beam; in both cases every refining operation is left to the fermentation of nature, for there is a divinity that shapes our ends, rough hew them how we may.

RICHARD FORD
Gatherings from Spain

Water=Wine

The following vintage, 1893, was also very remarkable, but in a different way. It was one of the sunniest years and one of the most plentiful vintages on record. The wells dried completely at the end of the summer and early autumn, when the grapes were being gathered and pressed, in the little villages on the slopes rising away from the river Marne. Water was badly needed to clean and cool the presses after each pressing, and he who had a cart, a horse and an empty cask, and would go to the river to fetch a caskful of water, could go home with his cask full of new wine, in return for the water supplied, no money passing; wine and water had for the time—a short time—the same value.

ANDRÉ L. SIMON
Vintagewise

Treading I

In the cuve (which is made use of but once a year) as well as all other parts of their making wine, they are, according to their manner, sufficiently nasty: the grapes often are also very rotten, and always full of spiders. Besides that, I have been told by those of the country, that they often put salt, dung, and other filthiness, in their wine to help, as they think, its purging. But, without these additions, the very sight of their treading and making their wine (walking without any scruple out of the grapes into the dirt, and out of the dirt into grapes they are treading) were enough to set one's stomach ever after against this sort of liquor.

JOHN LOCKE
Observations Upon the Growth and Culture of Vines and Olives
1679

Treading II

And now a word as to wine-treading. The process is universal in France, with the exception of the cases of the sparkling wines of the Rhône and Champagne, the grapes for which are squeezed by mechanical means, not by the human foot. Now, very venerable and decidedly picturesque as is the process of wine-treading, it is unquestionably rather a filthy one; and the spectacle of great brown horny feet, not a whit too clean, splashing and sprawling in the bubbling juice, conveys at first sight a qualmy species of feeling, which, however, seems only to be entertained by those to whom the sight is new. I looked dreadfully askance at the operation when I first came across it; and when I was invited—by a lady, too—to taste the juice, of which she caught up a glassful, a certain uncomfortable feeling of the inward man warred terribly against politeness. But nobody around seemed to be in the least squeamish. Often and often did I see one of the heroes of the tub walk quietly over a dunghill, and then jump—barefooted, of course, as he was—into the juice; and even a vigilant proprietor, who was particularly careful that no bad grapes went into the tub, made no objection. When I asked why a press was not used, as more handy, cleaner, and more convenient, I was everywhere assured that all efforts had failed to construct a wine-press capable of performing the work with the perfection attained by the action of the human foot. No mechanical squeezing, I was informed, would so nicely express that peculiar proportion of the whole moisture of the grape which forms the highest flavoured wine. The manner in which the fruit was tossed about was pointed out to me, and I was asked to observe that the grapes were, as it were, squeezed in every possible fashion and from every possible side, worked and churned and mashed hither and thither by the ever-moving toes and muscles of the foot. As far as any impurity went, the argument was, that the fermentation flung, as scum to the surface, every atom of foreign matter held in suspension in the wine, and that the liquid ultimately obtained was as exquisitely pure as if human flesh had never touched it.

ANGUS B. REACH
Claret and Olives

The Bad Old Days

Too much sentimentality has been wasted upon small producers— in the wine world at least. Dirt and disease are integral parts of peasant life; dirt in the winery and disease on the vines are common in peasant wine-growing and enormously hard to eradicate. Even in the aristocratic Médoc and St Emilion the quality of the ordinary wines has risen spectacularly during the last twenty years through the operation of the co-operatives. Third-rate vines which produce nasty fruit but a lot of it, mildewed grapes which the owner is too poor or obstinate to reject, dirty barns, foul vats, ancient and ill-smelling wine-presses, masses of flies and muck—all these are the tolerated plagues of makers of 'little local wines,' and it needs only a few old and obstinate owners to ruin the reputation of a whole commune. Official orders cannot enforce reform here. The only power that can work upon the stubborn peasant is the opinion of his colleagues in the co-op, who see their wine ruined and their money lost by his obstinacy.

RAYMOND POSTGATE
Portuguese Wine

A Port Vintage

The first lagar had been filled with grapes during the day and the solemn task of treading them began in the evening. The word *solemn* is correct, for the ceremony is traditional and unchanging. Twenty-two men, with bare legs and thighs, stood in two lines within the lagar; thirty inches deep in the lake of ripe fruit. They had taken their places against the opposite walls, erect, with their arms about each other, and were waiting when we entered the building. We passed the women and girls, dancing together, wearily, on the stone outside. My host looked at his watch and, sharp at 8.30, he raised his hand, lifting the tall silver-mounted stick, as a signal. The treading began: forty-four bare feet and legs, rising and falling—to the "Um! Dois! Esquerda! Direita!" of the leader. The monotonous, quiet, disciplined labour went on for two hours: very slowly, the two lines of men marched towards each other, through the deep swamp of grapes. When they met in the centre of the lagar they looked up, gravely, then turned and trod their way to the walls again. After fifteen minutes or so, the fruit juice began to lap against their legs; as they lifted them it seemed that they were wearing long stockings of purple silk. During all this time, while the hundreds of gallons of grapes began to move, as liquid, the women remained apart, as if this were some male and celibate ritual in which they were allowed no place.

At half-past ten, when the first two hours of treading were over and the men seemed as if they might sink into the juice, from exhaustion, the foreman made a signal. The forty-four arms fell away from the shoulders of their neighbours and the purple legs rested for a few moments: then there was leaping and singing—a polka in wine, and the song of freedom from toil. Then they shouted,

> Viva a Liberdade!
> Viva Inglaterra!
> Viva Portugal!
> Viva os nossos Patrões! . . .

Each man was then given a tot of raw spirit and a cigarette. Three of them stepped forward to the edge of the lagar and picked up a drum, a mouth organ and a concertina, and the wild dance began again. The women also danced, but still mildly and apart: the men clutched each other and pranced like drunken grasshoppers, singing,

> There is no purple like the iris,
> There is no green like the laurel tree;
> Nor is there white like the lily,
> Nor love like the first love. . . .

During almost two hours, the singing and dancing were innocent enough, but, about midnight, some witch of mischief rose from the purple foam: the men danced more madly than ever, so that the grape juice leapt also, and the scum of pips and skins made fantastic patterns on their thighs; and they sang a song of such wickedness that no one would translate it for me. My host looked at the pagan scene, a slightly astringent frown on his kindly face, and then admitted that the theme of the song was incest. His son straightened his Rifle Brigade tie and we left the dancers to their last prancing and notes of music, before they stepped from the lagar, ran their hands down their legs to wipe off the purple juice, and led their women and girls through the lenient shadows of the vineyard.

I leaned out of my window a long time, listening to distant singing and watching rockets, far up the valley, spluttering their patterns against the sky. A shooting star hurried down and died, and the train passed, cautiously, on its way back from Spain.

While I slept, the gallons of grape juice in the lagar began to ferment: the sugar was to change, slowly, into alcohol. The mysterious alchemy that would make it into wine had already begun.

HECTOR BOLITHO
The Wine of the Douro

Delicacy

But the wonderful memory I have of this indomitable woman concerns a certain phase of the vinification of red wines. At the time of the primary fermentation it used to be the practice in France for naked men to jump into the vats up to their armpits to break up the quickly forming crust, which if left alone would surely ruin the wine. This practice was abolished some years ago, not for sanitary reasons but because so many men were overcome by the fumes and drowned in the new wine. So as she was showing us around the winery and explaining her procedures we came to this point in the process.

"What happens here?" I asked.

"The men jump in the vats," she said.

"But isn't that illegal?"

With perfect aplomb she placed her hands an inch or so lower than her crotch and said, "They only jump in up to here, monsieur."

EVERETT CROSBY
The Vintage Years

Make Mine Beer

If any creature has fallen into the must and died there, such as a snake or a mouse or a shrewmouse, in order that it may not give the wine an evil odor, let the body in the condition in which it was found be burnt and its ashes when cool be poured into the vessel into which it had fallen and stirred with a wooden ladle; this will cure the trouble.

COLUMELLA
On Agriculture

A Practical Tip

And no man putteth new wine into old bottles; else the new wine will burst the bottles, and be spilled, and the bottles shall perish.

But new wine must be put into new bottles; and both are preserved.

St. Luke, Chapter 5

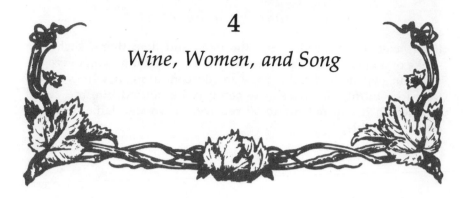

4
Wine, Women, and Song

Drinking songs make up a large part of the literature of drinking. Not many have specifically to do with wine, and even fewer are worth reprinting. I came across dozens in my reading, and most expressed the sentiment that it's better to be drunk today than dead tomorrow. Many of Anacreon's odes, for example, concern present pleasures, and here are the first lines of a song by John Fletcher:

> Drink to-day and drown all sorrow,
> You shall perhaps not do it tomorrow:
> Best, while you have it, use your breath;
> There is no drinking after death.

Perhaps the most famous of these poems is that of Abraham Cowley, which ends

> Crown me with roses whilst I live,
> Now your wines and ointments give,
> After death I nothing crave,
> Let me alive my pleasures have;
> All are stoics in the grave.

Another popular subject is heavy drinking. A few lines from the twelfth-century *Carmina Burana* will suffice:

> Fine drinkers, do your worst,
> you're thirsty with no thirst:

thus, joyously, you're cursed.
. . . He that can't keep the pace
must leave us in disgrace,
for faint-hearts we've no place.

A more humorous version of the tradition paean to drinking
can be summed up in the first and last lines of the anonymous
"Toper's Petition":

O grant me, kind Bacchus,
   The god of the vine,
Not a pipe nor a tun,
   But an ocean of wine. . . .

So that, living or dead,
   Both body and spirit
May float round the world
In an ocean of claret.

A typical heavy-handed drinking song is this seventeenth-century one by John Oldham that begins

Make me a bowl, a mighty bowl,
Large as my capacious soul.
. . . Let it of silver fashion'd be,
Worthy of wine, worthy of me!

The selections that follow include some of the livelier and more
imaginative drinking songs, along with some verses suggesting
that, despite the usual conjunction of "wine, women, and song,"
wine and women do not always agree.

Fill the Goblet Again!

Fill the goblet again! for I never before
Felt the glow which now gladdens my heart to its core;
Let us drink!—who would not?—since, through life's varied round,
In the goblet alone no deception is found.

I have tried in its turn all that life can supply;
I have bask'd in the beam of a dark rolling eye;
I have lov'd!—who has not?—but what heart can declare
That Pleasure existed while Passion was there?

In the days of my youth, when the heart's in its spring,
And dreams that Affection can never take wing,
I had friends!—who has not?—but what tongue will avow,
That friends, rosy wine! are so faithful as thou?

The heart of a mistress some boy may estrange,
Friendship shifts with the sunbeam—thou never canst change;
Thou grow'st old—who does not?—but on earth what appears,
Whose virtues, like thine, still increase with its years?

Yet if blest to the utmost that Love can bestow,
Should a rival bow down to our idol below,
We are jealous!—who's not?—thou hast no such alloy;
For the more that enjoy thee, the more we enjoy.

Then the season of youth and its vanities past,
For refuge we fly to the goblet at last;
There we find—do we not?—in the flow of the soul,
That truth, as of yore, is confined to the bowl.

When the box of Pandora was open'd on earth,
And Misery's triumph commenc'd over Mirth,
Hope was left,—was she not?—but the goblet we kiss,
And care not for Hope, who are certain of bliss.

Long life to the grape! for when summer is flown,
The age of our nectar shall gladden our own:
We must die—who shall not?—May our sins be forgiven,
And Hebe shall never be idle in Heaven.

LORD BYRON

Anacreontic Verse

Brisk methinks I am, and fine,
When I drink my cap'ring wine:
Then to love I do encline,
When I drink my wanton wine:
And I wish all maidens mine,
When I drink my sprightly wine:
Well I sup, and well I dine,
When I drink my frolic wine:
But I languish, lower, and pine,
When I want my fragrant wine.

ROBERT HERRICK

An Excuse for the Glass

CHARLES SURFACE: 'Fore heaven, 'tis true!—there's the great degeneracy of the age. Many of our acquaintance have taste, spirit, and politeness; but, plague on't, they won't drink.

CARELESS: It is so indeed, Charles! they give into all the substantial luxuries of the table, and abstain from nothing but wine and wit. O certainly society suffers by it intolerably; for now, instead of the social spirit of raillery that used to mantle over a glass of bright Burgundy, their conversation is become just like the Spa water they drink, which has all the pertness and flatulence of Champagne, without the spirit or flavour.

1ST GENT: But what are they to do who love play better than wine?

CARELESS: True: there's Sir Harry diets himself for gaming, and is now under a hazard regimen.

CHARLES SURFACE: Then he'll have the worst of it. What! you wouldn't train a horse for the course by keeping him from corn? For my part, egad, I am never so successful as when I am a little merry: let me throw on a bottle of Champagne, and I never lose—at least, I never feel my losses, which is exactly the same thing.

2ND GENT: Ay, that I believe.

CHARLES SURFACE: And then, what man can pretend to be a believer in love, who is an abjurer of wine? 'Tis the test by which the lover knows his own heart. Fill a dozen bumpers to a dozen beauties, and she that floats atop is the maid that has bewitched you.

SONG

Here's to the maiden of bashful fifteen;
   Here's to the widow of fifty;
Here's to the flaunting extravagant quean,
   And here's to the housewife that's thrifty.

CHORUS:
   Let the toast pass,
   Drink to the lass,
I'll warrant she'll prove an excuse for the glass.

Here's to the charmer whose dimples we prize;
   Now to the maid who has none, sir:
Here's to the girl with a pair of blue eyes,
   And here's to the nymph with but *one,* sir.

Here's to the maid with a bosom of snow;
   Now to her that's as brown as a berry:
Here's to the wife with a face full of woe,
   And now to the girl that is merry.

For let 'em be clumsy, or let 'em be slim,
   Young or ancient, I care not a feather;
So fill a pint bumper quite up to the brim,
   And let us e'en toast them together.

RICHARD BRINSLEY SHERIDAN
The School for Scandal

The Epicure

Fill the bowl with rosy wine,
Around our temples roses twine,
And let us cheerfully awhile,
Like the wine and roses, smile.
Crown'd with roses, we condemn
Gyges' wealthy diadem.
Today is ours; what do we fear?
Today is ours; we have it here.
Let's treat it kindly, that it may
Wish, at least, with us to stay.
Let's banish business, banish sorrow;
To the gods, belongs to-morrow.

ABRAHAM COWLEY

Thirst Comes with Summer

Thirst comes with Summer; Virgil, haste,
Comrade of noble youths and taste
Choice wine of Cales: my reward
One little shell of Syrian nard.
The mellow cask long-stored within
The depths of the Sulpician bin
Shalt then be thine, that nectar rare
Which brightens hope and drowns dull care.
Come taste my wine, but ere thou try it,
Remember, friend, that thou must buy it:
I cannot, like the rich man, give
Largess to all and nought receive.
Hence, sordid cares! Hence idle sorrow!
Death comes apace: to-day—to-morrow—
Then mingle mirth with melancholy,—
Wisdom at times is found in folly.

HORACE
Odes

The Toper

She tells me with claret she cannot agree,
And she thinks of a hogshead whene'er she sees me;
For I smell like a beast, and therefore must I
Resolve to forsake her or claret deny:
Must I leave my dear bottle that was always my friend,
And I hope will continue so to my life's end?
Must I leave it for her? 'tis a very hard task,—
Let her go to the Devil, bring the other whole flask!

Had she tax'd me with gaming and bade me forbear,
'Tis a thousand to one I had lent her an ear;
Had she found out my Chloris up three pair of stairs,
I had baulk'd her and gone to St. James's to pray'rs;
Had she bid me read homilies three times a day,
She perhaps had been humour'd with little to say;
But at night to deny me my flask of dear red,—
Let her go to the Devil, there's no more to be said!

TOM D'URFEY

Come, Thou Monarch of the Vine

Come, thou monarch of the vine,
Plumpy Bacchus with pink eyne!
In thy fats our cares be drown'd,
With thy grapes our hairs be crown'd.
Cup us till the world go round,
Cup us till the world go round!

WILLIAM SHAKESPEARE
Antony and Cleopatra

A Gourmet's Love-Song

Do I recall the night we met,
    With both our hearts *en feu?*
As if I ever could forget,
    Dear *Cordon Bleu!*

A lover's moon was in the sky.
    We dined alone, we twain.
Sole Véronique was partnered by
    A still Champagne.

You wore a bandeau on your hair,
    And with the *Coq au Vin*
Produced a magnum old and rare
    Of Chambertin.

Château d'Yquem, a last surprise,
    Was climax, crown and seal.
I might forget your lovely eyes,
    But not that meal.

                                    ERIC CHILMAN

The Flowing Bowl

Vulcan, contrive me such a cup
    As Nestor used of old;
Show all thy skill to trim it up,
    Damask it round with gold.

Make it so large that, filled with sack
    Up to the swelling brim,
Vast toasts on the delicious lake
    Like ships at sea may swim.

Engrave not battle on his cheek;
    With war I've naught to do.
I'm none of those that took Maestrich,
    Nor Yarmouth leaguer knew.

Let it no name of planets till
    Fixed stars or constellations,
For I am no Sir Sidrophel,
    Nor none of his relations.

But carve thereon a spreading vine,
    Then add two lovely boys;
Their limbs in amorous folds entwine,
    The type of future joys.

Cupid and Bacchus my saints are;
    May drink and love still reign!
With wine I wash away my care
    And then to love again.

JOHN WILMOT, Earl of Rochester

Ode on Himself

Replenish'd with liquor, well gladded my heart,—
    Such force has the juice of the vine,—
Inspir'd and inflam'd with the musical art,
    I sing to the praise of the Nine.

Replenish'd with liquor, the chaser of pain,
    I feel neither sorrow nor care,
But give the hoarse tempest, which ruffles the main,
    To waft and disperse them in air.

Replenish'd with liquor, my spirits restor'd,
    Then Bacchus, a lover of play,
While new-blowing roses their fragrance afford,
    Commands to be frolic and gay.

Replenish'd with liquor, I weave me a tire,
    In chaplets o'erjoy'd to be dress'd;
And, crowning my temples, I praise and admire
    Tranquillity, freedom, and rest.

Replenish'd with liquor, I take the perfume,—
    For beauty my bosom alarms—
Anoint me well over, a courage assume,
    And catch the dear nymph in my arms.

Replenish'd with liquor, high rais'd with a glass,
    My heart is so free and dilated,
From sages and grave to the cheerful I pass,
    And love with the young to be rated.

Good liquor alone is the gain we can have,
    The only fix'd pleasure we boast:
The rest are all flitting, submit to the grave,
    Forsaken, forgotten, and lost.

ANACREON

An Excuse for Drinking

Upbraid me not, capricious fair,
    With drinking to excess;
I should not want to drown despair,
    Were your indifference less.

Love me, my dear, and you shall find,
    When this excuse is gone,
That all my bliss, when Chloe's kind,
    Is fix'd on her alone.

The god of wine the victory
    To beauty yields with joy;
For Bacchus only drinks like me,
    When Ariadne's coy.

ANON.

A Toast

To her whose beauty doth excel
Story, we toss these cups and sell
Sobriety a sacrifice
To the bright lustre of her eyes.
Each soul that sips here is divine:
Her beauty deifies the wine.

THOMAS CAREW

Now I'm Resolv'd to Love No More

Now I'm resolv'd to love no more,
    But sleep by night, and drink by day;
Your coyness, Chloris, pray give o'er,
    And turn your tempting eyes away.
From ladies I'll withdraw my heart,
And fix it only on the quart. . . .

'Tis wine alone that cheers the soul,
    But love and ladies make us sad;

I'm merry when I court the bowl,
    While he that courts the madam's mad:
Then ladies, wonder not at me,
For you are coy, but wine is free.

ALEXANDER BROME

Advice

She's no mistress of mine
    That drinks not her wine,
Or frowns at my friends' drinking notions;
    If my heart thou wouldst gain,
    Drink thy flask of Champagne;
Twill serve thee for paint and love-potions.

SIR GEORGE ETHEREGE
She Would If She Could
1668

To Thea, at the Year's End
—with a Bottle of Gewürztraminer

I have no fancy to define
    Love's fullness by what went before;
I think the day we crossed the line
Was when we drank the sea-cooled wine
    Upon a sun-warmed shore.

The sun in sudden strength that day
    Inflamed the air, but could not reach
The steel-sharp sea of middle May
That brimmed with cold the breathless bay
    Below the sun-drowned beach.

The sun's heat laid its heavy hand
    On unaccustomed skins as we
Went tip-toe down the tilted strand
And set our bottle on the sand
    To cool it in the sea:

And watched as, where the sea-surge spent
  The last of its quiescent strength,
Stone-cold and circumambient,
The intermittent water went
  Along its polished length.

The bottle took the water's cold
  But did not let its wetness pass;
Glinting and green the water rolled
Against the wine's unmoving gold
  Behind its walls of glass.

We cooled it to our just conceit
  And drank. The cold aroma came
Almost intolerably sweet
To palates which the salt and heat
  Had flayed as with a flame.

We swam and sunned as well as drank,
  And found all heaven in a word;
But, dearest Thea, to be frank,
I think we had the wine to thank
  For most of what occurred.

And now the winter is to waste,
  I bring a bottle like the first;
And this in turn can be replaced,
As long as we have tongues to taste,
  And God shall give us thirst,

Lest with the year our love decline,
  Or like the summer lose its fire,
Before the sun resurgent shine
To warm the sea that cooled the wine
  That kindled our desire.

                              P. M. HUBBARD

More Wine!

Few things surpass old wine; and they may preach
Who please, the more because they preach in vain,—
Let us have wine and women, mirth and laughter,
Sermons and soda-water the day after.

LORD BYRON
Don Juan

5

Words About Wine

Surely one of the appeals of wine is that everyone who drinks a glass feels free to comment on its quality. S. Weir Mitchell's *A Madeira Party*, for example, a little volume published in 1895, includes remarks like this one: "Observe, Chestnut, the just perceptible smoke-flavor—a fine, clean-tasting, middle-aged wine—a gentleman, sir, a gentleman! Will never remind you to-morrow of the favor he did you last night." And, of course, wine merchants' catalogues are full of elaborate nonsense about wines. Here's a description of a red Bordeaux quoted by David Cecil:

Just the wine for those who like the smell of Verdi. Dark color, swashbuckling bouquet and ripe flavor. Ready for drinking, but will hold well, showing a gradual shift in style as it ages into graceful discretion.

Some short literary references to wine might qualify as tasting notes. Here's Michelangelo on the wine of San Gimignano: "It kisses, licks, bites, thrusts and stings." In the second part of *Henry IV*, Shakespeare has Mistress Quickly say, "But, i' faith, you have drunk too much canaries; and that's a marvelous searching wine, and it perfumes the blood ere one can say 'What's this?' " Jonathan Swift enjoyed wine, but he must have felt unsure of his tastes when he wrote in his *Journal to Stella*, "I love white Portugal wine better than claret, champagne, or burgundy; I have a sad vulgar appetite."

More recently, in John Updike's short story, "Farewell to the Middle Class," a man who has suddenly made a great deal of money spends five dollars for a bottle of wine for the first time in his life. "The strange thing is, the wine was great, really distinctly better than two-fifty Bordeaux, or dollar-sixty Almadén. Fuller, smokier, with more grape, more landscape, more sorrow in it." A different note is struck in Kingsley Amis' *The Green Man*, when an innkeeper describes some cheap white Burgundies as "closely resembling a blend of cold chalk soup and alum cordial with an additive or two to bring it to the colour of children's pee."

Of course, not every writer who drinks wine has managed to develop an adequate wine vocabulary right away. Washington Irving visited Bordeaux in 1826, and in his *Notebooks* he described Château Margaux as "a wine of fine flavour—but not of equal body. . . . Lafitte has less flavour than the former but more body—an equality of flavour and body. . . . La Tour has more body than flavour. . . .Haut Brion. A wine of fine flavour."

The selections that follow exhibit a somewhat greater range of expression, and they conclude with a number of notes by André L. Simon to give some sense of the imaginative and entertaining way he wrote about individual wines.

Two Undergraduates

One day we went down to the cellars with Wilcox and saw the empty bays which had once held a vast store of wine; one transept only was used now; there the bins were well stocked, some of them with vintages fifty years old.

"There's been nothing added since his Lordship went abroad," said Wilcox. "A lot of the old wine wants drinking up. We ought to have laid down the eighteens and twenties. I've had several letters about it from the wine merchants, but her Ladyship says to ask Lord Brideshead, and he says to ask his Lordship, and his Lordship says to ask the lawyers. That's how we get low. There's enough here for ten years at the rate it's going, but how shall we be then?"

Wilcox welcomed our interest; we had bottles brought up from every bin, and it was during those tranquil evenings with Sebastian that I first made a serious acquaintance with wine and sowed the seed of that rich harvest which was to be my stay in many barren years. We would sit, he and I, in the Painted Parlour with three bottles open on the table and three glasses before each of us; Sebastian had found a book on wine-tasting, and we followed its instructions in detail. We warmed the glass slightly at a candle, filled a third of it, swirled the wine round, nursed it in our hands, held it to the light, breathed it, sipped it, filled our mouths with it and rolled it over the tongue, ringing it on the palate like a coin on a counter, tilted our heads back and let it trickle down the throat. Then we talked of it and nibbled Bath Oliver biscuits, and passed on to another wine; then back to the first, then on to another, until all three were in circulation and the order of glasses got confused and we fell out over which was which, and we passed the glasses to and fro between us until there were six glasses, some of them with mixed wines in them which we had filled from the wrong bottle, till we were obliged to start again with three clean glasses each, and the bottles were empty and our praise of them wilder and more exotic.

". . . It is a little, shy wine like a gazelle."

"Like a leprechaun."

"Dappled, in a tapestry meadow."

"Like a flute by still water."

". . . And this is a wise old wine."

"A prophet in a cave."

". . . And this is a necklace of pearls on a white neck."

"Like a swan."

"Like the last unicorn."

And we would leave the golden candlelight of the dining-room for the starlight outside and sit on the edge of the fountain cooling our hands in the water and listening drunkenly to its splash and gurgle over the rocks.

"Ought we to be drunk *every* night?" Sebastian asked one morning.

"Yes, I think so."

"I think so too."

EVELYN WAUGH
Brideshead Revisited

Table Talk

The area where I suffered culture-shock most when I came to California was where I least expected it. I can talk about wine objectively with anyone—in the cellar, in the winery, in the tasting room. At the table I talk about wine subjectively—how I feel about it, what it reminds me of, the way it affects me. But in California I would sit down to dinner and had hardly taken the first sip of my wine when someone would lean across and say, "What do you think the pH is?"

I don't find talk of total acid, and residual sugar, and carbonic maceration stimulating to the sensual pleasure, the aesthetic, of wine. It's almost as if your hostess leaned across, just when you were about to taste her Hollandaise sauce, and started to discuss emulsions with you.

GERALD ASHER

Le Père Troisgros on Wine

The *patron* is very much at home here. He approaches a table at which two guests are starting their dinner. Without a word, the *patron* pours himself a little wine from their bottle.

"Undrinkable!" he exclaims, screwing his face into an expression of extreme distaste. "Are you *paid* to drink that? It's wood—all stalk and no grape—the wood of a cadaver. You like cadavers? Not possible!"

Peremptorily, he summons the sommelier and sends back the bottle, explaining that these guests are indignant at being served this atrocious wine. The maitre d'hôtel, who has enjoyed years of the *patron's* caprices, smoothly whisks away the offensive bottle and quickly returns with a different vintage. . . .

"Try the Fleurie," the *patron* is urging. "It's the wine of love, because it's diuretic. It disappears. There are some wines—the great Bordeaux, for example—if you drink them and you get drunk, the woman can't profit from it. But with Beaujolais you say, 'Ah, tomorrow I'll buy you a new dress.' You say anything at all to be pleasant. You're in a good mood."

. . . he pours more Beaujolais. "The Beaujolais is an intelligent wine—a scholarship student, not a mediocre one," he says. "The duck sauce has sugar, vinegar and lemon, and I was afraid the Beaujolais wouldn't be strong enough for the sauce."

"The wine is struggling," the tax inspector suggests. "I've never known it so strong."

"You see what's happened to France?" the *patron* rejoins. "Tax inspectors talk about gastronomy. Who's left to talk about taxes?"

"Not bad, your duck," he continues, as Pierre approaches the table.

"It's a very difficult dish for the wine," notes Pierre. . . .

As the waiter approaches with the cheese tray, the *patron* clearly has trouble restraining his appetite. "Ah!" he exclaims. "The cheese! Goat cheese and Roquefort! Give us a little from the white of the Roquefort, not the blue. And some of the ewe's cheese. This one is two months old. Go ahead, when the crust on the blue cheese is satiny, like that, you can eat it.

"So here we have goat's, ewe's, and cow's cheese. In France people think red wine goes with cheese, so let's make an experiment with the white wine—Sauvignon and Pouilly Fuissé—the same year—'71.

"We're going to eat with our hands, like the Indians. Take the blue cheese in your hand. Now break it gently. Drink some Sauvignon. It bangs you in the mouth—like an old peasant with his wooden shoe, a wooden shoe bangs you in the throat. Now some more cheese, and now try the Pouilly."

"What a difference!" the tax inspector exclaims. "An enormous difference!"

"In France the Sauvignon didn't implant itself well, except in Bordeaux," the *patron* resumes. "The red wine is good with the cheese, but it doesn't have the distinction of the white. It's not as good with these cheeses.

"The Sauvignon compared to the Pouilly? They're two sons, and the Sauvignon is the whipper-snapper. It's not solid enough. It's violent, it's sharp, it bites, it cries, it's like a ferocious dog you keep on a leash. The Pouilly is calm."

ISRAEL SHENKER
The New York Times

Hermitage 1846

But my Hermitage showed not the slightest mark or presage of enfeeblement. It was, no doubt (to translate, without 'betraying,' my friend's harsh epithet mildly), not a delicate wine; if you want delicacy you don't go to the Rhône or anywhere in France below Gascony. But it was the *manliest* French wine I ever drank; and age had softened and polished all that might have been rough in the manliness of its youth. . . . It had, like all its congeners, a heavy sediment, and required very careful decanting; but when properly brought to table it was glorious. The shade of its colour was browner (people used, *vide* Thackeray, to call the red hocks 'brown') than most of the Hermitages I have seen; but the brown was flooded with such a sanguine as altogether transfigured it. The bouquet was rather like that of the less sweet wall-flower. And as to the flavour one might easily go into dithyrambs. Wine-slang talks of the 'finish' in such cases, but this was so full and so complicated that it never seemed to come to a finish. You could meditate on it; and it kept up with your meditations. The 'gunflint' which, though not so strong in the red as in the white wines of the district, is supposed to be always there, was not wanting; but it was not importunate and did not intrude too much on the special Hermitage touch, or on that general 'red wine' flavour which in some strange way is common to every vintage from Portugal to Hungary, vary as they may in character and merit otherwise.

GEORGE SAINTSBURY
Notes on a Cellar-Book

Hermitage 1906

But at this particular hotel at Nîmes, selected at random, we were to drink one of the most notable wines of our career as amateur connoisseurs—a red Hermitage, 1906, from the firm of Labeaume, Alboussières, Berne et Cie, Saint-Péray. It might have been an even more epoch-making moment in our lives had it been served to us by a *sommelier* who realized that good wine should be treated, in the cradle, with the tenderness due to the seven months' heir of a great house, where no more are possible. But this wine-waiter, like so many others of his profession in France, treated the Hermitage, 1906, as though he were wielding Indian clubs in the gymnasium. His motto was obviously: "The hand that rocks the cradle rules the world!" Severely, we nicknamed him "Swingbottle" on the spot, and tasted the Hermitage with very little hope, though it was our first on the tour. Johnny and I had once tasted a very inferior Hermitage in some hotel on the French Riviera.

But this was transcendental. The gun-flint backwash was there, and all the other little subtle flavours that run up, one behind the other, elusively blending and disappearing again. For this is the peculiar excitement of a true Hermitage, that you have not yet done with it when you have relished the bouquet, and the rich flavour, and the silky texture, and the sight of its deep clear gold-and-red, shiningly blended. All these are straightforward appeals, but afterwards comes the fascination. You follow up your sensations with the thrill of a hunter after some live creature, with a will and a personality of its own, whom he would catch and tame and bring home. But it is no good; you cannot catch the wild charm of Hermitage, though you drink it and drink it again. You can only marvel at it gratefully.

G. B. STERN
Bouquet

Water Bore

What happens when you're told you can no longer drink wine is that you either continue but *pretend* you've given it up, or give it up and become a "water bore." (Choir sings: "Water bore where are you hi-iding.")

Water bores are as bad as wine bores but at least they have fresher breath. Their language is much the same, a mixture of jargon and lying.

"It's an impudent little water but I'm sure you'll be amused by its pretensions."

"A couple of chaps and I have invested in a little well in the Dordogne. The side of the valley that just soaks up the dew. Old Pierre manages it for us. Doesn't need much cultivating—they throw a dead sheep in every so often—helps the bouquet"—and so on. . . .

And how will the water snobs describe these fine table waters—"A trifle flinty"?—"A young water good for laying down"? If it came from Lake Windermere perhaps they'd say, "The 1970 rainfall produced some superlative waters in the classic style. They have depth and elegance; while they are already fine waters they will keep and develop further." Or if it comes from the Grand Union Canal, "An enormously full, rich water." The Severn? "A big, robust water with a very distinctive flavour . . . round . . . up-standing . . . a deliciously dry water." That's the one that everyone will go for obviously, the ultimate in chic—dry water. Once the marketing campaign is underway, water merchants will spring up everywhere. There'll be a water supermarket in every high street and the famous Fleet Street pub El Vino will be renamed El Eau. (I know it should be El Agua but El Eau sounds sillier.)

Every good restaurant will boast its water waiter, his status being denoted by a small silver divining rod on a chain round his neck—and everybody will slosh round full of water, alert, healthy and as dull as a Comedy Playhouse.

BARRY TOOK
"Water Works Wonders"

I'll Take a Case

Turin. The first nightingale I have heard this year, is to-day. There is a red wine of Nebiule made in the neighborhood, which is very singular. It is about as sweet as the silky Madeira, as astringent on the palate as Bordeaux, and as brisk as Champagne. It is a pleasing wine.

THOMAS JEFFERSON
Journals
1787

The Properties of Good Wine

. . . clear as the tears of a penitent, so that a man may see distinctly to the bottom of his glass. Its colour should represent the greenness of a buffalo's horn. When drunk, it should descend impetuously like thunder, sweet-tasted as an almond, creeping like a squirrel, leaping like a roebuck, strong like the building of a Cistercian monastery, glittering like a spark of fire, subtle as the logic of the schools of Paris, delicate as fine silk, and colder than crystal.

ALEXANDER NECKHAM
12th century

Candid

There is the true story of a firm of wine shippers who were giving a luncheon in their offices to one of the most distinguished of French growers whose agency they held. The purpose of the luncheon was that the Frenchman should show off some of his choicer wines. One of these was reverently produced and served first to the senior partner of the wine shippers to taste. He sipped the wine, rolled it round his tongue and swallowed it while the French principal seated at his right hand sat complacently waiting for the expected praise.

'Urine,' said the senior partner succinctly.

'I beg your pardon?' said the Frenchman.

'Urine,' he said more loudly, whereupon the Frenchman leapt to his feet, threw down his napkin and stormed out of the room.

'Where has he gone?' asked the senior partner in a surprised voice.

'Well, Sir,' explained a junior member of the firm, 'You did describe his Burgundy as er . . . urine.'

'Fussy old gentleman isn't he? Pass the potatoes,' said the senior partner, calmly getting on with his meal.

DOUGLAS SUTHERLAND
Raise Your Glasses

Now That's Old

Some find sepulchral vessels containing liquors, which time hath incrassated into jellies. For besides these lachrymatories, notable lamps with vessels of oils attended noble ossuaries, and some yet retaining a vinosity and spirit in them, which, if any have tasted, they have far exceeded the palate of antiquity. Liquors not to be computed by years of annual magistrates, but by great conjunctions and the fatal periods of kingdoms. The draughts of consulary date were but crude unto these, and Opimian wine but in the must unto them.

SIR THOMAS BROWNE

Here He Comes Again

Of course we know all about Fossbridge of the F.O. rinsing Amontillado around his teeth and gazing ceilingwards under eyelids lowered in illusionary rapture. Fossbridge with his 'clever little clarets' and 'rather over-bumptious burgundies' has been taken to task for his tedium so many a time and so oft, from James Thurber onwards, that it is surprising that he can still go on. And on, and on, and on. The insentient owl.

'The Paarl Valleys, now—do you realise that they've *almost* got it? They're mere striplings, of course, but I'd say they were beginning to breed true. I was agreeably surprised when I was out there for a week or two last year. Of course, like any wine, the Paarls are more eloquent *in situ*.'

Oh, they are, are they? Like the wine favoured of Rabelais with a bouquet mildly suggestive of raspberries which, fiendish old Fossbridge, you were boringly blethering about in here the other evening. *That*, you said, could be truly savoured only *in situ*, under a plane tree overlooking the lovely Loire in the castellated city of Chinon. And the 'plump' little *vins de Gaillac* which have to 'be called upon in their home,' since, 'alas! they die of sheer exhaustion should they ever go avisiting.'

'Same again, Fossbridge?'

'No, thank you, dear boy—no. To relish a sherry such as this must be only a single act of communion. Besides, I must hasten home. We have friends for dinner, and I have a rather sly little Vosne Romanée to decant for them.'

Belt up, then, Fossbridge, and beat it.

C. GORDON GLOVER
Boring at the Bar

A Palate Affair

I never drink now above three glasses of wine—and never any spirits and water. Though by the bye—the other day Woodhouse took me to his coffee house and ordered a bottle of claret—now I like claret, whenever I can have claret I must drink it,—'tis the only palate affair that I am at all sensual in. Would it not be a good spec to send you some vine roots—could it be done? I'll enquire. If you could make some wine like claret, to drink on summer evenings in an arbour! For really 'tis so fine—it fills one's mouth with a gushing freshness—then goes down cool and feverless—then you do not feel it quarrelling with your liver—no, it is rather a peacemaker, and lies as quiet as it did in the grape; then it is as fragrant as the queen bee, and the more ethereal part of it mounts into the brain, not assaulting the cerebral apartments like a bully in a bad-house look-ing for his trull and hurrying from door to door bounding against the wainscot, but rather walks like Aladdin about his enchanted palace so gently that you do not feel his step. Other wines of a heavy and spirituous nature transform a man into a Silenus: this makes him a Hermes—and gives a woman the soul and immortality of Ariadne, for whom Bacchus always kept a good cellar of claret—and even of that he could never persuade her to take above two cups. I said this same claret is the only palate-passion I have—I forgot game—I must plead guilty to the breast of a partridge, the back of a hare, the backbone of a grouse, the wing and side of a pheasant, and a woodcock *passim*.

JOHN KEATS
1819

On Wine and Hashish

It occurred to me to treat wine and hashish in the same article, because they do indeed have something in common: both cause an inordinate poetic evolvement in men. Man's greatness is attested by his frantic craving for all things—healthful or otherwise—that excite his individuality. He seeks always to rekindle his hopes, and rise to infinity. But we must examine the results. On the one hand, we have a beverage that aids digestion, strengthens the muscles, and enriches the blood. Even when taken in large quantities, it causes only relatively short-lived disorders. On the other hand, we have a substance that disturbs the digestive processes, weakens the limbs, and is capable of producing an intoxication that lasts up to twenty-four hours. Wine exalts the Will, hashish destroys it. Wine is a physical support, hashish a suicidal weapon. Wine makes a man good-natured and sociable; hashish isolates him. The one is indus-trious, as it were; the other, essentially lazy. Indeed, what point is there in working, toiling, writing, creating anything at all, when it is possible to obtain Paradise in a single swallow? In a word, wine is for the working man, who deserves to drink of it. Hashish be-longs to the class of solitary pleasures; it is made for the pitiful creatures with time on their hands. Wine is useful, it yields fruitful results. Hashish is useless and dangerous.

CHARLES BAUDELAIRE

No Comment

We dined at Saint-Remy, on the open veranda over the garden, and drank a Châteauneuf du Pape which tasted like nice chewed grass. This was Rosemary's definition, and Johnny and Humphrey said she was right. Personally, I found as little suggestion of chewed grass, even of nice chewed grass, as I had found of rose-petals in Tavel, or of gun-flint in Saint Péray. By this time I was growing humble about my indiscriminating olfactory nerves, and content to accept the verdicts of my friends.

G. B. STERN
Bouquet

Check One

You can talk about wine as if it were a bunch of flowers (fragrant, heavily perfumed); a packet of razor blades (steely); a navvy (robust, powerful); a troupe of acrobats (elegant and well balanced); a successful industrialist (distinguished and rich); a virgin in a bordello (immature and giving promise of pleasure to come); Brighton beach (clean and pebbly); even a potato (earthy) or a Christmas pudding (plump, sweet and round).

DEREK COOPER

My Cellar Book

The gentle melancholy with which the lover of good wine turns the reminiscent leaves of his cellar book is compounded of regrets for past glories and the memories of great vintages and golden years.

My cellar book goes back to 1930. I opened it when I laid down a half-dozen of Macgilligoody's Extra Ferruginous Tonic Wine (bottled in Blackfriars Road in 1929). I picked up the half-dozen for a mere song at the local chemist's annual sale, but they gave pleasure far out of proportion to what I paid for them. I had a bottle up when the manager of my department came to dinner, and served it with the Irish stew. Unfortunately the manager had to leave before the bottle was finished, but I could tell from the slow and reverent way in which he consumed it that my judgment had been fundamentally sound. He agreed with me that although it still showed traces of a certain juvenilism, it was pregnant with possibilities. I had the last bottle up only last year when my wife was recovering from a bad cold. It had lived up to its early promise and fully justified the confidence I had placed in it.

Parsnip wine I always regard as generous but rather frolicsome, always ready to play merry little pranks on you, but completely without malice. It is perhaps the best "all purpose" wine of all our native vintages. The best years in the 1930s were 1932, 1936, and of course the glorious 1938. I had a dozen of 1932 (bottled by my mother after six weeks in the copper). Unfortunately three bottles blew their corks in the first six months, but the remainder gave much pleasure to my friends and myself; perhaps, I might almost say, too much pleasure.

We had two magnums of the noble '38 vintage for the committee of the Working Men's Club on the occasion of a recent whist drive and dance. The wine was then "in perfection," friendly on the nose, generous on the palate, but insidious on the gait. A bottle my wife and I shared the night we had a flying bomb at the end of the road led to our removal, somewhat erroneously, as casualties suffering from acute "battle exhaustion." We have just drunk the last bottle, and I was unable to restrain myself from wondering whether we should ever see its like again. These suspicions are partly based on the fact that my mother is beginning to doubt if her wine is strictly non-alcoholic.

Many consider that in rhubarb wine our native vintages have achieved their choicest flowering. The richness of its velvet texture and the full flamboyancy of its bouquet have endeared it to generations of wine-lovers. I had some choice years in my cellar, but unfortunately the wine does not travel well, and we have had to move four times in the last eighteen months.

As all wine-lovers know, the severe attacks on the rhubarb plants by wireworm in the middle twenties had a disastrous effect on the output of rhubarb wine. The wireworm troubles are now largely over, and there have been some very good years in the "post wireworm" period. Memories of the famous "Coronation" vintage are with us yet. There were unfortunately no good years during the war; the labour shortage, coupled with the rationing of sugar, made things very difficult for the *Vignerons*. My sister-in-law, whose wine was adjudged a "first-growth" at the Flower Show, 1931, always relied on my brother to turn the mangle by which the fruit was crushed. Naturally, with my brother in the Army, the burden of turning the mangle fell entirely upon my sister-in-law herself. As a result the output for the war years was small in quantity and, owing to the scarcity of sugar, deficient in quality.

At my suggestion we used the whole of the 1944 output as a basis for a fortified wine, produced by blending the native product with two or three bottles of an interesting liquor known, I believe, as "potheen," very graciously presented by some American soldiers as a mark of appreciation for hospitality they had received. The resulting blend, which I named "potbarb," suffered from immaturity, since the donors of the "potheen" insisted on drinking the blend almost before I had entered the bottles in my cellar book. I like to think that this interesting blend strengthened them in their liberating mission, but we have lost touch with them, as we have with so many of our dear friends with whom we have shared a bottle of wine at one time or another.

L. W. DESBROW

Any Delivery Charge?

The following ambiguous advertisement of a wine merchant is taken from an Irish newspaper:—"The advertiser, having made an advantageous purchase, offers for sale, on very low terms, about six dozen of prime Port Wine, lately the property of a gentleman forty years of age, full in the body, and with a high bouquet."

CHARLES TOVEY
Wit, Wisdom and Morals

A Flight of Fancy

My reputation for giving good lunches in London was based on the fact that I knew more about the best qualities and the best years of French wines than most people. I have always had a passionate admiration for Rhine wines, too, and the wines of the Moselle. A long time ago now I once earned my living in London by tasting wines: we used to have an excellent lunch, three or four of us, and the six or eight bottles of wine that we had to taste were brought in after we had enjoyed an excellent beefsteak and had cleaned our palates with bread and salt and olives: then each of us had to give his opinion of the various wines and tell especially which would improve with keeping and so be the better purchase. Most of us could give the year of any special vintage. One man in London knew more about white wine even than I did, but I was a good second, and so I may be allowed to speak on French wines at least with some authority.

I remember making every one at table laugh one day by a comparison between wine and women as the two best things in the world. "Red Bordeaux," I said, "is like the lawful wife: an excellent beverage that goes with every dish and enables one to enjoy one's food, and helps one to live.

"But now and then a man wants a change, and champagne is the most complete and exhilarating change from Bordeaux; it is like the woman of the streets: everybody that can afford it tries it sooner or later, but it has no real attraction. It must be taken in moderation: too much of it is apt to give a bad headache, or worse. Like the woman of the streets, it is always within reach and its price is out of all proportion to its worth.

"Moselle is the girl of fourteen to eighteen: light, quick on the tongue with an exquisite, evanescent perfume, but little body; it may be used constantly and in quantities, but must be taken young.

"If you prefer real fragrance or bouquet, you must go to a wine with more body in it, such as Burgundy, Chambertin or Musigny. Burgundy I always think of as the woman of thirty: it has more body than claret, is richer, more generous, with a finer perfume; but it is very intoxicating and should be used with self-restraint.

"Port is the woman of forty: stronger, richer, sweeter than Burgundy; much more body in it but less bouquet; it keeps excellently and ripens with age and can only be drunk freely by youth; in maturity, more than a sip of it is apt to be heavy, and if taken every day it is almost certain to give gout. But if you are vigorous and don't fear the consequences, the best wine in the world is crusted Port, half a century old; it is strong with a divine fragrance, heady, intoxicating, but constant use of it is not to be recommended: it affects the health of even its strongest and most passionate admirers and brings them to premature death.

"At their best and worst, wines have curious affinities with women. Young men prefer Burgundy because of its sweetness and fire, while old men always choose Moselle because it is harmless, light, has a delicious perfume and no bad effect."

FRANK HARRIS
My Life and Loves

Falstaff on Sack

Good faith, this same young sober-blooded boy doth not love me; nor a man cannot make him laugh. But that's no marvel; he drinks no wine. There's never none of these demure boys come to any proof; for thin drink doth so over-cool their blood, and making many fish-meals, that they fall into a kind of male greensickness; and then, when they marry, they get wenches. They are generally fools and cowards—which some of us should be too, but for inflammation. A good sherris sack hath a twofold operation in it. It ascends me into the brain; dries me there all the foolish and dull and crudy vapours which environ it; makes it apprehensive, quick, forgetive, full of nimble, fiery, and delectable shapes; which delivered o'er to the voice, the tongue, which is the birth, becomes excellent wit. The second property of your excellent sherris is the warming of the blood; which before (cold and settled) left the liver white and pale, which is the badge of pusillanimity and cowardice; but the sherris warms it and makes it course from the inwards to the parts extremes. It illumineth the face, which, as a beacon, gives warning to all the rest of this little kingdom, man, to arm; and then the vital commoners and inland petty spirits muster me all to their captain, the heart; who great and puff'd up with this retinue, doth any deed of courage. And this valour comes of sherris: so that skill in the weapon is nothing without sack, for that sets it awork; and learning a mere hoard of gold kept by a devil, till sack commences it and sets it in act and use. Hereof comes it that Prince Harry is valiant; for the cold blood he did naturally inherit of his father, he hath, like lean, sterile, and bare land, manured, husbanded, and till'd with excellent endeavour of drinking good and good store of fertile sherris, that he is become very hot and valiant. If I had a thousand sons, the first humane principle I would teach them should be to forswear thin potations and to addict themselves to sack.

WILLIAM SHAKESPEARE
Henry IV, 2

Wine and Health: Three Views

I.

Sacke doth make men fat and foggy, and therefore not to be taken of young men. Being drunke before supper with store of sugar, it provoketh appetite, comforteth the spirits marvellously, and concocteth raw humours. Canary sacke is more full of spirits than any other. . . .

These kindes of wines [Muscadell, Malmesie, and Brown-Bastard] are onely for married folkes, because they strengthen the backe, yet I wish to be very chary in the drinking thereof, lest their often use fill the reines and seede-vessels with unnaturall, accidentall, windy, puft, or, as Philosophers speake, with adventicious heate, which in time will grow to a number of inconveniences. But for aged persons, these high and yellowish wines are wonderfull wholesome in the winter-time.

WILLIAM VAUGHAN
Directions for Health

II

Thus, *Red Port* of a moderate age, is astringent, good in diarrhœas, seminal weaknesses, gleets, etc. *Rhenish*, diuretick, and serviceable in the stone and gravel; *Canary*, or sweet wines purgative, and open obstructions in the lungs; *Mountain*, excellent in the colick, and *Champagne* affords a sudden flush of animal spirit and inspires vivacity.

DR. SHAW
The Juice of the Grape:
or, Wine Preferable to Water

III

White Wine and Rhenish, thin and penetrating, cut and attenuate gross humours; they are good to take in the morning, fasting, and also a little before dinner and supper, but they are hurtful when taken with meat, or at meals. Claret breedeth good humours, and is very good for young men with hot stomachs, but is hurtful for all that are of a cold and moist constitution. To rheumy people, it is of all wines most pernicious, but, verily, it being taken at meals, it is for temperate bodies, so it be a pure and quick wine, scarcely infe-

rior to any of the regal wines of France. Sack is hot and thin, wherefore it doth vehemently and quickly heat the body.

TOBIAS VENNER
The Straight Road to a Long Life

High Hopes

Curiously enough, he [an English wine writer] shows a foul and
preposterous ignorance when he comes to the wines of California.
Can it be that the English have reached such a state of mind that
everything American is obnoxious to them? . . . I give him Cresta
Blanca, as a Burgundy not to be matched at the price in Paris. I give
him the hocks of the Italian Swiss Colony, and even some of the
Moselles. . . . Can it be that like most wine bibbers he occasionally
swallows a label instead of the wine? I half suspect it. Certainly if
he had ever flooded his oesophagus with Cresta Blanca of a good
year he would not talk in so lordly and snooty a style of American
viniculture. We had still a long way to go, but we were assiduously
on our way. In another ten years our labels would have caught up
with our wines, and even Englishmen would have become aware of
Chateau Hollywood, Clos Mooney, and 1919er Rauenthaler-Sterlin-
ger Terrassenauslese. But I speak of what might have been.

H. L. MENCKEN
The Nation
1926

Catawba Wine

This song of mine
Is a Song of the Vine
To be sung by the glowing embers
Of wayside inns,
When the rain begins
To darken the drear Novembers.

It is not a song
Of the Scuppernong,
From warm Carolinian valleys,
Nor the Isabel
And the Muscadel
That bask in our garden alleys.

Nor the red Mustang,
Whose clusters hang
O'er the waves of the Colorado,
And the fiery flood
Of whose purple blood
Has a dash of Spanish bravado.

For richest and best
Is the wine of the West,
That grows by the Beautiful River;
Whose sweet perfume
Fills all the room
With a benison on the giver.

And as hollow trees
Are the haunts of bees,
For ever going and coming;
So this crystal hive
Is all alive
With a swarming and buzzing and humming.

Very good in its way
Is the Verzenay,
Or the Sillery soft and creamy;
But Catawba wine
Has a taste more divine,
More dulcet, delicious, and dreamy.

There grows no vine
By the haunted Rhine,
By Danube or Guadalquivir,
Nor on island or cape,
That bears such a grape
As grows by the Beautiful River.

Drugged is their juice
For foreign use,
When shipped o'er the reeling Atlantic,
To rack our brains
With the fever pains,
That have driven the Old World frantic.

To the sewers and sinks
With all such drinks,
And after them tumble the mixer:

For a poison malign
Is such Borgia wine,
Or at best but a Devil's Elixir.

While pure as a spring
Is the wine I sing,
And to praise it, one needs but to name it:
For Catawba wine
Has need of no sign,
No tavern-bush to proclaim it.

And this Song of the Vine,
This greeting of mine,
The winds and the birds shall deliver
To the Queen of the West,
In her garlands dressed,
On the banks of the Beautiful River.

HENRY WADSWORTH LONGFELLOW

Legendary Falernian

No wine has ever acquired such extensive celebrity as the Falernian, or more truly merited the name of 'immortal,' which Martial has conferred upon it. At least, of all ancient wines, it is the one most generally known in modern times: for, while other eminent growths are overlooked or forgotten, few readers will be found who have not formed some acquaintance with the Falernian; and its fame must descend to the latest ages, along with the works of those mighty masters of the lyre who have sung its praises. But, although the name is thus familiar to every one, scarcely any attempt has been made to determine the exact nature and properties of the liquor; and little more is understood concerning it, than that the ancients valued it highly, kept it until it became very old, and produced it only when they wished to regale their dearest friends. At this distance of time, indeed, and with the imperfect data which we possess, no one need expect to demonstrate the precise qualities of that or any other wine of antiquity; though, by collating the few facts already stated with some other particulars which have been handed down to us respecting the Falernian vintages, I am not without hope, that it may be possible to make some approach to a more correct estimate of their true characters, and, at the same time, to point out those modern growths to which they have the greatest resemblance.

In the first place, all writers agree in describing the Falernian wine as very strong and durable, and so rough, in its recent state, that it could not be drunk with pleasure, but required to be kept a great number of years, before it was sufficiently mellow. Horace even terms it a 'fiery' wine, and calls for water from the spring to moderate its strength; and Persius applies to it the epithet 'indomitum,' probably in allusion to its heady quality. From Galen's account, it appears to have been in best condition from the tenth to the twentieth year; afterwards it was apt to contract an unpleasant bitterness: yet we may suppose, that when of a good vintage, and especially when preserved in glass bottles, it would keep much longer, without having its flavour impaired. Horace, who was a lover of old wine, proposes, in a well-known ode, to broach an amphora, which was coeval with himself, and which, therefore, was probably not less than thirty-three years old. . . . As he bestows the highest commendation on this sample, ascribing to it all the virtues of the choicest vintages, and pronouncing it truly worthy to be produced on so happy a day, we must believe it to have been really of excellent quality. In general, however, it probably suffered, more or less, from the mode in which it was kept; and those whose taste was not perverted by the rage for high-dried wines, preferred it in its middle state. Thus Cicero, when animadverting on the style of the orations which Thucydides has introduced in his History, and which, he conceives, would have been more polished if they had been composed at a later period, takes occasion to illustrate the subject of his discourse by a reference to the effects of age upon wine. "Those orations," he remarks, "I have always been disposed to admire: but I neither would imitate them, if I could, nor could I, if I would; being, in this respect, like one who delights in Falernian wine, but chooses neither that which is so new as to date from the last consuls, nor that which is so old as to take the name of Annician, or Opimian. Yet the wines so entitled are, I believe, in the highest repute: but excessive age neither has the suavity which we require, nor is it even bearable."

ALEXANDER HENDERSON
1824

A Gentleman's Guide

Red with meat, white with fish except lox or herring. Rosé with any endangered species or an ice cream cone.

Wine should be stored in a cool, dry place. The glove compartment of a Jaguar or an abandoned washing machine are my personal favorites.

Good French wine should carry the phrase: *"Mise en bouteille au château."* This assures you that only the owner of the vineyard has had a chance to tamper with the wine. Labels stating, *"Mise en bouteille dans nôtre salle de bains"* or *"Fait dans nôtre baignoire"* are suspect.

The novice must be careful not to fall prey to the unscrupulous wine merchant. Some of the things to avoid include expensive wine sealed with a screw-off cap; Chianti bottles bearing the legend, *"Il Vino d'Il Duce"*; wine bottles made from lamps; wine labels stating "shake well before using" or "Caveat Emptor."

Before purchasing wine, turn bottle upside down. If cork slides out, do not buy—you might be taking a chance.

I have never come across a Chinese restaurant with a really great wine cellar.

The bottom of a good wine bottle is concave for a purpose. It enables you to drink the wine even if there are no glasses on hand. Merely remove the cork and pour the wine from the bottle directly into its concavity. This is a neat trick and does take some maneuvering, but the impression it creates is well worth the years of practice. Selwyn Stokes ruined a new ski parka and eleven suits on this one.

Among serious wine drinkers, you are what you say, and the importance of turning the correct phrase cannot be overemphasized. With this in mind, I have set forth below a few hints on gracious wine phraseology, especially useful at dinner parties.

You the guest after tasting the wine:

    "Ahh, the sting subsides almost immediately.

    "Obviously not a wine for boondoggling.

    "It fairly wears ballet shoes.

    "It literally belches heroism.

    "Shame on you."

You the host:

    "I double dare you to try it.

    "It's proudly humble.

    ("Humbly proud" also okay.)

"It travels quite well, I usually drink it on my bicycle.

"Here's a gay little vintage that actually wheezes contentment."

Wine, of course, does not exist only to satisfy the celebrants at dinner parties. Most wine drinkers, for instance, readily swear to the salubrious effects of wine. I myself favor a red burgundy, three drops in each nostril, whenever I feel a cold coming on.

Purchase of wine glasses: Always test their pitch before buying. Don't be shy, even in Georg Jensen's. In a truly matched set, each glass should sound a perfect A flat when smartly struck by a Mark Cross pen.

Trepanning the wine bottle: Choice A, known as the sissy method, consists of using a standard corkscrew in a standard manner. Choice B, known as the certifiably insane method, consists of holding the bottle upside down and delivering a sharp smack with the heel of the hand at the base of the bottle. Turn bottle right side up very quickly if cork actually becomes dislodged.

At what temperature should wine be drunk? Ideal, of course, is 98.6°F. But Stokes, during a bout with bubonic plague, ran his up to 103.4 degrees and nevertheless managed to down an entire bottle of excellent Sauternes with no apparent harm.

The down-to-earth effect created by presenting your host with a 49-cent bottle of cheap muscatel cannot be overestimated.

Should a great wine be stirred? No.

One should always serve good wine with originality and flamboyance. Stokes, for instance, when presenting a rare old Château au Pom Pom, would first stand the bottle on the sideboard and genuflect before it. He would then don a wimple and serve the wine either from a sterling silver gravy boat or an old milk carton, depending on his mood. Once, in a fit of plagiarism, Stokes had some labels made up stating, *Mise en bouteille pour Selwyn Stokes.* He then hired a layout man to paste these labels on all the bottles in his third-rate wine cellar. Eventually, Stokes went too far and pasted his labels on six cases of Dr. Pepper.

Stokes also had a shoddy little ploy in which, when serving terribly cheap wine, he would first hold a stethoscope to the bottle for a few seconds, breathe deeply, then nod sagaciously and proceed to open the bottle. Pure flimflam, of course, but it usually worked with relatives.

The fashionable wine drinker: Only diddlers favor the safari outfit for quaffing Beaujolais. The man who takes his wine seriously wears a tweedy sportcoat with slightly flared pants, opened shirt collar and a restrained ascot. This is a *de rigueur* outfit for any wine over $1.29 the bottle. Slight variations are, however, permitted. Well do I recall Stokes, who always wore an old shako when drinking Tokay.

"*Gesundheit*" is not a legitimate toast.

RICHARD SMITH

Easier Said Than Done

Choose your wine after this sort; it must be fragrant and redolent, having a good odour and flavour in the nose; it must sprinkle in the cup when it is drawn and put out of the pot into the cup; it must be cold and pleasant in the mouth; it must be strong and subtle of substance. And then moderately drunken it doth quicken a man's wits, it doth comfort the heart, it doth scour the liver; specially if it be white wine, it doth rejoice all the powers of man, and doth nourish them; it doth engender good blood, it doth comfort and nourish the brain and all the body, and it resolveth fleume; it engendereth heat, and it is good against heaviness and pensifulness; it is full of agility; wherefore it is medicinable, specially white wine, for it doth mundify and cleanse the wounds and sores.

ANDREW BOORDE
Dyetary of Helth
1562

White Wines

It would be a narrow and fanatical wine-lover who would exclude white wines from his appreciation, though in certain respects they cannot claim equality with the great red wines. They have, however, their own appointed times and moods. The very finest white wines are inclined to be too lavish with their favours. The *grande amoureuse* who gives herself utterly, nakedly, and does not keep back the deepest secret of her charm, may lose the irresistible enchantment of mystery and find herself with nothing in reserve to hold her lover when the first flood of passion is spent. So, in a chaster category of human pleasures, the great Rhine wines strike one speechless with amazement at the first glass, but succeeding glasses, which with red wines grow progressively more enthralling, never quite attain the pinnacle of artistic perfection with which the first taste dumbfounds the wine-lover. The very intensity of their qualities, their golden perfume and velvety sweetness, unless they are corrected with the austerity and aristocratic aloofness peculiar to the acidity of the Riesling grape, are apt to paralyse our perceptions and to cloy, so that disappointment mingles with our pleasure, since we can never quite recall the first rapture.

For this reason some wine-lovers prefer the less serious white wines, the Moselles, which have the attraction of a flower, and fade almost as rapidly. Their liveliness and gaiety tickles the palate without numbing it, and their simplicity never cloys.

H. WARNER ALLEN
The Romance of Wine

He Does His Best

My wife disappeared into the Civil Service Stores the other day and emerged not a million years later clutching a complete do-it-your-self wine-making kit. 'But I got it for a song!' she explained, as we belted down the Strand a pace and a half ahead of the store detective, who was still angrily waving the sheet music of 'Mountain Greenery.'

A perfectly respectable little wine it turned out to be, too. By the time we had spread the contents of the outfit over the kitchen floor and trodden them, with many a rollicking cry in Old Provençal (I dare say we could just have added water and stirred, but we had our sense of creative participation to think of), I really couldn't have told the difference between the finished product and, say, Pouilly Fuissé. Or Tasheimer Goldtröpfchen. Or Algerian cooking wine.

The more I thought about it, in fact, the wider became the range of things that I realised I couldn't have told the difference between. Look, the final bitter truth that I am trying to approach as tactfully as I can is this: if you took the labels off the bottles and distracted my attention slightly, I'm not sure that I could tell the difference between vintage champagne and high-octane petrol.

I mean, I do my best. When the waiter brings the bottle of wine, I hold it at arm's length and squint at it with my head slightly thrown back, as if to see the thing against the general background of mid-century Britain. I roll sips of wine around my mouth with a filthy smacking noise and a look of holy introspection while other people are talking to me. Oh, I rather enjoy the ritual, as agnostics say with hearty tolerance, paying patronising visits to Spanish cathedrals in baggy khaki shorts. All the same, a story being circulated in some quarters that I was seen in a restaurant in Curzon Street taking a critical sip from the finger-bowl and shouting offensively at the waiter 'Take it back—it's corked!' is completely false. The day I tell a wine-waiter to take something back because it's corked will be the day after I capture four enemy machine-gun posts single-handed.

The saddest thing is that I seem to be getting further and further away from my ideal of the mellow, well-rounded man-about-town, connoisseur of fine wines and pretty women. The nearest I ever got, in fact, was when I was a child. Clearing out a drawer recently I came across some short stories I wrote when I was a somewhat retarded adolescent. One of them turned out to be about a young man who takes his uncle—George Evesham, a fruity old bird by any standards—out for lunch on his birthday. They go to a place called Carlotti's, where the waiter's name is Giuseppe, and drink a bottle of Châteauneuf du Pape with the soup, a bottle of champagne with the chicken. and a goodly shot of Benedictine with the coffee. No mean lunch for men who have to be back in their offices at three. By the time they reach the champagne their conversation, and for that matter even the narrative, has taken on a rich, vinous hue.

'They drank. "Veuve Clicquot '43," winked Mr. Evesham over the rim of the glass.' I think he must have been going on to a fancy dress ball later dressed as one of Keats's Beaded Bubbles.

MICHAEL FRAYN

Aging

On . . . separate occasions within the space of a few weeks, I was reminded of the way wine surprises us in its aging. Just before Christmas at a dinner in Baltimore one of the wines served to me was a 1959 Romanée-Saint-Vivant, bottled at the *domaine* of General Marey-Monge—a distinguished wine from a year that had been presented to the world as the first in our recent spate of "vintages of the century." The 1959 Burgundies were products of a hot summer, one that inspires the layman, basking on Mediterranean beaches, to dream of grapes ripening in the sunshine to unprecedented perfection. But such a summer cautions professionals to expect wines of low acidity without the stamina to live long, often flattering when young but insipid when aged. Regrettably, our Romanée-Saint-Vivant was only an agreeable reminder of what it had been. It was tired—faded both in the pale brick of its color and in its fleeting aroma and flavor. The sadness is that our host had owned the bottle for a few years and had held it for a special occasion.

Then, only a week or two later, with this experience fresh in mind, I dined at the house of a grower in Volnay. We had drunk in succession two vintages of his *domaine*—1970 and 1964—and finally, with cheese, he poured a 1947 Volnay Champans. Like 1959, the year 1947 was a difficult one. Apart from the problems of the summer, the picking itself took place in intolerably hot weather, and in those immediate postwar days few growers had the equipment to control fermentation temperatures. Volnay wines mature more rapidly than any other wines of the Côte de Beaune in my experience, and aware that my host was known for the delicacy and lightness of his wines, I expected the 1947 to be well in decline. It was delicious; attenuated, a little blurred even, but still quite vigorous and with its flavor intact. The Romanée-Saint-Vivant, as long-lived a wine as any of Burgundy, had faded at thirteen years; the Volnay, a delicate wine, was still intact and lively at a quarter of a century.

GERALD ASHER

And Here Are the Critics . . .

And now we come to the wine. The wine we've been drinking this week is the Château Rougon Macquart of 1961, and here is Cecil Rye.

Well, I'm prepared to go out on a limb about this, and say that the 1961 is definitely the best thing Rougon Macquart has done. It's really an extraordinarily *finished* drink, and it's very remarkable how this estate's work can vary. I remember when I drank the 1956, at the Berkeley, I think it was, a year or so ago, I remember thinking that what the work of this estate really lacked was finish. But now it really has come on in the most interesting way. I don't know if anyone else here drank the 1956—

Yes, actually I drank it in—

But there's no doubt in *my* mind that that wine didn't hold the interest in the way that the wine we drank this week does. Perhaps I was rather lucky, I drank it with a rather decent *gigot de mouton* and *haricots verts* and *pommes à l'anglaise,* and I wonder if perhaps everyone got as good a performance as I did myself.

Did everyone get as good a performance as Cecil Rye? Teddy Clayton, what sort of a performance did you get?

On the whole I agree with Cecil Rye, I was interested continuously from the first sip, but I would like to make one point that he doesn't seem to have mentioned, and that is the bottle. I think the bottle this wine comes in is really most rewarding, a classic claret-shaped bottle with a pronounced angle, I suppose you would call it, a kind of angle between the neck and the main body of the bottle. And the label—

Yes, I was going to mention the—

Roland Postbox?

I was going to mention the label. I thought it had very great visual appeal, with the name of the estate laid out in big letters and the name of the shipper in rather smaller ones, and then the date of the vintage below the name of the estate, where the eye falls naturally.

Yes, it's very restful, isn't it? Anybody not *like the label? Clayton?*

I was only going to say that on the whole I think the public prefers the kind of label that has a picture of the château on it.

Oh well, the public, yes, I dare say they do.

Don't think I'm saying that it's necessarily at all important what the public thinks, but after all the wine-merchants have to live, don't they, ha ha ha.

I really don't know why, ha ha ha.

Cecil Rye drank his wine with a gigot de mouton. *Anyone got any comments to make about that? Clayton?*

Well, yes, I did think it a bit extraordinary that he called it a *gigot de mouton* and not a *gigot d'agneau.* My experience—

I called it a *gigot de mouton,* old boy, because it was a *gigot de mouton.* If it had been a *gigot d'agneau* I should have said so.

Did anyone have anything notably different from gigot de mouton? *Just briefly, we mustn't spend too much time on this.*

Actually I had *macaroni aux champignons* and *mille-feuilles au foie-gras,* but I think the wine performs much the same against either background.

Yes, well, we mustn't diverge too far. Anyone got any other points to raise about the 1961 Rougon Macquart? Roland Postbox, you look as if you wanted to say something.

I don't know if it's really important, but I would like just to say a word for the cork. I enjoyed the cork most tremendously. At the beginning of the evening it filled the mouth of the bottle with a fine sense of exact placing. I couldn't find a gap in it anywhere. And then later on it came out in a truly remarkable way.

I enjoyed the cork, too. It's enormously effective, isn't it, the way the underside takes on that red flush while the top stays a kind of rich nut-brown.

Cork-brown.

Yes, I suppose that's it. But it's tremendously effective, don't you agree?

Very effective, certainly. Cecil Rye, any points you want to raise before we pass on to our next subject?

Yes, there are one or two small points. It's all very well going to town about the cork and the label and the rest of it, but I think everybody's overlooking some of the rather more important things. As I made clear earlier on, this is a sixth-growth claret from the St. Marliac district that is strikingly mature for its age, with a charming rust-red colour and a full, elegant flavour with, I thought, an interesting after-taste of sarsaparilla—

Ipecacuanha, surely.

I thought sarsaparilla. I'd say sarsaparilla was much more characteristic of the wines of the St. Marliac district.

Yes, but surely this is exactly what it gives—

Personally I was more impressed by the nose, which—

Distinguished—

Balanced—

Graceful—

Classic—

Well, we mustn't launch out into a new discussion at this stage. Everyone seems to have enjoyed the Château Rougon Macquart of 1961, more or less, and now we must move on to our next subject, which is sauce. We have been tasting the Sauce Béchamel at the Savoy Grill, and here is Clement Jung . . .

B. A. YOUNG

Some Notes from André L. Simon

The oldest Hock that I ever had was a bottle of 1783 from the cellars of the last Duke of Nassau; it was given to me by Francis Berry, in 1906, and it was more interesting than enjoyable; the bouquet of the wine was still delightful, but the wine itself was flat, which is by no means the same thing as "still"; there is as much difference between a still and a flat wine as there is between sleep and death.

Probably the finest collection of Margaux ever assembled. A truly memorable as well as a most enjoyable evening. . . .

The 1905 was simply delightful: fresh, sweet and charming; a girl of fifteen, who is already a great artist, coming on tip-toes and curtseying herself out with childish grace and laughing blue eyes.

She probably never will be a Grande Dame; she may live long enough to be a sour old hag, but what does it matter to us to-day? I would not give such a wine a chance to get any older, had I the good fortune to call any of it my own.

The '11 was a better wine, but, to me, not so attractive: better, because it was fuller, with more bouquet as well as more body; still holding its fruit although somewhat harsh at the finish. A full-throated tenor with a splendid voice but hard, callous eyes: something admirable but not lovable. I believe that it is at the top of its form and will soon show its tannin and lose its fruit.

The '99 was also a wine at the top of its form, and its form a much higher one than that of the '11. There was in both plenty of sunshine, plenty of rich, sound, fine wine, but better tuned up, better balanced in the '99. Nothing hard; no jarring note; nothing but sweet harmony. The same full-throated tenor after he has fallen in love and found his soul.

The '75 was simply gorgeous! The most glorious sunset that ever fired the West! The bouquet clean, sweet, searching and wholly admirable. Its body free from fat and muscular enormities; attenuated; all in tracings, but wiry, crisp, lithe and lively. A beauty. Full marks.

The '70 was quite the gentleman of the party: no stooping; the eye clear and keen; the nose arched and aggressive; the cheekbones high; the lips full and red; a great aristocrat belonging to a generation now all but gone; a most admirable wine, with a fuller and harder body than that of the '75, by far the more lovable of the two.

The 1919 Burgundy [Chambertin] came in unannounced; it gave me rather a shock, but by no means an unpleasant one. It had a far greater volume of bouquet and a kind of caramelized sweetness; rather attractive but hardly natural. Probably a pasteurized wine; not a harlot but a painted lady.

The late bottled Graham [1909] followed very well: it had the same air of 'rouged' lips; it was enjoyable without being admirable.

The two Clarets were only moderate wines, wines of poor vintages, but they possessed breed and the inimitable charm of simplicity, which appeals to me more than all the 'make-up' used by the other two wines to show off.

The [1911 Romanée St. Vivant] was remarkably fresh and fragrant; neither heavy nor sugary; just what Burgundy ought to be; breed, bouquet, flavour and body in that order; the reverse order is, unfortunately, usually the case.

The Chambertin [1919] was a typical 'commercial' Burgundy, which would be described in the wine merchant's list as 'velvety' and in the grocer's as 'blood making.' There was some wine in it, of course, wine which was probably a fair specimen of some non-descript Beaune raised to the dignity of Chambertin by the addition of a little of the chemist's equivalents for body, sweetness and soft-ness. No post-War innovation, however; on the contrary, a type of wine identical to pre-War Burgundies of the same class. Painted lips have no age.

The [1865 Château Léoville] was very interesting—a fine old man, but, of course, an old man. It looked beautiful as it was poured out; its bouquet was alluringly puzzling; it was by no means dry, and the first impression it gave was that it was going to be a very great wine; but the impression did not last. It faded away in some unaccountable fashion; there was no life left: something like kissing a ghost; red lips that vanish the moment yours are going to meet them.

1933. A revised edition of 1923, at present in paper covers, but some copies, the Latour and Cheval Blanc among them, likely to be bound in full morocco by that great artist, Time. The chief feature of the wines is the gossamer texture of their as yet immature body. It will be a dangerous year, some wines not having enough in them to develop and grow to man's estate, whilst others, without ever being big wines, should be quite charming and ready to drink in a very few years.

1934. A revised edition of 1924, greatly enlarged. There was a considerable quantity of wine made in 1934, and many hours of sunshine stored in the grapes when they were picked. Sunshine means carbon; carbon means heat and energy. A wine made in such a year is like a child with a surplus amount of vitality and self-will; whether such a child grows up to be a genius or a criminal is chiefly a matter of education. The 1934 vintage will be likely to produce both, the genius and the criminal types of wine, some that will be exceptionally good and others no good at all, according to the way they will have been handled from the beginning.

Burgundies, on the whole, do not keep nearly so long as Clar-ets; they have more to give, more bouquet and greater vinosity, at first, but they exhaust themselves and fade away sooner than the less aromatic, more reserved Clarets. It is somewhat like some of the carnations which possess a far more pungent and assertive perfume, when first picked, than any rose; yet the more discreet, the gentler and sweeter perfume of the rose will abide with the bloom as long as the bloom will last. Of course, there are exceptions to all rules, and I remember a charming bottle of Chambertin '65, in September 1934.

ANDRÉ L. SIMON

6

In Praise of Older Wines

I can imagine that some wine drinkers would be bored, if not irritated, to read about old wines that they are unlikely ever to enjoy themselves. It seems to me, however, that just as one might read about the performance of an actor or musician who is no longer alive, so one might enjoy descriptions of classic old wines and the recollections of articulate enthusiasts.

This section includes a number of longer excerpts about bottles of old Burgundies, Bordeaux, and Madeira. Most of the wines are from the nineteenth century, and many of the Bordeaux described are pre-phylloxera, that is, older than 1879. There are passages about old wines in fiction—*The Egoist* of George Meredith and Bruce Todd's "The Greatest Bottle in the World," for example, both included in this anthology—but the notes in this section all refer to specific and real, not fictionalized, bottles. I find these descriptions fascinating, not only because very great wines are being described, but also because most of these commentaries were written by an earlier generation of wine writers, with their own attitudes and vocabulary, and with a less analytical and more leisurely approach to their subject.

Three Great Burgundies

For let there be no doubt about it: Burgundy at its best overtops Claret at *its* best. . . . You will only drink four or five bottles of truly first-class Burgundy in your whole life (and you will be lucky if you find so many; only three have rung the bell with me; good as the 1904 and the 1921 were, none of them was the really outstanding thing I have in mind). But you can drink Claret of the highest class several times in the year: Claret that should be drunk kneeling, with every sip consecrated as a libation to Heaven. I wonder if I can get an image from the orchestra. Everyone knows how tender and beautiful the flute can be in a solo part; but whosoever has had the luck to hear the solo played by the recorder recognizes a fullness, a roundness and a pathos of tone to which the flute cannot attain. Now Claret flutes for us all the time, while Burgundy is usually content to grate on its scrannel pipe of wretched straw. Occasionally it, too, will flute with grace and tenderness; but, once in a blue moon, it will produce the recorder, and then, indeed, our hearts are melted.

In September, 1926, I spent a few days in Paris; and I decided that I would try the merits of Lapré, in the Rue Drouot. I went early in the day to leave my order, and I ingratiated myself with the *sommelier* by ordering my wine first and then choosing the food that would show it at its best. The first wine was a Meursault; I cannot remember the vintage, but it was followed by a La Tâche 1904—oh! what shall I say about it that can give any idea of its excellence? So marvellous, so delicate was the bouquet, it seemed an impertinence to go further and taste this miraculous liquid; and yet, on the palate it almost made one regret as a waste of time the moments spent in taking in the perfume. This indeed was one of the Three Bottles; its excellence was beyond all description or recapture; yet I have never seen a good vintage year of La Tâche on a list since without making the vain effort to call back the past.

And what shall we say of Richebourg: Richebourg that has given me the most recent of my Three Great Bottles? It was far from the first occasion on which I had blessed the noble name; there was a Richebourg 1915 that I met in 1935 which caused me to think that twenty years was the ideal age of Burgundy; and there was another bottle, this time a 1911, that Guy Knowles had poured for me a year or two before, when it broke the lances of four other first growths, some of them of years that are usually set far above 1911. But the Bayard of Richebourgs was a 1923, drunk at the invitation of Sir Francis Colchester-Wemyss at his club on the night of Shrove Tuesday this year; and I have just had to refuse an invitation to the same hospitable table, when I feel sure another of these precious bottles is going to be drunk. Such are the horrors of war! For this, indeed, was a worthy rival to the La Tâche 1904 of which I have just been writing. Its colour arrested my attention at once. Claret can show the clearest limpidity; but a truly limpid Burgundy seems to have more substance in the colour; just as translucent, one feels that it would take more than a mere pebble to crack *that* glass. And this Richebourg had the true glow of the ruby; you were conscious of a lapidary worth. The bouquet did not fail to justify the clarity; it was almost spiced, so sweetly aromatic was it. And then the true glory revealed itself, not to the eye, not to the nose, but to the palate. It caressed the gullet; it spread its greeting over all the mouth, until the impatient throat accused the tongue of unfair delay. It was glorious, glorious, glorious; and a month later I had not yet stopped talking about it. For I had forgotten how good Burgundy could be. It was fourteen years since the La Tâche; and, although there had been many fine bottles in between, none of them had been of that rare outstanding merit that the Three Great Bottles reached. A grateful heart may be allowed a long chant of thanksgiving.

When I first joined the Windham Club in 1922 there were still a few bottles of Les Caillerets 1889 in the cellar. I drank one bottle with a good friend, and it was my first introduction to great wine. Now let me protest at once about the ordinary method of approach to a great wine. The average host bids you to dinner, and, without a word of warning, sets you drinking Lafite 1864, or something like that. The result is that he is robbing you and the wine of a great deal of your due. If you are going to drink a great wine, you should be told that you are going to drink a great wine. You should have an opportunity to prepare your palate and get it into a proper state of receptivity, and your mind into a proper state of reverence. You should drink barley water for lunch, and go without your tea; you should avoid the barber's shop and the Turkish bath, lest the first might spill his highly perfumed washes upon you, or the second create an unnatural dryness of the palate. You should go through the preliminary stages of your dinner with your mind fixed on the great moment, and you should not allow the conversation to be directed into controversial channels. Later, yes, but not until the wine has first had your whole attention. And you certainly ought not to fail to call to mind the goodness of God that has given you such a gift; and at least in this very reverent sense you should drink it in remembrance.

My good friend performed his duties like a true host. He began talking about the Volnay-Caillerets about a month before the dinner, and he drew such a picture of its marvellous greatness that I was all agog to drink it. He ordered it several days before, so that it had a good opportunity to stand up and let all the sediment get to the bottom of the punt, while it gradually took the temperature of the dining-room. Then he had it carefully decanted just before dinner; and he ordered the rest of the dinner so as to produce the gradual crescendo and avoid the anti-climax. And so the moment arrived when it was proper for me to raise my glass. This was nearly twenty years ago; but I still remember the magnificent shock of that bouquet, rich in mellow perfection, and entirely free from the infirmities of age. I took one sip; I closed my eyes, and every beautiful thing that I had ever known crowded into my memory. In the old fairy tales the prince drinks a magic potion, or looks into a magic crystal, and all the secrets of the earth are revealed to him. I have experienced that miracle. The song of armies sweeping into battle, the roar of the waves upon a rocky shore, the glint of sunshine after rain on the leaves of a forest, the depths of the church organ, the voices of children singing hymns, all these and a hundred other things seemed to be blended into one magnificence. I have since met two other bottles worthy to be compared with that one, and they were both bottles of Burgundy. Yes, I, a devotee of Bordeaux, solemnly declare that the three greatest bottles I have ever tasted were all from Burgundy.

MAURICE HEALY
Stay Me with Flagons

A Memorable Meal: Bordeaux, 1935

The fare, good; the wines, better; the host, best. Three score and ten busy years, full of difficulties of all sorts and with not a few tragedies thrown in, have not broken—nay, not even damped the spirit of this remarkable warrior—and best of friends. Jean Calvet is the last specimen of a type now all but extinct: a tireless man who never is tiresome. If ever he dies—which God forbid or put off for many years to come—he will die in harness. Even to-day there was no son or nephew or butler allowed to handle those wonderful old Clarets which we had for lunch. Papa Jean decanted every one of them himself and did it better than anybody else could have done it. And what wines!

The white Château Margaux 1928 was just for fun, an unexpected opening, and the right sort of rather neutral wine to dispose of the sole and spinach in an agreeable manner without in the least interfering with the more important wines that were to follow, two famous Clarets with the chicken and two even more famous with the foie gras. The Château Léoville-Poyferré, which opened the *Marche Triomphale du Médoc*, was no youngster, a '74, not one of the greatest among the classical pre-phylloxera years but one that was responsible for some exceedingly fine wines, including this best of the three Léovilles; it had not the volume of bouquet one might have expected after nearly sixty years spent under cork, nor had it any fruit—or sugar—left, but it was still as sound as a bell, deep of colour, full of real winey flavour in spite of being somewhat on the light side. A really delightful glass of wine by itself, and yet quite put in the shade the moment the Mouton appeared. The Mouton-Rothschild '71 was not much bigger, as to body, but the welcome of its bouquet was more gracious and the sweet smile of its farewell was most captivating. How such a wine, a light wine from the first, can have retained not only its life so long, but its sweetness, its fruitiness, passes not only my powers of expression but of comprehension.

The next two wines, both Château Latour, were also very remarkable. The 1869 was not only red but black, as rich in colour as if six and not sixty-six years old. It was sturdy and beautifully balanced, possessing power, breed and a very fine bouquet; an aristocrat to the end, but the end just a little austere. It shamed the '74, good as the '74 was when it first came in, but not the '71. To me, the '71 was still the Queen, and Queen in her own right, with the '69 as the handsome Prince Consort: it might have been fairer to make the '69 King outright, but even so the '71 holds first place in my heart. It did, until the '58 came in and claimed everybody's homage. It was just a perfect bottle of the most perfect wine imaginable; so great and yet so simple, so gentle, so get-at-able; on the very brink of the grave, of course, but unafraid and with the quiet majesty of the sun that has all but left a cloudless sky and will in another second or two have disappeared into the sea.

ANDRÉ L. SIMON

A Memorable Meal: London, 1935

Our host [Vyvyan Holland] asked me to come early to help him decant the Clarets, which we began doing an hour and a half before dinner. We used red-hot tongs to remove the necks of the older bottles. Although I have seen this neatly done with a tap from the back of a knife, the trick needs skill and always makes me apprehensive when a fine old claret is to be discovered—with such brisk discourtesy.

After a glass of fine Amontillado, which was, however, a trifle heavy for a perfect pre-prandial sherry, we sat down to the salmon-trout and the Bâtard Montrachet 1926. Cooled to just the right temperature, discreet and clean on the palate, it proved to be a very good bottle of a wine which will soon be past its best. Without pretensions to greatness, the Bâtard has endeared itself to a number of us lately by its fresh honesty at a time when reliable white wines from this part of France are becoming difficult to find. I did not inquire if the fish was steamed or poached in an artfully informed *court-bouillon* or just 'plain boiled.' It was cooked to perfection, and whether because of its excellent *Sauce Verte* or the precise accord of the Bâtard or simply that the freshness of northern stars was still in its pink flesh, I think of it as the best sea trout I have ever eaten.

It was nice to find an old friend next, Durfort-Vivens 1914, and to see how well it stood up in such proud company. Its fine Margaux nose was as delicate as ever, its body firm, though I was surprised that for some reason to-night it finished just a little tired, compared to other bottles I have seen recently.

With the cutlets and sea-kale we also looked at the Malescot, bearing the advantage of its birth in 1900. It presented itself ingratiatingly enough to the nose, but it promised more than it could give after the Durfort. In addition to the great Château itself, there are ten classified vineyards in the Margaux district, and Château Malescot St. Exupéry occupies its place among the Third Growths. I have yet to see a Margaux of older but lesser growth belittle a nobler younger cousin of any fine recent vintage. And so it was to-night, after the greater breed of the Durfort there was little to say for a wine whose only happy feature was its bouquet.

Guinea fowl is an underestimated bird in England. Properly roasted in spatchcock fashion, its slightly gamey flavour, when finer game are out of season, makes a suitable background to gauge the calibre of fine clarets. The battery of 'Soixante-quinzes' now trained before us was the delicate artillery to consider this evening. I should note that the 'crupoos' served with the pintades were a mistake, for although delightful in texture, their flavour is of fish.

The first of our '75's, a Château d'Issan, failed us completely. I had had misgivings when decanting it, but thinking it might be 'bottle stink' which could dissipate itself in an hour, I did confide my anxiety to Vyvyan, who now bravely decanted another bottle. This at first seemed equally disappointing. It almost misfired—but not quite. I decided to nurse it in the glass for a few minutes before passing judgment. It is interesting to record that this wine, which was dark for its age, stirred, stretched, yawned and came into life— a brief, tired and attenuated life—for only three or four minutes. Ian Campbell drank his glass, and I most of mine, while it was at its best—in another moment its sixty years proved too big a burden for its weary body and it passed irremediably over.

The Cos d'Estournel 1875 was a very different affair. Its body, though rather worn, had charm and poise. It had a bouquet of great delicacy and though not a superlative wine it had retained enough sugar to give it an impressive and graceful farewell. Ian Campbell stated it to be as good as when he saw it in 1892 and I was surprised to conclude on such authority that this specimen of St. Estèphe, charming as it was to-night, had not at some time been more wholly satisfying. Now we turned our attention to the peak of the evening: the Château Margaux 1875. This is the wine which our President, writing of a different occasion, once referred to as 'the most glorious sunset that ever fired the west.' Ours was a Château-bottled specimen and had decanted beautifully—its 'sang de bœuf' brilliance a delight to the eye.

Although it had originally less sugar probably than either of the other '75's, it had kept its qualities in far more perfect harmony. Breed, elegance, charm, all were there. There was sunshine and gaiety in its final courteous bow. James Laver could not have found a more apt moment to recall to us that Bordeaux had once been English.

The Guiraud 1914, served with the ice, was fruity and rich without being cloying, and suffered only from being an anti-climax. A glass of clean, dry brandy brought the royal procession to a close. I was left wondering whether three clarets of the famous 1875 vintage will ever be served again at the same dinner.

They will soon be only a memory, and I hope the guests will experience the same interest and enjoyment in knowing them as we did this evening.

CURTIS MOFFAT

Château Margaux 1869 or 1870?

This brief summary of the great pre-phylloxera Clarets demands a few words of more detailed description and of actual appreciation of specific wines of that Golden Age.

A short time ago five wine-lovers met around a fine apple-wood table in a quiet old-fashioned room looking out on Park Lane. There was a hush of religious expectation as we took our seats. Expectancy deepened, while our host, a Claret enthusiast, explained the purpose of his invitation. There was doubt as to the year of a bin of noble pre-phylloxera Claret. Château Margaux it undoubtedly was, and its vintage was either 1869 or 1870. Our host was in favour of 1870, but a great French expert pronounced it 1869. The company was invited to give its judgment, and some of the greatest wines the world has ever known awaited our attention, to compose and guide our judgment.

Léoville 1870, Margaux 1870 or 1869, Latour 1869 and Margaux 1871, were the masterpieces of Nature and the wine-grower's art offered to us that day. Their fascination was enhanced by a touch of melancholy that the tale of these great Clarets was nearly told. There are no Clarets worthy to take their place. They called for the same discriminating attention as the work of a great painter or musician. Their perfection would first create surprise which would deepen into the sympathy of full comprehension, as the wine developed with a pleasing coyness the most secret subtleties of its charm.

In a pleasant atmosphere of comradeship and mutual understanding which fitted with the ancient panelling of that quiet room, we cleansed our palates with a mouthful of very old and very dry Sercial Madeira, before doing honour to the 1870 Léoville. The food, the background against which the delicate harmonies of the wine were to be thrown into relief, was the best of simple fare with nothing that could clash with the bouquet and aroma of the most sensitive of Clarets. The deep dark purple of the Léoville enchanted the eye, but it had less subtle perfume than its age might have warranted, and in the mouth there was the faintest suspicion of that acidity that announces decay. As has been said, the 1870's which have been obstinate and very slow in attaining maturity, have proved exceptionally long-lived. Very full-bodied, with a wealth of sugar held concealed for over half a century, many of them are at their very best today—Lafite 1870, for instance—though they have exceeded by half the forty years that are the normal Claret's allotted span. The Léoville, however, had been overtaken by old age.

The Margaux of doubtful date that followed certainly belonged to a very great year. I think that by a majority vote it would have been awarded to 1869 on account of the richness of its bouquet and a certain grandeur which rarely belongs to Margaux. By itself it would have been a wine to linger over and to meditate lovingly upon, but there were greater still to follow.

The tapestry-like purples of the Latour 1869 contained that sheen of molten gold which only comes after many years of secret ripening in the still darkness of the cellar. The French call it "pelure d'oignon," a reference to onion peel, which recalls the homely simile in the Nineteenth Odyssey when Odysseus' purple tunic that glistened like the sun is compared to the sheen upon the skin of a dried onion. Beautiful to the eye, this great wine breathed forth a perfume worthy of the gods. It was compounded of a multitude of subtle fragrances, the freshness of the sun-ripened grape, etherealised by the patient work of Nature into a quintessence of harmonious scents. The palate recognised a heroic wine, such a drink as might refresh the warring archangels, and the perfection of its beauty called up the noble phrase "terrible as an army with banners." The full organ swell of a triumphal march might express its appeal in terms of music.

Its magnificence demanded comparison with other famous wines and a discussion on the ideal Claret, "the best wine for my beloved, that goeth down sweetly, causing the lips of those that are asleep to speak." If it be permissible to suggest a defect in the almost perfect, the Latour was a trifle—the merest trifle—too ponderous, too ostentatious, too grandiose, to reach the supreme height of Lafite 1864 with its perfect balance of every quality. Was there a slight exaggeration of the virtues that belong to dignity and pomp at the expense of the subtlest shades of delicacy? In truth, criticism shrinks abashed before the ambrosial qualities of that Latour '69 and can only excuse itself by the transcendent memory of the Lafite which remains the divine idea, in the Platonic sense, of Claret.

The Margaux 1871 that followed is a wine apart. After the thunderous heroism of the epic Latour, it comes with the dainty sweetness of lyric poetry. Its magic bouquet envelopes the senses in a cloud of airy fragrance, raspberry-scented like the breezes from the Islands of the Blest, a dream of grace and delicacy, the twinkling feet of dancing nymphs, suddenly set free in our tedious world. Here is nothing heavy, nothing ponderous, nothing clumsy. Its subtle symphony of ever-varied shades of beauty partakes of the poetry of speed, of the perfect lines that form and break and form again as dancers weave an agile pattern.

Some four hundred years before Christ, Hermippus, a poet of the Old Comedy, puts into the mouth of Dionysus a description of just such a wine as that Chateau Margaux 1871. "But there is," says Dionysus, "a wine which they call 'the mellow,' and from the mouth of its jar as it is opened, there comes a fragrance of violets, a fragrance of roses, a fragrance of hyacinth. A divine perfume pervades the high-roofed house, ambrosia and nectar in one."

As the last drops of the Margaux were being sipped, a guest, savouring preciously every fragrance, said with unaffected humility: "When I drink such wines as these, I ask myself in vain what merit I have acquired that I should be allowed to experience such beauty."

H. WARNER ALLEN
The Romance of Wine

A Lucullan Fantasy

One of the most notable events which has taken place in the last few years since Christie's, the famous London auctioneers, restarted their wine sales was when their director, Michael Broadbent, on Wednesday, the 31st May 1967, presented a range of remarkable old bottles; these had lain all their lives in the cellars of Dalmeny House and Hopetoun House, the Scottish seats of the Roseberry and Linlithgow families.

The wines, many of them quite fabulous, had remained in their original bins ever since the time they had been put into bottle. I remember the sale well, for I had been commissioned to buy a dozen bottles of Château Latour 1874 at almost any price on behalf of Keith Showering, whose family business [Harveys of Bristol] are part-owners of that well-known château. With a number of lots of similar calibre on offer, no wonder the sale made such a stir in the world of wine!

As was only to be expected, the sale room was crowded with a most distinguished gathering, and among them were my Californian friends Dr. Bernard L. Rhodes and Dr. Robert Kay Adamson, together with their wives. They were over for their annual visit to the European vineyards, and as the sale coincided with their visit, they had crossed to London with a view to acquiring some fine vintage port from the early years of the twentieth century; also, if possible, some of the pre-phylloxera claret, preferably in magnums or even larger sizes still. Amongst their purchases, and egged on by both Ronald Avery and myself, they bid for and obtained a triple magnum of 1865 Château Lafite, a wine made by Sir Samuel Scott, an Englishman, three years before he sold the Lafite property to the Rothschild family.

I had no compunction whatsoever in persuading Barney

Rhodes to go on bidding up to what was really a rather high figure, because in the private cellar at Latour, we still have a small bin of our own 1865 vintage. Although it is in bottles, the wine is still so extraordinarily virile and splendid that it seemed to me that a container six times the size, and of the same vintage, had an even greater chance of survival, particularly in view of its "case history," which is as follows:

This huge bottle was purchased by the first Earl of Roseberry from Cockburn's of Leith [Scotland], an old established firm of wine merchants, and in 1869 it was laid down in its original bin at Dalmeny House. Since then it has been moved only twice, the first time for the cork to be resealed with wax, done in 1930 by that distinguished firm of wine merchants, Berry Brothers of St. James's Street, London, and the second, of course, when it was shipped to California.

The vital factor for the good preservation of this 1865 Lafite was the very cold cellar in which it was stored. It is a well-known fact that when wine is kept at a cool, constant temperature such as this (around 50 degrees Fahrenheit) it takes longer to mature, but it does so under ideal conditions. Added to that, a triple magnum will take much longer to develop than a bottle, and thus should keep for a correspondingly longer time.

Having given the wine a year or so in which to settle down after its lengthy journey, tiring enough in any case for a young wine, but surely even more so for a centenarian, Barney Rhodes, Bob Adamson, and Ben Ichinose, the third partner in this Lucullan fantasy, decided to plan a gastronomic feast around this august and aristocratic bottle.

It was indeed fortunate for me that such *un grand diner* should coincide with one of my periodic visits to California, and a great honour indeed to be included among the group of distinguished guests, for once the word got out, there was a rush for attendance, and in spite of the high cost of each plate, quite a large number of people had to be disappointed. As it was, many of *les convives* came specially for the occasion, from as far away as Sacramento, Los Angeles, and one even from Aspen, Colorado.

As may be imagined, great were the preparations which went on beforehand. Apart from choosing a suitable menu to embellish the proceedings and other wines considered worthy to accompany this noble bottle, the transport and the decanting of such old treasures required the utmost attention. It was well perhaps that the three owners of the triple-magnum were all doctors, so that they could bring to bear all their technical skill to the decanting of the runner-up, a jeroboam of 1929 Château Bel Air (Saint-Emilion) and the triple-magnum which were so proudly set out for all to admire. So instead of tipping up the bottles in the usual manner, with the utmost expertise they siphoned off the contents into a number of decanters. Thanks to the unbroken wax which covered the tip of the neck of this outsize prima donna, the cork itself was in perfect condition, no mean feat after some forty years in contact with the wine within.

The fourth member of the committee, James F. Smith, an old friend of André Simon, had kindly arranged our presence at the Cercle de l'Union in San Francisco, together with the services of its excellent chef. As Monsieur Pompidou, the President of France, was in San Francisco on that very day, one cannot help feeling he would have preferred to spend his evening at the French Club, instead of at the state function which he had to attend!

When a wine reaches a venerable age, there is usually some evaporation, and the air-gap, or what is commonly called ullage, if excessive, can cause the contents of the bottle to become oxidised and thus spoiled. This is why the old vintages lying in Bordelais cellars are examined, refilled, and recorked approximately every twenty-five years, but when stood up, the extraordinary thing about this triple-magnum was that after over a hundred years and only one recorking, there was an air gap of less than an inch between the wine and the cork!

To describe the splendid food would take too long, but some remarks on the wines may not come amiss. The magnums of champagne were all excellent, and having been so recently disgorged, the Moët & Chandon 1952 was beautifully fresh and delightful. What was so unusual, however, were the magnums of Bollinger (1937 and 1934), for these had both been disgorged and corked in the regular manner, and under normal circumstances champagne of such an age would undoubtedly have taken on colour and generally be showing some grey hairs! Not a bit of it, though; each of these two wines had a very pale colour, and both were as fresh as a daisy. This must surely be due to the excellent conditions prevailing in Madame Bollinger's own cellar, where it had been housed for so long.

The 1870 Sercial, which accompanied the soup, had a superb bouquet and flavour, and the 1949 Montrachet, which followed, was equally well preserved. Just by looking at its pale colour, one could tell there would be no fear of oxidation there, something which at that age could easily have set in.

Nineteen-twenty-nine has always been my favourite vintage

for claret. In the late forties and early fifties the 1929's were quite unique. Their individual, almost unbelievable bouquet and flavour made them stand out amongst all others, but for a number of years now, time has set its seal upon them, and in most cases the glory has departed. Alas, good things do not go on forever! All the same, the 1929 Bel Air, decanted at the last minute from its jeroboam, had an excellent colour, a fine bouquet (though admittedly aged), and a lovely flavour as well. Sadly, though, it began to thin out towards the end of the taste. Even a few of the grey hairs had fallen, leaving that tell-tale patch of baldness!

There is no need to enlarge upon the apprehension surrounding the welfare of the triple-magnum, the *pièce de résistance* of the whole evening. In case the 1929 Bel Air had not come up to scratch, there was a jeroboam of 1923 Bel Air standing by, but what on earth can one have as a substitute for such *une grande bouteille* as 1865 Lafite?

There was considerable interest and much flashing of light bulbs attending the extraction of the cork, and one had to admire Doctors Adamson, Ichinose, and Rhodes for their ingenuity over the operation. Once the wax was chipped off, the top quarter of the cork was cut out. This was done just in case such an old cork should be pushed down into the bottle and the soiled top part of it come into contact with the wine. As mentioned before, the contents were then expertly siphoned out, leaving the sediment at the bottom of the bottle.

To say the least, the result was staggering. Such a beautiful deep colour was really unexpected in such a very old wine; the bouquet, too, was a delight—far, far younger than that of the 1929 Bel Air! The flavour was almost miraculous, so much fruit and such a lovely finish. There is something about these great pre-phylloxera clarets that no modern successor can equal, certainly not for longevity anyway.

The unfortunate 1928 Romanée-Saint-Vivant which followed, so overshadowed by its immediate predecessor, stood up wonderfully well under almost impossible circumstances, dark of colour, fine of bouquet, sturdy and full-bodied, and it even had some tannin still to brag about! A splendid bottle!

It was quite a task, too, for a very ancient vintage port to follow hard on the heels of anything so luscious and delectable as the double-magnum of 1953 Château d'Yquem, but what a glass of port that 1860 was! Bottled at Chard in Somerset by Mitchell Toms, its colour was unusually dark for a centenarian, and into the bargain it both tasted and smelled like fine vintage port. Except, perhaps, for the fact that it had lost most of its sugar, there was no need whatever to make polite noises in its defence. This was one of the finest really old bottles of vintage port I have ever tasted, and that together with the excellent cigars so kindly provided by Mr. Charles Woodruff of Dunhill's, rounded off this Lucullan feast in a most fitting manner.

HARRY WAUGH
Diary of a Winetaster

Château La Lagune 1858

I think Hugh Rudd, my vintner chief, had an eye to morale when he brought out for lunch a magnum of La Lagune 1858 from a bin whose other contents he hastily dispatched for safety to the country. I did know that La Lagune had a reputation for longevity, but I had never heard of its being put to such a test. At once it threw into the shade all my memories of the Lafite 1858 drunk many years before. Almost nonagenarian, it bore its years so lightly. I quote from the notes I made on the spot and incorporated in my book on *Natural Red Wines*. 'It was glorious without a trace of senility. Somehow it had preserved its sugar and finished on the palate with the most velvety sweetness. Its bouquet, as might be expected with so old a wine, was ethereal, and what was more surprising its aroma had *le moelleux* of a vigorous wine with a *finesse* of wonderful delicacy.'

When writing the first draft of this chapter and recalling the glorious old age of that magnum, I wondered what had happened to its five fellows so hurriedly snatched from peril to the security of the country cellar. In an inspired moment, I wrote to the present Directors of the firm whose friendship I had inherited from their forerunners, asking for news of them. The reply from Mr A. A. Berry began with an extract from his *Wine Diary*, recording his impressions of one of the magnums drunk in its hundredth year after a 1920 Claret. 'The 1858 was in superb form to celebrate its centenary. At first I feared it was dying in the glass, but it came round and finished in a blaze of glory. It had an amazingly full colour and a wonderful flavour and smell for so old a wine.'

The letter ended with an invitation. One magnum still remained and that generosity which prompts wine-lovers to share with their friends their rarest bottles was expressed in an invitation to play my part in the fulfilment of its destiny.

When the great day came [in 1960] we were five to do honour to that ancient, hand-blown magnum, inclined to wobble when upright, a delight to the eye. Invitation to make a sixth had been sent to several Claret-lovers, but in each case fate had forbidden acceptance. Perhaps I may whisper that there was a certain consolation in the thought that one-fifth is better than one-sixth of a magnum, but I trust that there will be no outbreak of suicide among those ill-fated connoisseurs if they learn what they have missed.

The first word over a glass of introductory Amontillado was reassuring. The magnum had decanted beautifully, the cork, quite a small one, intact. With an ingenuity worthy of their tradition my hosts had decided after due consideration to introduce the great wine with the second growth Rausan-Ségla of the vintage 1933, so charming in its time, but now well past its prime. It had always seemed to me rather stalky as compared to Beychevelle of that year, so long my favourite beverage, but its tannin had given it a longer life, though it was on its way downhill.

In the glasses the colours of the two wines with their contrast provided a study in themselves. Against the background of a white napkin the red of the Rausan-Ségla paled almost to pink in the presence of the dark glowing purple, which the alchemy of time had compounded in a hundred years with results like those wrought by millennia in precious stones. The bouquet of the Rausan-Ségla was attractive with that fragrance with which wines past their prime seek to compensate for their loss of appeal to the palate, but the first whiff of La Lagune reduced it to the tinkling of a musical box lost in the harmony of a great symphony. The centenarian was hale and hearty at the height of its form; the young wine of twenty-seven was fading into decrepitude.

There followed the judgment of the palate. At first it could not judge, only accept uncritically the multitudinous impact of—I can only use a vulgarism—'out of this world' sensations. They opened the gates to the Paradise which Swinburne fathered on Swedenborg where all senses were confounded and where music, colour and perfume were one. Jaded—Ian could never have used such a word for such a wine. It was applicable to the Rausan-Ségla, but the 1858 wine was as vigorous as it could be.

H. WARNER ALLEN
A History of Wine

1792 Bual Madeira

Before quitting Madeira, I must once more recount the story of the 1792 Bual which we had in the cellar of the Saintsbury Club in 1933.

In January 1933 I spent a few days as the guest of Mr. and Mrs. Edmund Leacock, near Funchal, and, dining one evening at Mrs. Blandy's—the uncrowned queen of the island at the time—we had some superb Madeiras which Mrs. Blandy almost apologized for, saying: "These are the best wines that I have, but not the best in the island. Uncle Michael has the best of all, but he will neither give it away nor drink it nor sell it." The next day, at the Funchal Club, Stephen Gaselee introduced me to "Uncle Michael," as Dr. Michael Grabham was known as to the Blandy family and to most people at Madeira. He was a well-beloved family doctor, but he was also a very gifted organist, and I gladly accepted his invitation to visit him that afternoon, when he played the organ to the smallest and most somnolent audience he probably had ever had. Then he came down into the "auditorium" and said to me: "Well, now let's have some tea." It was my chance and I took it. "You must pardon me, doctor, but please let me off, I do not like tea and never drink tea." He was a little surprised but quickly said: "Just as you like, but you can't just watch me drink tea; is there anything you would like?" That was, of course, exactly what I had hoped for. "Perhaps a small glass of Madeira, that is if you happen to have any in the house?" "What do you think?" the old gentleman chuckled. "Any Madeira in the house? I rather think I have, young man, and let me tell you, I have the very best Madeira there is in this island or anywhere else for that matter." Needless to say I was not in the mood to argue with him and presently the wine was opened and no tea for anybody that day. And this is how the wine was introduced by "Uncle Michael":

"This wine was made in 1792, a very good vintage, and by the way, the year when my father was born. When, in 1815, Napoleon called at Madeira on his way south, to St. Helena, this 1792 Madeira was picked out as being likely to become very fine, with age, and it was bought for the fallen Emperor, to help him forget the duress of exile. But, as you know, they found out that he suffered from some gastric trouble—some said that it was cancer of the stomach—and they would not let him drink this wine. As a matter of fact, the Emperor died in 1820, and this 1792 was hardly ready by then. The curious thing about it was that nobody had paid for the wine. That is to say, the English Consul at Funchal, a Mr. Veitch, had paid the merchant who had put the wine on board, in 1815. But he, Veitch, had never been able to get his money back. So he did the next best thing. He claimed the pipe of 1792 as his own, and he got it back in Madeira, in 1822, when he sold it to Charles Blandy. Charles Blandy's son, John, demijohned the wine in 1840, and that happens to be the year when I was born. I also married John's daughter, and that is how the wine came to me." There was not very much of it left, but Dr. Grabham was good enough to let me have twenty-four bottles for the members of the Saintsbury Club, and it so happened that on that very day of January 1933 Professor George Saintsbury passed away.

ANDRÉ L. SIMON
Vintagewise

On a Certain Madeira Boal 1792

The doomed and broken Bonaparte
To thaw the ice that bound his heart
Bore from Madeira to his jail
Islanded twixt sea and gale
The barrelled juice of grapes that grew
Twenty-three years ere Waterloo.
But Death was urging to his bed
Him who so richly Death had fed;
Aye, that more grim Napoleon
Was closing icy fingers on
The little body and great brain,
Bidding the haughty lip abstain
From comfort of the anodyne.
The weakening hand put by the wine,
And when at last the hand fell slack,
Homeward the cask was carried back
Unbroached, and when the wine had stood
Nigh half a century in wood,
They bottled it and duly laid
Cellared in its native shade.
The heart that hoped the world to gain
A century in dust has lain.
Yet we of these late times may sip
The wine forbid his dying lip.

MARTIN ARMSTRONG

Old Madeira

Years passed and little Madeira came my way. I was an old man when my senses were dumbfounded as if by a firework display by presentation to such a collection of glorious Madeiras as had never been seen before and will never again be seen. I had drunk the more than centenarian Madeira which the Saintsbury Club owed to the generosity of Sir Stephen Gaselee as the final of a sequence of fine vintage wines, with the reverence due to the rarest of pleasurable experiences, but it was not until May 1959 that I had a unique opportunity of judging the supreme heights to which the greatest of great Vintage Madeiras could rise.

In 1901 on his accession, King Edward VII startled his liege subjects by putting up to auction Vintage Madeiras and fine old Sherries from the royal cellars. Five thousand dozen brought in £18,000 and his mother's admirers wagged their heads sadly, wondering whether this wine sale was the first step in a Rake's Progress to be followed by submission to the hammer of all the white elephants conferred on the twice-Jubileed Queen and Empress by adoring subjects. Perhaps his successors sometimes wish that he had gone further on that path, but he may have found that he could buy nothing better with the price of his wines than the wines he had sold. André Simon considers that the King was well advised to give his people the chance of enjoying some of the Buckingham Palace old Madeiras and it is pleasant to imagine that His Majesty was moved by such altruistic magnanimity. 'There never had been—and there certainly never again will be—seen such Madeiras as those sold by order of the King.' For Simon writing thirty years later 'the memory of their concentrated essence of vinous perfection' was still as fresh as it was at the time he tasted those marvellous wines.

Nearly thirty years after Simon wrote, the grudge which I had harboured so long against the youth which deprived me of Simon's unwithering memory of the royal Madeiras was dissipated by an invitation to attend 'An Academy of Ancient Madeira Wines' with Senatorial Academicians quite worthy of the Buckingham Palace cellars. How Meredith's Doctor Middleton would have revelled in it, if only Madeira had been within his horizon!

Messrs Cossart Gordon of Funchal, the famous shippers, moved I feel sure by the same altruism as that of Edward VII, set out for tasting in the cellars of Messrs Evans Marshall nineteen ancient Madeira wines, some of which showed how the Wine God will persist in his beneficence even against the curses of Nature. Madeira early took kindly to the Spanish Solera system and I pass over as not strictly germane to my subject five excellent Solera wines including a magnificent Malmsey Solera laid down in 1808. Then there was a modern post-phylloxera Madeira Verdelho 1910, so fine that it might have justified Virgil's cry, *Redeunt Saturnia regna, The Golden Age returns,* with its promise that the old tradition had only been broken temporarily. Perhaps I passed over it too hastily in my eagerness to gain contact with the first Saturnian Golden Age.

Generally speaking, Madeira wines take their name from the vines from which they have been grown. There is the Sercial which yields the driest wine, so dry that it can challenge an Amontillado as an aperitif, and is regarded by Simon as the most typical of Madeiras for 'its distinction and the austerity of its farewell.' At the opposite extreme comes the Malmsey, so full and rich with the Hellenic classical restraint, that it is at once a rapture and a stimulant to the senses. Less luscious, but rich and full-bodied comes the Verdelho from white grapes, and between Sercial and Malmsey the Bual, which balances the qualities of one and the other with a delicacy of its own. There was also represented a grape which only once before had come my way, the Terrantez, no doubt because it was never replanted after the phylloxera of 1871. It is not mentioned by Simon nor in any other book known to me, yet it was responsible for two of the very finest wines shown, and perhaps in its day it claimed to be the most typical of all Madeira vines. A fine full body with a celestial bouquet is completed by an ozone-like finish so clean and dry as to be almost bitter, the perfect almond taste.

There were thirteen ancestral vintage wines, venerable patriarchs, any one of them worth to the wine-lover a king's ransom, and as if they had been submitted to the humiliation of sitting for an Honours Degree, Mr Noel Cossart's expert palate gave six of them a First, and to that select company I ventured to add a fancy of my own, Reserva Visconde Valle Paraiso—Bual 1844, which I was lucky enough to taste at the moment when the bottle in which it had lived for 23 years was opened. Mr Cossart faulted it for a bottle nose which wore off too quickly. These seven wines had an average age of 120 years, the youngest seventy-nine, the oldest a hundred and seventy. For myself I must confess that when I was called upon to classify the whole Academy in order of rank, I found myself as bewildered as Dionysius the False Areopagite ought to have been, when he set out to draw up the Gotha of the angelic hierarchy—and I lacked his self-confidence.

Several of these wines had passed part of their lives in large glass demijohns, wicker-covered bulging jars, a kind of halfway house between the cask and the bottle, ageing as it were after the wide open spaces of the cask in the closed community of a monastery before retiring to the hermit's cell in the solitude of the bottle. There was Sercial 1860, only withdrawn from demijohn to bottle fifteen months before; the date at which it left the cask was unknown. It was the driest Madeira I ever tasted, quite delightful I thought. Mr Cossart gave it alpha plus, but pronounced its days as numbered. Terrantez 1862 had spent 43 years in the wood, 31 years in demijohn and 23 years in bottle. It was the Terpsichore of Madeiras with all the elegance of the ageless Muse of Dance, and it tempted me to wonder whether perhaps with the disappearance of the Terrantez vine Madeira might not have lost an exquisite touch of spritely grace with which I had never associated it. The life history of the most famous of all Madeiras, that Methuselah of wine, Cama de Lobos 1789, covered 111 years in the wood, 50 years in demijohn and 9 years in bottle. It challenged and defeated all the legends of the immortal Opimian Falernian, for it was glory on the palate and in the nose—another thirty years and it would certainly not have been reduced to the likeness of rough honey, precious as attar of roses in a blend but quite undrinkable, the condition of Pliny's Opimian after 200 years. What joy would it have given to that learned wine-lover, Sir Edward Barry, if he could have known that a wine made fourteen years after the publication of his *Observations* would justify to posterity his theory that something like the amphora was needed to restore the classic tradition, by maturing for half a century in a vessel very like the receptacle he had suggested.

Cama de Lobos 1789, with its majestic presence was embalmed history. Had not its grapes been pressed only a month or so after the fall of the Bastille and just before Louis XVI and his queen were brought by the mob from Versailles to Paris with the guillotine three years ahead? Napoleon Bonaparte was only twenty and unknown. George Washington had just been inaugurated as the first President of the newly born United States of America. George III was on the throne and Pitt Prime Minister. All the world upheavals during the centuries which had elapsed since the Fall of the Roman Empire were to be mere child's play compared to those which were to befall mankind during the next hundred and seventy years, the still unfinished span of the life of Cama de Lobos 1789.

Possibly its junior by six years, Terrantez 1795, the year of Napoleon's 'whiff of grape-shot,' bore up its age with equal sturdiness and even an additional hint of the Terrantez grace after 133 years in the wood. The mere stripling Verdelho 1844 took its place with the others as a perfect example of its type, the triumph over time of the golden mean.

H. WARNER ALLEN
A History of Wine

7

Too Much Wine

If some wine is good, more wine must be better. While some eno-philes discuss the merits of fine old bottles, others drink whatever they can put their hands on and as fast as possible. Literature is full of drunks and debauches, and I've selected a few entertaining accounts that specifically concern wine, and not drinking in general. The eighteenth century seems particularly to have been a period of heavy drinking, and a few excerpts from Boswell's *Journal* give the flavor of the times, as does Ned Ward's account of an evening out. Although bacchanalian frenzy is somewhat removed from the drinking of Boswell, Lamb, or Waugh, I thought it would be a shame to leave Bacchus out of a book about wine. I have therefore included references to the god of wine from the works of Bulfinch and Frazer.

Poets and wine are no strangers to each other. Rayner Heppenstall recalls an occasion when Dylan Thomas visited him in Cornwall. One morning Thomas was "sipping from a flagon of 'champagne wine tonic' . . . Dylan talked copiously and then stopped. 'Somebody's boring me,' he said. 'I think it's me.' "

William Blake also enjoyed drinking, and it was claimed that he would drink anything with alcohol in it. In his biography of the poet, Alexander Gilchrist writes, "When he drank wine, which, at home, of course, was seldom, he professed a liking to drink off good draughts from a tumbler, and thought the wine glass system absurd: a very heretical opinion in the eyes of your true wine drinkers." Not so heretical as all that, actually, since André Simon enjoyed drinking champagne from a silver tankard.

Captain Gronow's story of Fiennes' instructions to a new servant is included here. A similar story concerns Sir Hercules Langrish. When asked whether he had any assistance in finishing three bottles of port, he replied that he had the assistance of a bottle of Madeira. More recently, George Mikes has commented, "I have often thought that the aim of port is to give you a good and durable hangover, so that during the next day you should be reminded of the splendid occasion the night before."

The most unfortunate example of someone having had too much wine, surely, concerns the Duke of Clarence and the butt of malmsey. As dramatized by Shakespeare in *Richard III*, Clarence, in prison, asks for a cup of wine. "Thou shalt have wine enough, my lord, anon," replies the First Murderer. Ignoring Clarence's pleas, the First Murderer finally stabs Clarence and the scene ends with his words "If all this will not do, / I'll drown you in the malmsey butt within."

Some of the accounts that follow may involve almost as much wine but with less fatal results.

He Was the First

And Noah began to be an husbandman, and he planted a vineyard:

And he drank of the wine, and was drunken; and he was uncovered within his tent.

And Ham, the father of Canaan, saw the nakedness of his father, and told his two brethren without.

And Shem and Japheth took a garment, and laid it upon both their shoulders, and went backward, and covered the nakedness of their father; and their faces were backward, and they saw not their father's nakedness.

And Noah awoke from his wine, and knew what his younger son had done unto him.

Genesis, Chapter 9

. . . and Others Followed

So Noah, when he anchor'd safe on
The mountain's top, his lofty haven,
And all the passengers he bore
Were on the new world set ashore,
He made it next his chief design
To plant and propagate a vine,
Which since has overwhelm'd and drown'd
Far greater numbers, on dry ground,
Of wretched mankind, one by one,
Than all the flood before had done.

SAMUEL BUTLER
"Satire upon Drunkenness"

An Awkward Moment

Butlers, we were told, were always notoriously drunk. When one of
the great Edwardian hostesses died and left her great cellar to her
eldest son, it was discovered that it had long since ceased to exist.
The famous wines had been drunk by her famous butler. Only a
half-dozen bottles of *vin ordinaire* remained. That same butler, it
was said, had been passed a note during a distinguished dinner
party. The note was from his lady. It said: 'You are disgustingly
drunk. Leave the table.' With drunken solemnity he had handed
the note (on a silver salver) to Sir Austen Chamberlain.

LADY ELIZABETH MONTAGU

Clear Instructions

Twisleton Fiennes was a very eccentric man, and the greatest epicure of his day. His dinners were worthy of the days of Vitellius or Heliogabalus. Every country, every sea, was searched and ransacked to find some new delicacy for our British Sybarite. I remember, at one of his breakfasts, an omelette being served which was composed entirely of golden pheasants' eggs! He had a very strong constitution and would drink absinthe and curaçoa in quantities which were perfectly awful to behold. These stimulants produced no effect upon his brain; but his health gradually gave way under the excesses of all kinds in which he indulged. He was a kind, liberal, and good-natured man, but a very odd fellow. I never shall forget the astonishment of a servant I had recommended to him. On entering his service, John made his appearance as Fiennes was going out to dinner, and asked his new master if he had any orders. He received the following answer,—"Place two bottles of sherry by my bed-side, and call me the day after to-morrow."

REES HOWELL GRONOW
Reminiscences

It Wasn't the Wine

Mr. Pickwick, with his hands in his pockets and his hat cocked completely over his left eye, was leaning against the dresser, shaking his head from side to side, and producing a constant succession of the blandest and most benevolent smiles without being moved thereunto by any discernible cause or pretence whatsoever; old Mr. Wardle, with a highly-inflamed countenance, was grasping the hand of a strange gentleman muttering protestations of eternal friendship; Mr. Winkle, supporting himself by the eight-day clock, was feebly invoking destruction upon the head of any member of the family who should suggest the propriety of his retiring for the night; and Mr. Snodgrass had sunk into a chair, with an expression of the most abject and hopeless misery that the human mind can imagine, portrayed in every lineament of his expressive face.

"Is anything the matter?" inquired the three ladies.

"Nothin' the matter," replied Mr. Pickwick. "We—we're—all right.—I say, Wardle, we're all right, ain't we?"

"I should think so," replied the jolly host.—"My dears, here's my friend Mr. Jingle—Mr. Pickwick's friend, Mr. Jingle, come 'pon—little visit."

"Is anything the matter with Mr. Snodgrass, Sir?" inquired Emily, with great anxiety.

"Nothing the matter, Ma'am," replied the stranger. "Cricket dinner—glorious party—capital songs—old port—claret—good— very good—wine, Ma'am—wine."

"It wasn't the wine," murmured Mr. Snodgrass, in a broken voice. "It was the salmon." (Somehow or other, it never *is* the wine, in these cases.)

CHARLES DICKENS
The Pickwick Papers

Bacchus

The god Dionysus or Bacchus is best known to us as a personification of the vine and of the exhilaration produced by the juice of the grape. His ecstatic worship, characterised by wild dances, thrilling music, and tipsy excess, appears to have originated among the rude tribes of Thrace, who were notoriously addicted to drunkenness. Its mystic doctrines and extravagant rites were essentially foreign to the clear intelligence and sober temperament of the Greek race. Yet appealing as it did to that love of mystery and that proneness to revert to savagery which seem to be innate in most men, the religion spread like wildfire through Greece until the god whom Homer hardly deigned to notice had become the most popular figure of the pantheon. The resemblance which his story and his ceremonies present to those of Osiris have led some enquirers both in ancient and modern times to hold that Dionysus was merely a disguised Osiris, imported directly from Egypt into Greece. But the great preponderance of evidence points to his Thracian origin, and the similarity of the two worships is sufficiently explained by the similarity of the ideas and customs on which they were founded.

JAMES G. FRAZER
The Golden Bough

. . . and a Bacchanal

Bacchus was the son of Jupiter and Semele. Juno, to gratify her resentment against Semele, contrived a plan for her destruction.

Assuming the form of Beroë, her aged nurse, she insinuated doubts whether it was indeed Jove himself who came as a lover. Heaving a sigh, she said, "I hope it will turn out so, but I can't help being afraid. People are not always what they pretend to be. If he is indeed Jove, make him give some proof of it. Ask him to come arrayed in all his splendours, such as he wears in heaven. That will put the matter beyond a doubt." Semele was persuaded to try the experiment. She asks a favour, without naming what it is. Jove gives his promise, and confirms it with the irrevocable oath, attesting the river Styx, terrible to the gods themselves. Then she made known her request. The god would have stopped her as she spake, but she was too quick for him. The words escaped, and he could neither unsay his promise nor her request. In deep distress he left her and returned to the upper regions. There he clothed himself in his splendours, not putting on all his terrors, as when he overthrew the giants, but what is known among the gods as his lesser panoply. Arrayed in this, he entered the chamber of Semele. Her mortal frame could not endure the splendours of the immortal radiance. She was consumed to ashes.

Jove took the infant Bacchus and gave him in charge to the Nysæan nymphs, who nourished his infancy and childhood, and for their care were rewarded by Jupiter by being placed, as the Hyades, among the stars. When Bacchus grew up he discovered the culture of the vine and the mode of extracting its precious juice . . .

As he approached his native city Thebes, Pentheus the king, who had no respect for the new worship, forbade its rites to be performed. But when it was known that Bacchus was advancing, men and women, but chiefly the latter, young and old, poured forth to meet him and to join his triumphal march. . . .

Pentheus would take no warning, but instead of sending others, determined to go himself to the scene of the solemnities. The mountain Citheron was all alive with worshippers, and the cries of the Bacchanals resounded on every side. The noise roused the anger of Pentheus as the sound of a trumpet does the fire of a war-horse. He penetrated through the wood and reached an open space where the chief scene of the orgies met his eyes. At the same moment the women saw him; and first among them his own mother, Agave, blinded by the god, cried out, "See there the wild boar, the hugest monster that prowls in these woods! Come on, sisters! I will be the first to strike the wild boar." The whole band rushed upon him, and while he now talks less arrogantly, now excuses himself, and now confesses his crime and implores pardon, they press upon him and wound him. In vain he cries to his aunts to protect him from his mother. Autonoe seized one arm, Ino the other, and between them he was torn to pieces, while his mother shouted, "Victory! Victory! we have done it; the glory is ours!"

THOMAS BULFINCH
Mythology

Plenty of Port

But the subject of this memoir had not such excuses to plead for his excess in drinking, neither will I endeavour to find them for him. It was, however, to him the Circean cup—the bane of his respectability, his health, his happiness, and every thing that was dear to him as a man and a gentleman; and can this be marvelled at? It is written of Hercules, that he acquired his immense strength by feeding on the marrow of lions, and how powerful must have been the stimulus of the almost unheard-of quantity of from *four* to *six* bottles of port wine *daily*, on that volcanic excitability of mind, which was, not only by nature, Mr. Mytton's, but which had been acted upon, and increased, by a severe affection of the brain, at an early period of life! Thus, then, although I offer no excuse for his drinking, his drinking—for men are tried by wine, says the proverb, as metals are by fire—furnishes excuses, I should rather have said apologies, for his conduct, inasmuch as his reason was, to a certain extent, lost in delirium, caused by the fumes of wine, on an already somewhat distempered brain. Many of his acts were not the acts of John Mytton but of a man *mad, half by nature, and half by wine*, and I think his best and dearest friends are decidedly of my opinion.

From this account of its Host, it may be supposed that Halston was a scene of general dissipation and riot. By no means. In short, I cannot bring to my recollection a single instance of being one of what may be termed a drunken party, during my frequent visits to the house. But this is accounted for in more ways than one. The host had always the start of his friends, in the first place; and in the next, long sittings were not in accordance with his restless disposition. In the summer he would jump out of the window, and be off. In the winter, he was anxious to get to the billiard table, which was always lighted up after coffee, for the amusement of himself and his friends, and here he was in his element. How then, it may be asked, did he consume that quantity of port wine? Why this question is easily answered. He shaved with a bottle of it on his toilet; he worked steadily at it throughout the day, by a glass or two at a time, and at least a bottle with his luncheon; and the after dinner and *after supper* work—not losing sight of it in the billiard room—completed the Herculean task. . . . He is, however, a memorable example of the comparatively harmless effects of *very good wine*, which he always had, and just of a proper age—about eight years old—for, assisted by exercise, such as he took, it was many years before it injured him.

"NIMROD"
Memoirs of the Life of John Mytton

Drunk Too Soon

Today before a goblet of wine I was shamed,
My third cup unfinished, I couldn't pour another.
Wondering why I am always drunk beneath the flowers,
Perhaps the spring breeze has made me tipsy.

YÜAN CHEN
9th century

A Bad Bargain

Addison used often to walk from Holland House to the White Horse, Kensington, to enjoy his favourite dish, a fillet of veal, his bottle, and perhaps a friend. There is a story that the profligate Duke of Wharton plied him one day at table so briskly with wine, in order to make him talk, that he could not keep it on his stomach, which made his Grace observe, that "he could get wine, but not wit, out of him."

CHARLES TOVEY
Wit, Wisdom and Morals

Stages of Drunkenness

All the world's a pub,
And all the men and women merely drinkers;

They have their hiccoughs and their staggerings;
And one man in a day drinks many glasses,
His acts being seven stages. At first the gentleman.
Steady and steadfast in his good resolves;
And then the wine and bitters, appetiser,
And pining, yearning look, leaving like a snail
The comfortable bar. And then the arguments,
Trying like Hercules with a wrathful frontage
To refuse one more two penn'orth. Then the mystified.
Full of strange thoughts, unheeding good advice,
Careless of honour, sudden, thick, and gutt'ral,
Seeking the troubled repetition
Even in the bottle's mouth; and then quite jovial,
In fair good humour while the world swims round,
With eyes quite misty, while his friends him cut,
Full of nice oaths and awful bickerings;
And so he plays his part. The sixth stage shifts
Into the stupid, slipping, drunken man,
With 'blossoms' on his nose and bleery-eyed,
His shrunken face unshaved, from side to side
He rolls along; and his unmanly voice,
Huskier than ever, fails and flies,
And leaves him—staggering round. Last scene of all.
That ends this true and painful history,
Is stupid childishness, and then oblivion—
Sans watch, sans chain, sans coin, sans everything.

ANON.

Keep It Coming

The wines were chiefly port, sherry and hock; claret, and even Burgundy, being then designated 'poor thin washy stuff.' A perpetual
thirst seemed to come over people, both men and women, as soon
as they had tasted their soup; as from that moment everybody was
taking wine with everybody else till the close of the dinner; and
such wine as produced that class of cordiality which frequently
wanders into stupefaction. How all this sort of eating and drinking
ended was obvious, from the prevalence of gout, and the necessity
of every one making the pill-box their constant bedroom
companion.

REES HOWELL GRONOW
Reminiscences

Dead and Alive

His Wife she was a Woman,
   that lov'd a cup of Sack,
And she would tipple soundly,
   behind her Husband's back;
A bottle she had gotten that
   would hold two quarts or more,
Well fill'd with wine she hang'd it
   behind her chamber door:
And she told unto her Husband
   that it was poyson strong,
And bad him not to touch it,
   for fear of doing wrong:
If thou drink but one drop on't,
   (quoth she) 'twill end thy life;
Therefore in time take heed,
   and be ruled by thy Wife. . . .

When's Wife came in the dairy-house,
   and saw what there was done,
A strong and fierce encounter
   she presently begun;
She pull'd him by the ears,
   and she wrung him by the nose,
And she kickt him on the belly,
   while the tears ran down his hose.
And she vow'd to be revenged
   before the morrow day,
For all the brood of chickens,
   which the kite had carried away:
Poor *Simon* stood amazed,
   being weary of his life,
For he good Man was tired
   with his unruly Wife.

For when that he perceived
    his Wife in such a rage,
Nor knowing how, nor which way
    his fury to asswage:
He cunningly got from her,
    and to the chamber went,
Thinking himself to poyson,
    for that was his intent;
So coming to the bottle,
    which I spoke of before,
He thought it to be poyson,
    which hung behind the door:
He vow'd to drink it all up,
    and end his wretched life,
Rather than live in thraldom,
    with such a cursed Wife.

So opening of a window, which
    stood towards the South,
He took the bottle of sack,
    and set it to his mouth:
Now will I drink this poyson,
    (quoth he) with all my heart;
So that the first draught he drunk on't
    he swallowed near a quart:
The second time that he set
    the bottle to his snout,
He never left off swigging,
    till he had suckt all out:
Which done, he fell down backward
    like one bereft of life,
Crying out, I now am poysoned
    by means of my cursed Wife.

Quoth he, I feel the poyson
    now run through every vein,
It rumbles in my belly,
    and it tickles in my brain;
It wambles in my stomack,
    and it molifies my heart,
It pierceth through my members,
    and yet I feel no smart;
Would all that have curst wives,

example take hereby,
   For I dye as sweet a death sure,
     as every man did dye:
   'Tis better with such poyson,
     to end a wretched life,
   Than to live, and be tormented
     with such a wicked Wife.

ANON.
17th Century

In His Cups

It is an observation of a wise man that 'moderation is best in all things.' I cannot agree with him 'in liquor.' There is a smoothness and oiliness in wine that makes it go down by a natural channel, which I am positive was made for that descending. Else, why does not wine choke us? could Nature have made that sloping lane, not to facilitate the down-going? She does nothing in vain. You know that better than I. You know how often she has helped you at a dead lift, and how much better entitled she is to a fee than yourself sometimes, when you carry off the credit. Still there is something due to manners and customs, and I should apologise to you and Mrs. Asbury for being absolutely carried home upon a man's shoulders thro' Silver Street, up Parson's Lane, by the Chapels (which might have taught me better), and then to be deposited like a dead log at Gaffar Westwood's, who it seems does not 'insure' against intoxication. Not that the mode of conveyance is objectionable. On the contrary, it is more easy than a one-horse chaise.

CHARLES LAMB
Letter to Dr. J. V. Asbury

. . . and Again

A glimpse of Lamb in his cups is given by Mrs. Procter in a letter to Mrs. Jameson in 1830 or thereabouts. "Charles Lamb," she writes (from 25 Bedford Square), "dined here on Monday at 5, and by seven he was so tipsy he could not stand. Martin Burney carried him from one room to the other like a sack of coals, he insisting on saying 'Diddle diddle dumpty, my son John'—he slept until 10, and then awoke more tipsy than before—and between his fits of bantering Martin Burney, kept saying, 'Please God I'll never enter this cursed house again.' He wrote a note next day begging pardon and asking when he may come again. Poor Miss Lamb is ill."

E. V. LUCAS
The Life of Charles Lamb

A False Friend

CASSIO: Reputation, reputation, reputation! O, I have lost my reputation! I have lost the immortal part, sir, of myself, and what remains is bestial.—My reputation, Iago, my reputation.

IAGO: As I am an honest man, I thought you had received some bodily wound; there is more offence in that than in reputation. Reputation is an idle and most false imposition; oft got without merit, and lost without deserving: You have lost no reputation at all, unless you repute yourself such a loser. What, man! there are ways to recover the general again: you are but now cast in his mood, a punishment more in policy than in malice; even so as one would beat his offenceless dog, to affright an imperious lion: sue to him again, and he is yours.

CASSIO: I will rather sue to be despised, than to deceive so good a commander, with so slight, so drunken, and so indiscreet an officer. Drunk? and speak parrot? and squabble? swagger? swear? and discourse fustian with one's own shadow?—O thou invisible spirit of wine, if thou hast no name to be known by, let us call thee—devil!

IAGO: What was he that you followed with your sword? What had he done to you?

CASSIO: I know not.

IAGO: Is it possible?

CASSIO: I remember a mass of things, but nothing distinctly; a quarrel, but nothing wherefore,—O, that men should put an enemy in their mouths, to steal away their brains! that we should, with joy, revel pleasure, and applause, transform ourselves into beasts!

IAGO: Why, but you are well enough: How came you thus recovered?

CASSIO: It hath pleased the devil, drunkenness, to give place to the devil, wrath: one unperfectness shows me another, to make me frankly despise myself.

IAGO: Come, you are too severe a moraler: As the time, the place and the condition of this country stands, I could heartily wish this had not befallen; but, since it is as it is, mend it for our own good.

CASSIO: I will ask him for my place again; he shall tell me, I am a drunkard! Had I as many mouths as Hydra, such an answer would stop them all. To be now a sensible man, by and by a fool, and presently a beast! O strange!—Every inordinate cup is unblessed, and the ingredient is a devil.

IAGO: Come, come, good wine is a good familiar creature, if it be well used; exclaim no more against it.

WILLIAM SHAKESPEARE
Othello

Looking Back

There were six or seven clubs [at Oxford] with their own premises; some, like the Grid, highly respectable, others, Hogarthian drinking dens. The most notable of the dens was named the Hypocrites, in picturesque Tudor rooms over a bicycle shop in St Aldates (now of course demolished). There the most popular drink was red Burgundy drunk from earthenware tankards. A standing house rule was: 'Gentlemen may prance but not dance.' The oddest of these clubs with premises was the New Reform at the corner of the Cornmarket on Ship Street. This was subsidized by Lloyd George in the belief that it would be a nursery for earnest young Liberals. It became a happy centre of anarchy and debauch. Habits of extravagance grew and in my last year we drank a good deal of champagne in mid-morning at the New Reform and scoffed from the windows at the gowned figures hurrying from lecture to lecture. There was a vogue for whisky and crumpets at tea-time in the Union. I think it is no exaggeration to say that, in my last year, I and most of my friends were drunk three or four times a week, quite gravely drunk, sometimes requiring to be undressed and put to bed, but more often clowning exuberantly and, it seemed to us, very funnily. We were never pugnacious or seriously destructive. It took very little to inebriate at that age and high spirits made us behave more flamboyantly than our state of intoxication really warranted. Not many of us have become drunkards.

We were not discriminating. In a novel I once gave a description of two undergraduates sampling a cellar of claret. I never had that experience at that age. Indeed I do not think that at twenty I could distinguish with any certainty between claret and burgundy. Port was another matter. The tradition of port drinking lingered. Many of the colleges had ample bins of fine vintages of which undergraduates were allowed a strictly limited share. Port we drank with reverence and learned to appreciate. The 1904s were then at their prime, or, at any rate, in excellent condition. We were not ashamed (nor am I now) to relish sweet wine. Yquem had, of course, a unique reputation. Starting to drink it in a mood of ostentation, I was led to the other white Bordeaux. Tokay was then procurable and much relished. Bristol Milk, and a dark sherry named Brown Bang were also favourites. We tried anything we could lay hands on, but table-wines were the least of our interests. We drank them conventionally at luncheon and dinner parties but waited eagerly for the heavier and headier concomitants of dessert.

Nowadays, I am told, men privately drink milk and, when they entertain, do so to entice girls. It is tedious for the young to be constantly reminded what much finer fellows their fathers were and what a much more enjoyable time we had. But there you are; we were and we did.

EVELYN WAUGH
"First Faltering Steps: Drinking"

Drinking with Boswell

I

THURSDAY 14 JULY. . . . When we went into the Mitre tonight, Mr. Johnson said, "We will not drink two bottles of port." When one was drank, he called for another pint; and when we had got to the bottom of that, and I was distributing it equally, "Come," said he, "you need not measure it so exactly." "Sir," said I, "it is done." "Well, Sir," said he, "are you satisfied? or would you choose another?" "Would you, Sir?" said I. "Yes," said he, "I think I would. I think two bottles would seem to be the quantity for us." Accordingly we made them out. . . .

FRIDAY 15 JULY. A bottle of thick English port is a very heavy and a very inflammatory dose. I felt it last time that I drank it for several days, and this morning it was boiling in my veins. Dempster came and saw me, and said I had better be palsied at eighteen than not keep company with such a man as Johnson.

II

FRIDAY 4 NOVEMBER. Colonel Campbell and I set out in his chaise about eight. I was not much indisposed. We breakfasted at the North Ferry, stopped at Queensferry, and drank a glass at Bailie Buncle's; drove to town, and came out of our chaise at the Exchange, that all who were at the Cross might see us after our victory. I went home and saw my wife and Veronica, then dined with the Colonel at his lodgings, and, as he was to be busy, just drank half a bottle of port; then sallied forth between four and five with an avidity for drinking from the habit of some days before. I went to Fortune's; found nobody in the house but Captain James Gordon of Ellon. He and I drank five bottles of claret and were most profound politicians. He pressed me to take another; but my stomach was against it. I walked off very gravely though much intoxicated. Ranged through the streets till, having run hard down the Advocates' Close, which is very steep, I found myself on a sudden bouncing down an almost perpendicular stone stair. I could not stop, but when I came to the bottom of it, fell with a good deal of violence, which sobered me much. . . .

III

FRIDAY 10 NOVEMBER. I dined with Mr. Alexander Mackenzie, Writer to the Signet, with Barrock, a Caithness laird, and his lady and two daughters, my client Ardross and his lady, and my cousin Lieutenant Graham. I got into a Highland humour and drank first plentifully of port and then of claret, which cost only £16 a hogshead; and, as intoxication rose, I disregarded my solemn engagement of sobriety to my friend Temple, and pushed the bottle about with an improper keenness, as I was not the entertainer. About nine Graham and I drank tea with Mr. and Mrs. Mackenzie. I was able to be decent then. But when I got into the street I grew very drunk and miserably sick, so that I had to stop in many closes in my way home, and when I got home I was shockingly affected, being so furious that I took up the chairs in the dining-room and threw them about and broke some of them, and beat about my walking-stick till I had it in pieces, and then put it into the fire and burnt it. I have scarcely any recollection of this horrid scene, but my wife informed me of it. She was in great danger, for it seems I had aimed at her both with chairs and stick. What a monstrous account of a man! She got me to bed, where I was excessively sick.

SATURDAY 11 NOVEMBER. My intemperance was severely punished, for I suffered violent distress of body and vexation of mind. I lay till near two o'clock, when I grew easier, and comforted myself by resolving vigorously to be attentively sober for the future. There is something agreeably delusive in fresh resolution.

JAMES BOSWELL
Journals

Bad Habits

Now give my argument fair play,
And take the thing the other way:
The youngster, who at nine and three
Drinks with his sisters milk and tea,
From breakfast reads till twelve o'clock,
Burnet and Heylin, Hobbes and Locke;
He pays due visits after noon
To cousin Alice and uncle John;
At ten from coffee-house or play
Returning, finishes the day.
But, give him port and potent sack,
From milksop he starts up mohack;
Holds that the happy know no hours;
So through the street at midnight scours,
Breaks watchmen's heads, and chairmen's glasses,
And thence proceeds to nicking sashes;
Till, by some tougher hand o'ercome,
And first knock'd down, and then led home,
He damns the footman, strikes the maid,
And decently reels up to bed.

MATTHEW PRIOR
"Alma, or the Progress of the Mind"
1715

Revels

From thence . . . we adjourned to the sign of the Angel in Fen-
church Street. . . . There my friend had the good fortune to meet
some of his acquaintances, with whom we join'd, and made up
together as pretty a tippling society as ever were drawn into a cir-
cumference round the noble center of a punch bowl, tho' our liquor
was the blood of the grape, in which we found such delectable
sweetness that as many thirsty pigs round a troughful of ale-
grounds could not have expressed more satisfaction in their grunts
than we did in our merry songs and catches.

NED WARD
The London Spy
1703

Beware the Bright Juice

See Inebriety! her wand she waves,
And lo! her pale, and lo! her purple slaves!
Sots in embroidery, and sots in crape,
Of every order, station, rank, and shape:
The king, who nods upon his rattle throne;
The staggering peer, to midnight revel prone;
The slow-tongued bishop, and the deacon sly,
The humble pensioner, and gownsman dry;
The proud, the mean, the selfish, and the great,
Swell the dull throng, and stagger into state.
Lo! proud Flaminius at the splendid board,
The easy chaplain of an atheist lord,
Quaffs the bright juice, with all the gust of sense,
And clouds his brain in torpid elegance;
In china vases, see! the sparkling ill,
From gay decanters view the rosy rill;
The neat-carved pipes in silver settle laid,
The screw by mathematic cunning made:
Oh, happy priest! whose God, like Egypt's, lies,
At once the deity and sacrifice.

GEORGE CRABBE
"Inebriety"
1775

A Hair of the Beast

If the Head complaine itself of too much Drinke, there may be made a Frontlet of wild Time, Maiden Haire; Roses, or else to drinke of the shavings of Hart's horne with Fountain or River water, or if you see that your stomach be not sicke, thou mayst take of the hair of the Beast that hath made thee ill, and drink off a good glasse of Wine.

JEAN LIÉBAULT
Maison Rustique

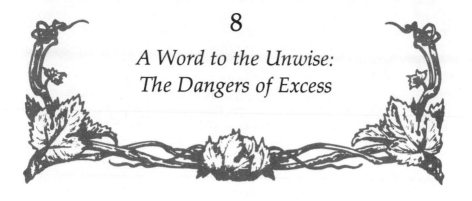

8

A Word to the Unwise:
The Dangers of Excess

Along with the literature of drunkenness, there is, it seems, a special category that consists of advice. Much of it is straightforward; some, like Lamb's essay on drunkenness, is tongue in cheek; and some, like De Quincey's reasons for preferring opium to wine, approach the problem from an unusual perspective. Adam Smith and Thomas Jefferson have both suggested that the best way to avoid excessive drinking is to make wine cheaper, not more expensive, and their comments are included in this section.

Drink Not the Third Glass

Drink not the third glass, which thou canst not tame
  When once it is within thee, but before
May'st rule it as thou list; and pour the shame,
  Which it would pour on thee, upon the floor,
It is most just to throw that on the ground,
Which would throw *me* there, if I keep the round.

GEORGE HERBERT

A Warning

The art of taking wine is the science of exciting agreeable conversation and eliciting brilliant thoughts for an idle hour between the repast and the dining-room, after the ladies retire. Wine makes some men dull; such persons should on no account drink the strong brandied wines of the south, but confine themselves to the light red French growths, or the white, pregnant with carbonic gas. If these fail to promote cheerfulness; if with the light Burgundy, with La-fitte, or the ethereal sparkle of champagne, a man continue un-moved, he may depend the innocent use of wine cannot be his. He may excite himself by the stronger kinds, and half intoxicate him-self to rise a leaven of agreeability which is altogether artificial;—he may woo mirth "sorrowfully," but he will only injure his stomach and cloud his brain. Oftentimes Englishmen drink themselves into taciturnity below-stairs, and, ascending to the drawing-room, sit silent and solemn as so many quakers, among the fair sex. Such are past the stage of innocent excitement by a rational quantity of the juice of the grape. They take it because the effect is a temporary indifference, an agreeable suspense between pleasure and pain. Such are not the true enjoyers of wine in its legitimate use; and they should always rise and retire with the ladies, for the effect upon them is but that of a narcotic.

ALEXANDER HENDERSON
Every Man His Own Butler
1878

Choose Carefully

All black wines, over-hot, compound, strong, thick drinks, as mus-cadine, malmsey, alicant, rumney, brown bastard, metheglin, and the like, of which they have thirty several kinds in Muscovy, all such made drinks are hurtful in this case, to such as are hot, or of a sanguine, choleric complexion, young, or inclined to head-melan-choly. For many times the drinking of wine alone causeth it. . . . Guianerius tells a story of two Dutchmen, to whom he gave enter-tainment in his house, "that in one month's space were both mel-ancholy by drinking of wine, one did naught but sing, the other sigh."

ROBERT BURTON
The Anatomy of Melancholy

Against Drunkenness

You wish for truth and virtuous days you'd spend?
Shun tearing wine, for death's its bosom-friend.
Recklessly drunk, it leaves the body cursed
more than a fever. Yes, the drug comes first,
wickeder far than fire or fetid snake.
Worse pangs than snake-bite wine can quickly wake.
Think of the trembling limbs, the void for mind,
the hamstrung shambling walk, the eyes half-blind,
the deafened ears, the tongue that none can mark,
losing its powers to gain a babbling bark.
Speak, drunkard, are you dead or living now?
You're pallid, but no peace has calmed your brow;
a sickly rest is pressing on your eyes;
good, bad, soft, hard, you cannot recognize;
you might be stretched out in the night of death
save that your limbs heave faintly at your breath.

EUGENIUS, Bishop of Toledo
7th Century

The Wine of Lepe

Now keep ye from the white and from the red,
And namely from the white wine of Lepe,
That is to sell in Fish Street or in Chepe.
This wine of Spain creepeth subtilly
In other wines, growing fast by,
Of which there riseth such fumositee,

That when a man hath drunken draughtes three,
And weneth that he be at home in Chepe,
He is in Spain, right at the town of Lepe,
Not at the Rochelle, nor at Bordeaux town.

GEOFFREY CHAUCER
"The Pardoner's Tale"

Who Hath Woe?

Who hath woe? who hath sorrow? who hath contentions? who hath babbling? who hath wounds without cause? who hath redness of eyes?

They that tarry long at the wine; they that go to seek mixed wine.

Look not thou upon the wine when it is red, when it giveth his color in the cup, when it moveth itself aright.

At the last it biteth like a serpent, and stingeth like an adder.

Proverbs, Chapter 23

Socrates Speaks

Here Socrates again interposed. "Well, gentlemen," said he, "so far as drinking is concerned, you have my hearty approval; for wine does of a truth 'moisten the soul' and lull our griefs to sleep just as the mandragora does with men, at the same time awakening kindly feelings as oil quickens a flame. However, I suspect that men's bodies fare the same as those of plants that grow in the ground. When God gives the plants water in floods to drink, they cannot stand up straight or let the breezes blow through them; but when they drink only as much as they enjoy, they grow up very straight and tall and come to full and abundant fruitage. So it is with us. If we pour ourselves immense draughts, it will be no long time before both our bodies and our minds reel, and we shall not be able even to draw breath, much less to speak sensibly; but if the servants frequently 'besprinkle' us—if I too may use a Gorgian expression—with small cups, we shall thus not be driven on by the wine to a state of intoxication, but instead shall be brought by its gentle persuasion to a more sportive mood."

XENOPHON
Symposium

Before It's Too Late

Could the youth, to whom the flavor of his first wine is delicious as the opening scenes of life or the entering upon some newly discovered paradise, look into my desolation, and be made to understand what a dreary thing it is when a man shall feel himself going down a precipice with open eyes and a passive will,—to see his destruction and have no power to stop it, and yet to feel it all the way emanating from himself; to perceive all goodness emptied out of him, and yet not to be able to forget a time when it was otherwise; to bear about the piteous spectacle of his own self-ruins;—could he see my fevered eye, feverish with last night's drinking, and feverishly looking for this night's repetition of the folly; could he feel the body of the death out of which I cry hourly with feebler and feebler outcry to be delivered,—it were enough to make him dash the sparkling beverage to the earth in all the pride of its mantling temptation.

CHARLES LAMB
"Confessions of a Drunkard"

Wine vs. Opium

First, then, it is not so much affirmed as taken for granted by all who ever mention opium, formally or incidentally, that it does or can produce intoxication. Now, reader, assure yourself, *meo periculo*, that no quantity of opium ever did, or could, intoxicate. As to the tincture of opium (commonly called laudanum), *that* might certainly intoxicate, if a man could bear to take enough of it; but why? Because it contains so much proof spirits of wine, and not because it contains so much opium. But crude opium, I affirm peremptorily, is incapable of producing any state of body at all resembling that which is produced by alcohol; and not in *degree* only incapable, but even in *kind*; it is not in the quantity of its effects merely, but in the quality, that it differs altogether. The pleasure given by wine is always rapidly mounting, and tending to a crisis, after which as rapidly it declines; that from opium, when once generated, is stationary for eight or ten hours: the first, to borrow a technical distinction from medicine, is a case of acute, the second of chronic, pleasure; the one is a flickering flame, the other a steady and equable glow. But the main distinction lies in this—that, whereas wine disorders the mental faculties, opium, on the contrary (if taken in a proper manner), introduces amongst them the most exquisite order, legislation, and harmony. Wine robs a man of his self-possession; opium sustains and reinforces it. Wine unsettles the judgment, and gives a preternatural brightness and a vivid exaltation to the contempts and the admirations, to the loves and the hatreds, of the drinker; opium, on the contrary, communicates serenity and equipoise to all the faculties, active or passive; and, with respect to the temper and moral feelings in general, it gives simply that sort of vital warmth which is approved by the judgment, and which would probably always accompany a bodily constitution of primeval or antediluvian health. Thus, for instance, opium, like wine, gives an expansion to the heart and the benevolent affections; but, then, with this remarkable difference, that, in the sudden development of kindheartedness which accompanies inebriation, there is always more or less of a maudlin and a transitory character, which exposes it to the contempt of the bystander. Men shake hands, swear eternal friendship, and shed tears—no mortal knows why; and the animal nature is clearly uppermost. But the expansion of the benigner feelings incident to opium is no febrile access, no fugitive paroxysm; it is a healthy restoration to that state which the mind would naturally recover upon the removal of any deep-seated irritation from pain that had disturbed and quarrelled with the impulses of a heart originally just and good. True it is that even wine up to a certain point, and with certain men, rather tends to exalt and to steady the intellect; I myself, who have never been a great wine-drinker, used to find that half-a-dozen glasses of wine advantageously affected the faculties, brightened and intensified the consciousness, and gave to the mind a feeling a being 'ponderibus librata suis'; and certainly it is most absurdly said, in popular language, of any man, that he is *disguised* in liquor; for, on the contrary, most men are disguised by sobriety, and exceedingly disguised; and it is when they are drinking that men display themselves in their true complexion of character; which surely is not disguising themselves. But still, wine constantly leads a man to the brink of absurdity and extravagance; and, beyond a certain point, it is sure to volatilise and to disperse the intellectual energies; whereas opium always seems to compose what had been agitated, and to concentrate what had been distracted. In short, to sum up all in one word, a man who is inebriated, or tending to inebriation, is, and feels that he is, in a condition which calls up into supremacy the merely human, too often the brutal, part of his nature; but the opium-eater (I speak of him simply *as* such, and assume that he is in a normal state of health) feels that the diviner part of his nature is paramount—that is, the moral affections are in a state of cloudless serenity, and high over all the great light of the majestic intellect.

THOMAS DE QUINCEY
Confessions of an English Opium-Eater
1821

The Pursuit of False Pleasure

Bacchus is represented by Hesiod as the dispenser of joys and sorrows. It may be remarked, however, that his gifts are distributed very unequally among those who repair to his altars; that the unallayed joys are confined to a few, and, though lively, are substantial and fleeting in their nature,—while the sorrows are real and permanent, and generally become the portion of his most ardent votaries. They revel, for a time, in feverish gaiety; but the period at length arrives, when the dream of happiness dissolves, and they awake to melancholy and despair. Doomed, for the remainder of their days, to endure the anguish of remorse and irremediable disease, they discover, when it is too late, that, in the pursuit of false pleasure, they have drained the cup of life to its bitterest dregs. If they should happily escape the more formidable bodily ills which follow in the train of intemperance, they never fail to experience its baneful influence on the mind. Perception is blunted; imagination decays; the memory and judgment are enfeebled; the temper becomes irritable and gloomy; and a degree of moral callousness is superinduced, which steels the heart against all the tender feelings and refined sympathies of our nature. Moreover, as every fresh debauch occasions a temporary aberration of intellect, it often happens, especially when a disposition to insanity pre-exists, that reason is shaken from her seat for ever. But, dreadful as this calamity appears in all its forms, it is perhaps an enviable fate, compared to the lot of those victims of imprudence who retain the full consciousness of their own errors. To them premature death is the least of the evils which they inflict on themselves.

ALEXANDER HENDERSON
1824

To His Son

Take especial care that thou delight not in wine, for there was not any man that came to honour or preferment that loved it; for it transformeth a man into a beast, decayeth health, poisoneth the breath, destroyeth natural heat, brings a man's stomach to an artificial heat, deformeth the face, rotteth the teeth, and, to conclude, maketh a man contemptible, soon old, and despised of all wise and worthy men; hated in thy servants, in thyself, and companions; for it is a bewitching and infectious vice. A drunkard will never shake off the delight of beastliness; for the longer it possesses a man, the more he will delight in it; and the older he groweth, the more he will be subject to it; for it dulleth the spirits, and destroyeth the body, as ivy doth the old tree; or as the worm that engendereth in the kernel of a nut. Take heed, therefore, that such a cureless canker pass not thy youth, nor such a beastly infection thy old age; for then shall all thy life be but as the life of a beast, and after thy death thou shalt only leave a shameful infamy to thy posterity, who shall study to forget that such a one was their father.

SIR WALTER RALEIGH

Old Before Their Time

Now the great drinkers are very dull, inactive fellows, no women's men at all; they eject nothing strong, vigorous, and fit for generation, but are weak and unperforming, by reason of the bad digestion and coldness of their seed. And it is farther observable that the effects of cold and drunkenness upon men's bodies are the same,— trembling, heaviness, paleness, shivering, faltering of tongue, numbness, and cramps. In many, a debauch ends in a dead palsy, when the wine stupefies and extinguisheth all the heat. And the physicians use this method in curing the qualms and diseases gotten by debauch; at night they cover them well and keep them warm; and at day they anoint and bathe, and give them such food as shall not disturb, but by degrees recover the heat which the wine hath scattered and driven out of the body. Thus, I added, in these appearances we trace obscure qualities and powers; but as for drunkenness, it is easily discerned what it is. For, in my opinion, as I hinted before, those that are drunk are very much like old men; and therefore great drinkers grow old soonest, and they are commonly bald and gray before their time.

PLUTARCH
Morals

Cheaper Wine I

I rejoice as a moralist at the prospect of a reduction of the duties on wine, by our national legislature. It is an error to view a tax on that liquor as merely a tax on the rich. It is a prohibition of its use to the middling class of our citizens, and a condemnation of them to the poison of whiskey, which is desolating their houses. No nation is drunken where wine is cheap; and none sober, where the dearness of wine substitutes ardent spirits as the common beverage. It is, in truth, the only antidote to the bane of whiskey. Fix but the duty at the rate of other merchandise, and we can drink wine here as cheap as we do grog; and who will not prefer it? Its extended use will carry health and comfort to a much enlarged circle. Every one in easy circumstances (as the bulk of our citizens are) will prefer it to the poison to which they are now driven by their government. And the treasury itself will find that a penny apiece from a dozen, is more than a groat from a single one. This reformation, however, will require time.

THOMAS JEFFERSON

Cheaper Wine II

Though in every country there are many people who spend upon such liquors more than they can afford, there are always many more who spend less. It deserves to be remarked too, that, if we consult experience, the cheapness of wine seems to be a cause, not of drunkenness, but of sobriety. The inhabitants of the wine countries are in general the soberest people in Europe; witness the Spaniards, the Italians, and the inhabitants of the southern provinces of France. People are seldom guilty of excess in what is their daily fare. Nobody affects the character of liberality and good fellowship, by being profuse of a liquor which is as cheap as small beer. On the contrary, in the countries which, either from excessive heat or cold, produce no grapes, and where wine consequently is dear and a rarity, drunkenness is a common vice.

ADAM SMITH
The Wealth of Nations

Discouraging Words

As soon as the wine has entered into the stomach it commences to swell up and boil over; then the spirit of that man commences to abandon his body, and rising as though to the sky it reaches the brain, which causes it to become divided from the body; and so it begins to infect him and cause him to rave like a madman; so he perpetrates irreparable crimes, killing his own friends.

LEONARDO DA VINCI

Bacchus' Son

Bacchus, that first from out the purple grape
Crushed the sweet poison of misused wine,
After the Tuscan mariners transformed,
Coasting the Tyrrhene shore, as the winds listed,
On Circe's island fell. (Who knows not Circe,
The daughter of the Sun, whose charmèd cup
Whoever tasted lost his upright shape,
And downward fell into a grovelling swine?)

This Nymph, that gazed upon his clustering locks,
With ivy berries wreathed, and his blithe youth,
Had by him, ere he parted thence, a son
Much like his father, but his mother more,
Whom therefore she brought up, and Comus named:
Who, ripe and frolic of his full-grown age,
Roving the Celtic and Iberian fields,
At last betakes him to this ominous wood,
And, in thick shelter of black shades imbowered,
Excels his mother at her mighty art;
Offering to every weary traveller
His orient liquor in a crystal glass,
To quench the drouth of Phœbus; which as they taste
(For most do taste through fond intemperate thirst),
Soon as the potion works, their human count'nance,
The express resemblance of the gods, is changed
Into some brutish form of wolf or bear,
An ounce or tiger, hog, or bearded goat,
All other parts remaining as they were.
And they, so perfect in their misery
Not once perceive their foul disfigurement,
But boast themselves more comely than before,
And all their friends and native home forget,
To roll with pleasure in a sensual sty.

JOHN MILTON
Comus

A Mocker

Wine is a mocker, strong drink is raging: and whosoever is deceived thereby is not wise.

Proverbs, Chapter 20

9

Hosts and Guests: Vinous Encounters

One of the pleasures of wine derives from sharing a bottle. Some vinous encounters are more convivial than others, and not all hosts are equally generous with their wine. In a poem attributed to Longfellow, he writes,

> When you ask one friend to dine,
> Give him your best wine!
> When you ask two,
> The second best will do!

Serving ordinary wine is one thing, serving spoiled wine another. Alexander Pope summed up in two lines the misplaced thrift that would compel anyone to drink bad wine:

> One half-pint bottle serves them both to dine,
> And is at once their vinegar and wine . . .

The *Fifth Satire* of Juvenal contains a description of a host whose best wines are reserved for a few privileged guests, while others drink inferior wines from plain vessels. Here are two couplets from the seventeenth-century translation by John Dryden, which conveys Juvenal's scorn so well:

> For him is kept a liquor more divine
> You sponges must be drunk with lees of wine . . .
> Thou may'st at distance gaze, and sigh in vain
> A crack'd black pot's reserved for thee to drain.

Byron complained of the stingy landlord and "a lingering bottle . . . leaving all claretless the unmoistened throttle." A similar note is struck in Robertson Davies' *The Fifth Business*: ". . . the very best champagne flowed like the very best champagne under the care of a good caterer (which is to say, not more than three glasses to a guest unless they made a fuss)."

Martha and Catherine Wilmot attended quite a different party in Russia in 1802. In their *Russian Journals* they describe a reception at Count Ostrowman's at which a trumpet blast announced the arrival of a crystal vase filled with champagne. "The Master of the Castle stood up and quaff'd the sparkling draught to the health of the Lady of the feast"; and then each guest in turn repeated the ceremony, drinking from the same crystal vase, "and as there were a party of 46 you may judge the time which all the pomp and parade took up."

Sometimes a guest is unlucky. In his essay "Uncle Ned's Wine Preferences," Lucius Beebe recalls:

At the conclusion of luncheon and dinner at Monrepos, the butler would pass a tall vase of scented water for washing the hands; he was assisted in the process by a footman with a broad basin. My sister from Boston, who had never seen such goings-on, at first encounter held her champagne glass out under the warm water. It was a moment that we never again mentioned in public.

And sometimes a host is unlucky. When H. Warner Allen was at Oxford he spent more than he could afford on a case of Lafite-Rothschild 1864, most of which he enjoyed. Three of the bottles, however, were drunk in his absence by friends who raided his rooms "and did nothing to appease my injured feelings by congratulating me on my 'quite decent red ink.' "

No host is more unlucky, however, than one who has hoarded his best bottles too long. One result of such stinginess may be that the fine wines so carefully held back may be wasted by one's heir, as prophesied in the final lines of one of Horace's *Odes*:

> The worthier heir thy Caecuban shall squander,
> Bursting the hundred locks that guard its treasure,
> And wines more rare than those
> Supped at high feasts by pontiffs dye thy floors.

Wine and hospitality usually go together, but not always: there are occasional references to the solitary enjoyment of wine. Theodore Hook, for example, said, "When one is alone the bottle does come around so often," and we learn from John Aubrey's *Brief Lives* that Andrew Marvell "would drink liberally by himself to refresh his spirits and exalt his muse." Another reference to enjoying wine alone is found in Hemingway's *The Sun Also Rises*: "I drank a bottle of wine for company. It was Château Margaux. It was pleasant to be drinking slowly and to be tasting the wine and to be drinking alone. A bottle of wine was good company." Come to think of it, there's also a moment in James Joyce's *Ulysses* when Leopold Bloom muses alone over a glass of Burgundy in Davy Byrne's pub:

Glowing wine on his palate lingered swallowed. Crushing in the winepress grapes of Burgundy. Sun's heat it is. Seems to a secret touch telling me memory. Touched his sense moistened remembered.

These remarks about enjoying wine alone, however charming or evocative, are exceptions to the rule, as the following selections will illustrate.

Wine Talk

But at quite an early stage I learned one important lesson, and that is that the pleasure of wine consists only partly in itself; the good talk that is inseparable from a wine dinner is even more important than the wines that are being served. Never bring up your better bottles if you are entertaining a man who cannot talk. Keep your treasures for a night when those few who are nearest to your heart can gather round your table, free from care, with latchkeys in their pockets and no last train to catch.

MAURICE HEALY
Claret

A Few Words of Advice

At length I am come to the consideration of that important accompaniment to dinner—wine, in the management of which there is ordinarily a lamentable want of judgment, or rather a total absence of it. Besides an actual want of judgment, there is frequently a parsimonious calculation on the one hand, or an ostentatious profusion and mixture on the other, both destructive, in their different ways, of true enjoyment. The art in using wine is to produce the greatest possible quantity of present gladness, without any future depression. To this end, a certain degree of simplicity is essential, with due attention to seasons and kinds of food, and particularly to the rate of filling the glass. Too many sorts of wines confuse the palate and derange digestion. The stronger wines, unless very sparingly used, are apt to heat in hot weather, and the smaller kinds are unsatisfactory when it is cold. The rate at which to take wine is a matter of great nicety and importance, and depends upon different circumstances at different times. Care and observation can alone enable any one to succeed in this point. The same quantity of wine, drunk judiciously or injudiciously, will produce the best or the worst effects. Drinking too quick is much more to be avoided than drinking too slow. The former is positively, the latter negatively, evil. Drinking too quick confuses both the stomach and the brain; drinking too slow disappoints them. . . .

What I have hitherto said has been with a view principally to individual guidance in the use of wine, though much of it may be applied to the management of parties. In the management of parties, so far as relates to wine, judgment, liberality, attention, and courage, are necessary; and calculation, inattention, ostentation, profusion, and excess, are the vices to be guarded against.

THOMAS WALKER
The Original
1850

No Decanters Needed

When my dear aunt's parlormaid very carefully brought the first bottle of Burgundy into the dining room, carrying it horizontally and taking infinite pains, as she explained, to avoid disturbing the sediment, the old lady exclaimed, "Silly girl, it's the sediment that contains all the nourishment": whereupon she took the bottle by the neck, turned it upside down and gave it a good hearty shaking.

I. M. CAMPBELL
Reminiscences of a Vintner

A Memorable Meal: London, 1935

A baked trout and a cold chicken salad, nothing could have been better or half as good on a hot summer's day, in London. Both were perfect of their kind. A glass of fresh Berncasteler was all that the most fastidious connoisseur could have wished for and would have been grateful for. We had a glass of fresh 1929 Berncasteler, a wine of Feldheim's shipping, just the sort of wine for such a fine day. But we did not stop there. It was followed by a magnum of 1884 Pommery which was wonderful. Its cork was covered up with a thick blob of yellow wax which took a lot of time to knock off, and when it was off, the head of the cork also came off, the wire that once upon a time held it down having been eaten up by rust. But the 'cheville' inside the neck of the bottle still held on like grim death; it had to submit to the indignity of a corkscrew after fifty years of good service, and when it came out, the wine within sent out a distinct bang of pleasure. It poured out with life and bubbles and it drank very well indeed. It had no 'old stink' on the nose, but a sweet caramel-like smell, absolutely clean and free from any sign of decay. The colour of the wine was deep yellow gold, without any trace of mahogany red in it. It had both body and power and it finished sweet to the last: quite an incredible *tour de force* of Nature. After such a wine, there was nothing to do but say Grace with due gratefulness. Our host had other views. He was anxious to have our help in deciding which was the better of the two, a fine white Burgundy and a first-class Hock. The Burgundy was a bottle of the real Montrachet, from Baron Thénard, and of the 1929 vintage. It was beautiful and above all perfectly balanced, just right, the bouquet very fine but the body and flavour and the very farewell of the wine quite equal to the bouquet, equal and not greater. The magnum of 1884, which had just preceded it, did not upset it in the least: it may have made it taste a little fresher than if it had followed a very young wine, but that was all to the good. It deserved and received fuller marks than the 1917 Marcobrunn, a remarkable wine indeed, but one with so superb and so much of a bouquet that the wine itself failed to live up to it: its noble nose had worn out its less noble body. Of course, the more we assured Curtis Moffat that we had been only too happy to give him the benefit of our opinion in the most disinterested spirit, the more he insisted upon rewarding us for our valuable assistance, and he gave us a bottle of one of the most extraordinary, as well as rarest, wines which millionaires could still buy to-day, had not their sense of beauty been dulled by a surfeit of money. It was a Moselle like a light tawny Port in colour, like an Yquem in sweetness and more like a Tokay in its concentrated essence of grape. It was the last wine made by the Widow Thanisch's son, in 1921, from the famous Berncasteler Doctor vineyard, from the sun-dried last berries—Trockenbeeren Auslese—and much more of a liqueur than a wine, although it could not be called a liqueur, it was too gentle; to call it a freak would be an insult: let us call it a miracle.

ANDRÉ L. SIMON

A Difficult Guest

Rather than love, than money, than fame, give me truth. I sat at a table where were rich food and wine in abundance, and obsequious attendance, but sincerity and truth were not; and I went away hungry from the inhospitable board. The hospitality was as cold as the ices. I thought that there was no need of ice to freeze them. They talked to me of the age of the wine and the fame of the vintage; but I thought of an older, a newer, and purer wine, of a more glorious vintage, which they had not got, and could not buy.

HENRY THOREAU
Walden

Wine Conversations

The wine was excellent: the Port was of some famous vintage, I forget which; the Madeira was forty years old; the Claret was a present from Bordeaux. As a matter of course, we talked wine. No company of Englishmen can assemble together for an evening without doing that. Every man in this country who is rich enough to pay income-tax, has, at one time or other of his life, effected a very remarkable transaction in wine. Sometimes he has made such a bargain as he never expects to make again. Sometimes he is the only man in England, not a peer of the realm, who has got a single drop of a certain famous vintage which has perished from the face of the earth. Sometimes he has purchased, with a friend, a few last left dozens from the cellar of a deceased potentate, at a price so exorbitant that he can only wag his head and decline mentioning it—and, if you ask his friend, that friend will wag his head and decline mentioning it also. Sometimes he has been at an out-of-the-way country inn; has found the Sherry not drinkable; has asked if there is no other wine in the house; has been informed that there is some "sourish foreign stuff that nobody ever drinks;" has called for a bottle of it; has found it Burgundy, such as all France cannot now produce; has cunningly kept his own counsel with the widowed landlady, and has bought the whole stock for "an old song." Sometimes he knows the proprietor of a famous tavern in London; and he recommends his one or two particular friends, the next time they are passing that way, to go in and dine, and give his compliments to the landlord, and ask for a bottle of the brown Sherry, with the light blue—as distinguished from the dark blue—seal. Thousands of people dine there every year, and think they have got the famous Sherry when they get the dark blue seal; but—and, by no means let it go any further—the real wine, the famous wine, is the light blue seal; and nobody in England knows it but the landlord and his friends. In all these wine conversations, whatever variety there may be in the various experiences related, one of two great first principles is invariably assumed by each speaker in succession. Either he knows more about it than anyone else—or he has got better wine of his own even than the excellent wine he is now drinking. Men can get together sometimes without talking of women, without talking of horses, without talking of politics; but they cannot assemble to eat a meal together without talking of wine; and they cannot talk of wine without assuming to each one of themselves an absolute infallibility in connexion with that single subject, which they would shrink from asserting in relation to any other topic under the sun.

CHARLES TOVEY
Wit, Wisdom, and Morals

He Knows Its Place

'I think we had better stay with this champagne, don't you?' said Theodorescu. It was a 1953 Bollinger; they were already near the end of this first bottle. 'Harmless enough, not in the least spectacular, but I take wine to be a kind of necessary bread, it must not intrude too much into the meal. Wine-worshipping is the most vulgar of idolatries.'

ANTHONY BURGESS
Tremor of Intent

Samuel Johnson on Wine

Johnson harangued against drinking wine. "A man (said he) may choose whether he will have abstemiousness and knowledge, or claret and ignorance." Dr. Robertson (who is very companionable) was beginning to dissent as to the proscription of claret. JOHNSON (with a placid smile). "Nay, Sir, you shall not differ with me; as I have said that the man is most perfect who takes in the most things, I am for knowledge and claret."

"Wine makes a man better pleased with himself. I do not say it makes him more pleasing to others. Sometimes it does. But the danger is, that while a man grows better pleased with himself, he may be growing less pleasing to others."

"This is one of the disadvantages of wine; it makes a man mistake words for thoughts."

"I did not leave off wine because I could not bear it; I have drunk three bottles of port without being the worse for it. University College has witnessed this."

"I now no more think of drinking wine, than a horse does. The· wine upon the table is no more for me, than for the dog that is under the table."

I at last had recourse to the maxim, *in vino veritas*, a man who is well warmed with wine will speak truth. JOHNSON. "Why, Sir, that may be an argument for drinking, if you suppose men in general to be liars. But, Sir, I would not keep company with a fellow who lies as long as he is sober, and whom you must make drunk before you can get a word of truth out of him."

"I also admit, that there are some sluggish men who are improved by drinking; as there are fruits which are not good until they are rotten."

A gentleman having to some of the usual arguments for drinking added this: "You know, Sir, drinking drives away care, and makes us forget whatever is disagreeable. Would you not allow a man to drink for that reason?" JOHNSON. "Yes, Sir, if he sat next *you*."

On Wednesday, April 7, I dined with him at Sir Joshua Reynolds's. I have not marked what company was there. Johnson harangued upon the qualities of different liquors; and spoke with great contempt of claret, as so weak, that "a man would be drowned by it before it make him drunk." He was persuaded to drink one glass of it, that he might judge, not from recollection, which might be dim, but from immediate sensation. He shook his head, and said, "Poor stuff! No, Sir, claret is the liquor for boys; port for men; but he who aspires to be a hero (smiling) must drink brandy. In the first place, the flavour of brandy is most grateful to the palate; and then brandy will do soonest for a man what drinking *can* do for him. There are, indeed, few who are able to drink brandy. That is a power rather to be wished for than attained. And yet (proceeded he) as in all pleasure hope is a considerable part. I know not but fruition comes too quick by brandy. Florence wine I think the worst; it is wine only to the eye; it is wine neither while you are drinking it, nor after you have drunk it; it neither pleases the taste, nor exhilarates the spirits."

JAMES BOSWELL
Life of Samuel Johnson

Old Friends Know What I Like

Old friends know what I like:
They bring wine whenever they come by.
We spread out and sit under the pines;
After several rounds, we're drunk again.
Old men chatting away—all at once;
Passing the jug around—out of turn.
Unaware that there is a "self,"
How do we learn to value "things"?
We are lost in these deep thoughts;
In wine, there is a heady taste.

T'AO CHI'EN
5th Century

A Warm Welcome

Up till now, most of these reminiscences and instructions have consisted of—or been illustrated by—anecdotes against myself. It will be pleasant for once to tell a story against someone else. My wife and I some years ago were invited to dinner by a fairly high B.B.C. official at his house in Kent. "I know you are fond of wine," he said, with that unvarying radio suavity, "so I have got some Chablis to go with the salmon." I indicated my pleasure, and he added: "I have put it to warm in the next room; it is standing in front of the gas fire." There was at this point a slight but distinct report; a cork had blown out. "I should think it's warm enough by now," he said, in a connoisseur's tone. "Yes," I replied, which was a marvel of understatement and self-control.

RAYMOND POSTGATE
"Oinoposiai"

Old Madeira

"Where's Warmson?" he said suddenly. "I should like a glass of Madeira to-night."

"There's champagne, James."

James shook his head. "No body," he said. "I can't get any good out of it."

Emily reached forward on her side of the fire and rang the bell.

"Your master would like a bottle of Madeira opened, Warmson."

"No, no!" said James, the tips of his ears quivering with ve-
hemence, and his eyes fixed on an object seen by him alone. "Look
here, Warmson, you go to the inner cellar, and on the middle shelf
of the end bin on the right you'll see seven bottles; take the one in
the centre, and don't shake it. It's the last of the Madeira I had from
Mr. Jolyon when we came in here—never been moved; it ought to
be in prime condition still; but I don't know, I can't tell."

"Very good, sir," responded the withdrawing Warmson.

"I was keeping it for our golden wedding," said James suddenly, "but I shan't live three years at my age."

"Nonsense, James," said Emily, "don't talk like that."

"I ought to have got it myself," murmured James, "he'll shake
it as likely as not." And he sank into silent recollection of long
moments among the open gas-jets, the cob-webs and the good
smell of wine-soaked corks, which had been appetiser to so many
feasts. In the wine from that cellar was written the history of the
forty odd years since he had come to the Park Lane house with his
young bride, and of the many generations of friends and acquaintances who had passed into the unknown; its depleted bins preserved the record of family festivity—all the marriages, births,
deaths of his kith and kin. And when he was gone it would be
there, and he didn't know what would become of it. It'd be drunk
or spoiled he shouldn't wonder.

JOHN GALSWORTHY
The Forsyte Saga

Forgetful Authors: Generosity . . .

This I say is the interest of every diner-out. An unguarded passage
in the above description, too, might give rise to a fatal error, and be
taken advantage of by stingy curmudgeons who are anxious for any
opportunity of saving their money and liquor,—I mean those cul-
pably careless words, "*Where hock, champagne, &c. &c., are served,
they are handed round between the courses.*" Of course they are
handed round between the courses; but they are handed round
during the courses too. A man who sets you down to a driblet of
champagne—who gives you a couple of beggarly glasses between
the courses, and winks to John who froths up the liquor in your
glass, and screws up the remainder of the bottle for his master's

next day's drinking,—such a man is an imposter and despicable snob. This fellow must not be allowed an excuse for his practice— the wretch must not be permitted to point to Joseph Bregion and Anne Miller for an authority, and say they declare that champagne is to be served only between the courses. No!—no! you poor lily-livered wretch! If money is an object to you, drink water (as we have all done, perhaps, in an angust state of domestic circumstances, with a good heart); but if there is to be champagne, have no stint of it, in the name of Bacchus! Profusion is the charm of hospitality; have plenty, if it be only beer. A man who offers champagne by driblets is a fellow who would wear a pinchbeck breastpin, or screw on spurs to his boots to make believe that he kept a horse. I have no words of scorn sufficiently strong to characterise the puny coward, shivering on the brink of hospitality, without nerve to plunge into the generous stream!

WILLIAM THACKERAY
"Barmecide Banquets"

. . . and Thrift

As for the wine, that depends on yourself. Always be crying out to your friends, "Mr. So-and-so, I don't drink myself, but pray pass the bottle. Tomkins, my boy, help your neighbour, and never mind me. What! Hopkins, are there two of us on the doctor's list? Pass the wine; *Smith* I'm sure won't refuse it;" and so on. A very good plan is to have the butler (or the fellow in the white waistcoat who "behaves as sich") pour out the wine when wanted (in half-glasses, of course), and to make a deuced great noise and shouting, "John, John, why the devil, sir, don't you help Mr. Simkins to another glass of wine?" If you point out Simkins once or twice in this way, depend upon it, *he* won't drink a great quantity of your liquor. You may thus keep your friends from being dangerous, by a thousand innocent manœuvres; and, as I have said before, you may very probably make them believe that they have had a famous dinner. There was only one man in our company of ten the other day who ever thought he had not dined; and what was he? a foreigner,—a man of a discontented inquiring spirit, always carping at things, and never satisfied.

WILLIAM THACKERAY
"Memorials of Gormandising"

A Little Wine

"And what do you think of my little wine?" Mme. B. asked M. Clicquot. "I'm so anxious for your professional opinion—as a rival producer, you know."

The wine was a thin *rosé* in an Art Nouveau bottle with a label that was a triumph of lithography; it had spires and monks and troubadours and blondes in wimples on it, and the name of the *cru* was spelled out in letters with Gothic curlicues and pennons. The name was something like Château Guillaume d'Aquitaine, *grand vin.*

"What a madly gay little wine, my dear!" M. Clicquot said, repressing, but not soon enough, a grimace of pain.

"One would say a Tavel of a good year," I cried, "if one were a complete bloody fool." I did not say the second clause aloud.

My old friend looked at me with new respect. He was discovering in me a capacity for hypocrisy that he had never credited me with before.

The main course was a shoulder of mutton with white beans—the poor relation of a gigot, and an excellent dish in its way, when not too dry. This was.

For the second wine, the man from the Midi proudly produced a red, in a bottle without a label, which he offered to M. Clicquot with the air of a tomcat bringing a field mouse to its master's feet. "Tell me what you think of this," he said as he filled the champagne man's glass.

M. Clicquot—a veteran of such challenges, I could well imagine—held the glass against the light, dramatically inhaled the bouquet, and then drank, after a slight stiffening of the features that indicated to me that he knew what he was in for. Having emptied half the glass, he deliberated.

"It has a lovely color," he said.

"But what is it? What is it?" the man from the Midi insisted.

"There are things about it that remind me of a Beaujolais," M. Clicquot said (he must have meant that it was wet), "but on the whole I should compare it to a Bordeaux" (without doubt unfavorably).

Mme. B.'s agent was beside himself with triumph. "Not one or the other!" he crowed. "It's from the *domaine*—the Château Guillaume d'Aquitaine!"

The admirable M. Clicquot professed astonishment, and I, when I had emptied a glass, said that there would be a vast market for the wine in America if it could be properly presented. "Unfortunately," I said, "the cost of advertising . . ." and I rolled my eyes skyward.

"Ah, yes," Mme. B. cried sadly. "The cost of advertising!"

I caught Mirande looking at me again, and thought of the Pétrus and the Cheval Blanc of our last meal together *chez* Mme. G. He drank a glass of the red. After all, he wasn't going to die of thirst.

A.J. LIEBLING
Between Meals

Self-Criticism

Her stories about Brahms's rudeness and wit amused me in particular. For instance, I loved the one about how a great wine connoisseur invited the composer to dinner. "This is the Brahms of my cellar," he said to his guests, producing a dust-covered bottle and pouring some into the master's glass. Brahms looked first at the color of the wine, then sniffed its bouquet, finally took a sip, and put the glass down without saying a word. "Don't you like it?" asked the host. "Hmm," Brahms muttered. "Better bring your Beethoven!"

ARTHUR RUBINSTEIN
My Young Years

Have Some Madeira, M'Dear

She was young! She was pure! She was new! She was nice!
She was fair! She was sweet seventeen!
He was old! He was vile and no stranger to vice!
He was base! He was bad! He was mean!
  He had slyly inveigled her up to his flat
  To see his collection of stamps,
  And he said as he hastened to put out the cat,
  The wine, his cigar and the lamps . . .

'Have some Madeira, m'dear!
You really have nothing to fear;
I'm not trying to tempt you—it wouldn't be right—
You shouldn't drink spirits at this time of night,

Have some Madeira, m'dear!
It's very much nicer than Beer:
I don't care for Sherry, one cannot drink Stout,
And Port is a wine I can well do without,
It's simply a case of *Chacun a son GOUT!*
Have some Madeira, m'dear!'

Unaware of the wiles of the snake in the grass,
Of the fate of the maiden who topes,
She lowered her standards by raising her glass,
Her courage, her eyes—and his hopes.
   She sipped it, she drank it, she drained it, she did,
     He quietly refilled it again
   And he said as he secretly carved one more notch
   On the butt of his gold-handled cane . . .

'Have some Madeira, m'dear!
I've got a small cask of it here,
And once it's been opened you know it won't keep,
Do finish it up—it will help you to sleep;
Have some Madeira, m'dear!
It's really an excellent year;
Now if it were Gin, you'd be wrong to say yes,
The evil Gin does would be hard to assess . . .
(Besides, it's inclined to affect my prowess!)
Have some Madeira, m'dear!'

Then there flashed through her mind what her mother had said
With her antepenultimate breath:
'Oh, my child, should you look on the wine when it's red
Be prepared for a fate worse than death!'
   She let go her glass with a shrill little cry . . .
   Ah! Crash, tinkle! It fell to the floor.
   When he asked: 'What in heaven . . . ?' She made no reply,
   Up her mind, and a dash for the door. . . .

'Have some Madeira, m'dear!'
Rang out down the hall loud and clear.
A tremulous cry that was filled with despair,
As she paused to take breath in the cool midnight air;
'Have some Madeira, m'dear!'
The words seemed to ring in her ear . . .
Until the next morning she woke up in bed,
With a smile on her lips and an ache in her head—

And a beard in her earhole that tickled and said:
'Have some Madeira, m'dear!'

MICHAEL FLANDERS

Curious

"Will you take a glass of wine?"

"Yes."

"That's right; what shall it be?"

"Madeira!"

The magistrate gave a violent slap on his knee; "I like your taste," said he, "I am fond of a glass of Madeira myself, and can give you such a one as you will not drink every day; sit down, young gentleman, you shall have a glass of Madeira, and the best I have."

Thereupon he got up, and, followed by his two terriers, walked slowly out of the room.

I looked round the room, and, seeing nothing which promised me much amusement, I sat down, and fell again into my former train of thought. "What is truth?" said I.

"Here it is," said the magistrate, returning at the end of a quarter of an hour, followed by the servant, with a tray; "here's the true thing, or I am no judge, far less a justice. It has been thirty years in my cellar last Christmas. There," said he to the servant, "put it down, and leave my young friend and me to ourselves. Now, what do you think of it?"

"It is very good," said I.

"Did you ever taste better Madeira?"

"I never before tasted Madeira."

"Then you ask for a wine without knowing what it is?"

"I ask for it, sir, that I may know what it is."

GEORGE BORROW
Lavengro

Table Talk: Bordeaux

An interval of this and that:—
The virtues of the plastic vat;
The lunacy of Monsieur Y,
Who's tried to make his sweet wine dry;
The wickedness of Baron G,
Who's advertising Burgundy
Right in the heart of the Médoc.
(Why, one might just as well drink Hock!
He's sold—)
              That's done it. In a flash
The conversation's back on cash:—
Will the good English go on paying
The prices caused by three dismaying
Seasons? 'Fifty-two and three—
Remember?—they got almost free;
And what about old Monsieur L
Who bought his own wine back to sell
At more than top price for his *cru*
Attained by his great rival, Q?

The talk flows on from franc to franc,
One might as well be in a bank!

PETER DICKINSON

Red Wine

With fish, which always is served first,
White wine may slake the proper thirst.
Red wine, however, we postpone—
The nearer the sweet, the meeter the Beaune.

JUSTIN RICHARDSON

Fastidious

Adolphe objected to claret for a breakfast wine, as being too weak to restore the damage done to the constitution over-night, and banished burgundy from the dinner-table, as being too hot, and apt to overload the mental faculties. He would not allow champagne at breakfast, but he admitted no other wine at supper. He esteemed iced madeira to be one of the most brilliant conquests of modern times.

EUGÈNE BRIFFAULT
"The Viveur"
1840

Wine and Food I

I often wonder whether those who so vehemently proscribe certain wine and food combinations do so from unhappy experience or from an untested acceptance of "rules" that are often found to have little meaning. In any case, the whole point of wine and food, even in the finest and most formal of circumstances, is the joy of eating and drinking in agreeable company, and I do not see how that end can be achieved if there is exaggerated concern over the rightness of wine or dish. There are certain mixtures of wine and food that I have found to be better than others, and these discoveries have often resulted from circumstances that cannot be repeated. For example, I remember crossing the Alps by the Simplon Pass one June day with an appetite sharpened by the sight of sun on crisp snow in midsummer. I pulled off the road at a small inn and dined there on a piquant veal and cheese dish with a jug of light red wine, scented almost to the point of spiciness as mountain wines often are. I was exquisitely happy, but which wine and food guide could possibly have led me to such an experience?

Another time, just a few years ago, I was lunching in the offices of some fellow wine merchants in London when the steward, usually a careful man, made a mistake. A bottle of Sauternes, a 1923 Château de Rayne-Vigneau with which we were to finish our luncheon, was opened and poured instead of the dry white wine that was to accompany the preceding courses. We were eating smoked salmon at the time and didn't notice what the steward had done. When we raised our glasses there was a delighted murmur from each of us at the quite unexpected taste sensation produced by this dry-sweet old wine—rich in flavors rather than sugars—in combination with the delicate richness of the fish. What rule would have told me to drink fine old Sauternes with smoked salmon?

GERALD ASHER

Wine and Food II

Wine also presents certain complexities. The first is the question of which wine to serve with which food. Wine professors sometimes try to dismiss this issue as unimportant. It does not really matter, they say, how you match wine to food provided you, the consumer, like the combination.

This may work for Alexis Lichine, but anyone less authoritative who adopts it as a principle of wine drinking will be inviting the contempt of all other wine drinkers. Recent studies of the French Revolution, to illustrate how severe this contempt may be, suggest that the French never thought for a moment of overthrowing Louis XVI until word spread through Paris that he invariably drank muscatel with his lobster.

Robespierre, by contrast, was worshipped by Parisians, even though he drank red Chianti with everything—clams on the half shell, grilled catfish, everything. Chianti is an Italian wine and Parisians knew their wine code. When drinking in the Italian mode, it is uncivilized to make a fuss about wine color.

Perfectionists, however, will not accept Robespierre's facile solution. They will go to the great wine masters for education and be told that, in general, a red wine is drunk with a red meat while a white wine is drunk with a white meat.

This sounds childishly easy until one starts trying to apply it. Red wine with red meat, white wine with white meat—fine. But what about brown meat? It is disheartening to discover how much brown meat there is. Chili. Hot dogs and beans. Well done roast beef. Or is that gray meat?

There's a good bit of gray meat too. Certain veal cutlets. Well fried pork chops. The oilier segments of the bluefish.

Is it correct to drink a brown wine—a Bristol cream sherry, say—with brown meats? A gray wine with gray meats? Nothing could be more naive. Important men have been thrown out of excellent French restaurants in New York for ordering sherry with their hot dogs.

Probably the wisest thing to do if you have ordered hot dogs is to tell the wine steward to bring you some mustard.

RUSSELL BAKER
"Tread and Vine"

Wine and Food III

What, if anything, should be taken and eaten with after-dinner wine? . . .

Nuts pass, of course, but most "soft" fruit is questionable. Grapes go not ill, but I have sometimes felt a moral qualm, in marrying a grape too nearly to what is in a way its grandmother.

GEORGE SAINTSBURY
Notes on a Cellar-Book

Wine and Food IV

And still the film folk can be suave on occasion. Producer Arthur Hornblow, Jr., who was more famed for the finesse of his social functions than of his films, once threw a sumptuous dinner party for a gathering of Hollywood notables. The late Herman Mankiewicz, writer and wit, tippled a little too much at the affair, with the result that he became ill in the midst of the repast and committed the unpardonable social error of losing his food at the beautifully set table. A deadly hush descended over the assembled guests. Finally Mankiewicz broke the silence himself. Not too sick to get off a good line, he managed to say to his host, "It's all right, Arthur, the white wine came up with the fish."

EZRA GOODMAN
The Fifty Year Decline and Fall of Hollywood

A Night Out

Our host had replenished his sideboard with fine wines from his father's cellars and wine merchants in town; but having, unluckily, forgotten port, a few bottles of black-strap had been obtained for the nonce from the adjacent inn at Highgate; and sooth to say it was not of the first quality. To add to this grievance, the glasses appertaining to the lodgings were of a diminutive capacity, and when they came to be addressed to champagne and hock, were only tolerable and not to be endured. Thus, in the midst of dinner, or rather more towards the close, we were surprised by Hook's rising, and asking us to fill our bumpers to a toast. It was not difficult to fill these glasses, and we were pledged to follow the example of our leader in draining them. In a brief but most entertaining address he

described the excellent qualities of Reynolds, and above all his noble capacity for giving rural dinners, but—there was always a but,
not a butt of wine, but a but, a something *manqué*. On this occasion
it was but too notorious in the size of those miserable pigmies, out
of which we were trying to drink his health etc. etc. etc. The toast
was drunk with acclamation, and then followed the exemplary can-
nikin clink, hob-nobbing, and striking the poor little glasses on the
table till every one was broken save one, and that was reserved for a
poetical fate.

Tumblers were substituted, and might possibly contribute their
share to the early hilarity and consecutive frolic of the night; for ere
long Coleridge's sonorous voice was heard declaiming on the extraordinary ebullitions of Hook—'I have before in the course of my
time met with men of admirable promptitude of intellectual power
and play of wit, which, as Stillingfleet tells,

> The rays of wit gild whereso'er they strike;

but I never could have conceived such amazing readiness of mind,
and resources of genius to be poured out on the mere subject and
impulse of the moment.' Having got the poet into this exalted
mood, the last of the limited wine-glasses was mounted upon the
bottom of a reversed tumbler, and, to the infinite risk of the latter,
he was induced to shy at the former with a silver fork, till after two
or three throws he succeeded in smashing it into fragments, to be
tossed into the basket with its perished brethren. . . . The exhibi-

tion was remembered for years afterwards by all who partook of it; and I have a letter of Lockhart's alluding to the date of our witnessing the roseate face of Coleridge, lit up with animation, his large grey eye beaming, his white hair floating, and his whole frame, as it were, radiating with intense interest, as he poised the fork in his hand, and launched it at the fragile object (the last glass of dinner) distant some three or four feet from him on the table!

WILLIAM JERDAN
Autobiography

The Wine of the House

That evening the President [Richard Nixon] entertained ten conservative Congressmen from both parties aboard his yacht. . . .

There was beef tenderloin for dinner. The President had become something of a wine buff during his New York City days, and the *Sequoia* was stocked with his favorite, a 1966 Château Margaux which sold for about thirty dollars a bottle. He always asked for it when beef was served. And he had issued orders to the stewards about what to do when large groups of Congressmen were aboard: His guests were to be served a rather good six-dollar wine; his glass was to be filled from a bottle of Château Margaux wrapped in a towel.

BOB WOODWARD AND CARL BERNSTEIN
The Final Days

Shocking

ALGERNON: Oh! . . . by the way, Lane, I see from your book that on Thursday night, when Lord Shoreham and Mr. Worthing were dining with me, eight bottles of champagne are entered as having been consumed.
LANE: Yes, sir; eight bottles and a pint.
ALGERNON: Why is it that at a bachelor's establishment the servants invariably drink the champagne? I ask merely for information.
LANE: I attribute it to the superior quality of the wine, sir. I have often observed that in married households the champagne is rarely of a first-rate brand.
ALGERNON: Good heavens! Is marriage so demoralizing as that?

OSCAR WILDE
The Importance of Being Earnest

Ten Little Bottle Boys

Ten little bottle boys
Setting out to dine,
One had a faulty cork,
Then there were nine.

Nine little bottle boys
Looking so sedate,
One had a broken crust,
Then there were eight.

Eight little bottle boys,
Cherubim from Heav'n,
One couldn't stand upright,
Then there were seven.

Seven little bottle boys
Always in a fix,
A Cloete swallowed one,
Then there were six.

Six little bottle boys,
Very much alive,
One decanted all alone,
Then there were five.

Five little bottle boys
Out of half a score,
One caught the weevil bad,
Then there were four.

Four little bottle boys
From the cellar free,
One ullaged by himself,
Then there were three.

Three little bottle boys
Wond'ring what to do,
One enticed the butler,
Then there were two.

Two little bottle boys
When the day was done,

One was taken up to bed,
Then there was one.

One little bottle boy
Standing all one,
Winked at his Master there,
Then there was none.

CHARLES WALTER BERRY

Advice

In some families the master often sends to the tavern for a bottle of wine, and you are the messenger: I advise you, therefore, to take the smallest bottle you can find; but, however, make the drawer give you a full quart, then you will get a good sup for yourself, and your bottle will be filled. As for a cork to stop it, you need be at no trouble for the thumb will do as well, or a bit of dirty chewed paper.

JONATHAN SWIFT
"Directions to Servants"

A Glass of Sunshine

"One cause, however, of the longer and healthier life of my forefathers was, that they had many pleasant customs, and means of making themselves glad, and their guests and friends along with them. Nowadays we have but one!"

"And what is that?" asked the sculptor.

"You shall see!" said his young host.

By this time, he had ushered the sculptor into one of the numberless saloons; and, calling for refreshment, old Stella placed a cold fowl upon the table, and quickly followed it with a savory omelet, which Girolamo had lost no time in preparing. She also brought some cherries, plums, and apricots, and a plate full of particularly delicate figs, of last year's growth. The butler showing his white head at the door, his master beckoned to him.

"Tomaso, bring some Sunshine!" said he.

The readiest method of obeying this order, one might suppose, would have been, to fling wide the green window-blinds, and let the glow of the summer noon into the carefully shaded room. But, at Monte Beni, with provident caution against the wintry days, when there is little sunshine, and the rainy ones, when there is none, it was the hereditary custom to keep their Sunshine stored away in the cellar. Old Tomaso quickly produced some of it in a small, straw-covered flask, out of which he extracted the cork, and inserted a little cotton wool, to absorb the olive-oil that kept the precious liquid from the air.

"This is a wine," observed the Count, "the secret of making which has been kept in our family for centuries upon centuries; nor would it avail any man to steal the secret, unless he could also steal the vineyard, in which alone the Monte Beni grape can be produced. There is little else left me, save that patch of vines. Taste some of their juice, and tell me whether it is worthy to be called Sunshine! for that is its name."

"A glorious name, too!" cried the sculptor.

"Taste it," said Donatello, filling his friend's glass, and pouring likewise a little into his own. "But first smell its fragrance; for the wine is very lavish of it, and will scatter it all abroad."

"Ah, how exquisite!" said Kenyon. "No other wine has a bouquet like this. The flavor must be rare, indeed, if it fulfil the promise of this fragrance, which is like the airy sweetness of youthful hopes, that no realities will ever satisfy!"

This invaluable liquor was of a pale golden hue, like other of the rarest Italian wines, and, if carelessly and irreligiously quaffed, might have been mistaken for a very fine sort of champagne. It was not, however, an effervescing wine, although its delicate piquancy produced a somewhat similar effect upon the palate. Sipping, the guest longed to sip again; but the wine demanded so deliberate a pause, in order to detect the hidden peculiarities and subtle exquisiteness of its flavor, that to drink it was really more a moral than a physical enjoyment. There was a deliciousness in it that eluded analysis, and—like whatever else is superlatively good—was perhaps better appreciated in the memory than by present consciousness.

One of its most ethereal charms lay in the transitory life of the wine's richest qualities; for, while it required a certain leisure and delay, yet, if you lingered too long upon the draught, it became disenchanted both of its fragrance and its flavor.

The lustre should not be forgotten, among the other admirable endowments of the Monte Beni wine; for, as it stood in Kenyon's glass, a little circle of light glowed on the table round about it, as if it were really so much golden sunshine.

"I feel myself a better man for that ethereal potation," observed the sculptor. "The finest Orvieto, or that famous wine, the Est Est Est of Montefiascone, is vulgar in comparison. This is surely the wine of the Golden Age, such as Bacchus himself first taught mankind to press from the choicest of his grapes. My dear Count, why is it not illustrious? The pale, liquid gold, in every such flask as that, might be solidified into golden scudi, and would quickly make you a millionnaire!"

Tomaso, the old butler, who was standing by the table, and enjoying the praises of the wine quite as much as if bestowed upon himself, made answer,—

"We have a tradition, signore," said he, "that this rare wine of our vineyard would lose all its wonderful qualities, if any of it were sent to market. The Counts of Monte Beni have never parted with a single flask of it for gold. At their banquets, in the olden time, they have entertained princes, cardinals, and once an emperor, and once a pope, with this delicious wine, and always, even to this day, it has been their custom to let it flow freely, when those whom they love and honor sit at the board. But the grand duke himself could not drink that wine, except it were under this very roof!"

"What you tell me, my good friend," replied Kenyon, "makes me venerate the Sunshine of Monte Beni even more abundantly than before. As I understand you, it is a sort of consecrated juice, and symbolizes the holy virtues of hospitality and social kindness?"

"Why, partly so, Signore," said the old butler, with a shrewd twinkle in his eye; "but, to speak out all the truth, there is another excellent reason why neither a cask nor a flask of our precious vintage should ever be sent to market. The wine, Signore, is so fond of its native home, that a transportation of even a few miles turns it quite sour. And yet it is a wine that keeps well in the cellar, underneath this floor, and gathers fragrance, flavor, and brightness, in its dark dungeon. That very flask of Sunshine, now, has kept itself for you, sir guest (as a maid reserves her sweetness till her lover comes for it), ever since a merry vintage-time, when the Signore Count here was a boy!"

"You must not wait for Tomaso to end his discourse about the wine, before drinking off your glass," observed Donatello. "When once the flask is uncorked, its finest qualities lose little time in making their escape. I doubt whether your last sip will be quite so delicious as you found the first."

And, in truth, the sculptor fancied that the Sunshine became almost imperceptibly clouded, as he approached the bottom of the flask. The effect of the wine, however, was a gentle exhilaration, which did not so speedily pass away.

NATHANIEL HAWTHORNE
The Marble Faun

Sorry I Can't Join You

It is a fact, which some philosophers may think worth setting down, that Scott's organization, as to more than one of the senses, was the reverse of exquisite. He had very little of what musicians call an ear; his smell was hardly more delicate. I have seen him stare about, quite unconscious of the cause, when his whole company betrayed their uneasiness at the approach of an over-kept haunch of venison; and neither by the nose or the palate could he distinguish corked wine from sound. He could never tell Madeira from Sherry; nay, an Oriental friend having sent him a butt of *sheeraz*, when he remembered the circumstance some time afterwards, and called for a bottle to have Sir John Malcolm's opinion of its quality, it turned out that his butler, mistaking the label, had already served up half the binn as *sherry*. Port he considered as physic: he never willingly swallowed more than one glass of it, and was sure to anathematize a second, if offered, by repeating John Home's epigram—

> "Bold and erect the Caledonian stood,
> Old was his mutton, and his claret good;
> Let him drink port, the English statesman cried—
> He drank the poison, and his spirit died."

In truth, he liked no wines except sparkling champagne and claret; but even as to this last he was no connoisseur; and sincerely preferred a tumbler of whisky-toddy to the most precious "liquid ruby" that ever flowed in the cup of a prince. He rarely took any other potation when quite alone with his family; but at the Sunday board he circulated the champagne briskly during dinner, and considered a pint of claret each man's fair share afterwards. I should not omit, however, that his Bordeaux was uniformly preceded by a small libation of the genuine *mountain dew*.

J. G. LOCKHART
The Life of Sir Walter Scott

Walpole and Wine

In red wines it is quite clear that he preferred claret to port, or his guests did, for claret dominates the years 1732 and 1733 for which complete bills exist. And it is the only wine which Walpole bought during these years by the cask. Ordinary claret was £36 per hogshead and the best £45, and Walpole preferred the very best, buying four hogsheads of Château Margaux at a time and a hogshead of Lafite regularly every three months. The clerk of his wine merchant, James Bennett, must have known Bordeaux, for he is the only early eighteenth-century clerk, whom I have yet met with, who spells both Margaux and Lafite correctly; usually Margaux appears in the most extraordinary forms—Margoose, Margos, Margon, in fact any way but the right way. The only other named claret in Walpole's bills is Pontac, a popular wine in England at that time. From the frequency of purchase it would seem that the wine was quickly drunk, whilst young, and there is no reference to any purchase of old claret. The same is not true of burgundy. On the very rare occasions when Walpole bought this wine, it is always described as 'old burgundy' and at 4s. the bottle (24s. in modern money), it was by far the most expensive wine which he possessed. Red port occurs, of course, quite frequently, but it occupied only a modest position in his cellar.

From these bills, too, we can get an idea of the very large yearly expenditure of Walpole on wine. In 1733, he spent £1,118 12s. 10d. with James Bennett, and £48 2s. 0d. with Schaart & Co. And there may have been accounts with other merchants which have not survived—certainly there were purchases of arrack at Lynn, possibly of brandy and various wines, too. But even if nothing had been bought at Lynn, the expenditure with these two merchants alone would be equivalent to about £7,700 today. From the return of empties, carefully kept and audited, we know that the consumption was prodigious. During 1733, 552 dozen empty bottles were returned to James Bennett. This represents probably only the major part of the consumption of Walpole's household.

Nor was wine Walpole's only drink. Very early in life he was famed for his hogan of which three or four casks were brewed every year at Houghton. This, and arrack punch, were always in plentiful supply at his famous Norfolk Congresses. At times, when his friends were using his house during his absence, they were so tempted by his hogan that they broached a cask and got his permission afterwards. But principally he drank wine, and wine of limited range, but certainly judged with a connoisseur's palate. Obviously he was not very interested in variety and his cellar does not compare with the Duke of Chandos's with its wines, ranging from Samos to Kill Priest. On occasion Walpole would ask a friend to send him anything of interest, discovered on a journey abroad, and, in 1716, William Willis sent him white Sieges from Barcelona, Banibofar from Majorca, and a hogshead of Hermitage from Avignon, but Walpole stuck in the main to his Lafite and Margaux with the obstinate loyalty which was so much a part of his nature.

From these bills can be gleaned a little knowledge of how the wine trade worked and of current prices. Claret was usually bottled at Walpole's cellar by his merchant, and the merchant charged 4s. for drawing a hogshead; bottles were half-a-crown a dozen, 2d. a dozen returnable on empties; long French corks, half-a-crown a gross; wine bottled at the merchants was sent out in hampers which were far from cheap—3s. for a four-dozen hamper. In fact there was nothing really cheap about wine in the early eighteenth century: even labour was expensive—fifty dozen bottles cost 6s. to be carried from London to Chelsea—no free delivery in those days. But one aspect of a wine merchant's life remains unchanged. In 1736 Walpole's merchant was still waiting patiently for settlement of his 1733 bill.

J. H. PLUMB
"Sir Robert Walpole's Wine"

Fit for a King

[Louis XIV] had formerly suffered from long attacks of gout, and to prevent their recurrence Fagon swathed him every night between feather-beds, which made him perspire so violently that he had to be rubbed down in the morning before the Grand Chamberlain and Gentlemen of the Bedchamber could enter. Instead of the best champagne, which at one time was the only wine he drank, he had for years drunk nothing but Burgundy and water, and the wine was so old that it had become sour; he used to say, laughing, that he had often seen foreign noblemen well taken in when they wished to taste his own particular wine. He never at any time drank wine unmixed with water; nor did he ever drink any sort of liqueur, not even tea, coffee, or chocolate.

DUC DE SAINT-SIMON
Memoirs

Careful

The Rev. Dr. Folliott. . . . But a glass of wine after soup is, as the French say, the *verre de santé*. The current of opinion sets in favour of Hock: but I am for Madeira; I do not fancy Hock till I have laid a substratum of Madeira.

THOMAS LOVE PEACOCK
Crotchet Castle

Jorrocks at Ease

"And wine?" asked the housekeeper; adding, "the butler's away with Sir Archey, but I 'ave the key of the cellar."

"That's all right!" exclaimed our friend, adding, "I'll drink his 'ealth in a bottle of his best."

"Port?" asked Mrs. Markham.

"Port in course," replied Mr. J., with a hoist of his eyebrows, adding, "but, mind, I doesn't call the oldest the best—far from it—it's oftentimes the wust. No," continued he, "give me a good fruity wine; a wine with a grip o' the gob, that leaves a mark on the side o' the glass; not your weak woe-begone trash, that would be water if it wasn't wine."

"P'r'aps you'd like a little champagne at dinner," suggested Mrs. Markham.

"Champagne," repeated Mr. Jorrocks thoughtfully, "champagne! well, I wouldn't mind a little champagne, only I wouldn't like it hiced; doesn't want to 'ave all my teeth set a-chatterin' i' my 'ead; harn't got so far advanced in gentility as to like my wine froze. . . .

The wine circulated languidly, and Mr. Jorrocks in vain tried to get up a conversation on hunting. The Professor always started his stones or Mr. Muleygrubs his law, varied by an occasional snore from Mr. Slowman, who had to be nudged by Jones every time the bottle went round. Thus they battled on for about an hour.

"Would *you* like any more wine?" at length inquired Mr. Muleygrubs, with a motion of rising.

"Not any more I'm obleged to you," replied the obsequious Mr. Jacob Jones, who was angling for the chaplaincy of Mr. Marmaduke's approaching shrievalty.

"*Just another bottle!*" rejoined Mr. Jorrocks encouragingly.

"Take a glass of claret," replied Mr. Muleygrubs, handing the jug to our master.

"Rayther not, thank ye," replied Mr. Jorrocks, "not the stuff for me. By the way now, I should think," continued Mr. Jorrocks, with an air of sudden enlightenment, "that some of those ancient ancestors o' yours have been fond o' claret."

"Why so?" replied Mr. Muleygrubs pertly.

"Doesn't know," replied Mr. Jorrocks, musingly, "but I never hears your name mentioned without thinking o' small claret. But come, let's have another bottle o' black strap—*it's good strap*—sound and strong—got wot I calls a good grib o' the gob."

"Well," said Mr. Muleygrubs, getting up and ringing the bell, "if you must, you must, but I should think you have had enough."

"PORT WINE!" exclaimed he, with the air of a man with a dozen set out, to his figure footman, as he answered the bell.

ROBERT SMITH SURTEES
Handley Cross

Thanks

To Angus Fletcher

Dear Angus: We broke out tonight
In the unconcentrated light
Of eight black candles (lamps of hell?)
Your lovely bottle of Beychevelle,
Sprung and fallen, reaped and conceived
In the same gentle, many-leaved
Summer of nineteen sixty-seven
(My thirty-eighth quick year to heaven).
It tasted of its family tree
And chemical biography
In vine, in wood and in—alas—
Its veritable gaol of glass
—Not of that past year of its birth
When I lay on the grass-rich earth
Beside the trivial, moving Cam,
Unbuilding me toward what I am,
—Not of the ravages and tears
Of seven intervening years
That helped unbuild a world of hope

To its decaying isotope:
The history of this dark wine
Is, thankfully, untouched by mine.
But as the candles gutter out,
The bottle emptied beyond doubt
Down to its common sediment,
We wonder, breathless, where it went,
The claret of our middling years
Remembered; as it disappears,
Inside the green glass shadows fall.
It is dark. Emptiness is all
Toward which we stare with eyes yet bright
That make a little, glooming light,
Recalling, just before the end
(As the last breaths of flame descend)
The gift, the giver and the friend.

JOHN HOLLANDER

Ode

My dear Maecenas, noble knight,
You'll drink cheap Sabine here tonight
From common cups. Yet I myself
Sealed it and stored it on the shelf
In a Greek jar that day the applause
Broke out in your recovery's cause,
So that the compliment resounded
Through the full theatre and rebounded
From your own Tiber's banks until
The echo laughed on Vatican hill.
At your house you enjoy the best—
Caecuban or the grape that's pressed
At Cales. But whoever hopes
My cups will taste of Formian slopes
Or of the true Falernian
Must leave a disappointed man.

HORACE

A Dilemma

"And while I think of it," I once heard him say, "we haven't had any woodcock for days, or truffles baked in the ashes, and the cellar is becoming a disgrace—no more '34s and hardly any '37s. Last week, I had to offer my publisher a bottle that was far too good for him, simply because there was nothing between the insulting and the superlative."

A. J. LIEBLING
Between Meals

Democracy

It would be a long story, and of no importance, were I to recount too particularly by what accident I (who am not at all fond of society) supped lately with a person, who in his own opinion lives in splendour combined with economy; but according to mine, in a sordid but expensive manner. Some very elegant dishes were served up to himself and a few more of the company; while those which were placed before the rest were cheap and paltry. He had apportioned in small flagons three different sorts of wine; but you are not to suppose it was that the guests might take their choice: on the contrary, that they might not choose at all. One was for himself and me; the next for his friends of a lower order (for, you must know, he measures out his friendship according to the degrees of quality); and the third for his own freed-men and mine. One who sat next me took notice of this, and asked me if I approved of it. "Not at all," I told him. "Pray, then," said he, "what is your method on such occasions?" "Mine," I returned, "is, to give all my company the same fare; for when I make an invitation, it is to sup, not to be censored. Every man whom I have placed on an equality with myself by admitting him to my table, I treat as an equal in all particulars." "Even freed-men?" he asked. "Even them," I said; "for on these occasions I regard them not as freed-men, but boon companions." "This must put you to great expense," says he. I assured him not at all; and on his asking how that could be, I said "Why you must know my freed-men don't drink the same wine I do—but *I* drink what *they* do."

PLINY THE YOUNGER
Letters

Raise Your Glasses

What's dirty land or hoarded coin
To him that fears to purchase wine?
He's curs'd with all his useless chink,
And damn'd alive, that durst not drink,
Or trespass on his ill-got treasure,
For one short day's expensive pleasure.
Give me the generous soul that dares
To drown in wine all worldly cares,
The jolly heart who freely spends
His surplus with his bottle friends,
And envies not those South-Sea noddies
That loll in coaches with their dowdies,
Nor all the glitt'ring pomp that waits
On powers, titles, and estates,
But one that does for pleasure choose
Some tavern where good-fellows use,
And ne'er seems backward, when he's there,
Of spending what he well can spare,
But hugs the flask, and frankly bends
To all the motions of his friends,
Those bosom ministers of ease,
So hard to find and hard to please.
Let stingy mortals rail at wine,
And angry wives reproach the vine,
. . . I'll laugh at the penurious knave,
And honor Bacchus to my grave.

NED WARD
"The Delights of the Bottle"
1720

Once Is Enough

There was a man, much my senior, learned in his own branch of science, innocent, hospitable, nobly fanatical about Claret, proud to remember that Sir Walter Scott had liked his grandfather's wines. I had won his kind heart by contradicting a man who asserted that the Scottish knew nothing but whisky; without having a drop of Scotch blood in me, and never having been in Scotland, I yet knew—what should be common knowledge—that the ancient amity between Scotland and France made the Scottish gentry very good judges of Claret. Amusingly amazed to find this grain of knowledge in a sterile Southerner, he repeatedly gave me great Clarets. Then, one long-promised evening, I introduced him at the end of dinner to a very great Château Yquem. We were never to meet again; and I keep the memory of my old friend, rotund, pink, and getting pinker in his discreet excitement, joy in his genial old face, passing into rapture as the wine took him, his eyes sparkling behind his strong glasses. "I have never cared for sweet wine, but you are right. This *is* wine. I will never drink it again. I will keep it as a memory of our evening together."

T. EARLE WELBY
The Cellar Key

Classical Wines

So Luke appeared for the Sunday lunch in Brown's rooms, once more effacing himself into discretion again, dressed with a subfusc taste more cultivated than that of anyone there except Roy Calvert. Unobtrusively he inhaled the bouquet of his glass of Montrachet.

Brown had placed Chrystal at one end of the table, and took the other himself. After we had sipped the wine, Brown said contentedly:

"I'm glad most of you seem to like it. I thought it was rather suitable. After all, we don't meet for this purpose very frequently."

Brown's parties were always modest. One had a couple of glasses of a classical wine, and that was all—except once a year, when his friends who had a taste in wine were gathered together for an evening. This Sunday there was nothing with lunch but the Montrachet, but afterwards he circulated a bottle of claret. "I thought we needed something rather fortifying," said Brown, "before we started our little discussion."

We were content after our lunch. Pilbrow was a gourmet, young Luke had the sensuous gusto to become one; Chrystal and Roy Calvert and I enjoyed our food and drink. Pilbrow was chuckling to himself.

"Much better than the poor old Achaeans——" I distinguished among the chuckles. We asked what it was all about, and Pilbrow become lucid:

"I was reading the *Iliad*—Book XI—again in bed—Pramnian

wine sprinkled with grated goat's cheese—Pramnian wine sprinkled with grated goat's cheese——Oh, can anyone imagine how *horrible* that must have been?"

C. P. SNOW
The Masters

Circe

So he spoke to them, and the rest gave voice, and called her,
and at once she opened the shining doors, and came out, and
    invited
them in, and all in their innocence entered; only
Eurylochos waited outside, for he suspected treachery.
She brought them inside and seated them on chairs and benches,
and mixed them a potion, with barley and cheese and pale honey
added to Pramnian wine, but put into the mixture
malignant drugs, to make them forgetful of their own country.
When she had given them this and they had drunk it down, next
    thing
she struck them with her wand and drove them into her pig pens,
and they took on the look of pigs, with the heads and voices
and bristles of pigs, but the minds within them stayed as they had
    been
before. So crying they went in, and before them Circe
threw down acorns for them to eat, and ilex and cornel
buds, such food as pigs who sleep on the ground always feed on.

HOMER
The Odyssey

The Prosecution Rests

The defense attorney alone held aloof from the general uproar. He pushed the platter of cheese in front of Traps. "Take some," he urged. "We may as well eat hearty. There's nothing left for us to do."

A Château Margaux was brought in, and the dusty bottle, vintage of 1914, restored quiet. Everyone gazed respectfully at the judge as he cautiously and with great deliberation began removing the cork, employing a curious, old-fashioned corkscrew that enabled him to draw the cork from the bottle as it lay on its side in the little basket. They watched in breathless suspense, for the cork had to be removed with the least possible damage, as it was the only proof of the age of the wine. (After four decades there was little left of the label.) The cork did not come out quite whole, and the remainder had to be scraped out with delicate care. But enough of the cork was left for the date to be legible. It was handed around the table, sniffed, admired, and finally solemnly presented to the sales manager as a memento, the judge said, of their wonderful evening. The judge now tasted the wine, licked his lips, and filled the other glasses. The rest of the company smelled the wine, sipped it, burst into cries of ecstasy and praise. The cheese was handed around again, and the judge requested the prosecutor to make his little speech and present the "case for the prosecution."

FRIEDRICH DUERRENMATT
Traps

Fussy

A hard drinker, being at table, was offered grapes at dessert.

'Thank you,' said he, pushing the dish away from him, 'but I am not in the habit of taking my wine in pills.'

ANTHELME BRILLAT-SAVARIN
The Physiology of Taste

A Mad Tea-Party

There was a table set out under a tree in front of the house, and the March Hare and the Hatter were having tea at it: a Dormouse was sitting between them, fast asleep, and the other two were using it as a cushion, resting their elbows on it, and talking over its head. "Very uncomfortable for the Dormouse," thought Alice; "only as it's asleep, I suppose it doesn't mind."

The table was a large one, but the three were all crowded together at one corner of it. "No room! No room!" they cried out when they saw Alice coming. "There's *plenty* of room!" said Alice indignantly, and she sat down in a large arm-chair at one end of the table.

"Have some wine," the March Hare said in an encouraging tone.

Alice looked all round the table, but there was nothing on it but tea. "I don't see any wine," she remarked.

"There isn't any," said the March Hare.

LEWIS CARROLL
Alice's Adventures in Wonderland

The Marriage in Cana

And the third day there was a marriage in Cana of Galilee; and the mother of Jesus was there:

And both Jesus was called, and his disciples, to the marriage.

And when they wanted wine, the mother of Jesus saith unto him, They have no wine.

Jesus saith unto her, Woman, what have I to do with thee? mine hour is not yet come.

His mother saith unto the servants, Whatsoever he saith unto you, do it.

And there were set there six water pots of stone, after the manner of the purifying of the Jews, containing two or three firkins apiece.

Jesus saith unto them, Fill the waterpots with water. And they filled them up to the brim.

And he saith unto them, Draw out now, and bear unto the governor of the feast. And they bare it.

When the ruler of the feast had tasted the water that was made wine, and knew not whence it was: (but the servants which drew the water knew;) the governor of the feast called the bridegroom,

And saith unto him, Every man at the beginning doth set forth good wine; and when men have well drunk, then that which is worse: but thou hast kept the good wine until now.

This beginning of miracles did Jesus in Cana of Galilee, and manifested forth his glory; and his disciples believed on him.

St. John, Chapter 2

10

Water vs. Wine

It may seem odd to include references to water in a book about wine, but there are a number of entertaining descriptions to be found of the pleasures of water compared to those of wine, as well as accounts—by confirmed wine drinkers—of the dangers of water. In addition to the selections that follow, there is the misleadingly titled "Drinking Song" by Longfellow that turns out to be in praise of water:

> Youth perpetual dwells in fountains,
> Not in flasks, and casks, and cellars . . .
>
> Then with water fill the pitcher
>   Wreathed about with classic fables;
> Ne'er Falernian threw a richer
>   Light upon Lucullus' tables.

James Nicholson took a much stronger, and somewhat melodramatic, stand against wine in a poem which begins,

> Our homes are invaded with dark desolation,
> There's danger wherever the wine-cup doth flow . . .

G. K. Chesterton, on the other hand, wrote a famous poem with the refrain "I don't care where the water goes if it doesn't get into the wine," but the rest of it doesn't seem to me worth quoting.

I have, however, included Benjamin Franklin's facetious letter to the Abbé Morellet imploring him not to put water into the wine. This attitude about water and wine is also reported by Richard Ford in his nineteenth-century travel book on Spain: "Of good wine," he writes, "the Spaniards are almost as good judges as of good water; they rarely mix them, because they say it is spoiling two good things."

Baudelaire's attitude toward people who shun wine was clear when he wrote, "A man who drinks only water has a secret to hide from his fellow men." And then there's the old story about the teetotaler who was offered a glass of port. "I would rather commit adultery than drink port," he said.

"And who wouldn't," replied his host.

A Wise Man's Drink

I believe that water is the only drink for a wise man; wine is not so noble a liquor; and think of dashing the hopes of a morning with a cup of warm coffee, or of an evening with a dish of tea! Ah, how low I fall when I am tempted by them! Even music may be intoxicating. Such apparently slight causes destroyed Greece and Rome, and will destroy England and America.

HENRY THOREAU
Walden

Too Spartan

Note also how the Spartans fell. They added to their other brutish qualities an abstinence from wine. With what result? That they died out and their power was extinguished. Some brief generations after their chief victories they had dwindled to a few hundred men and, soon after, none were to be found. They had perished. Nor have they left any memory or monument. Athens, august in the use of wine, is immortal gloriously, but who reads or remembers Lacedaemon? Where are its songs, its visions, its philosophy, its laughter, or its marbles? There are none known, for they had none. Lacking wine the Spartans could not create, and their city was transformed

into a squalid hamlet, which it remains to this day. So much for the
Spartans.

HILAIRE BELLOC
"Advice to a Young Man
in the Matter of Wine"

A Sober Pledge

I'll pledge thee not in wassail bowl,
  With rosy madness filled;
But let us quaff the nobler wine,
  By Nature's hand distilled.
Where to the skies the mountains rise
  In grandeur to the view,
Where sparkling rills leap down the hills,
  Our Scotia's mountain dew.

JAMES NICHOLSON

No Water, Please

You have often enlivened me, my dear friend, by your excellent
drinking-songs; in return, I beg to edify you by some Christian,
moral, and philosophical reflections upon the same subject.

In vino veritas, says the wise man,—*Truth is in wine*. Before the
days of Noah, then, men, having nothing but water to drink, could
not discover the truth. Thus they went astray, became abominably
wicked, and were justly exterminated by *water*, which they loved to
drink.

The good man Noah, seeing that through this pernicious beverage all his contemporaries had perished, took it in aversion; and
to quench his thirst God created the vine, and revealed to him the
means of converting its fruit into wine. . . .

We hear of the conversion of water into wine at the marriage in
Cana as of a miracle. But this conversion is, through the goodness
of God, made every day before our eyes. Behold the rain which
descends from heaven upon our vineyards, and which incorporates
itself with the grapes, to be changed into wine; a constant proof
that God loves us, and loves to see us happy. The miracle in question was only performed to hasten the operation, under circumstances of present necessity, which required it. . . .

My Christian brother, be kind and benevolent like God, and do not spoil his good work. He made wine to gladden the heart of men; do not, therefore, when at table you see your neighbor pour wine into his glass, be eager to mingle water with it. Why would you drown *truth*? It is probable that your neighbor knows better than you can what suits him. Perhaps he does not like water; perhaps he would only put in a few drops for fashion's sake; perhaps he does not wish any one to observe how much he puts in his glass. Do not, then, offer water, except to children; 't is a mistaken piece of politeness, and often very inconvenient. I give you this hint as a man of the world; and I will finish as I began, like a good Christian, in making a religious observation of high importance, taken from the Holy Scriptures. I mean that the apostle Paul counselled Timothy very seriously to put wine into his water for the sake of his health; but that not one of the apostles or holy fathers ever recommended *putting water to wine.*

B. FRANKLIN.

P.S.—To confirm still more your piety and gratitude to Divine Providence, reflect upon the situation which it has given to the *elbow.* You see in animals, who are intended to drink the waters that flow upon the earth, that if they have long legs, they have also a long neck, so that they can get at their drink without kneeling down. But man, who was destined to drink wine, is framed in a manner that he may raise the glass to his mouth. If the elbow had been placed nearer the hand, the part in advance would have been too short to bring the glass up to the mouth; and if it had been nearer the shoulder, that part would have been so long that when it attempted to carry the wine to the mouth it would have overshot the mark, and gone beyond the head; thus, either way, we should have been in the case of Tantalus. But from the actual situation of the elbow, we are enabled to drink at our ease, the glass going directly to the mouth. Let us, then, with glass in hand, adore this benevolent wisdom;—let us adore and drink!

BENJAMIN FRANKLIN
Letter to the Abbé Morellet
1779

Hence Burgundy, Claret, and Port!

Hence Burgundy, Claret, and Port,
　　Away with old Hock and Madeira,
Too earthly ye are for my sport;
　　There's a beverage brighter and clearer.
Instead of a pitiful rummer,
My wine overbrims a whole summer;
　　My bowl is the sky,
　　And I drink at my eye,
　　Till I feel in the brain
　　A Delphian pain—
Then follow, my Caius! then follow:
　　On the green of the hill
　　We will drink our fill
　　Of golden sunshine,
　　Till our brains intertwine
With the glory and grace of Apollo!

　　　　　　　　　　　　　JOHN KEATS

Hence Burgundy, Claret, and Port*

Hence Burgundy, Claret, and Port,
For the Duty per Gallon is crippling—
A Poet is bound to go short
When it costs him so much for his tippling.

Away with old Hock and Madeira—
When each Chancellor opens his throttle,
Each bottle is one-and-six dearer,
And no Poet drinks less than a bottle.

Too earthly are ye for my sport—
That is, out of this world is your price now,
For a Poet's resources are short,
And Bank Managers seldom are nice now.

There's a beverage brighter and clearer
Than Hippocrene, sparing its blushes,

* A contemporary English poet imagines how Keats would have reacted to the present duty on imported wine, increased no less than a dozen times in as many years.

Only fit for the Bards of this era—
You turn on the tap and it gushes.

And so, with their heads in the sink,
Overcome by this Government fiddle,
Our Poets become what they drink,
And all that they write is pure piddle.

ROBERT GITTINGS

Horrible, Horrible

Full many a man, both young and old,
　Is brought to his sarcophagus
By pouring water, icy cold,
　Adown his warm æsophagus . . .

And if from man's vile arts I flee
And drink pure water from the pump,
I gulp down infusoria
And quarts of raw bacteria,
And hideous rotatoræ,
And wriggling polygastricæ,
And slimy diatomaceæ,
And hard-shelled ophryocercinæ,
And double-barrelled kolpodæ,
Non-loricated ambœdæ,
And various animalculæ,
Of middle, high and low degree.

ANON.

How's That Again?

Any article to which Providence has given those properties which
nourish or refresh the human system, man may, when in health,
use in moderation. The unadulterated juice of the grape, of wine
before it undergoes that chemical decomposition and internal action by which alcohol is produced, is such an article, and may
therefore be drank with propriety. But adulterated wines or wines
mingled with alcohol, are nowhere allowed in scripture, and are in
any quantity, to a person in health, always injurious. At the marriage in Cana of Galilee, our Saviour turned water into pure wine,

which was therefore nourishing and refreshing, *not* into that which contained alcohol and was therefore pernicious. He therefore evidently allowed men to drink wine uncontaminated with alcoholic poison.

DOCTOR SPRINGWATER
The Cold-Water-Man
1832

Let Water Its Own Frigid Nature Retain

Let water its own frigid nature retain;
Since water it is, let it water remain!
Let it ripple and run in meandering rills,
And set the wheels going in brook-sided mills.
In the desert, where streams do but scantily run,
If so much they're allowed by the thirsty old sun,
There water *may* be, as it's quaff'd by each man,
Productive of fun to a whole caravan.

Yes, water, and welcome, in billows may rise,
Till it shiver its feathery crest 'gainst the skies;
Or in dashing cascades it may joyously leap,
Or in silvery lakes lie entranced and asleep;—
Or, e'en better still, in full showers of hope,
Let it gaily descend on some rich vineyard's slope,
That its sides may bear clusters of ripening bliss,
Which in Autumn, shall melt into nectar like this.

Let it bear up the vessel that bringeth us o'er
Its freight of glad wine from some happier shore.
Let it run through each land that in ignorance lies:
It the Heathen will do very well to baptize.
Yes, water shall have ev'ry due praise of mine,
Whether salt, like the ocean, or fresh, like the Rhine,
Yes, praised to the echo pure water shall be,
But wine, wine alone is the nectar for me!

ANON.

Wine But Water Sublim'd

It is without controversie that in the nonage of the world, men and beasts had but one buttery which was the fountaine and river, nor do we read of any vines or wines till two hundred years after the flood, but now I do not know or hear of any nation that hath *water* only for their drink except the *Japonois*, and they drink it hot too; but we may say that what beverage soever we make either by brewing, by distillation, decoction, percolation or pressing, it is but *water* at first, nay *wine* it self is but water sublim'd, being nothing else but that moysture and sap which is caus'd either by rain or other kind of irrigations about the roots of the vine and drawn up to the branches and berries by the virtuall attractive heat of the Sun, the bowells of the earth serving as a limbec to that end, which made the Italian vineyard-man (after a long drouth, and an extream hot summer, which had parch'd up all his grapes,) to complain that *per mancamento d'acqua, bevo del' acqua, se io havessi acqua beverei el vino,* for want of water, I am forc'd to drink water, if I had water I would drink wine . . .

JAMES HOWELL
Drinks of all Nations
1634

No, Thanks

[Water] may be very suitable for people living in hot countries; but in England, it is in no wise agreeable, for it doth very greatly deject the appetite, destroy the natural heat, and overthrow the strength of the stomach; and, consequently, confounding the concretion, is the cause of crudities, fluctuations, and windiness in the body.

TOBIAS VENNER
The Straight Road to a Long Life

The Horse of Parnassus

If with water you fill up your glasses,
You'll never write anything wise
But wine is the horse of Parnassus,
That carries a bard to the skies.

ATHENÆUS
The Deipnosophists

What, Never? No, Never

An old French gentleman, a great gourmet, was preaching the gospel of the grape to an American. "Wine is the only safe and sanitary beverage," he declared. "Look at me. At the age of eighty-seven I am in perfect health. And why? Because water has never passed my lips."

"You mean that literally?"

"Absolutely, monsieur."

"What about brushing your teeth?"

"For that," replied the old gentleman blandly, "I use a very light, dry wine."

JULIAN STREET
Table Topics

11
Tasting

We take it for granted that a wine has to be tasted before it can be commented on, but since many people are intrigued by wine tasting itself, I thought it would be fun to group together some accounts of varied tasting experiences. In addition, three longer accounts of wine tasting will be found in the section "Extended Diversions": in "Winesmanship," Stephen Potter makes a distinction between commenting on wines and "Tastingmanship"; Art Buchwald's "It Puckers Your Mouth" is about tasting wines in Bordeaux; and probably the most famous wine story of all, Roald Dahl's "Taste," revolves around a wine tasting at a dinner party.

In *The Devil's Dictionary*, Ambrose Bierce defines "connoisseur" with an anecdote of a winebibber who was in a railway accident. A glass of wine was put to his lips, and he said, "Pauillac, 1873," and expired. The English wine merchant Allan Sichel, a connoisseur with curiosity, once had claret for breakfast "to see what it had to say to me." An unusual reference to tasting wine can be found in William Butler Yeats' poem, "All Souls' Night," in which he says that it is a ghost's right "To drink from the wine-breath / While our gross palates drink from the whole wine."

The selections that follow are drawn from both fact and fiction, take place in the cellar and at the dinner table, and include some anecdotes about blind tastings, at which an expert is challenged to identify the vineyard and vintage of the wine put before him.

A Tasting Party

Vulgaria was now about to launch about twenty new wines upon the export market. Advance intelligence from old Baron Hisse la Juppe, the Military Attaché (who had practically lived down there while experiments were going on) suggested that something most promising had taken place. Vulgaria, he said (rather precariously), was on the point of exporting wines which would equal anything the French and Italians could do. . . . We were incredulous, of course, but were glad to assist in the send-off of the new wines. The whole Corps accepted the invitation to the *Vin d'Honneur* with alacrity.

The day dawned bright and fair, and it was a merry party of carefree dips who took the train north to the vineyards. The whole *vieillesse dorée* of diplomacy, old man. In sparkling trim. For once, the whole thing was admirably worked out; we were carried in vine-wreathed carriages to the great main cellars of the place—more like a railway tunnel than anything, where warm candle-light glowed upon twinkling glasses and white linen; where the music of minstrels sounded among the banks of flowers. . . . I must say, I was transported by the beauty of the scene. There lay the banks of labelled bottles, snoozing softly upon the trestles with the candles shining upon their new names. Our hosts made speeches. We cheered. Then corks began to pop and the wine-tasting began. One of the French specialists led us round. He tried to get us to take the thing rather too professionally—you know, shuffling it about in the mouth, cocking the chin up to the ceiling and then spitting out into a kind of stone draining-board. Well as you know, one is trained to do most things in the F.O. But not to spit out good wine. No. We simply wouldn't demean ourselves by this niggardly shuffling and spitting out. We swallowed. I think you would have done the same in our place. What we were given to taste, we tasted. But we put the stuff away.

And what stuff, my dear boy. Everything that Hisse la Juppe had said proved true. What wines! Wines to set dimples in the cheeks of the soul. Some were little demure white wines, skirts lifted just above the knee, as it were. Others just showed an elbow or an ankle. Others were as the flash of a nymph's thigh in the bracken. Wines in sables, wines in mink! What an achievement for the French! Some of the range of reds struck out all the deep bass organ-notes of passions—in cultured souls like ours. It was ripping. We expanded. We beamed. Life seemed awfully jolly all of a sudden. We rained congratulations upon our hosts as we gradually wound along the great cellars, tasting and judging. What wines! I couldn't decide for myself, but after many trials fell upon a red wine with a very good nose. You see, we each had to pick one, as a free crate of it was to be given to each member of the Corps. Sort of Advertisement.

And as we went along the French specialist enchanted us by reading out from his card the descriptions of the wines which we were trying. What poetry! I must hand it to the French, though they tend to make me suspicious in lots of ways. There was one, for example, a sort of hock, which was described as *"au fruité parfait, mais présentant encore une légère pointe de verdeur nullement désagréable."* Another was described as *"séveux et bien charpenté."* And then there was a sort of Vulgarian Meursault which was *"parfait de noblesse et de finesse, une petite splendeur."* I must say, for a moment one almost succumbed to culture, old man. The stuff was damned good. Soon we were all as merry as tom-tits, and I even smiled by mistake at the Bulgarian Chargé.

LAWRENCE DURRELL
Stiff Upper Lip

A Clever Parrot

I was having supper with [Herbert Beerbohm] Tree there one day, when the conversation turned upon wine and upon the extent to which the real connoisseur of wine could accurately distinguish between one vintage port and another.

"Well," observed Tree, "I had a sister-in-law who lived in the country and was very fond of Port, of which her husband had a fine cellar. And she possessed a remarkable parrot which shared her appreciation of good Port and which, when given a sip, could always identify it. 'Cockburn 1870,' the parrot would say, or 'Dow 1884.' One day a neighbour, who was sceptical about this, declared that he would produce a wine which my sister-in-law's parrot would not be able to place. In due course a decanter of Port appeared and, after sampling it, the parrot said, 'Cockburn 1878.' Whereupon the neighbour laughed and said: 'I'm afraid your parrot has let you down this time. I brought this Port at the grocer's shop in the village this afternoon.' My sister-in-law, feeling chagrined, but not at all disturbed, replied: 'No, there must be a mistake somewhere; my parrot could never be deceived to that extent.' And, being of a suspicious disposition, she went to the village shop next morning and asked for a bottle of their best Port. There was a slight panic and my sister-in-law, being a woman of strong character, eventually got the grocer to admit that he had been buying my uncle's vintage Port from his butler, and that the wine they had drunk the evening before was indeed Cockburn 1878.''

I asked Tree whether this phenomenal bird was still alive, as I would like to see it in action, but Tree said no, it had unfortunately died at about the same time as his sister-in-law. This story always intrigued me and, after Tree died, I met his charming niece, Marie Beerbohm, and asked her whether she knew the story. She went into peals of laughter and said: "That's so like Uncle Herbert! He had the story all wrong; it was my mother's *palate,* not her *parrot,* that was never deceived.''

VYVYAN HOLLAND
Time Remembered

An American Buyer

The waiter recommended the Auberge de l'Etoile, at Gevrey-Chambertin, a village of blessed associations. At the Auberge, I fell in with the greatest host of my life—a retired second lieutenant *de carrière* named Robaine, who had risen from the ranks in the course of thirty years in the colonial Army. Robaine took me to all the cellars of the commune and the communes adjoining, representing me as a rich American bootlegger come to the Côte d'Or, the Golden Slope of Burgundy, to buy wine for the cargo of a fabulous *bateau-cave*—a wine-cellar ship that would be sailed into New York Harbor and hoisted by night ("like a lifeboat but on a huge scale, understand?") into a skyscraper with a specially prepared false front. In that way, I got to drink more good wine than most men are able to pay for in their lives, and Robaine drank along with me— "pushing" the merchandise as he drank, and winking grossly at the proprietors of the vineyards, to indicate that he was conspiring with *them* to get a good price from *me*. . . .

One day, I varied the hospitality of the *cavistes* of Gevrey-Chambertin, Fixin, and Vougeot, the nearest communes, with a pedestrian expedition to Nuits-Saint-Georges, six miles away. There, in the restaurant of one of the two local hotels, I sat at the common table, where I was soon joined by a young man of my own age—a scholarly chap interested in foreigners—who said that he was bookkeeper-manager for a local wine merchant. Presently, he asked me how I liked the wine I had before me. The wine was a superb bottle of Grands-Echézeaux, but with a presence of mind learned from Robaine, I said that while it was good, it had limitations. Prodded, I even confessed to a trifle of disappointment. I said I had drunk as good bottles of Burgundy in Paris, even in Ireland; one expected that when one came to the birthplace of wine and asked the proprietress to furnish her best bottle . . . It was one of the most mendacious moments of my life.

The young Frenchman, appalled, said that he would speak to Madame. I begged him not to. He bit his lip. Finally, he said, "I cannot tolerate that you should carry away such a mediocre impression of our cellars. I invite you to sample what we call good wines at *our* place." Looking at the label on my now empty bottle—which was fortunately not that of his firm—he whispered, "Between you and me, the fellow who bottled that, although he is my boss's cousin, is a sharp chap. Doubtful integrity." After that, of course, he had to start me off on something that he considered better than the wine I had downed.

The afternoon I spent in the cellars of his firm was one of the happiest of my life. I regret that I have forgotten the firm's name. I was lucky to remember my own. After sipping the first glass he poured for me, I said, "It certainly beats the other for velvet, but the Echézeaux had a certain vigor, all the same, that is not to be despised." The next, I conceded, had an eternally youthful masculinity—but the Echézeaux, much as I had depreciated it, had had a certain originality. When I had drunk myself as tight as a New Year's Eve balloon, I admitted that the last wine he offered was indeed clearly superior to the bottle at the hotel. This was polite, but a lie. "*That*," I said, "is what I call Burgundy." It was a Romanée-Conti of some sort, and first-rate. "Well worth a voyage from North America to taste. Thunderously superior to that stuff I had with lunch." My benefactor was pale with gratitude. But the bottle at the hotel had been the best of the day.

A. J. LIEBLING
Between Meals

On the Evidences of Having Spat Too Close
in the Tasting-Room of a First-Growth Château

This purplish spot
Upon my shirt
That otherwise appears so neat—
This mark is not,
As *you* think, dirt:
No, it is '63 Lafite.

One couldn't swallow
This shrivelling brew,
Smelling of sawdust, harsh as brine.
The years that follow
Will turn it to
The fabled, violet-hinting wine.

Its price will rise
With every year
Far from my pocket as star from star;
And so I prize
The shirt I wear,
Stained with this honourable scar.

PETER DICKINSON

Tasting Tips

I am always sorry to come up again from a cellar. They have an architecture of their own, their own smell, temperature, light. They even have their own vegetation. There is a kind of fungus which sprouts from barrels, living exclusively on the fumes of good wine.

But we are not yet coming up from the cellar. It is during its schoolboy age—one, two, or three years—that the wine is judged and bought by the merchants. You too will be given wine to taste and judge; and the chief cellarman, not knowing how unimportant you are, will watch your face and listen to everything you say most seriously.

It takes twenty years of hard work to develop a discriminating palate for wine. Having been brought up on gin and beer and also being poor, I certainly will never know much more than that wine is good. But I must have tasted wines a score of times in the company of experts, and I developed a technique which deceived the most critical *Maître de chai* or *Chef de caves*. For what they are worth I will pass on my notes. (A *chai*, by the way, is a ground-cellar where barrels are kept; a *cave* is an underground cellar.)

The first rule is to say nothing. Actions and expressions are more significant and much safer than words. A mistake most amateurs make at first is to behave as if they were being judged by the wine and by the company. That may be true. But behave as if you were doing the interviewing—with dignity, courtesy, keen interest, and decision.

When the wine-glass is handed to you, do not take it by the stem but by the base, between forefinger and thumb. Bow to the man who gives it to you. Hold the glass up to the light, peer at it, frowning slightly and swilling the wine round and round in the glass. You must not spill it, of course, but it is most impressive if you can learn—with a glass of water in your bedroom—to make it swish round just below the rim, as fast as a motor-cyclist on the wall of death. Having done this, you study your wine-glass again, this time with the expression you might wear while reading small type. What you are looking at is the speed or slowness with which the last of the wine drains down the sides of the glass.

Then swish it round again and immediately afterwards cup your two hands about the bowl and bury your nose in it as if you were inhaling something for a cold. When you lift your face again the fumes of the wine, the bouquet at the back of your nose, will of their own accord have given you the right expression. But you may accentuate the effect by throwing up your eyes and then bowing your head. After this, swish the wine round the glass, frowning thoughtfully.

Now take a mouthful. A mistake most novices fall into is to take a sip, which gives them away at once. You must take a great hungry gulp of wine. But you don't swallow it, of course. You chew it. You push it forward through your teeth with the tongue and suck it back to the back-door of your nose. If the *Maître de chai* is watching you at this time, as he certainly will be, make sure that all your facial muscles are working. But look at nobody yourself. Your eyes must be far away in the dim recesses of the cellar.

You should practise this chewing, for you must be able to keep it up for a long time without swallowing, which is not easy. Your face works more and more strongly. You have now appeared to appreciate the wine with all your sensory nerves. You have reached your decision. The moment of climax has come.

The climax is the spit. Again and again I have seen a good

performance ruined by the spit. It is disastrous to bend down in a corner and merely open your mouth. It is little better to purse your lips as if you were getting rid of a cherry stone.

You have reached your decision, remember; so your spit must underline it. It must be bold and emphatic as an exclamation mark. The way to do it is to draw your shut lips wide as if you were about to whistle for a taxi, and with a tremendous flick of the tongue send the stuff jetting out so that it strikes the floor like a fist banged on a table. Then look round at everybody happily and proudly, because you have been allowed to share in a tremendous secret.

If you are unable to perfect the spit, then swallow. But don't do it steadily. Do it as if carried away by passion, and afterwards slap your chest gaily to emphasize your independence. But there are disadvantages in swallowing if there are many wines to taste during the morning. There are always disadvantages about being carried away by passion.

All this, you notice, has been done without a word. Only at the moment of leaving the cellar need you speak. You step impulsively up to the *Maître de chai* and wring his hand and mutter, *"Merci, Maître, merci, merci,"* then hurry out-of-doors.

In the sunlight there may be discussion about the wines. This need not alarm you, for your sense of hearing has been as busy as the rest and you have probably overheard some safe opinions. *"Très souple"* is generally a safe one. But unless asked a direct question, it is best to maintain a sphinx-like silence, smiling knowingly at the whole world from half-shut eyes.

J. M. SCOTT
The Vineyards of France

A Critical Group

Wing opened the crucial bottle and sloshed wine into the glasses, with no more to-do than if it were water from the tap. And with no more to-do it was sipped.

"Dryer," said Jule, who was the youngest.

"Steely," said Cleve.

The bouquet was unwavering. It even seemed to increase in the glass. Port gave a nod and his customary grunt, then looked at Blanqui, who was the oldest, who had tasted more Regolberg than anyone in the den. Cleve held his breath. Alda had gone back to the hybrid she had grown four years ago, which had fullness, crossed into that, and come into something else. It had strangeness. And it also had struck him as would a face vanishing in a mist after it had looked at him with familiarity. He was nervous. It crossed his mind that Alda, too, was over-tense. She went to the window and without sound adjusted the slats of the French blind. But she made the room neither lighter nor darker. The least change would have disturbed Blanqui's silent interrogation in the corridor of his memory. The others, not touching their glasses, remained as still as chess players who had made their last move.

Cleve stared at Blanqui, and waited. The wine was already beyond the Chardonnay he had tasted with Port in the old farmer's bower up at the skyline. And when Blanqui spoke, the verdict would be true. He had his vanity. But in greater measure he had wonder and rectitude. He raised his glass and tasted again, as if he were nibbling at the edge of a dream. Then he set down his glass, and without change in expression filled his pipe.

"That pretty near it?" asked Port, holding out a light.

"*Oui*," nodded the Swiss, bending his face to the match. "More near." He held up his gnarled hands and fanned them apart. "Li'l bit more full—li'l bit more stone taste, and rocks and flowers—and she pretty near there."

He sank back, holding his pipe, and exhaled with satisfaction.

"So I thought," smiled Alda. "But I wasn't quite sure. There's a little more grafting I want to do. Nurse it along to more sweet-acid. I think I know now."

"Well," said the schoolmaster, "I can't say anything. It's going too deep for me. But I know—I think I know—what you're groping for."

"I've a dozen vines ripening to what I had in mind," she said. "And perhaps—next year—"

"It's been a long journey for you," said Mr. Wedge.

"A long journey for Montino," she smiled. "I would like to bring it back—the farm and the pasture—to where he remembered Montino at its best, long before it was changed."

IDWAL JONES
The Vineyard

Ways of Drinking

The act itself of drinking is varied divers manner of ways. I will allege a few circumstances: As for example, it pleaseth some to lift up the glass unto their mouth. Others hang down their lip, that they might drink with their heads inclining downward. Some join two cups one upon another, and drink them together. Others take not up the cup in their hand, but enwreathe it in the crook of their arm. There are, who set the glass to their brow, that by little and little it might descend down by their nose as by a conduit to their mouth; wherein such men have a singular faculty above others, who are well nos'd, as having their noses bending down with a beaker after the manner of a parrot's bill.

RICHARD BRATHWAITE
1626

Joyce's Favorite

He was sensitive enough to her complaints, however, to decide to give up absinthe, which he liked very much, in favor of wine. He did not care for red wine, which he said was 'beefsteak,' and greatly preferred white, which was 'electricity.' Several evenings were spent in tasting various *crus*, until one night drinking with Ottocaro Weiss, who had returned from the army in January 1919, he sampled a white Swiss wine called Fendant de Sion. This seemed to be the object of his quest, and after drinking it with satisfaction, he lifted the half-emptied glass, held it against the window like a test tube, and asked Weiss, 'What does this remind you of?" Weiss looked at Joyce and at the pale golden liquid and replied, '*Orina.*' '*Si,*' said Joyce laughing, '*ma di un'arciduchessa*' ('yes, but an archduchess's'). From now on the wine was known as the Archduchess, and is so celebrated in *Finnegans Wake*.

RICHARD ELLMANN
James Joyce

Taster's Choice

My favorite story of wine guessing games, because it distills the ethos of certain wine-trade encounters, is told by Peter Sichel about his cousin Charles. Guests at a luncheon in Paris, they were asked to guess the wine. Almost without pausing Charles identified it as La Tâche '29, and their host congratulated him. When they left the house Peter turned to his cousin and asked why he had answered as he had, adding, "The wine was no more La Tâche than it was 1929. It wasn't even Burgundy."

"I just wanted to see if D—— is really as excessively polite as everyone says he is," said Charles.

GERALD ASHER

Blind Tasting

It is my firm opinion (one of the few these days unwhittled by doubts!) that to assess the qualities of a wine by tasting it completely blind, without any hint of what it might be, is the most useful and salutory discipline that any self-respecting taster can be given. It is not infrequently the most humiliating. The first thing it does is to concentrate the thoughts, and expose fresh and unprejudiced senses to the problem of analysing the colour, bouquet and flavour. To know what the wine is before one starts is like reading the end of a detective novel first; it satisfies the curiosity but dampens the interest.

Should blind tastings and guessing games be conducted at the dinner table? This is perhaps the most vexed question of all. I am sure that my colleagues in the English wine trade, particularly fellow Masters of Wine, will be the first to agree that it is one of the hazards of their occupation to be expected to 'perform' before any anonymous looking glass of wine, and before only too un-anonymous and hideously expectant hosts and fellow guests: to pronounce vineyard, vintage and the name of the cellar-master in ten seconds flat. It is not that it *cannot* be done, even in this time. It can, but only in rare and exceptional circumstances, and I exclude all known methods of cheating, like bribing the butler. The point is that unless there is an immediate and quite positive 'click' of recognition the only alternative is an extremely elaborate round-the-houses process of elimination, an intellectual exercise which takes time and may well be acutely boring for those waiting and watching. At a dinner party, particularly, the surest way of offending one's hostess is to undergo these mental contortions, letting one's meal go cold, and possibly even delaying subsequent courses.

Broad-minded professionals don't mind making fools of themselves in the company of others in the business. At least, they reassure themselves, their friends in the trade *know* how really difficult it is to identify wines, and they all have comforting knowledge of their common manifold blunders. It is another thing to be ex-

posed before, and caught out by, amateurs—perhaps their own customers—who simply don't understand the complexity and problems involved.

I personally subscribe to 'blind' tasting, at least of the principal
wines, at a dinner party, but only on the following conditions:

☐ that the occasion is an appropriate one—good and carefully
planned wines with appropriate food.

☐ that the company should be like-minded, otherwise the
whole thing becomes a bit tedious and unbalanced; off-putting for
expert and non-expert alike.

☐ that reasonable time be allowed for thinking about the wine.
The host and hostess must time the service of wine and food to
accommodate this. *Nothing* is more irritating and fatuous, in my
opinion, than for a host to say 'what is it?' and then blurt out the
answer in whole or in part before one has had a chance to examine
the wine properly.

☐ that the length of time is *not* dragged out and that one is
never forced to a complete and final answer if one is not naturally
forthcoming. Indeed, in mixed (not just 'genders,' but professional
and lay) company I think it is probably tactless of the host to try to
extract nearest answers in a competitive manner. If people *want* to
be sporting, let them have a go. (This can be a good thing, for one
is stimulated into thinking along fresh lines by hearing other people's reactions, and one finds perhaps a new point of view engen-
dered.) It should be remembered on the other hand, that some people can no more guess wines in public than they can stand on a
table and sing; their minds become blank as panic sets in!

MICHAEL BROADBENT
Wine Tasting

Alexis Lichine Challenged

Connoisseurs are forever engaging in the pastime of "guessing"
wines—their year and their place of origin—which is an exclusive
form of entertainment, as appealing to wine experts as scaling a
peak in the Himalayas is to mountain climbers. Lichine has guessed
a good many wines, for both pleasure and profit, and he has been
known to make mistakes, since it is easy to be deceived by a wine
that, for instance, has been prematurely bottled, or has freakishly
failed to run true to type, or is too young to possess the identifying
characteristics that appear with age. But he has also come through

with some memorable demonstrations of guessing, among them one he put on in Bordeaux a couple of years ago at a dinner of local winegrowers. Given an unlabelled bottle of wine to guess, he was told only that it was true and that it was a product of one of the great years. "You pinpoint your wine by a process of elimination, starting with the region and working down through the district to the commune," Lichine explained to a friend after the test was over. "So I identified this wine first as a Bordeaux, then as a Médoc, and then as a Saint-Estèphe. After that, I put the geographical problem aside temporarily and turned to the question of the year. It wasn't one of the '40s or '50s—that was elementary—and I knew it wasn't a '34 or a '37, the two great years of that decade. It just didn't have the right characteristics. And gradually I became convinced that it could only be from one of the four great years of the '20s—a '24, a '26, a '28, or a '29. I eliminated '26 and '28, because the wines of those years have a pronounced hardness and this wine didn't. It might be a weak '24, or a soft '29. I tasted again. The wine was full and round and slowly dying out, which is typical of a '29, so I eliminated the '24. Now, then, where did it come from, exactly? There are only three great châteaux in the commune of Saint-Estèphe—Chateau Calon-Ségur, Château Montrose, and Château Cos-d'Estournel. In a second, I eliminated Montrose. Thirty seconds more, and I eliminated Calon-Ségur. I can't really explain what goes on in my head at such times. My brain is filled with names and years, and the ones I eliminate just drop out, as if they were falling through a strainer, and in the end only one name and one year remain. So I said, 'This is a Cos-d'Estournel '29.' And it was."

JOSEPH WECHSBERG
"A Dreamer of Wine"

Mirandol '93

The proprietor brought tenderly to the table a black bottle in a wicker cradle, and laid it down as though it were a baby and he its loving nurse.

"I thought that it would be appropriate on this night of all nights," said Hanaud, "if we drank a bottle of old Mirandol. It is a second growth, to be sure, but according to many judges should be classed with the first. You shall tell me!"

Yes, it was Mr. Ricardo's turn to tell. He was on his own ground. The red wines of the Médoc! Not for nothing had he travelled once a year from Bordeaux to Arcachon! Hanaud tipped a tablespoonful first into his own glass and then filled Mr. Ricardo's. Mr. Ricardo beamed. Good manners and good wine—could there be a more desirable conjunction? He held the glass up to the light. The wine was ruby-red, ruby-clear. He lowered it to his nostrils and savoured its aroma.

"Exquisite," he said.

Then religiously he drank of it.

"Adorable," he cried; and drank again. He swam upwards into rosy clouds. That little affair at Suvlac would be settled in no time. "A wine for two friends to drink in a rapturous silence by the side of an historic square in la belle France."

It was a pity that he must end his flight of poesy with so dreadful a banality as "la belle France." But that was his way, and Hanaud took the compliment to himself as though he *was* la belle France all in one. And that was Hanaud's way, too.

"The cellar here is not so bad," he remarked.

Ricardo drank again, and after much rolling of the wine upon his tongue, put down the glass with a vigour which threatened to break the stem.

"It is '93," he declared; and Hanaud bowed in admiration of the subtle palate of his friend. Oh, certainly, Mr. Ricardo reflected, stretching out his legs beneath the table, with the great detective of France to begin with, and a friend who could announce right off the year of a '93 claret to help him, the mystery of Suvlac was as good as solved, the criminals practically in the dock.

A. E. W. MASON
The Prisoner in the Opal

A Delicate Palate

It is in the mouth that one may perhaps trace an aspect of T. E. [Lawrence] that is more misunderstood than any other—an extreme sensuousness that is entirely unsensual, in the accepted meaning. . . . He has occasionally tasted wine, but prefers water as being more varied in flavor. This is not a jest: his senses are very highly developed—but different. He says himself that he hunts *sensation*— in the deeper sense of the word. . . . in his judgment "the more elemental you can keep sensations, the better you feel them." A taste for wine mars the more subtle appreciation for water.

LIDDELL HART
Colonel Lawrence

A Claret Party

At that time we were a little ashamed of ourselves, and I thought, when I next saw Brown, that he was going a roundabout way to atone. "I'm wondering about enlarging the claret party this year." Brown's claret party took place each year at the beginning of June. "I'm inclined to think it would be rather statesman-like. After all, we've got to live with the present society even if we slide Jago in. Mind you, I'm all against trying to make arrangements with the other side over the election. But I should regard it as reasonable to remind them that we're still capable of enjoying their company. It would be a decent gesture to invite some of them to the party."

And so the claret party consisted of Winslow, Crawford, Pilbrow, Roy Calvert, me and Brown himself. Like so much of that summer, it tantalised me. The night was tranquil, the college had never looked more beautiful. I should be lucky if I had the chance to drink wine so good again. But Roy's melancholy had got worse, and all the time I was fearing one of his outbursts. Most of that night, I could think of nothing else.

Twice I managed to signal to Roy that he must keep quiet. He was enough in control of himself to do so, though he was affected by the sight of another unhappy man. For Winslow was worried by his son's examination, which had just finished. As soon as the party began, Brown asked him how the boy had got on, and Winslow snubbed him:

"My dear Tutor, I cannot answer for the prospects of the semi-illiterate. I hope the wretched youth managed to read the questions."

Roy heard the sadness in that answer, and it nearly touched the trigger of his own. But, to my momentary relief, we settled down to wine. It was ten o'clock, but the sun had only just set, and over the roof opposite Brown's window there was a brilliant afterglow. From one of the May week balls, we could just hear the throbbing of a band. There was the slightest of breezes stirring, and on it came the scent of acacia from the court beneath.

Pilbrow took charge of the party. He was an authority on wine, and had been Brown's master. His bald head gleamed in the fading light, shone when, towards midnight, Brown switched on the lamps; the ruddy cheeks flushed, but otherwise Pilbrow did not change at all as one decanter after another was left empty. He fixed one of us with a lively brown eye and asked what we noticed at each sip—at the beginning, middle and end of each sip. The old man rang all the changes possible with ten bottles of claret. When we were half-way through, he said with extreme firmness:

"I don't think any of you would ever be quite first-class. I give our host the benefit of the doubt—"

"I don't claim it," said Brown. "I shall never be anything like as good as you."

Brown insisted on drinking to young Winslow's success.

"Let me fill your glass. Which shall it be? You've gone a bit light on the Latour '24."

We each had ten glasses in front of us, labelled to match the decanters. Brown selected the right one from Winslow's set.

"That will do very nicely. If you please. If you please."

Crawford surveyed the glasses, the decanters, the gleam of crystal and silver, the faces all flushed, the scene of luxury and ease. Out of the window there was still a faint glow in the west. Girls' laughter came up from the court, as a party moved out of college to a ball.

C. P. SNOW
The Masters

Practice, Practice

As tastes and smells reside not in the objects themselves, but in the senses by which they are perceived, so they are liable to be modified by the habits and conditions of these organs. The difference of tastes, in this view of the subject, is proverbial; and much of the diversity undoubtedly proceeds from the way in which the palate has been exercised. Thus, strong liquors blunt its sensibility, and disqualify it for the perception of the more delicate flavours of the lighter wines. A person accustomed only to bad wines will often form but a very erroneous estimate of the better growths, and sometimes, even, give the preference to the former. Whole nations may be occasionally misled by this prejudice.

ALEXANDER HENDERSON
1824

A Little Experiment

The same thought struck us simultaneously, 'Was there any connection between the vintage of olive oil and that of wine?' And with this thought the idea of vintage sardines came into being.

Here were the sardines, for the past twenty years at least, on Mr Moar's shelves, waiting for our experiment. The sardines were incidental; it is true that they contributed to the oil, which would hardly have been preserved but for them, in airtight tins. I am no ichthyologist, but I am pretty sure that the weather in the Mediterranean Sea and the Atlantic Ocean does not make much difference to the fish in them, and he would be a very clever naturalist who could distinguish the sardine of one year from that of another.

But the oil was another matter, and we reasoned that if the alternation of sun and rain could so affect the grape as to cause the wine made from it to be of really excellent quality or very poor, it might easily affect the olives as well. So we went to see Mr Moar and we each bought one tin of all the sardines available back to 1906. Mr Moar had only begun collecting them a short time before, so he had not got every year. I think someone must have given him the idea and helped him with his stock; still, we had enough to experiment upon. . . .

We now became more critical and we wondered whether the olive-oil harvest years followed the great years of any particular wine—Sauternes, for instance. This was a very interesting theory, but we were not going to become confused into wishful thinking and, proceeding on the principle that sardines tinned early in any particular year would have been put into the previous year's oil, we selected eight tins of the years between 1919 and 1930 and removed their dates, substituting signs by which we alone could know them. We then collected a symposium of gourmets, consisting of André Simon, Col. Ian Campbell and Barry Neame and asked them to adjudicate.

I must say that a feast of sardines, particularly when helped down, as this one was, by Sauternes, sounds a little bilious, but we had selected men of strong stomach, particularly André Simon, who once confessed to me that he had eaten six dozen Colchester oysters with brown bread and butter and goblets of champagne as a preliminary snack before a city banquet. But that is another story. Anyway, they unanimously placed the sardines in the following order, with the rest nowhere: 1921, 1929, 1924, 1914; thus *exactly following the years of good Sauternes.*

VYVYAN HOLLAND
"Sardines and Sauternes"

Tasting Note

It was in Saumur, where we were tasting wines with a group of wine merchants from the Isle of Jersey, that we heard one of the most amusing phrases to describe taste which has ever come our way. The year in question had no distinction we could discover, and we handed the problem to a colleague.

He sniffed, tasted, considered; then, with a slow nod of agreement, said: "Nothing there—like kissing your aunt."

JULIAN STREET
Table Topics

A Cynic

In olden times, when I was dock clerk and salesman for one of the first port and sherry houses, I occasionally amused myself by experimenting upon the truth of the wonderfully correct taste attributed to a few old stagers, whose opinion was regarded as law, and whose wisdom and judgment were shown, like Lord Burleigh's, by a shake of the head. I remember three constant frequenters of the docks, Joe Reynolds, Samuel Linnott, and John Colgrave, who used to express themselves in their peculiar oracular way, so authoritatively, that I resolved to put their judgment to the test. Often when they were laying down the law, and discovering differences in casks of the same mark, which I knew to have been shipped as exactly the same, I used to tell the cooper to draw two glasses from the same pipe, and to hand them as if they were from different numbers. I may say that the trick upon them was invariably successful; for they were sure, after tasting, and retasting, and much profound thought, to pronounce the verdict that, although similar, one possessed rather more of this, or that, than the other. I kept my own counsel, but was convinced forty years ago, and the conviction remains to this day, that in wine-tasting and wine-talk there is an enormous amount of humbug.

T. G. SHAW
Wine, the Vine, and the Cellar
1864

12

Waiter, the Wine List!

The selections in this chapter are perhaps unfairly chosen, since they mostly involve imperious sommeliers or careless waiters. The occasions when a bottle was properly presented and thoroughly enjoyed seem to have found their way into other parts of this book. One exception is Harry Waugh's account of ordering good Burgundy in a Bordeaux restaurant; another is J.-K. Huysmans' description, from his novel *Against Nature*, of Des Esseintes' visit to an English wine bar in Paris.

For reasons of space, I left out a long chapter titled "Felix Poubelle 1884" from *Trent's Own Case*, a mystery novel by E. C. Bentley and H. Warner Allen. It concerns Trent's search for the restaurant in which a particular bottle of old champagne had been served to the murder victim and includes this description of a wine waiter: "He was grey-haired, with the white whiskers appropriate to his office; and he appeared to belong to that nameless tribe which talks all languages equally fluently and incorrectly, and has none of its own."

Let me add two anecdotes to those that follow. I found a reference to a scene in a recent novel, which I was unable to track down, in which the sommelier brings out a bottle and shows it to the host, who says, "Yes, that's nice and full."

The second confrontation with a sommelier is one at which I was present. I was a guest at a fancy restaurant, and the sommelier went through the entire ritual of serving a bottle of wine, ending, of course, by pouring some into my host's glass. He tasted the wine, turned to the sommelier, and said, "You win."

A Good Question

Reluctantly the Captain entered the ship's dining room for the second sitting at nine o'clock, expecting the worst. He regarded, smelled, and tasted a glass of available red wine. "This is perfectly sound Algerian wine," he said to the wine steward. "Why should they put this Beaujolais label on the bottle?"

"Our passengers enjoy trying to pronounce the French, sir," the wine steward explained.

RICHARD CONDON
Arigato

A Little Knowledge . . .

Talking of ordinary, or more properly *ordinaire*, as the Bordelais habitually term such wines, calls to my mind a story told by my father of dining at a certain London restaurant. As usual, he called for a wine list and turned at once to the "Clarets": he was highly amused to see the list of clarets headed by

Bordeaux, ordinaire, 2s. 6d. a bottle
Bordeaux, très ordinaire, 3s. 6d. a bottle

I. M. CAMPBELL
Wayward Tendrils of the Vine

A Delicate Decision

The restaurant was simple and expensive, designed for eating, not for gazing at the decor. Partly because he felt festive, and partly to impress Jemima, Jonathan ordered a bottle of Lafite.

"May I suggest 1959?" the wine steward asked, with the rhetorical assumption that his guidance was impeccable.

"We're not French," Jonathan said, not taking his eyes from Jemima.

"Sir?" The arch of the eyebrow had that blend of huff and martyrdom characteristic of upper echelon servants.

"We're not French. Prenubile wines hold no fascination for us. Bring a '53 if you have it, or a '55 if not."

As the steward departed, Jemima asked, "Is this Lafite something special?"

"You don't know?"

"No."

Jonathan signaled the steward to return. "Forget the Lafite. Bring us an Haut-Brion instead."

Assuming the change was a fiscal reconsideration, the steward made an elaborate production of scratching the Lafite off his pad and scribbling down the Haut-Brion.

"Why did you do that?" Jemima asked.

"Thrift, Miss Brown. Lafite is too expensive to waste."

"How do you know, I might have enjoyed it."

"Oh, you'd have enjoyed it all right. But you wouldn't have appreciated it."

Jemima looked at him narrowly. "You know? I have this feeling you're not a nice person."

TREVANIAN
The Eiger Sanction

Provincial Logic

The great staple of the Mountain States, of course, is still red meat. And it is expected to be washed down with beer or bourbon.

When two city rubes recently ordered handsome T-bones at the Hilltop Tavern in Hardin, Mont., for example, they inquired whether the restaurant had a bottle of California burgundy to go with it. The waitress looked dubious. "Yeah, but it's not open," she said.

The New York Times
1976

The Good Old Days

Before the war there were *bistros* (and many of them) in the south of France, where wine was sold by the hour rather than by the glass or bottle; you paid four or five *sous* an hour and drank as much as your conscience (or your wife) would let you. Naturally, the wine was pretty bad—it was new and rough and it tasted of the grape. But, after all, what could you expect for a nickel an hour?

FRANK SCHOONMAKER
Come with Me Through France

A Word of Advice

I see that my time has come to talk about wine.

There is one only course to pursue if you wish to taste the best wines of France. I have drunk French wines ever since I was eight and ought therefore to know all about it. It is to ask the proprietor of any restaurant in which you may eat, what wines he suggests should go with the dishes you have ordered . . . Of course if you go to gilded and famous palaces you will get your deserts as a fool. . . . Nevertheless, wanting one day to impress a publisher, I took him to a famous place on the Quais and gave him *caneton Rouennais au sang*—a gross dish whose distensive powers I detest. And I asked the proprietor what wine to order with that horror. He said: You will take my *vin d'Arbois* 1929. . . . According to the wine-publicity-agents *vin d'Arbois* is a third or fourth grade wine. I have known really great connoisseurs who have never tasted it. . . . Even Mr Shand confesses to that. . . .

I looked then at the wine-card and finding that that wine cost only seven francs I asked that proprietor if he could not make it something a little more expensive. He said:

"You will take my *vin d'Arbois* 1929."

I explained that my fortune for the next year or so depended on my giving my friend either something out of a gilded bottle or the disgusting treacle they call *Château Yquem*. I said I knew it was a shame to disgrace his restaurant in the eyes of the connoisseurs who were dining all round us. I apologised from the depths of my heart but he could see my predicament. He said:

"You will take my *vin d'Arbois* 1929. . . . Or a carafe of my *vin ordinaire*."

The contract that that publisher offered me was so derisory that my income ever since has been much reduced.

FORD MADOX FORD
Provence

The Syncopated Song of a Sour Sommelier

They gaze a little blankly at the wine-list that I hand 'em
 And run up and down the pages with their thumbs.
I long to get a sign that they really dig the wine,
 But it's always just the same when it comes—
Neglectful of the claims of such estimable names
 As Deidesheimer, Dão, Desmirail,
They choose a wine at random (the way I understand 'em)
 And ask 'Is it dry?'

 Is it dry, man?
 Is it dry?
 They haven't got a clue what it means.
They seem to think that dryness in a wine is meant to rate as
A kind of handy measure of its gastronomic status.
 Still, it's no use arguing with customers;
 It only makes embarrassing scenes;
So, smothering my feelings with a veil of British phlegm,
I tell myself, Well *really*, if you have to deal with *them*,
Then everything's the driest up to Château Yquem—
 Yeah, it's dry, man, dry!

I'd be patient with a customer who blinded me with science;
 I'd pardon him the gibberish he talked
If now and then a fellow would just say 'Is it mellow?'
 'Is it fruity?' 'Is it smooth?' or 'Is it corked?'
I read gastronomic books in attempts to get my hooks
 In some adjectives for customers to try,

But I can't exact compliance from my monoglottal clients
   Who simply ask 'Is it dry?'

      Is it dry, man?
      Is it dry?
   Well, it's dry, in another sense, for me
To try to be a teacher to a creature in a rut
Who couldn't tell a Forster from a fizzy Something Brutt.*
   But I'll reap my reward in the hereafter
      When the Lord has dried up the sea.†
   I shall take my *carte des nectars* that I've had since Judgement Day
To where four angel-oenophiles are ordering *déjeuner*—
André Simon, Warner Allen, Raymond Postgate, Cyril Ray—
   And they'll know what's dry!

                                                    B. A. YOUNG

* As the poet Kipling hath it.
† cf. Revelation xxi. 1.

The Last Word

ROBERT: Cherries for Madame, and for me (*greedily*) wild straw-berries with thick cream. Send me the wine waiter. Mitsou, shall we have burgundy, claret or champagne?

MITSOU: It's all the same to me; I don't care what countries wine comes from.

ROBERT: I think they've got a very attractive claret here; it has a light bouquet of coffee and of violets in the glass.

MITSOU (*horrified*): How dreadful! Fancy a thing like that here!

ROBERT: I'm not suggesting burgundy, which wouldn't go with lobster, and is too full for the chicken—

MITSOU: Does burgundy sparkle?

ROBERT: People sometimes make it do so. But there. I can see we shall end up having champagne.

MITSOU: Oo, yes! A champagne that doesn't taste! (*The wine waiter is present and visible, but he has long lost any interest in the conversation.*)

ROBERT (*shocked*): That doesn't taste! Mitsou, where on earth were you brought up?

MITSOU (*annoyed, because of the wine waiter*): Not in a wineshop, anyway.

                                                    COLETTE
                                                    Mitsou

Ordering Carefully

The real reason, however, that Frank preferred Nino to all the other waiters in "Pothillippo's" establishment was that he liked the sound of the word "Nino," and pronounced it beautifully.

"Nino!" Frank would cry, in a high, strange, and rather womanish voice—"Nino!"

"Si, signor," Nino would breathe unctuously, and would then stand in an attitude of heavy and prayerful adoration, awaiting the young lord's next commands.

"Nino," Frank would then go on in the tone and manner of a sensuous and weary old-world sophisticate. "Quel vin avez-vous? . . . Quel vin—rouge—du—très—bon. Vous—comprenez?" said Frank, using up in one speech most of his French words, but giving a wonderful sense of linguistic mastery and complete eloquence in two languages.

"Mais si, signor!" Nino would answer immediately, skilfully buttering Frank on both sides—the French and the Italian—with three masterly words.

"Le Chianti est *très, très* bon! . . . C'est parfait, monsieur," he whispered, with a little ecstatic movement of his fingers. "Admirable!"

"Bon," said Frank with an air of quiet decision. "Alors, Nino," he continued, raising his voice as he pronounced these two words, which were among his favorites. "Alors, une bouteille du Chianti—n'est-ce pas—"

THOMAS WOLFE
Of Time and the River

Wining Boy

Hilma Burt's was on the corner of Custom House and Basin Street, next door to Tom Anderson's Saloon—Tom Anderson was the king of the district and ran the Louisiana legislature, and Hilma Burt was supposed to be his old lady. Hers was no doubt one of the best-paying places in the city and I thought I had a very bad night when I made under a hundred dollars. Very often a man would come into the house and hand you a twenty- or forty- or a fifty-dollar note, just like a match. Beer sold for a dollar a bottle. Wine from five to ten, depending on the kind you bought. Wine flowed much more than water—the kind of wine I'm speaking about I don't mean sauterne or nothing like that, I mean champagne, such as Cliquot and Mumm's Extra Dry. And right there was where I got my new name—Wining Boy.

When the place was closing down, it was my habit to pour these partly finished bottles of wine together and make up a new bottle from the mixture. That fine drink gave me a name and from that I made a tune that was very, very popular in those days . . .

> I'm a wining boy, don't deny my name,
> I'm a wining boy, don't deny my name.

ALAN LOMAX
Mister Jelly Roll

A Brave Man

In France the good provincial restaurants usually concentrate on the local wine, whatever it may be and, in such cases the selection from other districts is more often than not pretty second-rate. The Hotel Splendid is a remarkable exception to this rule, for there are some fabulous red Burgundies in the cellar. I hardly dare mention the word Burgundy in Bordeaux, but the short list is almost past belief. Glancing casually through it a year or so ago, my eyes were riveted by seeing Château Gris 1937, a property that is part of the Nuits les Crots vineyard of Nuits St. Georges. Feeling very guilty and disloyal to Bordeaux I ordered a bottle. I was well rewarded though for it was sheer heaven, and because of the lack of demand, the wine was offered at an absurdly low price. I feel sure that few of the great restaurants of the Côte d'Or can offer anything much finer than this 1937 Château Gris, and certainly not at so modest a price as 28 francs a bottle.

Although a guest on this occasion I was asked to choose the wine, and I am afraid there was rather a shocked silence from my Bordelais host as I asked the sommelier to decant a red Burgundy! Quite naturally, both the Burgundians and the Bordelais are rather chauvinistic concerning their own wines; no true Bordelais would ever dream of drinking any red wine other than claret in his own citadel, consequently this fine Burgundy has lain untouched in this cellar for many years. When the bottle arrived at the table it gave me a wicked enjoyment to watch our Bordelais host having, admittedly somewhat reluctantly, to concede the fine quality of this Château Gris!

On another evening, and again to the consternation of other Bordelais friends, we tried a further bottle of this same wine and drank it alongside a delightful Latricières Chambertin of the same year. To say they were astonished is to put it mildly. These two wines are listed at about two-thirds of the price of the second and third growth clarets of 1959. Of course I was foolish not to keep this information to myself, because other delights such as Musigny 1929 are still to be tried. I must return to Bordeaux quickly before all these gems have disappeared.

HARRY WAUGH
Bacchus on the Wing

Château Pavie 1914 . . . I think

I will tell you what Mr Belloc calls a Cautionary Tale that when you next visit France will be worth to you ten times the library subscription on which you have obtained this book. . . .

It was before the Crisis. . . . I was at Villeneuve les Avignon with crowds of charming American friends settled around the immediate landscape. . . . There came down a lady almost *too* generous and almost *too* beautiful from the countryside where the Studebakers grow.

Nothing would content her but that she must take out and treat the whole crowd. . . . That was all right. . . . I led them to the Avignon tavern where you can get the best wine in all Provence. Then the disaster occurred. That lady who was beautiful enough to hold the eyes of everyone in that place of entertainment would have it that we must drink champagne. We must have champagne: she had never heard of anyone dining without champagne. Champagne it must be. . . .

You should have seen the incredulous faces of my Avignonnais friends sitting round. . . . Champagne may be all very well in its place—but I do not know what may be its place. . . . Perhaps at a very young child's birthday party with an iced cake or after two, at a dance, as a before-supper cocktail. . . .

But on the next day came the tragedy. . . . Wanting to be quiet after that whirlwind I lunched at the same place. It was a special occasion and I ordered—there were two of us—a famous Bordeaux, bottled at the Château in the year 1914. . . . I had eaten at that place often enough to know its wine card and the proprietor very well. The sommelier however was new.

Now mark. . . . That fellow brought the wine in its wicker carrier, already uncorked. He showed me the cork which had the brand of the Château all right. He made to pour out the wine but as we were still eating an exquisite *soupe de poisson*—which is one of the specialties of Avignon—and drinking one of the little local white wines which goes very agreeably with fish and saffron, I told him I would pour the wine myself later.

Now listen very attentively. . . . When with reverential hand I tried to pour out that wine . . . *it would not pour*. . . . In the neck of the bottle was part of a perfectly new cork.

I called the proprietor who, as I have said, was a very old friend of mine and signed to him to pour out the wine, showing him at the same time the Château cork and the date on the label of the bottle. . . . I did not say a word. . . . He peeped into the neck of the bottle.

I have never seen a man become so suddenly distracted or pallid. He caught at his throat. . . . He really caught at his throat. . . . When he was a little recovered he shouted at that sommelier in a voice of shaky thunder to fetch the cellarman.

That procession of two threaded its way between the tables of the appalled diners. And M. le Patron shouted:

"Take off your aprons. . . . There is the door!"

Then, as their crestfallen shades obscured the doorway, he went himself to his deep cellar and came back, bearing with his own hands a bottle of Château Pavie 1914.

I don't know if you see the point. Americans are said never to be able to see an Englishman's point and the English never to see the point of any story at all for a week, when they telegraph to the teller the two vocables "Ha! Ha!"

The point isn't merely that that sommelier, taking me for an ignorant Briton, had, with the connivance of the cellarman, poured a bottle of local wine at frs 1.90 into an empty Château Pavie bottle which he had re-corked with a *bouchon* so new that, unknown to him, half of it had remained, when he re-uncorked it, in the neck of the bottle. . . . Château Pavie is a very expensive wine when it is of the year 1914 so he and the cellarman would have made a handsome profit. . . . They would of course have reserved several authentic corks from real bottles previously opened. . . .

But you had seen that already. . . . There is of course the other point that the sommelier had never seen me before, being new, and had observed me the day before to drink champagne—but positively *champagne!* with a titianesque Bacchante from Studebakerville. So naturally he had taken me for one of those other Anglo-Saxon "brutes."

But even *that* is not the point. . . . *Je vous le donne en mille!* . . . The real point is that, if that bottle *had* poured I might have gone through all the ceremonies of turning the wine under my nose, swirling it round in the glass, regarding the light through, and finally sipping and respiring it. . . . And might quite possibly have been taken in and have lectured my unfortunate—for once Antipodean!—disciple as to its colour, bouquet, body and the rest. Do not think that that would have been the result merely of snobbishness. . . . I do really know something of Bordeaux and Mosel wines. I am not one of the great writers on wines, like Mr William Bird or Mr Shand or M. Monot. . . . But Château Pavie is my favourite wine and I ought to know something about it. And you have to consider that I was in a restaurant that I had known for years; that I was entirely convinced of the probity of the proprietor and the excellence of his kitchen and cellar. And who can really pledge his personal taste against such overwhelming things as the cork and bottle of the Château? Not I!

I should probably have smelt, tasted, and looked through that wine and have thought that there was something the matter with my liver and eyes. . . . And I should have delivered a perfectly correct lecture on Château Pavie to that disciple from down under . . . who perhaps would not have got any harm from it.

FORD MADOX FORD
Provence

Service à la Mode

A gourmet ordered with dinner in a restaurant a bottle of magnificent old vintage Burgundy. The waiter who brought it handled the bottle carelessly.

"Look here," exclaimed the gourmet, "you haven't shaken that bottle, have you?"

"No, sir," replied the waiter, "but I will." And he suited the action to the word.

JULIAN STREET
Table Topics

Literal Minded

It was early in 1918. I was entertaining at a certain Club two brother officers and had ordered a bottle, an Imperial Quart, of Krug Champagne. I forget the vintage; I rather think that it was 1895. I thought an Imperial Quart, quite an uncommon size, would about suffice. The bottle was duly brought, placed upon the table, and I took hold of it—"warm!"—so I ventured to ask for an ice bucket.

This was brought after a considerable lapse of time, and as the waiter was going away, I called him back, saying, "Put the wine on the ice."

A minute after, I instinctively looked round to see that it was all right, when to my amazement, what do you think was happening? He was pouring the wine into the bucket.

What the . . . , etc., etc., naturally followed, when, with a more or less blank look on his face, he replied, "You told me to put the wine on the ice, didn't you?"

CHARLES WALTER BERRY
Viniana

Des Esseintes Visits an English Bodega in Paris

Outside, he found it bitterly cold and wet, for the wind was blowing across the street and lashing the arcades with rain.

"Drive over there," he told the cabby, pointing to a shop at the very end of the gallery, on the corner of the Rue de Rivoli and the Rue Castiglione, which with its brightly lit windows looked like a gigantic night-light burning cheerfully in the pestilential fog.

This was the Bodega. The sight which greeted Des Esseintes as he went in was of a long, narrow hall, its roof supported by cast-iron pillars and its walls lined with great casks standing upright on barrel-horses. Hooped with iron, girdled with a sort of pipe-rack in which tulip-shaped glasses hung upside-down, and fitted at the bottom with an earthenware spigot, these barrels bore, besides a royal coat of arms, a coloured card giving details of the vintage they contained, the amount of wine they held, and the price of that wine by the hogshead, by the bottle, and by the glass.

In the passage which was left free between these rows of barrels, under the hissing gas-jets of an atrocious iron-grey chandelier, there stood a line of tables loaded with baskets of Palmer's biscuits and stale, salty cakes, and plates heaped with mince pies and sandwiches whose tasteless exteriors concealed burning mustard-plasters. These tables, with chairs arranged on both sides, stretched to the far end of this cellar-like room, where still more hogsheads could be seen stacked against the walls, with smaller branded casks lying on the top of them.

The smell of alcohol assailed Des Esseintes' nostrils as he took a seat in this dormitory for strong wines. Looking around him, he saw on one side a row of great casks with labels listing the entire range of ports, light or heavy in body, mahogany or amaranthine in colour, and distinguished by laudatory titles such as "Old Port," "Light Delicate," "Cockburn's Very Fine," and "Magnificent Old Regina"; and on the other side, standing shoulder to shoulder and rounding their formidable bellies, enormous barrels containing the martial wine of Spain in all its various forms, topaz-coloured sherries light and dark, sweet and dry—San Lucar, Vino de Pasto, Pale Dry, Oloroso, and Amontillado.

The cellar was packed to the doors. Leaning his elbow on the corner of a table, Des Esseintes sat waiting for the glass of port he had ordered of a barman busy opening explosive, eggshaped soda bottles that looked like giant-sized capsules of gelatine or gluten such as chemists use to mask the taste of their more obnoxious medicines.

All around him were swarms of English people. There were pale, gangling clergymen with clean-shaven chins, round spectacles, and greasy hair, dressed in black from head to foot—soft hats at one extremity, laced shoes at the other, and in between, incredibly long coats with little buttons running down the front. There were laymen with bloated pork-butcher faces or bulldog muzzles, apoplectic necks, ears like tomatoes, winy cheeks, stupid bloodshot eyes, and whiskery collars as worn by some of the great apes. Further away, at the far end of the wine-shop, a tow-haired stick of a man with a chin sprouting white hairs like an artichoke, was using a microscope to decipher the minute print of an English newspaper. And facing him was a sort of American naval officer, stout and stocky, swarthy and bottle-nosed, a cigar stuck in the hairy orifice of his mouth, and his eyes sleepily contemplating the framed champagne advertisements on the walls—the trademarks of Perrier and Rœderer, Heidsieck and Mumm, and the hooded head of a monk identified in Gothic lettering as Dom Pérignon of Reims.

Des Esseintes began to feel somewhat stupefied in this heavy guard-room atmosphere. His senses dulled by the monotonous chatter of these English people talking to one another, he drifted into a daydream, calling to mind some of Dickens' characters, who were so partial to the rich red port he saw in glasses all about him, and peopling the cellar in fancy with a new set of customers—imagining here Mr. Wickfield's white hair and ruddy complexion, there the sharp, expressionless features and unfeeling eyes of Mr. Tulkinghorn, the grim lawyer of *Bleak House*. These characters stepped right out of his memory to take their places in the Bodega, complete with all their mannerisms and gestures, for his recollections, revived by a recent reading of the novels, were astonishingly precise and detailed. The Londoner's home as described by the novelist— well lighted, well heated, and well appointed, with bottles being slowly emptied by Little Dorrit, Dora Copperfield, or Tom Pinch's sister Ruth—appeared to him in the guise of a cosy ark sailing snugly through a deluge of soot and mire. He settled down comfortably in this London of the imagination, happy to be indoors, and believing for a moment that the dismal hootings of the tugs by the bridge behind the Tuileries were coming from boats on the Thames. But his glass was empty now; and despite the warm fug in the cellar and the added heat from the smoke of pipes and cigars, he shivered slightly as he came back to reality and the foul, dank weather.

He asked for a glass of Amontillado, but at the sight of this pale dry wine, the English author's soothing stories and gentle lenitives gave place to the harsh revulsives and painful irritants provided by Edgar Allan Poe. The spine-chilling nightmare of the cask of Amontillado, the story of the man walled up in an underground chamber, took hold of his imagination; and behind the kind, ordinary faces of the American and English customers in the Bodega he fancied he could detect foul, uncontrollable desires, dark and odious schemes. But then he suddenly noticed that the place was emptying and that it was almost time for dinner; he paid his bill, got slowly to his feet, and in a slight daze made for the door.

J.-K. HUYSMANS
Against Nature

13
Travelers' Tales

This is a mixed bag of observations and recollections drawn from both fact and fiction. Byron wrote that "the very best of vineyards is the cellar," but most of the writers represented here would disagree. Not all are quite as enthusiastic as the anonymous author of "An Invitation to Lubberland" (1684), reporting on the riches of the New World:

> The rivers run with claret fine,
>   the brooks with rich Canary,
> The ponds with other sorts of wine,
>   to make your hearts full merry.

Few travelers find rivers of claret, but travelers occasionally discover inexpensive bottles of fine wines on a provincial wine list or in the back of a grocery store. Francis Colchester-Wemyss described a typical incident in his *Souvenirs Gastronomiques*: He came across thirty-five bottles of Château Latour 1899 in a New Zealand hotel and the owner was delighted to get rid of this old "French Burgundy" for less than he was charging for his youngest Australian wines.

Here are some vinous reports from such different writers as Homer and Hemingway, Jefferson and Pepys, and Rabelais and Henry James.

A Squirt of Wine

A Basque with a big leather wine-bag in his lap lay across the top of the bus in front of our seat, leaning back against our legs. He offered the wine-skin to Bill and to me, and when I tipped it up to drink he imitated the sound of a klaxon motor-horn so well and so suddenly that I spilled some of the wine, and everybody laughed. He apologized and made me take another drink. He made the klaxon again a little later, and it fooled me the second time. He was very good at it. . . .

The Basque lying against my legs was tanned the color of saddle-leather. He wore a black smock like all the rest. There were wrinkles in his tanned neck. He turned around and offered his wine-bag to Bill. Bill handed him one of our bottles. The Basque wagged a forefinger at him and handed the bottle back, slapping in the cork with the palm of his hand. He shoved the wine-bag up.

"Arriba! Arriba!" he said. "Lift it up."

Bill raised the wine-skin and let the stream of wine spurt out and into his mouth, his head tipped back. When he stopped drinking and tipped the leather bottle down a few drops ran down his chin.

"No! No!" several Basques said. "Not like that." One snatched the bottle away from the owner, who was himself about to give a demonstration. He was a young fellow and he held the wine-bottle at full arms' length and raised it high up, squeezing the leather bag with his hand so the stream of wine hissed into his mouth. He held the bag out there, the wine making a flat, hard trajectory into his mouth, and he kept on swallowing smoothly and regularly.

"Hey!" the owner of the bottle shouted. "Whose wine is that?"

The drinker waggled his little finger at him and smiled at us with his eyes. Then he bit the stream off sharp, made a quick lift with the wine-bag and lowered it down to the owner. He winked at us. The owner shook the wine-skin sadly.

ERNEST HEMINGWAY
The Sun Also Rises

Don't Leave Home Without It

Having thus disposed of these matters on the front bow of his saddle, to which we always added a *bota*—the pocket-pistol of Hudibras—one word on this *bota,* which is as necessary to the rider as a saddle to his horse. This article, so Asiatic and Spanish, is at once the bottle and the glass of the people of the Peninsula when on the road, and is perfectly unlike the vitreous crockery and pewter utensils of Great Britain. A Spanish woman would as soon think of going to church without her fan, or a Spanish man to a fair without his knife, as a traveller without his *bota.* . . .

The shape is like that of a large pear or shot-pouch, and it contains from two to five quarts. The narrow neck is mounted with a turned wooden cup, from which the contents are drunk. The way to use it is thus—grasp the neck with the left hand and bring the rim of the cup to the mouth, then gradually raise the bag with the other hand till the wine, in obedience to hydrostatic laws, rises to its level, and keeps always full in the cup without trouble to the mouth. The gravity with which this is done, the long, slow, sustained, Sancho-like devotion of the thirsty Spaniards when offered a drink out of another man's *bota,* is very edifying, and is as deep as the sigh of delight and gratitude with which, when unable to imbibe more, the precious skin is returned. No drop of the divine contents is wasted, except by some newly-arrived bungler, who, by lifting up the bottom first, inundates his chin. . . .

As the *bota* is always near every Spaniard's mouth who can get at one, all classes being ever ready, like Sancho, to give "a thousand kisses," not only to his own legitimate *bota,* but to that of his neighbour, which is coveted more than wife: therefore no prudent traveller will ever journey an inch in Spain without getting one, and when he has, will never keep it empty, especially when he falls in with good wine.

RICHARD FORD
Gatherings from Spain
1846

Henry James in Bordeaux

For the rest, Bordeaux is a big, rich, handsome, imposing commercial town, with long rows of fine old eighteenth-century houses, which overlook the yellow Garonne. I have spoken of the quays of Nantes as fine, but those of Bordeaux have a wider sweep and a still more architectural air. The appearance of such a port as this makes the Anglo-Saxon tourist blush for the sordid waterfronts of Liverpool and New York, which, with their larger activity, have so much more reason to be stately. Bordeaux gives a great impression of prosperous industries, and suggests delightful ideas, images of prune-boxes and bottled claret. As the focus of distribution of the best wine in the world, it is indeed a sacred city—dedicated to the worship of Bacchus in the most discreet form. The country all about it is covered with precious vineyards, sources of fortune to their owners and of satisfaction to distant consumers; and as you look over to the hills beyond the Garonne you see them in the autumn sunshine, fretted with the rusty richness of this or that immortal *clos*. . . .

The whole town has an air of almost depressing opulence, an appearance which culminates in the great *place* which surrounds the Grand-Théâtre—an establishment in the highest style, encircled with columns, arcades, lamps, gilded cafés. One feels it to be a monument to the virtue of the well-selected bottle. If I had not forbidden myself to linger, I should venture to insist on this, and, at the risk of being considered fantastic, trace an analogy between good claret and the best qualities of the French mind; pretend that there is a taste of sound Bordeaux in all the happiest manifestations of that fine organ, and that, correspondingly, there is a touch of French reason, French completeness, in a glass of Pontet-Canet. The danger of such an excursion would lie mainly in its being so open to the reader to take the ground from under my feet by saying that good claret doesn't exist. To this I should have no reply whatever. I should be unable to tell him where to find it. I certainly didn't find it at Bordeaux, where I drank a most vulgar fluid; and it is of course notorious that a large part of mankind is occupied in vainly looking for it. There was a great pretence of putting it forward at the Exhibition, which was going on at Bordeaux at the time of my visit, an "exposition philomathique," lodged in a collection of big temporary buildings in the Allées d'Orléans, and regarded by the Bordelais for the moment as the most brilliant feature of their city. Here were pyramids of bottles, mountains of bottles, to say nothing of cases and cabinets of bottles. The contemplation of these glittering tiers was of course not very convincing; and indeed the whole arrangement struck me as a high impertinence. Good wine is not an optical pleasure, it is an inward emotion; and if there was a chamber of degustation on the premises, I failed to discover it.

HENRY JAMES
A Little Tour in France

The Fountain of Wines

She then ordered mugs with lids, cups, and goblets to be handed to us, of gold, silver, crystal, and porcelain; and we were graciously invited to drink of the water that gushed from that fountain; which we willingly did. For, to be frank with you, we are by nature different from a herd of cattle, who—like the sparrows, which only feed when you tap their tails—never eat or drink unless you whack them hard with a big stick. We never refuse anyone who courteously invites us to drink.

Bacbuc then asked us what we thought of the liquor, and we answered her that it seemed like good fresh spring-water to us, more limpid and silvery than the water of Argyrontes in Aetiolia, of Peneus in Thessaly, of Axius in Mygdonia, or of Cydnus in Cicilia; which last Alexander of Macedon found so beautiful, so clear and cool in the midst of summer that he preferred the luxury of bathing in it to the harm that he saw would ensue for him from this transitory pleasure.

'Ha,' said Bacbuc, 'that is what comes of not reflecting, and of not understanding the movements of the muscular tongue, when the drink flows over it on its way down, not into the lungs by the tracheal artery, as was supposed by the good Plato, Plutarch, and others, but into the stomach by way of the oesophagus. Are your throats lined, paved, and enamelled, noble strangers, as Pithyllus, nicknamed Theutes, had his of old, that you have not recognized the taste or savour of this godlike liquor? Bring me those scourers of mine,' she called to her ladies-in-waiting, 'so that we can rake, clear, and clean their palates.'

Then there were brought fine, jolly great hams; fine, jolly, great smoked ox-tongues, excellent salt-meats, saveloys, botargoes, caviar, excellent venison sausages, and other such gullet-sweepers; and, by her command, we ate of these until we confessed that our stomachs were thoroughly scoured and that we were now pretty grievously tormented by thirst. Upon this she observed:

'As a certain Jewish captain of old, a learned and valiant man, was leading his people across the desert in utter famine, he received manna out of the skies, which to their imagination tasted exactly as food had tasted in the past. Similarly here, as you drink of this miraculous liquor you will detect the taste of whatever wine you may imagine.'

This we did, and Panurge cried out: 'By God, this is the wine of Beaune, and the best that ever I tasted, and may a hundred and six devils run away with me if it isn't! How grand it would be to have a neck six foot long, so as to taste it longer, which was Philoxenus's wish; or as long as a crane's, as Melanthius desired!'

'I swear as a Lanterner,' exclaimed Friar John, 'that it's Graves wine, gay and sparkling. Pray teach me, lady, the way you make it like this.'

'To me,' said Pantagruel, 'it seems like wine of Mirevaux. For that's what I imagined before I drank. The only thing wrong with it is that it is cool. Colder than ice, I should say, colder than Nonacris or Dirce water, colder than the fountain of Cantoporeia in Corinth, which froze the stomach and digestive organs of those who drank it.'

'Drink,' said Bacbuc, 'once, twice, and three times. And now again, changing your thoughts, and each time you'll find the taste and savour of the liquor just as you imagined it. After this you must confess that to God nothing is impossible.'

'We never said that anything was,' I replied. 'We maintain that he is all-powerful.'

FRANÇOIS RABELAIS
Gargantua and Pantagruel

A Shared Pleasure

Montrose always seems to me to have a touch of lovely sweetness, a trace of some very generous and kindly quality, kept back by the elegant balance of a great and classic wine. No doubt memories have coloured it in my mind, for it was here that, on my first visit, M. Charmolüe quietly put half a dozen bottles of his wine in the back of my car before I drove away. The next weekend I was on my own up in the lovely remote country of the Dordogne, staying and eating my evening meal at a *routiers* café. I drank one of the bottles of Montrose with my dinner, and was so happy with it that I went out to the car to get the other five and gave them (it makes me sound mad) to the lorry-drivers who were in the café eating their stew. They evidently thought I was mad, too: they had probably never drunk a château-bottled second-growth claret before. In any case, they raised their glasses politely, and were about to empty them, when they stopped in mid-swallow. A look of immense pleasure, the expression of a true connoisseur face to face with a masterpiece, came over their faces. It was the scent of the wine, the clean, sweet, exquisite breath of autumn ripeness, which held them rapt. I do not think I exaggerate. It was a wonderful sight to see those great *onze-degrés* men, those pushers of gigantic trucks and trailers, breathing in the bouquet of a wine which spoke straight to them.

HUGH JOHNSON
Wine

A Serious Drinker

The numerous persons who attend at the sideboard of his Majesty, and who serve him with victuals and drink, are all obliged to cover their noses and mouths with handsome veils or cloths of worked silk, in order that his victuals or his wine may not be affected by their breath. When drink is called for by him, and the page in waiting has presented it, he retires three paces and kneels down, upon which the courtiers, and all who are present, in like manner make their prostration. At the same moment all the musical instruments, of which there is a numerous band, begin to play, and continue to do so until he has ceased drinking, when all the company recover their posture. This reverential salutation is made as often as his Majesty drinks.

The Travels of Marco Polo

Puzzling

There was one thing, however, which I had not expected to see [in the sherry bodegas], of which I had never read. I had not expected to see at floor level by one of the casks a grill work to which were attached pieces of dry toast. These, I was informed, were for the mice. Mice were encouraged, and cats kept off the premises. I saw a number of mice who were appreciating the care that had been taken for their safety and their comfort. They were extremely small. It seemed to me that it would be very easy for them to push aside the light covering of the bungholes. I remembered being told years ago that at one time rabbits were put into sherry casks, that the alcohol in the wine fed on them and was enriched. I wondered, watching those midget mice, but I decided it was more prudent not to be inquisitive.

ALEC WAUGH
In Praise of Wine

Ulysses and the Cyclops

At that time I told the rest of my eager companions
to stay where they were beside the ship and guard it. Meanwhile
I, choosing out the twelve best men among my companions,
went on, but I had with me a goatskin bottle of black wine,
sweet wine, given me by Maron, son of Euanthes
and priest of Apollo, who bestrides Ismaros; he gave it
because, respecting him with his wife and child, we saved them
from harm. He made his dwelling among the trees of the sacred
grove of Phoibos Apollo, and he gave me glorious presents.
He gave me seven talents of well-wrought gold, and he gave me
a mixing bowl made all of silver, and gave along with it
wine, drawing it off in storing jars, twelve in all. This was
a sweet wine, unmixed, a divine drink. No one of his servants
or thralls that were in his household knew anything about it,
but only himself and his dear wife and a single housekeeper.
Whenever he drank this honey-sweet red wine, he would pour out
enough to fill one cup, then twenty measures of water
were added, and the mixing bowl gave off a sweet smell;
magical; then would be no pleasure in holding off. Of this
wine I filled a great wineskin full, and took too provisions
in a bag, for my proud heart had an idea that presently
I would ecounter a man who was endowed with great strength,
and wild, with no true knowledge of laws or any good customs. . . .

With the evening he [Cyclops] came back again, herding his fleecy
flocks, but drove all his fat flocks inside the wide cave
at once, and did not leave any outside in the yard with the deep
    fence,
whether he had some idea, or whether a god so urged him.
When he had heaved up and set in position the huge door stop,
next he sat down and started milking his sheep and his bleating
goats, each of them in order, and put lamb or kid under each one.
But after he had briskly done all his chores and finished,
again he snatched up two men and prepared them for dinner.
Then at last I, holding in my hands an ivy bowl
full of the black wine, stood close up to the Cyclops and spoke out:
"Here, Cyclops, have a drink of wine, now you have fed on
human flesh, and see what kind of drink our ship carried
inside her. I brought it for you, and it would have been your
    libation

had you taken pity and sent me home, but I cannot suffer
your rages. Cruel, how can any man come and visit
you ever again, now you have done what has no sanction?"
    So I spoke, and he took it and drank it off, and was terribly
pleased with the wine he drank and questioned me again, saying:
"Give me still more, freely, and tell me your name straightway
now, so I can give you a guest present to make you happy.
For the grain-giving land of the Cyclops also yields them
wine of strength, and it is Zeus' rain that waters it for them;
but this comes from where ambrosia and nectar flow in
        abundance."
    So he spoke, and I gave him the gleaming wine again. Three
        times
I brought it to him and gave it to him, three times he recklessly
drained it, but when the wine had got into the brains of the
        Cyclops,
then I spoke to him, and my words were full of beguilement:
"Cyclops, you ask me for my famous name. I will tell you
then, but you must give me a guest gift as you have promised.
Nobody is my name. My father and mother call me
Nobody, as do all the others who are my companions."
    So I spoke, and he answered me in pitiless spirit:
"Then I will eat Nobody after his friends, and the others
I will eat first, and that shall be my guest present to you."
    He spoke and slumped away and fell on his back, and lay there
with his thick neck crooked over on one side, and sleep who
        subdues all
came on and captured him, and the wine gurgled up from his gullet
with gobs of human meat. This was his drunken vomiting.

HOMER
The Odyssey

A Happy Surprise

Nor is it necessary for white wines to be particularly rich in sugar
or alcohol in order to age (though an 1893 Vouvray, plentiful in
both, was one of the most exciting wines I have ever tasted).
Spurred by a reference in H. Warner Allen's book *White Wines and
Cognac* when I was still a wine-trade student completing my training in France, I went off to the Dordogne region to find a wine that
the author had described. It had no controlled appellation, not even

one of the simpler kind, and I knew only that it was produced somewhere on the hilly watershed between the Dordogne and the Lot. It is savage country, wild and twisted, and the vineyard I was looking for, called Bonnecost, was difficult to find. When I finally arrived, the proprietor was sitting under a tree enjoying a glass of wine with the local priest. He made me welcome and gave me a glass of his white wine. It was dry and very light with a slightly herby bouquet. Cool from the cellar rather than cold, it was both refreshing to drink and satisfying to savor. He poured another glass, urging me to drink. Seeing my eye travel to my car, the proprietor told me to stay for lunch and, in any case, the wine was very low in alcohol. "A wine to drink young then," I said. He smiled and went into the house to fetch another bottle. I noticed the next glass had a deep lemony gleam, and as I raised it there was an overpowering aroma of fresh-picked ripe fruits. The old man watched with obvious satisfaction while I tasted it. "That wine," he said, "has only nine percent alcohol, but it is forty years old." It was a valuable lesson to me, and I have never enjoyed one more.

GERALD ASHER

Serendipity

Then there is an odd bottle of Mouton '69 which came to me in the oddest possible way. I was in New York. I was lonely and miserable (this was in 1949) and one needs to be alone in New York to know how lonely one can be. I found myself passing the 21 Club, of which I had heard a great deal, one wet and foggy night in November. I presented myself at the door, I was admitted. I asked if I'd be allowed to buy a meal, and I was given this privilege. Over the meal, because I had no companion and bought a modest half bottle, I spent my time looking at the really wonderful wine list.

Among the items on the wine list of small quantities (prices were available on application) there was the 1869 Mouton, so I asked the sommelier, who was extremely intelligent and pleasant, what it could possibly be like and how much it would cost. The price quoted was impossible for me, but I took leave to doubt whether '69 Mouton would have stayed the course. He then said 'Perhaps, sir, you would like to see our cellars.' I was, in those days, somewhat green and had no idea of the significance of this particular cellar, so I said that I would, and after I finished my meal I was escorted down to the cellar, which I have since learned is world-famous. It is an old bootleggers' cellar of the 'twenties; entrance is obtained by inserting a thin piece of wire through a perfectly harmless-looking brick. A great door swings open, rather like a Chubb safe, and one enters an air-conditioned perfectly arranged cellar, and in due course I arrived before a bin of 1869 Mouton. There were perhaps eight or nine bottles. I was allowed to take them out and hold them up to the light. They were not ullaged, they were beautiful in colour and I congratulated the sommelier upon the way in which they were kept. Later, I was taken back to the bar and introduced to Mr. Kreindler, who was part-owner of the 21 Club. He gave me an excellent brandy and we chatted about wine for some time, then he regretted he had to leave me, and with a gesture, he said he hoped I would take with me, an unknown insignificant stranger in New York, some little memento of the 21 Club, and presented me with a bottle of the Mouton '69, which I had never hoped to drink, and could not possibly hope to buy. So I brought it back to England with a song in my heart and in due course it was served at a rather special luncheon. It turned out to be marvellous in every possible way, only beaten in memory by a Margaux 1870 which I drank a year or two before. A wonderful wine and a wonderful story. Where else in the world could such a magnificent gesture be made?

GEORGE RAINBIRD
"Old Wine and Old Bottles"

A Tricky Customer

So home and late at the office; and then home and there find Mr. Batelier and his sister Mary, and we sat chatting a great while, talking of witches and spirits; and he told me of his own knowledge, being with some others at Bordeaux, making a bargain with another man at a tavern for some clarets, they did hire a fellow to thunder (which he had the art of doing upon a deale board) and to rain and hail; that is, make the noise of—so as did give them a pretence of undervaluing their merchant's wines, by saying this thunder would spoil and turn them—which was so reasonable to the merchant that he did abate two *pistolls* per Tun for the wine, in belief of that—whereas, going out, there was no such thing. This Batelier did see and was the cause of, to his profit, as is above said.

SAMUEL PEPYS
Diary
1666

Vinous Philosophy

A farmer of ten arpents has about three laborers engaged by the year. He pays four louis to a man, and half as much to a woman, and feeds them. He kills one hog, and salts it, which is all the meat used in the family during the year. Their ordinary food is bread and vegetables. At Pommard and Volnay, I observed them eating good wheat bread; at Meursault, rye. I asked the reason of this difference. They told me that the white wines fail in quality much oftener than the red, and remain on hand. The farmer, therefore, cannot afford to feed his laborers so well. At Meursault, only white wines are made, because there is too much stone for the red. On such slight circumstances depends the condition of man!

THOMAS JEFFERSON
Journal
1787

An Italian Vineyard

A beautiful feature of the scene today, as the preceding day, were the vines growing on fig-trees and often wreathed in rich festoons from one tree to another, by and by to be hung with clusters of purple grapes. I suspect the vine is a pleasanter object of sight under this mode of culture than it can be in countries where it produces a more precious wine, and therefore is trained more artificially. Nothing can be more picturesque than the spectacle of an old grape-vine, with almost a trunk of its own, clinging round its tree, imprisoning within its strong embrace the friend that supported its tender infancy, converting the tree wholly to its own selfish ends, as seemingly flexible natures are apt to do, stretching out its innumerable arms on every bough, and allowing hardly a leaf to sprout except its own. I must not yet quit this hasty sketch, without throwing in, both in the early morning, and later in the forenoon, the mist that dreamed among the hills, and which, now that I have called it mist, I feel almost more inclined to call light, being so quietly cheerful with the sunshine through it. Put in, now and then, a castle on a hilltop; a rough ravine, a smiling valley; a mountain stream, with a far wider bed than it at present needs, and a stone bridge across it, with ancient and massive arches,—and I shall say no more, except that all these particulars, and many better ones which escape me, made up a very pleasant whole.

NATHANIEL HAWTHORNE
French and Italian Notebooks

A Visit to Mouton

We shall take as an example a visit to Mouton, one of the best-managed and most welcoming of vineyards, whose wines, relatively heavy for the Médoc, have a certain bull-like grace and solidity. '*Ça fait très Mouton,*' as they say of some particularly noble specimen.

As a region, the Médoc illustrates all the subtlety of the Bordeaux climate. Until the seventeenth century it was unreclaimed marsh, and compared to the great names of Saint Emilion, whose wines were prized by Ausonius, its châteaux seem absurdly *nouveau riche*. The vine-ripening belt is a narrow strip running north-northwest; on one side lie the salt marshes and the brown estuary, on the other the sandy Landes with their commons and pine-forest. Between the sand and the mud runs the magic vein of stony soil. The flints, the light earth, the rainy spring, the hot blue summer and the lingering autumn have all contributed to this perfection of the grape: fruit of sunny sea-wind radiance, of Dutch polders silver-gilt by the warmth of the Midi. To understand the Médoc is to begin to love Bordeaux, to which it forms a companion-piece.

Flat, bright, dusty—subject to sudden storms and lowering clouds which as suddenly clear—the plain, between the tidal water and the dark belt of forest, is peppered with sacred names: Latour, Lafite, Margaux, Cantenac; each vineyard marked out by an army of knotted green bushes whose powdery clusters dangle among the pebbles, whose wine gives out the most delicate of civilized aromas; fragrant, light and cavernous as myrtle-berries from an Etruscan tomb, the incomparable *bouquet du vieux Médoc,* offspring of sunshine and hard work, parent of warmth, wit, and understanding.

The châteaux are strung out irregularly along the strip. Two at all costs must be seen, Beychevelle and Margaux. They are the loveliest of the region, the one Louis Quinze (1753), the other Louis Seize. As befits the age of Adam, Margaux is the statelier pile, while Beychevelle is lower and more rambling, with a garden pavilion to each wing and fine wrought-iron gates. Classical perfection or rococo charm? We must examine both from as near at hand as impertinence will take us and then forever take our stand. Other enchanting neighbours are Issan, with its moat, the British-owned Léoville-Barton, with its cypress, and the eighteenth-century tower of Château Latour, stoniest of all vineyards, most perfect of all wines.

Mouton seems more like a pleasant English villa—until we enter the group of low buildings across the courtyard. The first room, which one might call an ante-chapel, contains old prints, decanters, documents and statues likely to induce a mood of reverence: vestry would be a better term for it, the robing-room of Bacchus. Great doors silently open and we look across an enormous low nave with the heraldic sheep of Mouton emblazoned on the far wall over the pew-like rows of silent barrels in which the new wine rests for three years, before being bottled, numbered, labelled and sent out to the world on its goodwill mission.

We walk down the nave to its far end, rinse our mouths with the sharp new wine and, lighting our pious candles, descend to the crypt. Here stand the enormous vats in which the newly pressed wine ferments before being stored in barrels, each vat as big as a Nissen hut, with the temperature-chart and case-history of its tumultuous inmate pinned up outside. Here also is an electric wind-machine which will dry grapes gathered in wet weather; and at the end of the crypt, in greater darkness, heavy iron doors which lead to the catacombs, the long dry cellars where the bottles themselves mature in their cobwebby cages.

A vista of shiny black disks recedes before us, the bottled vintages of the last few years, then come the years we covet most, the *reserve de Monsieur le Baron* and lastly the 'museum' of rare and ancient wines from this and neighbouring properties, where fabulous bottles, too precious to drink, may peacefully end their days like kings in the Escurial. '*Ça fait très Mouton.*'

At last we must climb back from catacombs to crypt, crypt to cathedral, cathedral to vestry to visit the winepresses themselves, where the grapes are poured in by the pickers, then sifted and trodden by labourers with wooden rakes and paddles who shuffle round to the music of a fiddle. M. Marjory, the enchanting manager, will imitate the motions for us as a special favour. This age-old sifting of the grape and pressing of the wine (before it flows into the huge vats below) is performed by human hands, or rather feet, and wooden implements. More complicated modern machinery has been tried and found wanting, and the process illustrates the archaic and dedicated life of the great vineyards, where quantity is sacrificed to quality and where the munificent owners sometimes prefer to carry on the business at a loss rather than lower the standard or destroy the tradition to suit the declining taste and coarsening palate of our frantic epoch.

It is always hard to keep awake at Mouton; the sea-air, the sun, the wines (decanted and served again from their own bottles) and the simple but outrageous perfection of the cooking—*risotto aux truffes, gigot de pré salé*—deal one knock-out blow after another—or I would recommend a prolonged stay in the district to all painters and writers. But the region is anti-art and the villages lack the Romanesque beauties and pastoral surroundings of those across the estuary. Tennis, hospitality and big business occupy the claret-kings, with their American cars and English nicknames, and there are few walks and fewer books in the artificial landscape. Fleecy clouds drift across the high blue sky, slow carts with spraying machines pass between the squat regiments of vines, 'ole man liver' rumbles a warning against *galanteries vinicoles;* it is time to go.

CYRIL CONNOLLY
"Bordeaux-Dordogne"

Napoleon and His Chambertin

It is well known that Napoleon seldom drank anything but Chambertin. We may presume that he formed his liking for Burgundy when stationed as a young artillery officer at the Southern extremity of the Côte d'Or. By 1798 he had become addicted to this agreeable wine, and with the exception of a little Champagne (usually as a stimulant), he seldom drank anything else. Bourrienne tells us that 'before his departure [for Egypt] Bonaparte laid in a considerable stock of Burgundy. It was supplied by a man named James, of Dijon. I may observe, that on this occasion we had an opportunity of ascertaining that good Burgundy, well racked off, and in casks hermetically sealed, does not lose its quality on a sea voyage. Several cases of this Burgundy twice crossed the desert of the Isthmus of Suez on camels' backs. We brought some of it back with us to Fréjus, and it was as good as when we departed. James went with us to Egypt.' Taking his wine merchant all over Europe to look after the Chambertin became customary with Napoleon. Later the wine was supplied by Soupé et Pierrugues, 338 rue Saint-Honoré, and one of the two partners went on every campaign. As there were no cellars in the Tuileries or any of the palaces, the wine was supplied from the rue Saint-Honoré on sale or return. It was usually about six years old and cost 72 francs a dozen. Like all the wines and liqueurs used in the palaces, it was sent in porcelain bottles made at Sèvres with the imperial cypher. There are few occasions on which Napoleon is known to have drunk anything else. One is said to have been with Elchingen, when his baggage was pillaged—though how it had strayed into Ney's column is not clear. This, he said, was the first time he had done without it, 'even amid the sands of Egypt.' Another, Maurice Healy tells me, was the night before Jena, when his baggage got lost and he had to try the local wine, which he said was not bad. That brute Hudson Lowe supplied only claret at St. Helena, and the fact that the distinguished prisoner was forced to drink this instead of Chambertin is held against the Governor by Napoleonophiles as one of his innumerable inhumanities.

Whatever Napoleon drank he always liked chilled, and usually diluted with water.

DESMOND FLOWER
"Napoleon's Table"

Wine in America

Then the dinner comes early; at least it always does so in New England, and the ceremony is much of the same kind. You came there to eat, and the food is pressed on you almost *ad nauseam*. But as far as one can see there is no drinking. In these days, I am quite aware, that drinking has become improper, even in England. We are apt at home to speak of wine as a thing tabooed, wondering how our fathers lived and swilled. I believe that as a fact we drink as much as they did; but nevertheless that is our theory. I confess, however, that I like wine. It is very wicked, but it seems to me that my dinner goes down better with a glass of sherry than without it. As a rule I always did get it at hotels in America. But I had no comfort with it. Sherry they do not understand at all. Of course I am only speaking of hotels. Their claret they get exclusively from Mr. Gladstone, and looking at the quality, have a right to quarrel even with Mr. Gladstone's price. But it is not the quality of the wine that I hereby intend to subject to ignominy, so much as the want of any opportunity for drinking it. After dinner, if all that I hear be true, the gentlemen occasionally drop into the hotel bar and "liquor up." Or rather this is not done specially after dinner, but without prejudice to the hour at any time that may be found desirable. I also have "liquored up," but I cannot say that I enjoy the process. I do not intend hereby to accuse Americans of drinking much, but I maintain that what they do drink, they drink in the most uncomfortable manner that the imagination can devise.

ANTHONY TROLLOPE
North America

Napa Wine

I was interested in California wine. Indeed, I am interested in all wines, and have been all my life, from the raisin-wine that a school-fellow kept secreted in his play-box up to my last discovery, those notable Valtellines, that once shone upon the board of Cæsar. . . .

If wine is to withdraw its most poetic countenance, the sun of the white dinner-cloth, a deity to be invoked by two or three, all fervent, hushing their talk, degusting tenderly, and storing reminiscences—for a bottle of good wine, like a good act, shines ever in the retrospect—if wine is to desert us, go thy ways, old Jack! Now we begin to have compunctions, and look back at the brave bottles squandered upon dinner-parties, where the guests drank grossly, discussing politics the while, and even the schoolboy "took his whack," like liquorice-water. And at the same time we look timidly forward, with a spark of hope, to where the new lands, already weary of producing gold, begin to green with vineyards. A nice point in human history falls to be decided by Californian and Australian wines.

Wine in California is still in the experimental stage; and when you taste a vintage, grave economical questions are involved. The beginning of vine-planting is like the beginning of mining for the precious metals: the wine-grower also "prospects." One corner of land after another is tried with one kind of grape after another. This is a failure; that is better; a third best. So, bit by bit, they grope about for their Clos Vougeot and Lafite. Those lodes and pockets of earth, more precious than the precious ores, that yield inimitable fragrance and soft fire; those virtuous Bonanzas, where the soil has sublimated under sun and stars to something finer, and the wine is bottled poetry: these still lie undiscovered; chaparral conceals, thicket embowers them; the miner chips the rock and wanders farther, and the grizzly muses undisturbed. But there they bide their hour, awaiting their Columbus; and nature nurses and prepares them. The smack of Californian earth shall linger on the palate of your grandson.

Meanwhile the wine is merely a good wine; the best that I have tasted—better than a Beaujolais, and not unlike. But the trade is poor; it lives from hand to mouth, putting its all into experiments, and forced to sell its vintages. To find one properly matured, and bearing its own name, is to be fortune's favourite. . . .

Napa Valley has been long a seat of the wine-growing industry. It did not here begin, as it does too often, in the low valley lands along the river, but took at once to the rough foothills, where alone it can expect to prosper. A basking inclination, and stones, to be a reservoir of the day's heat, seem necessary to the soil for wine; the grossness of the earth must be evaporated, its marrow daily melted and refined for ages; until at length these clods that break below our footing, and to the eye appear but common earth, are truly and to the perceiving mind a masterpiece of nature. The dust of Richebourg, which the wind carries away, what an apotheosis of the dust! Not man himself can seem a stranger child of that brown, friable powder, than the blood and sun in that old flask behind the fagots.

A Californian vineyard, one of man's outposts in the wilderness, has features of its own. There is nothing here to remind you of the Rhine or Rhône, of the low Côte d'Or, or the infamous and scabby deserts of Champagne; but all is green, solitary, covert. . . .

Mr. Schram's . . . is the oldest vineyard in the valley, eighteen years old, I think; yet he began a penniless barber, and even after he had broken ground up here with his black malvoisies, continued for long to tramp the valley with his razor. Now, his place is the picture of prosperity; stuffed birds in the verandah, cellars far dug into the hillside, and resting on pillars like a bandit's cave:—all trimness, varnish, flowers, and sunshine, among the tangled wildwood. Stout, smiling Mrs. Schram, who has been to Europe and apparently all about the States for pleasure, entertained Fanny in the verandah while I was tasting wines in the cellar. To Mr. Schram this was a solemn office; his serious gusto warmed my heart; prosperity had not yet wholly banished a certain neophyte and girlish trepidation, and he followed every sip and read my face with proud anxiety. I tasted all. I tasted every variety and shade of Schramberger, red and white Schramberger, Burgundy Schramberger, Schramberger Hock, Schramberger Golden Chasselas, the latter with a notable bouquet, and I fear to think how many more. Much of it goes to London—most, I think; and Mr. Schram has a great notion of the English taste.

In this wild spot I did not feel the sacredness of ancient cultivation. It was still raw; it was no Marathon, and no Johannisberg; yet the stirring sunlight, and the growing vines, and the vats and bottles in the cavern, made a pleasant music for the mind. Here, also, earth's cream was being skimmed and garnered; and the London customers can taste, such as it is, the tang of the earth in this green valley. So local, so quintessential is a wine, that it seems the very birds in the verandah might communicate a flavour, and that romantic cellar influence the bottle next to be uncorked in Pimlico, and the smile of jolly Mr. Schram might mantle in the glass.

But these are but experiments. All things in this new land are moving farther on: the wine-vats and the miner's blasting tools but picket for a night, like Bedouin pavilions; and tomorrow, to fresh woods! This stir of change and these perpetual echoes of the moving footfall haunt the land. Men move eternally, still chasing Fortune; and, Fortune found, still wander. As we drove back to Calistoga the road lay empty of mere passengers, but its green side was dotted with the camps of travelling families: one cumbered with a great waggonful of household stuff, settlers going to occupy a ranch they had taken up in Mendocino, or perhaps Tehama County; another, a party in dust coats, men and women, whom we found camped in a grove on the roadside, all on pleasure bent, with a Chinaman to cook for them, and who waved their hands to us as we drove by.

ROBERT LOUIS STEVENSON
The Silverado Squatters

Cellar in the Sky

The conquest of space may be a fine thing for the reputation of the human race, but it promises nothing but frustration for those to whom one of the most splendid of all achievements is the sight of a glass being filled gently yet majestically with some rare and well-aged liquid.

The fact that the stuff will not pour at all is one of the most immediate yet most sinister of the horrors that space-travel holds for those who drink wine. The obvious trouble is that space-travellers are either strapped in a foetal posture on a foam-rubber couch, with their stomachs pressed hard against their vertebrae and their faces contorted as in some nasty fun fair, or they are floating freely with nothing to tell them which is up and which is down.

You can still take a cork from a bottle, but there is no particular reason why the wine should run out, no matter which way the neck is pointing. To be sure, you can get the liquid out by shaking the bottle, much as a vinegar-bottle is manipulated in a chip-shop, but then there is no knowing where the wine will finish up. In these circumstances it will clearly be impossible to drink a toast, either to Bacchus or to the first man—the first real man—in the Moon.

Those who drink wine had better take notice that they will be able to practise their art only if the growers mature their wines in handy squeezee bottles rather like those in which washing-up detergents now find their way into the shops. For those who would savour the bouquet first, there will have to be an atomizer, like a kind of scent-spray. It is, as will be evident, a prospect to make multitudes turn in their graves.

Opening a bottle of champagne will be a hazard compared with which the occasional collision with a meteorite will seem mere child's play. The cork will fly off right enough, but the bubbles will have no particular incentive to move towards the neck of the bottle. As a result, tiny bubbles will not easily encounter others so as to amalgamate into larger bubbles. And the liquid will escape as easily as the gas. And so there will come shooting out of the champagne bottle not a heady froth of bubbles but a thick foam with the colour and consistency of shaving cream. Those who must will have to eat champagne from ice-cream cones.

But these most obvious impediments to a proper appreciation of wine in space are only, unfortunately, a beginning. A more fundamental matter is that the absence of gravity will make the maturation of all wines virtually impossible. If there is no up and no down, the sediments will stay where they are, floating muddily throughout each bottle, making each drop of nectar into a kind of ink. Far from being a wine fit for astronauts to drink, only astronauts will be fit to drink the stuff.

JOHN MADDOX
"Wine in Space"

An Optimist at Château Latour

Wine of the vintage of 1865 was uncommonly good, and so was the regisseur to give me some of it. He took me into the dark and musty inner apartment where it lay, and there, on the very spot of its origin, I saw it drawn from the original package. Of course I found it the best wine, either red or white, I had ever tasted. Nevertheless, I was not dismayed, and I turned away from the precincts of Latour with more hope and faith than ever in the Norton's Virginia Seedling.

WILLIAM J. FLAGG
Three Seasons in European Vineyards
1869

The Wine of Georgia: Pro

With nobler products see thy Georgia teems,
Cheered with the genial sun's director beams;
There the wild vine to culture learns to yield,
And purple clusters ripen through the field.
Now bid thy merchants bring thy wine no more
Or from the Iberian or the Tuscan shore;
No more they need the Hungarian vineyard's drain,
And France herself may drink her best Champagne.
Behold! at last, and in a subject land,
Nectar sufficient for thy large demand; . . .

SAMUEL WESLEY
"Georgia"
1736

. . . and Con

Two things proposed by the colony [Georgia] was to raise silk and wine . . . as to wine, he believed it would be well to give it to the inhabitants for their own drinking, and wished them good luck with it, for it would be all would ever be seen of their wine, and if the people of the place drank no other, they would be the soberest subjects in the world.

JOHN MORDAUNT
1740

Stendhal in Bordeaux

Gently undulating terrain which, on the whole, forms a plain, but where you would seldom find five hundred feet of level ground. From a distance, the land appears to be bare. Vines cover everything that is not pine woods. They stretch out in long straight rows of vine arbors, scarcely a foot above the ground which, in turn, is divided into an endless number of little elevations shaped like a capital A, the highest point being covered by lines of vine stocks.

The arbor is supported by vertical stakes eighteen inches long, six inches of which are hidden in the ground. Young pines, no thicker than a thumb, are used for the horizontal line. They are sown as thick as hemp and half of them are pulled up when they become ten or twelve feet high.

First I found, in this rather deserted land, several large trees surrounding a sort of chateau with a tower. A little later I came to a strange building which had only a ground floor. "Those are stables belonging to a rich landowner whose chateau is a quarter of a mile from the road," the postilion told me. I thought that it was more probably a *chai*: that is what the people in this region call a wine cellar or a wine factory! This very elegant building, brilliant light yellow in color, was not, to tell the truth, in any particular style, neither Greek nor Gothic; but it was very gay and rather in the Chinese style. On the façade you could read the single word: *Cos.* Among the vineyards were round crenelated towers; shelters for the vine grower's tools and for himself during a storm. These towers, which I have already seen in the neighborhood of Blaye, are a very pretty sight.

The undulating plain went on and on. Then we came to great pine forests, not very high but mixed with clumps of oak trees and cuttings of underbrush. Very few houses or men in this flat countryside. I look admiringly at everything that is not woods and vineyards in this great name of Médoc. . . .

This evening, charming picnic dinner at the Café de Paris. These pleasant Bordelais lead a wholly physical, carefree, out-of-doors life, admirable at a time when hypocrisy is polluting the moral life of France.

One of the diners, a winebroker, was being teased about the good life he led. The only capital these gentlemen put in their business is a horse and a tilbury in which they run all over Médoc, a land that produces good wine, from Bordeaux to the Tour de Cordouan on the left bank of the Gironde. They taste the wines of the various proprietors and, with a piece of chalk, mark the quality on the casks. You can imagine how the proprietors pay court to them! And woe betide the owner who would dare to rub out the broker's chalk mark! No broker would take it upon himself to sell that man's wine.

After he has received his mail, a merchant will say to a broker: "I need 200 casks of wine, of such and such a quality, at such and such a price."

The winebroker replies: "There are some in this place and that place." He then goes to the proprietors and charges 2 per cent above the price paid by the merchant, in addition to gifts from the proprietors who are always eager to sell. These brokers are like ministers: they always call on people who need them. Many of them make 8–10,000 francs a year from their travels around Médoc and by allowing themselves to be urged to accept good dinners. Besides they can never lose.

STENDHAL
Travels in the South of France

. . . and Burgundy

The men I pass on the roads near Dijon are small, spare, lively, ruddy. You see that their good wine governs their whole makeup. So, to make a superior man, a logical head is not enough. There must be a certain fiery temperament.

As I left Dijon I stared hard at the famous Côte d'Or, so celebrated throughout Europe. I had to recall the verse, "Are witty people ever ugly?" for, without its wonderful wines, I would find nothing uglier than the Côte d'Or. According to the system of M. Elie de Beaumont, it was one of the first mountain ranges to emerge on our globe when the crust began to cool.

The Côte d'Or, then, is only a small mountain, quite ugly and barren, but they mark the vineyards with little stakes, and at every instant you find an immortal name, Chambertin, Clos-Vougeot, Romanée, St. Georges, Nuits. With the aid of so much fame, you end by getting accustomed to the Côte d'Or.

When General Bisson was a colonel, he was on his way to join the Army of the Rhine with his regiment. As he was passing the Clos-Vougeot, he made them halt, ordered them left into line of battle, and made them present arms.

As my fellow traveler was telling me this honorable anecdote, I saw a square, walled enclosure of about four hundred acres sloping gently to the south. We came to a wooden door which bore in rough, ugly characters "Clos-Vougeot." This name was furnished by the Vouge, a brook that winds a little way away. This immortal enclosure once belonged to the monks of the Abbey of Citeaux. The good fathers did not sell their wine. They gave away what they did not drink. No merchant tricks in those days.

STENDHAL
Memoirs of a Tourist

Les Trois Glorieuses

The town of Beaune is protected in its entirety by the French state: Every steeple, every gateway, and every crooked roof tile is a *monument historique*. On the Sunday of the Hospices sale Beaune becomes a fairground as well. All day crowds of small winegrowers from the surrounding villages visit the stands of agricultural machinery and household goods, view the sideshows, and eat *saucissons chauds*. In the chaste elegance of the seventeenth-century Hôtel de Ville there are usually booths at which wines from a number of growers can be tasted, to be compared with the cuvées of the Hospices and to give a broader impression of the vintage.

Yet above all else, this third weekend in November is devoted to *Les Trois Glorieuses*, the three great feasts of Burgundy, each offering a different face of the region. First, on the Saturday evening before the auction, there is a banquet organized by the Confrérie des Chevaliers du Tastevin at Clos de Vougeot. The most formal of the three feasts, it is intended to show the international face of Burgundy. The guests are largely ambassadors, ministers, and other distinguished foreign visitors from outside the world of wine. The dinner sets the tone for the auction and for the new vintage.

On Sunday evening, after the auction, a more *sympathique Dîner aux Chandelles* is held in the huge cellars under the old bastion towers of the town. Several hundred sit down to dinner— mostly the wine merchants of Beaune, the vineyard owners, and their guests. Despite the numbers there is a great family feeling, and everyone joins in the singing of the *ban bourguignon* between courses. Perhaps the tradition of noisily waving the hands in the air to the beat of the music is to show the rest of the assembly that fingers can be trusted in the sauce.

The noise and chatter of arriving guests is deafening, so the silence when everyone is at last seated and the lights are extinguished is all the more dramatic. Suddenly, from a small doorway, the young men who are to wait on table file into the vast cellars carrying lighted candles. It is very simple but grandly effective. Each course and each wine is presented with a well rehearsed flourish and impeccable precision. The last time I was present we started with a *consommé Célestine* and then drank a Beaune Blanc '64 with a partridge tart. This was followed by a *suprême de saumon à la norvégienne* with a Puligny-Montrachet Clos du Cailleret '64. Diners regained their breath on a *salmis* of wild duck with a Pommard cuvée Dames de la Charité '64 of the Hospices de Beaune. Then there was a *côte de charolais* accompanied by a 1962 Corton in magnums, which we continued to drink with the selection of cheeses. A Champagne Brut '61 was served with an enormous frosted cake (I can never understand why the French, logical in all else, drink dry Champagne with sweet dishes), and we toyed with *petits fours,* coffee, and *prunelle de Bourgogne*—the white brandy distilled from the little Burgundy plums—into the small hours. As well as the wines officially accompanying each course, the menu listed twenty-six others, which were presented by growers and merchants and were available, on request, as extra or alternative choices.

Monday morning comes too soon if the *Dîner aux Chandelles* has been preceded by the Chevaliers du Tastevin banquet at Clos de Vougeot. But gastronomically undaunted, we set off to Meursault for *La Paulée,* a Rabelaisian luncheon that concludes *Les Trois Glorieuses.* The origins of *La Paulée* are lost, but essentially it is a vineyard workers' banquet, presenting the third and most basic of the three faces of Burgundy. Each guest brings his own bottle, which is to say that each brings several, and there is a great deal of sipping and sampling of one another's wines. An atmosphere of *fête champêtre* reigns: Most of the participants are from the little town of Meursault and the surrounding area.

In 1967 I was a guest there of Mlle. Berthe Morey, and we drank the Meursault and Volnay from her vineyards. We started with a *jambon persillé,* a specialty of the region, and followed it with a *pâté en croûte* before reaching a glorious *pochouse verdunoise,* a stew of delicate river fish in white wine, savory with garlic. There was a charming little ceremony of marrying the *pochouse*—from the other side of the river Saône—with the white wine of Meursault. *"Je vous annonce gastronomiquement mariés,"* sang out the mayor of Meursault to the fish cauldron and the bottle, and we all agreed. At least, no one could think of any reason why the two should not be joined in gastronomic matrimony.

Then a huge wild boar was carried round the hall in triumph, head and fur replaced for decoration. (I was provoked to rather ungastronomic thoughts, I must confess.) While we dined, the Joyeux Bourguignons, a local glee club, sang Burgundian refrains, and we all joined in with the finger-waggling choruses of the *ban bourguignon,* essential to all Burgundian merrymaking. We finished with cheese and cakes and were astonished to find ourselves in the dark of evening.

After *La Paulée* all the growers throw open their cellars and expect their neighbors to come and taste. Nobody feels very much like eating supper that night.

GERALD ASHER

Sherry in Seaton

Seaton must be one of the most excellently quiet seaside resorts in England. It has no pier, no band, nothing beyond the beach, the sea and its comfortable beds. For us, however, it offered both less and more than these things. We took our apéritif of dry cider in a handsome inn whose landlord, though unable to put us up, recommended a nearby boarding house. Having secured our lodging for the night (as we thought) we sallied out in search of dinner. Moved by an impulse that might well justify a claim to second sight, Wyndham insisted that the Royal Clarence Hotel was likely to have good wine behind its blank façade. We entered; we ordered dinner; we asked for the wine list. Unimpressed by the selection offered, we enquired of the manager if there were not some old bottles left over and unlisted. To our delight there were. The proprietor's permission to visit the cellars was soon obtained, and down we went, eager and thirsty. Behold, in a dark corner nestled no fewer than four different 1914 clarets; a few bottles of antique but uninteresting hock; and half a dozen of sherry, with capsules stamped Mitchell & Toms, Chard, obviously a remnant of long standing. Careful inquiry established that the sherry had lain in its dark bin for at least thirty years. After congratulating our stars, we ordered a bottle of Beychevelle 1914, a Durfort Vivens of the same date, and a bottle of sherry. 1914 was not a happy year, either for Europe or Claret; it was too eventful for comfort, too hot for red wine; nevertheless, the two survivors set before us (ourselves survivors) were delicious; light, a trifle dry in the finish, but still admirably disciplined and worthy representatives of the soil that raised and the hands that made them. And we came to them in a good temper, for the sherry was superb. Most of the sherry that we drink nowadays is fresh from the cask, and lacks the bottle age that gives bouquet and forms character. This was very otherwise. Thirty, perhaps forty, years under cork had given a wine, that must always have been good, a perfume and distinction lacking in youth. It had absorbed its grape sugar, to the vast advantage of its flavour and its style; and though perhaps too robust a preliminary for light clarets, it set the key to a wholly happy evening, which even the anticlimax did not disturb. For there was an anticlimax: our beds, when we hilariously returned to them, were, as we were almost gleefully told, already occupied by two tired commercial travellers! The reason for this accident lay in the extreme good nature of the innkeeper who had recommended us. He had not only recommended us, but the travellers also; and they, industrious while we were revelling, had overcome the landlady's doubts and secured the beds. For a moment we were almost disconsolate. To find beds in August in a crowded seaside town is possible, though not easy, at seven o'clock; at eleven it is possible, though not likely. Fortunately it was a fine night; and in the end Wyndham slept soundly on a camp bed in the garden, while I dreamed cheerfully in the attic of an obliging auctioneer nearby.

A. J. A. SYMONS
"Walking in Wessex"

Two Visits to Champagne:
1909 with André L. Simon

For our first lunch we were the guests of Charles Heidsieck on 27 August 1909, a very hot day, really too hot for me, much as I love sunshine; my friends felt the heat even more than I did, more particularly the older ones, Roland Lane, the wine buyer of Booth Distillery and Arthur Spencer, the Walter Symons of Mark Lane. When we arrived sweating and panting just after 1 o'clock, rather late by French standards, we went straight down the deep *crayères*, the old Roman chalk pits which serve as cellars, and there was a beautifully laid table on trestles with such tempting plain carafes full of pale gold wine waiting for us. No speeches, no cocktails; we sat down anywhere we liked. Charles Heidsieck *père* asked me to sit next to him; some of his sons and senior members of his firm each took a member of our party in charge, but the first thing that was given to us was not Champagne but a rug to put over our knees, and then came a black woollen shawl for our shoulders. The temperature was just about 10° Centigrade or 50° Fahrenheit, a wonderful rest for us all but a real danger of catching a bad cold, after coming down from some 90° above ground. The *vin blanc en carafe* on the table was our first drink of the day and absolute nectar. We had taken for granted, or at any rate I had, that it was a *vin ordinaire pour la soif*; but it was very far from *ordinaire*. It was a truly delicious Cramant 1900 still *blanc de blancs,* the best still Champagne I could remember having drunk when I lived in Reims and had lunch *chez* Monsieur Puisard, Pommery's Steward for the Côte des Blancs Vineyard. Of course, none of my party had ever tasted a still Champagne and they were amazed. It was lesson No. 1 of the Education Committee on tour. *Grand succès.* The food, of course, was cold and excellent, the only wine served with the meal was Charles Heidsieck 1900, at cellar temperature, of course, just right, and we all enjoyed this lunch enormously. We were most reluctant when the time came to go. We had asked a Spanish firm who made Champagne corks, near the Porte de Paris, to show our party how Champagne corks were cut out of the cork bark and made to the size and shape any client asked for. Four cabs had been ordered to wait for us outside Charles Heidsieck's office, take us to the Porte de Paris, wait for us and bring us back to our garage home.

When we emerged from the cold *crayères* into the terrific heat of that August day we were hardly able to goose-step our way to the cabs only a short way away. We were so wobbly—quite sober, of course—that we were glad to have a seat in a cab to sit down, and, so far as I was concerned, go to sleep. I never saw, but I can so well visualize how those four cabs looked in single file, like a funeral procession having lost the hearse. I am sorry to say that I cannot remember if and when we arrived at the Spanish cork firm. I suppose that we must have done so, but I am afraid that none of us were in the right mood to take an intelligent interest in Champagne corks. . . .

The next day . . . we had the most spectacular meal of our trip when we were the guests of Heidsieck Dry Monopole Champagne for lunch at the Moulin de Verzenay, perched on a spur of the Montagne de Reims, overlooking thousands of acres of vines from the main Reims to Châlons-sur-Marne road up the hills as far as and beyond the villages below the woodlands which cover the top of the Montagne. There is but one large, long room in the Moulin, three of its sides all glass, so that one can enjoy the truly magnificent panorama. Year after year, day after day, visitors from all parts of the world have come to this unique observatory and admired the view that we admired, but there was on this last day of August 1909 another view which, I believe, had never been seen before and was never seen again. Upon a long refectory table almost as long as the room, there stood twenty-four Magnums of Dry Monopole 1892, one Magnum for each of the twenty-four men who sat down to lunch, fourteen of us and ten others; some of them members of the firm, others their guests. The fare was cold and very good and nobody was in a hurry. As far as I could tell the only cheating, if cheating it may be called, was Otto Winterschlaøden of Middlesbrough, the youngest member of the party, helping Roland Lane, the oldest of us, who found a Magnum rather more than he could drink.

ANDRÉ L. SIMON
In the Twilight

. . . and 1975 with Punch

"Hitler," said Dickinson with the forceful logic which so entranced Selhurst Grammar School when he taught there, "was a teetotaller. Churchill was a bottle-a-day man. So let's have another."

I nodded. You can't argue with experts. And if there is one subject on which cartoonists are acknowledged authorities it's drink.

We were in El Vino's, training for our forthcoming expedition to Epernay. An earlier foray to the vineyards of Italy had shown us that one cannot, or should not, embark on inspection tours of places where they actually make the stuff without the most careful preparation. It's not just a matter of packing the right sort of equipment: corkscrew, liver pills, Fernet Branca. The French—and to a lesser extent, the Italians—have an unshakable faith in their ability to outdrink everyone else and invariably turn these kind of visits into drinking contests. The choice of weapons is theirs, and I don't have to tell you how vital it is to do one's training in the local tipple. A beer drinker, however proficient, is no more likely to shine in, say, Bordeaux than an Olympic sprinter is to win the high jump. . . .

The first contest took place before, during, and after dinner that evening, at the splendid Château de Saran. It wasn't billed as such, of course (the French would never be that crude) but Dickinson and I were not deceived. There were, or seemed to be, two waiters for every guest and our glasses were refilled after every sip. They were pouring not from bottles but *magnums* and we caught our host's expectant look: any moment *ces faibles anglais* would start singing *God Save the Queen* and collapse helplessly onto the overstuffed sofa in the corner.

Two American guests had already succumbed. Reared on bourbon and dry martinis, they were no match for the Champenois. One, a reserve lieutenant in the San Diego police force (no, I am not making this up) was so far gone that he was busy swearing in everyone in the room—including Dickinson and me—as deputy sheriffs in the San Diego police force. (So if you ever find yourself in that delightful city, watch out.) The other was even further along the road to blissful oblivion. Listing heavily to starboard, he was telling an attractive young Frenchwoman, who did not speak a word of English, a long and complex joke about some Kentucky racehorse whose name, goddammit, he just couldn't remember.

I don't wish to boast, but I think I can safely claim that we managed to hold the French to a draw. As I recall, I said as much to this man who was approaching us from several directions all at once.

WILLIAM DAVIS
"Champagne with Everything"

The Last Word

I was advised to visit a cellar [in Epernay] containing fifteen hundred thousand bottles of wine; but on the road I chanced upon a field so beautifully bespangled with wild flowers, and so bright with sunshine, that I could not tear myself away to proceed to a cellar.

VICTOR HUGO
The Rhine

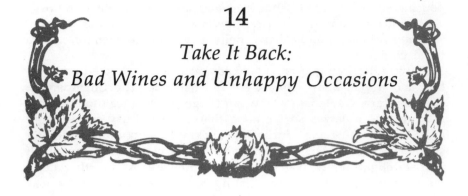

14

Take It Back:
Bad Wines and Unhappy Occasions

Although most wine writing is in praise of fine bottles, there are references enough to poor wines or wines mishandled. One of the earliest references in English to bad wine concerns the beverage served at the court of Henry II in the twelfth century, a wine so filthy that "a man need close his eyes, and clench his teeth, wry-mouthed and shuddering, and filtering the stuff rather than drinking." In 1644 John Evelyn wrote in his *Diary* that the wine of Orléans "is so gross and strong that the King's cup-bearers are sworn never to give the King any of it." Fifty years later, when the wines of Portugal had begun to replace the increasingly expensive wines of France, the anonymous author of "Farewell to Wine" describes Portuguese wines:

> Mark how it smells. Methinks, a real pain
> Is by its odour thrown upon my brain.
> I've tasted it—'tis spiritless and flat,
> And has as many different tastes
> As can be found in compound pastes.

A few years later tastes had changed to such an extent that, in *The Spectator* of 1711, Richard Steele has a character complain about "plaguy French claret" as compared to "good, solid edifying Port."

Whatever wine may be in fashion, no one likes to be served a bad wine. Nathaniel Hawthorne writes in his *Notebooks*, "I have nothing more to say of Arezzo, except that [we found] the ordinary

288

wine very bad, as black as ink, and tasting as if it had tar and vinegar in it . . ." The qualities that dismayed Hawthorne, however, seem to have been prized two thousand years earlier, judging by the descriptions quoted here of ancient wines. More recently, Osbert Sitwell praised Lambrusco as preferable to "that murky Chianti, which tastes of searing red ink with walnut shells melted into its sultry and sulky stream."

I admit to having cheated when compiling this section because it includes references to wines not made from grapes. The final entries concern fruit wines, as well as a description of kava, a Polynesian "wine" made by . . . well, why not read it for yourself?

A Welcome Change

"I think I shall go down to Hampton Court and play tennis," said Lord Eugene. "As it is the Derby, nobody will be there."

"And I will go with you, Eugene," said Alfred Mountchesney, "and we will dine together afterwards at the Toy. Anything is better than dining in this infernal London."

"Well, for my part," said Mr. Berners, "I do not like your suburban dinners. You always get something you can't eat, and cursed bad wine."

"I rather like bad wine," said Mr. Mountchesney; "one gets so bored with good wine."

BENJAMIN DISRAELI
Sybil

An Old Favorite

I had first met H. G. Wells at his house in Church Row, Hampstead, in the summer of 1908. I was living in London at the time and Wells asked Robert Ross, who was his closest friend, to bring me to dinner. As I was a great admirer of Wells's work and had read all his books once and most of his imaginative scientific stories at least twice, I was naturally delighted by this invitation. While driving up to Hampstead with Robert Ross he told me that I would get a good dinner, but that the wine, if any, might not be so good, because H. G. never drank it himself and therefore knew nothing about it. "The last time I dined with H. G.," he went on, "he produced a bottle of wine which had probably been delivered that afternoon with the groceries. I wouldn't have minded that so much, but it was corked and I had not the heart to tell him about this as it was almost certainly the only bottle he had in the house; and in any case I don't suppose he would have understood what I meant; so I had to drink a couple of glasses. However, this time I have taken the precaution of bringing him a bottle of good wine as a gift."

As soon as I had been introduced to H. G., and before Ross had time to produce his bottle, H. G. said: "I've got a treat for you, Robbie. You remember that wine you liked so much the last time you were here? Well, I wouldn't let anyone else have it and I have kept the rest of it for you!" And he pointed proudly to the offending bottle standing on the mantelpiece and which was of course by this time the finest corked vinegar.

VYVYAN HOLLAND
Time Remembered

A Story from the Duke of Wellington

It is said that the Iron Duke, dining on one occasion in his old age at the mess of a regiment of which he was the honorary colonel, grew anecdotal when the Port was passed to him for the —th time: "I remember," he began, "that when we were in the lines of Torres Vedras they brought me a bottle of Port one night which, on being opened, was found to contain a dead rat." "It must have been a very small rat, Sir," interjected a nervous subaltern. "It was a damned *big* rat, Sir!" came the irascible answer. "Perhaps it was a very large bottle, then!" commented the unhappy subaltern, trying to retrieve his error, only to be annihilated with "Damme, I tell you, it was a damned *small* bottle!"

P. MORTON SHAND

Ancient Wines

I

The dinner and dessert passed away. The ladies retired to the drawing-room: the gentlemen discoursed over their wine. Mr. MacBorrowdale pronounced an eulogium on the port, which was cordially echoed by the divine in regard to the claret.

Mr. Falconer.—Doctor, your tastes and sympathies are very

much with the Greeks; but I doubt if you would have liked their wine. Condiments of sea-water and turpentine must have given it an odd flavour; and mixing water with it, in the proportion of three to one, must have reduced the strength of merely fermented liquor to something like the smallest ale of Christophero Sly.

The Rev. Dr. Opimian.—I must say I should not like to put either salt-water or turpentine into this claret: they would not improve its bouquet; nor to dilute it with any portion of water: it has to my mind, as it is, just the strength it ought to have, and no more. But the Greek taste was so exquisite in all matters in which we can bring it to the test, as to justify a strong presumption that in matters in which we cannot test it, it was equally correct. Salt-water and turpentine do not suit our wine: it does not follow that theirs had not in it some basis of contrast, which may have made them pleasant in combination. And it was only a few of their wines that were so treated.

THOMAS LOVE PEACOCK
Gryll Grange

II

They loved old wine, too, did those old people. Wine, as old as the years to which ravens are reported to attain,—a century, or even two,—was served up at Rome. It was in consistency something like the clotted cream of Devonshire. But there was wine of a more solid consistency than this. I have elsewhere spoken of wine chopped in pieces by an axe, before it could be used. This was because of an accident which had happened to the wine; but the Romans had various preparations which were served up in lumps; and we hear of wines being kept in the chimney like modern bacon, and presented to the guests "as hard as salt." The ancients are also reported to have been able to change red wine into white, by means of white of egg and bean-flour, shaken together with the red wine in a flagon. It would require much shaking before a degenerate modern could effect the mutation in question. But if Cato could imitate the best Chian by means of his own gooseberries, the other feat may hardly be disputed. It is certain that the ancients could boldly swallow some questionable mixtures. Thus they drank their wine with sea-water, in order to stimulate and whip up energies exhausted by being overdriven the night before.

JOHN DORAN
Table Traits
1855

From the preceding details it must be sufficiently evident, that the ancients bestowed great attention and care on the management of their vineyards; that they were familiar with the most approved rules for the culture of the vine; that they were fully instructed in the processes necessary for giving to their wines a high degree of perfection; and that they were particularly curious in the means which they employed for bringing them to a proper degree of maturity, and for preserving them during a long term of years. Of these processes several have been handed down to their descendants, and are still practised in Italy and Greece; while others, either from their inadequacy to the purpose, or from being superseded by recent improvements, have fallen into merited disrepute. At first sight, indeed, it seems difficult to explain on any principles consistent with a refined taste, how a predilection should come to be entertained for wines to which a quantity of sea-water had been added, or which were highly impregnated with pitch, rosin, turpentine, and a multitude of powerful aromatic ingredients; nor can we well imagine, that their strong wines, even when mellowed by age, could be rendered very exquisite by being exposed in smoky garrets, until reduced to a syrup, and rendered so muddy and thick, that it was necessary to strain them through a cloth in order to free them from impurities, or to scrape them from the sides of the vessels, and dissolve them in hot water, before they were fit to be drunk. But, when we consider the effects of habit, which soon reconciles the palate to the most offensive substances, and the influence of fashion and luxury, which leads us to prefer every thing that is rare and costly to articles of more intrinsic excellence and moderate price, we may readily conceive, that the Greeks and Romans might have excused their fondness for pitched and pickled wines on the same plea by which we justify our attachment to tea, coffee, and tobacco. It was long ago observed by Plutarch, that certain dishes and liquors, which at first appeared intolerable, came,

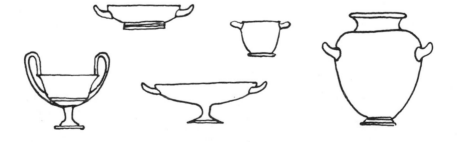

in the course of time, to be reckoned the most agreeable: and surely the charge of indulging a perverted taste in wine would proceed with an ill grace from the people of this country, where a notorious partiality exists in favour of a liquor, of which the harshness, bitterness, acidity, and other repulsive qualities, are only disguised by a large admixture of ardent spirit, but which long use has rendered so palatable to its admirers, that they fancy it the best of all possible wines.

ALEXANDER HENDERSON
1824

Piquette

The wine-makers are terrible hands for getting at the very last get-at-able drop. To this end, somewhat on the principle of rinsing an exhausted spirit bottle, so as, as it were, to catch the very flavour still clinging to the glass, they plunge the doubly-squeezed *rape* into water, let it lie there for a short time, and then attack it with the press again. The result is a horrible stuff called *piquette*, which, in a wine country, bears the same resemblance to wine as the very dirtiest, most wishy-washy, and most contemptible of swipes bears to honest porter or ale. Piquette, in fact, may be defined as the ghost of wine!—wine minus its bones, its flesh, and its soul!—a liquid shadow!—a fluid nothing!—an utter negation of all comfortable things and associations! Nevertheless, however, the peasants swill it down in astounding quantities, and apparently with sufficient satisfaction.

ANGUS B. REACH
Claret and Olives

Put It on the Bill

Desirous of knowing what sort of wine the future clergy get at the Universities, I procured specimens from Oxford, and some information withal as to the drinking customs of the place. I am glad to learn that a wholesomer taste is beginning to prevail. "Claret," says my informant, "is much drunk when friends meet after dinner; more so now than port or sherry. An average price I should say is 2s. the bottle. It is rough, but pure and wholesome." My friend tells me that very little positively bad wine is bought, except by young men who are in debt with the local wine-merchant.

ROBERT DRUITT
Report on the Cheap Wines

No More for Me

A year or two before I had had an opportunity of tasting at Mr. Blandy's dinner-table at Funchal some madeira, the authentic age of which was upwards of a century. I was cautioned beforehand not to attempt to swallow it, as I should find the flavour the reverse of agreeable. The warning was certainly not superfluous, for the liquid had lost all its vinosity, and had acquired the nauseous flavour which I should conceive a diluted mixture of creosote and petroleum to possess.

HENRY VIZETELLY
Glances Back Through Seventy Years

Tale of Three Wines

"Well," resumed Knudtzen, "we were in a wild part of the country,—weary, hungry, cold, and in the dark. Wanderers could not be in a worse plight. We were as *flûté* as Juno's columns, near the church of St. Helia; and the skeleton doing duty there for that of St. Simeon of Judæa, the pride and palladium of the people of Zara, looked in far better condition, and in, especially, better raiment, than could be boasted of by us humble pedestrians. We had walked many leagues, when we reached a sorry inn kept by a Gipsy, where we hoped to find rest and refreshment, but were permitted to enjoy neither. Our swarthy host stood in his door-way, like Horatius Cocles at the head of the bridge. Beds he did not even profess to find for travellers. He had not slept for years, and was none the worse, he said, for the privation. Leopold asked for wine.

" 'We have three sorts of wine,' said the Gipsy, 'which travellers like yourselves once tasted and paid for. I have the very wines which the seven Schwaben asked for in the Goldenes Kreutz at Ueberlingen.'

" 'What! old Sauerampfer?' cried Löwenskiold.

" 'The same,' said our singular host. 'It is not quite so sour as vinegar, but it will pierce the marrow of your bones like a sword; and it will so twist your mouth, that you shall never get it straight again.'

" 'We will try something better than this acid water,' said I: 'we will'—

" 'Try the Dreimännerswein? I am sorry there are only women in the house!'

" 'What, in the name of all your saints in Zara, have your women to do with the refreshment we need?'

" 'Do! nothing in the world! that is precisely it! You will want three men each of you. For Dreimännerswein is three times as rough and ten times as sour as vinegar; and he who drinks it must be held fast by two men, while a third pours the liquid down his throat!'

" 'And what of the third of these Olympic beverages?' said I.

" 'It is called Rachenputzer, and has peculiar qualities too. He who lies down to sleep with a flask of it in his body, must be aroused every half-hour, and turned over. Otherwise a pint of Rachenputzer would eat a hole right through his side!' "

JOHN DORAN
Table Traits
1855

Private Reserve

While some of the soldiery in World War II may have been fighting the battle for freedom, democracy and peace in their time, the armoured regiment doomed to suffer my military period fought only the battle for the booze. Our commander, Colonel Arkdust, was a saturated oenophile and his operational maps in the Italian campaign were marked up with the location and tipple-appellation of every vineyard, distillery or bodega within wheel-reach of the main axis. The red arrows of our indomitable advance drove not, as the top brass intended, straight through strongholds of Boche, but zigzagged forward between citadels of Bacchus.

"There's an interesting white chianti chateau just to the west of Doppodemani," the colonel instructed me deep in the heart of Tuscany. "Take your troop up there and bring me back some samples."

We had a tough time capturing Doppodemani. The Germans had sensibly pulled out two days before, but we had to fight off three counter-attacks by a fellow booze-chasing posse from the American Fifth Army. The chianti was stored in mighty stone vats as big as Bethesda chapels. When we tapped the first one the vino didn't come out the expected straw colour, but spouted in a pale green stream as if it were heavily laced with creme-de-menthe. It was white chianti all right to the palate but it tickled the taste-buds with a strange, herbaceous tang. I hastened back to the colonel with a couple of carboys and he called a senior officers wine-tasting right away.

"A most intriguing bouquet," pronounced the second-in-command. "Such verdant panache. Such marrow. And that subtle nuance of young vine-leaves."

"It positively sings," acclaimed the adjutant, "with an earthy meadow fragrance. All the gaunt bravura of a fine chianti pierced with the sharpness of aquamarine."

"A truly memorable wine," decided the headquarters squadron commander. "Noble, eloquent and yet with a haunting sea-green finesse."

"Green Chianti!" cried Colonel Arkdust. "It's the wine of a lifetime! Muster every watercart, bottle and gazogene we've got at Doppodemani and we'll corner the world market."

The regiment, ever-avid for alcoholic novelty, knocked back our Green Chianti as fast as we could unload it and devoted oenophiles came by bush telegraph from all over the division begging to try a bottle at 2,000 lire a time. But the bottom dropped out of the market when, as we were filling our third watercart, the emerald tinge faded from the vino and it came out the standard straw colour of white chianti. And our palate for the regimental stock vanished away when we took the lid off the vat and found a dead German in the bottom, nicely pickled, smiling seraphically, and with the normal grey-green of his field uniform drained white as chicken-feathers.

PATRICK RYAN

Taking His Lumps

Turning to the other guest in the library, I remarked: "That beats anything you can imagine as being offered to drink."

"I'm not so sure," he replied, "I think I can cap it from personal experience.

"Not very long since, a friend of mine who lives in a pleasant little suburban villa invited me to come over one Sunday and lunch with him, excusing himself that, as he only lived in a humble way, I must take him as I found him. He is a good sort of fellow, and I promised to go. True to time, I turned up, an excellent joint of beef was served at lunch, with roast potatoes.

" 'Tom, old chap, what will you drink?' he inquired, 'I have a little wine if you would care for it.' 'Thanks very much, old boy,' I answered, in order to place myself, as it were, on the same footing.

"He proceeded to open a small cupboard from which he produced a half-bottle of claret, which had been already opened and left standing on the shelf. 'I hope you will like it,' he said, as he placed the bottle on the table. 'Help yourself, old chap.' 'Thanks old boy,' I said. I attacked the joint with seemly hunger and then thought of my bottle of wine; I noticed that he was indulging in a glass of ale.

"The wine seemed a little thick as I poured it out, when suddenly, without warning, a large lump of something fell into the glass. You never saw or smelt anything so disgusting; the mildew and scum on the 'wine' was 'barking.' Looking toward my friend, I said—'I'll swap with you, old boy. I don't see why you should drink beer while I am being spoilt with wine.' 'Don't mention it, old chap,' he said; 'I'd just as soon have the beer; besides, I had my share out of the bottle, you know, and as we don't often indulge in wine I thought I'd keep it for this special occasion,' and rising, he slapped me on the shoulder and said: 'Don't worry about me, old chap, you go on and enjoy the wine.'

"I said nothing but later helped myself to water from a jug near at hand. Returning home, the thought passed through my mind that it was small wonder that some people speak of wine as 'that nasty stuff.'"

CHARLES WALTER BERRY
A Miscellany of Wine

Room Temperature?

At the next level, you come to the provision made in certain back-waters of sound radio, and in certain frontwaters of television, for a hot meal from the BBC kitchens served in somebody's office before the programme. The food here consists usually of chicken that would be refused indignantly as tasteless by a cannibal broiler-fowl, accompanied by peas that are clearly the lineal descendants of Napoleon's whiff of grapeshot, preceded by grapefruit of an acidity that necessitates its being served by a waitress wearing asbestos gloves, followed by a compote of the contents of five different tins, no two of which go together in any way, the whole being washed down by claret served so cold that I am ready to swear that I have on occasion cut my lip on the ice formed on the surface.

BERNARD LEVIN
"They Call It Hospitality"

Waste Not, Want Not

Wine for the hands to drink through the winter: Pour into a jar 10 quadrantals of must, 2 quadrantals of sharp vinegar, 2 quadrantals of boiled must, 50 quadrantals of fresh water. Stir with a stick thrice a day for five consecutive days. Then add 64 sextarii of old sea-water, cover the jar, and seal ten days later. This wine will last you until the summer solstice; whatever is left over after the solstice will be a very sharp and excellent vinegar.

CATO
On Agriculture

A Bad Bottle?

That night Prince Aribert dined with his august nephew in the superb dining-room of the Royal apartments. Hans served, the dishes being brought to the door by other servants. Aribert found his nephew despondent and taciturn. On the previous day, when, after the futile interview with Sampson Levi, Prince Eugen had despairingly threatened to commit suicide, in such a manner as to make it "look like an accident," Aribert had compelled him to give his word of honour not to do so.

"What wine will your Royal Highness take?" asked old Hans in his soothing tones, when the soup was served.

"Sherry," was Prince Eugen's curt order.

"And Romanée-Conti afterwards?" said Hans. Aribert looked up quickly.

"No, not to-night. I'll try Sillery to-night," said Prince Eugen.

"I think I'll have Romanée-Conti, Hans, after all," he said. "It suits me better than champagne."

The famous and unsurpassable Burgundy was served with the roast. Old Hans brought it tenderly in its wicker cradle, inserted the corkscrew with mathematical precision, and drew the cork, which he offered for his master's inspection. Eugen nodded, and told him to put it down. Aribert watched with intense interest. He could not for an instant believe that Hans was not the very soul of fidelity, and yet, despite himself, Racksole's words had caused him a certain uneasiness. At that moment Prince Eugen murmured across the table:

"Aribert, I withdraw my promise. Observe that, I withdraw it."

Aribert shook his head emphatically, without removing his gaze from Hans. The white-haired servant perfunctorily dusted his napkin round the neck of the bottle of Romanée-Conti, and poured out a glass. Aribert trembled from head to foot.

Eugen took up the glass and held it to the light.

"Don't drink it," said Aribert very quietly. "It is poisoned."

"Poisoned!" exclaimed Prince Eugen.

"Poisoned, sire!" exclaimed old Hans, with an air of profound amazement and concern, and he seized the glass. "Impossible, sire. I myself opened the bottle. No one else has touched it, and the cork was perfect."

"I tell you it is poisoned," Aribert repeated.

"Your Highness will pardon an old man," said Hans, "but to

say that this wine is poison is to say that I am a murderer. I will prove to you that it is not poisoned. I will drink it."

And he raised the glass to his trembling lips. In that moment Aribert saw that old Hans, at any rate, was not an accomplice of Jules. Springing up from his seat, he knocked the glass from the aged servitor's hands, and the fragments of it fell with a light tinkling crash partly on the table and partly on the floor. The Prince and the servant gazed at one another in a distressing and terrible silence. There was a slight noise, and Aribert looked aside. He saw that Eugen's body had slipped forward limply over the left arm of his chair; the Prince's arms hung straight and lifeless; his eyes were closed; he was unconscious.

"Hans!" murmured Aribert. "Hans! What is this?"

ARNOLD BENNET
The Grand Babylon Hotel

Looking Back

Before Prohibition the American people drank very little wine. They were, in fact, just beginning to appreciate their excellent California wines when the Eighteenth Amendment was passed. Some of the California grape-growers, in despair, plowed up their vineyards and planted oranges and olives. Now they wish that they had been less hasty. Last Autumn wine was made in hundreds of thousands of American households, and the price of grapes rose to $125 a ton. I know of no American home, indeed, in which some sort of brewing, wine-making or distilling is not going on. Even in the country, where belief in Prohibition still persists, practically every housewife at least makes a jug or two of blackberry cordial. Every known fruit is expectantly fermented; in the cities raisins and currants are in enormous demand. Even the common dandelion, by some process unknown to me, is converted into a beverage that gently caresses.

H. L. MENCKEN
"Souvenirs of a Journalist"

Who Needs Grapes?

It's some years now since I last went as an observer to a national amateur wine-making conference. It was in Brighton, hard by the

Regency pavilion, and the vast hall was crammed with people. Nearly 2,000 bottles of wine had been entered for judging in the 42 different classes and they varied in colour from urine gold to cough mixture pink. I saw bottles of Indian tea, primrose, passion fruit, birch sap, oak leaf, clover, rose petal, clementine, artichoke and nettle tip alongside the more everyday varieties such as apple, plum, cherry, damson, rhubarb, gooseberry, blackcurrant and potato.

Winemakers in conclave are a jolly lot, very proud of their ancient mystery, the little miracle by which a bucketful of foul-looking fruit and veg. can be transformed into liquid sunshine. Each winemaker usually brings a couple of his best bottles to the lunch so no one goes thirsty. Sitting next to me at one of these lunches a Pickwickian old solicitor exchanged wines with his neighbour: 'You try that nettle,' he beamed, 'you'll find it nice and nutty.' At another table a red-faced gentleman was appraising a glass of what looked Arbois. He inhaled the bouquet, sipped a little and a smile broke over his face: 'Bless my soul, you can smell the roses in this; what a breath of summer!'

As the lunch progresses the level of chatter rises, there is much moving from table to table bottle in hand. Here a fat man with a gold watch-chain is pressing the last of his mint and horseradish wine on four merry ladies. 'Not as good as your mangel-wurzel,' one chides him. 'You should try my dried fig,' he roars and they all collapse into peals of mirth. I met a Hertfordshire expert who has 400 gallons of wine in his cellar. He told me that a white wine is drinkable in 18 months and at its peak when two years old; a red wine will take slightly longer to achieve perfection.

Another winemaker reckoned that he had a big enough cache of wines to provide a perfect accompaniment to any meal: 'If you were dining with me I'd offer as an *aperitif* the golden warmth of a really good runner bean. With the *hors d'oeuvre* a light dry pear and perhaps if we were having chicken as the main course I'd open a bottle of my '59 gorse flowers, chilled of course.' I asked him if there was anything outstanding in his cellar that might complement the cheese: 'Pumpkin wine with the cheese, no doubt about it, and there's nothing to beat a really full-blooded blackberry liqueur with the coffee.'

When I went down to see Mr. Berry at his editorial offices in Andover I recalled this conversation and asked him if he could improve on it. 'No, I wouldn't say "improve," everyone to his taste, but if you asked *me* I'd offer you an apple sherry as an aperitif, either a *fino* or an *oloroso*. With the soup a lightish elderflower or perhaps a gooseberry—the Hairy Grape, we call it—that produces a very nice Moselle type wine. With the fish I'd serve a dry apricot very much like a Pouilly Fuissé. If we were having beef for the main course I'd offer a bilberry-redcurrant, that's as near a dry claret as you'd get. And then if you wanted a Sauternes type wine with the sweet, I'd suggest a heavy peach or an orange wine.'

DEREK COOPER
The Beverage Report

May I Have the Recipe?

The most extraordinary concoction we ever met with, or heard of, is the following:—A very worthy old lady of our acquaintance prided herself upon her "Home-made" manufacture, candidly confessing that she never drank them herself, as they disagreed with her— which was not to be wondered at. She was fond of making experiments upon new materials, and was in the habit of asking our opinion upon the results. The smell of these abominations was enough for us, although out of respect for the old lady's feelings, we endeavoured by a little cheerful banter to avoid passing sentence upon them. It happened on one occasion, when we called upon our venerable acquaintance, that some of these unfortunate wines were, with the usual intended hospitality brought forward, and our attention was particularly directed towards a dark, inky-looking liquid, which we were informed was a new discovery. We were prudently satisfied with its appearance and smell, as decomposition had evidently been going on at a rapid rate. "Now, do try it," said the old lady. "What do you think it is made of?" We pleaded ignorance, and speculated upon mushrooms. "No," said the old lady, "it is real Hock and I made it from Holly Hocks." A friend who had accompanied us was too polite to decline the invitation to taste it, and he drank a portion of a glass, and, but for the immediate assistance of a medical man, he would probably have died from the effects of the poison. His sufferings induced her subsequently to destroy what stock remained, and we elicited from her a promise to make no more such experiments.

CHARLES TOVEY
Wine and Wine Countries

Strong Stuff

Kava is the ancient national "wine" of Polynesia and Melanesia. In the old days in Tahiti, Marquesas, Samoa, Tonga, Fiji, Hawaii and hundreds of the other Pacific Islands, the natives used to make Kava in this way. Girls with sound teeth and excellent health chewed pieces of kava root—it is a sort of pepper plant—and spat them out into a bowl. In Samoa, the taupo or beauty of the village, chief's daughter and virgin of unblemished character, often mixed the Kava. Now the chips of kava root are pressed and put into a vessel, water is poured over them and they are left to ferment.

The ceremony of drinking Kava is generally held in the chief's house. The guests sit round, dressed in their bark-cloth lava-lava petticoats, but naked to the waist, their bushy black hair and beautiful copper skins shining with coco-nut oil. When all is ready, the host hands the Kava in a coco-nut shell, and it is passed round to the clapping of hands.

It was in a native house in Samoa that I tasted this liquor. It has a muddy appearance, rather like *café au lait*, or a greenish hue if made with leaves. The taste is at first sweet, then pungent and acrid. The usual dose is a couple of mouthfuls. Intoxication follows in about twenty minutes. This, however, only happens to those who are not inured to the use of the liquor.

The drunkenness produced by Kava is of the melancholy, silent, drowsy type; it affects the limbs, causing them to become temporarily paralysed. Excessive Kava drinking is said to lead to skin and other diseases, but on the other hand many medicinal virtues are ascribed to the preparation. It is supposed to be very refreshing and wholesome in these hot climates.

FRANK HEDGES BUTLER
Wine and Wine Lands of the World

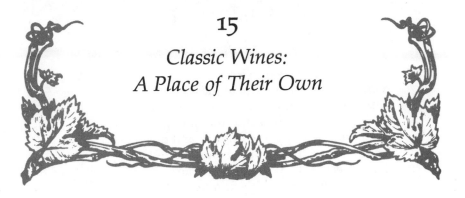

15

Classic Wines:
A Place of Their Own

Four classic wines—champagne, Bordeaux, Burgundy and port—have been written about more often than any others, and it seemed fitting to me that they should be singled out for special attention.

The section begins, appropriately enough, with champagne, and includes a charming account by Henry Vizetelly of the effects of champagne on a dinner party. There are also appreciations by Thackeray and Hemingway, a compliment from Bismarck, an acknowledgment by George Bernard Shaw, and more.

The Bordeaux selections include a recollection by Baron Philippe de Rothschild of his first morning at Mouton-Rothschild, an early appreciation of Margaux 1784 by Thomas Jefferson, a historical account of Château Palmer, and a description of a dinner at Château Latour by Harry Waugh.

Burgundy is next. Evelyn Waugh's evocation of Clos de Bèze 1904, an ingenious bottle-shaped poem by John Hollander, and a story about the English wine trade by André Simon provide three different views of this wine, among others.

Finally, some comments about port. Thackeray on the pleasures of after-dinner wine, several appreciations of the rituals associated with port, an excerpt from Dorothy L. Sayers' *Busman's Honeymoon* describing how Lord Peter Wimsey's vintage port was appallingly mishandled, and a firm negative vote from P. Morton Shand are all included.

CHAMPAGNE

Champagne

Lulled in a nine year's sleep
A child of Dionysus here abides
Imprisoned in this keep
Of dark green glass with round and glossy sides,
The entrance stopped with cork and metal cap
And muzzled like a dog with cage of wire—
Grim skeleton bedizened in a wrap
Of golden foil like kingly shroud that hides
Disintegration in a proud attire.
But loose the wire, and, lo, the prisoned slave
Stretches his muscles, heaves at the tight-closed door,
Heaves yet again and, like the whispering wave
That bursts frost-sparkling on a summer shore,
Leaps out, a fount of foam; then, changed again,
Dissolves to liquid sunlight. Golden wine
Brims every glass. Seen through each crystal pane,
In tall straight jets or whirled in spiral twine
The hurrying air-beads to the surface strain,
An April shower of bright inverted rain.

MARTIN ARMSTRONG

A Discriminating Palate

(Candida comes in with glasses, lemons, and a jug of hot water on a tray.)

CANDIDA: Who will have some lemonade? You know our rules: total abstinence. (She puts the tray on the table, and takes up the lemon squeezer, looking enquiringly round at them.)

MORELL: No use, dear. They've all had champagne. Pross has broken her pledge.

CANDIDA (to Proserpine): You don't mean to say you've been drinking champagne!

PROSERPINE (stubbornly): Yes I do. I'm only a beer teetotaller, not a champagne teetotaller.

GEORGE BERNARD SHAW
Candida

A Dinner Party

We certainly do not approve of Mr. Charles Dickens's dictum that Champagne's proper place is not at the dinner-table, but solely at a ball. 'A cavalier,' he said, 'may appropriately offer at propitious intervals a glass now and then to his danceress. There it takes its fitting rank and position amongst feathers, gauzes, lace, embroidery, ribbons, white-satin shoes, and eau-de-Cologne, for Champagne is simply one of the elegant extras of life.' This is all very well; still the advantageous effect of sparkling wine at an ordinary British dinner-party, composed as it frequently is of people brought indiscriminately together in accordance with the exigencies of the hostess's visiting-list, cannot be gainsaid. After the preliminary glowering at each other, *more Britannico,* in the drawing-room, everybody regards it as a relief to be summoned to the repast, which, however, commences as chillily as the soup and as stolidly as the salmon. The soul of the hostess is heavy with the anxiety of prospective dishes, the brow of the host is clouded with the reflection that our rulers are bent upon adding an extra penny to the income-tax. Placed between a young lady just out and a dowager of grimly Gorgonesque aspect, you hesitate how to open a conversation. Your first attempts are singularly ineffectual, only eliciting a dropping fire of monosyllables. You envy the placidly languid young gentleman opposite, limp as his fast-fading camellia, and seated next to Belle Breloques, who is certain, in racing parlance, to make the running for him. But even that damsel seems preoccupied with her fan, and, despite her *aplomb,* hesitates to break the icy silence. The two City friends of the host are lost in mute speculation as to the future price of indigo or Ionian Bank shares, while their wives seem to be mentally summarising the exact cost of each other's toilettes. Their daughters, or somebody else's daughters, are desperately jerking out monosyllabic responses to feeble remarks concerning the weather, the theatres, operatic *débutantes,* the people in the Row, æstheticism, and kindred topics from a couple of F.O. men. Little Snapshot, the wit, on the other side of the Gorgon, has tried to lead up to a story, but has found himself, as it were, frozen in the bud. When lo! the butler softly sibillates in your ear the magic word 'Champagne,' and as it flows, creaming and frothing, into your glass, a change comes over the spirit of your vision.

The hostess brightens, the host coruscates. The young lady on your right suddenly develops into a charming girl, with becoming appreciation of your pet topics and an astounding aptness for repartee. The Gorgon thaws, and implores Mr. Snapshot, whose jests are popping as briskly as the corks, not to be so dreadfully funny, or he will positively kill her. Belle Breloques can always talk, and now her tongue rattles faster then ever, till the languid one arouses himself like a giant refreshed, and gives her as good as he gets. The City men expatiate in cabalistic language on the merits of some mysterious speculation, the prospective returns from which increase with each fresh bottle. One of their wives is discussing church decoration with a hitherto silent curate, and the other is jabbering botany to a red-faced warrior. The juniors are in full swing, and ripples of silvery laughter rise in accompaniment to the beaded bubbles all round the table.

HENRY VIZETELLY
A History of Champagne

Beloved Sparkler

Yes, beloved sparkler, you are an artificial, barley-sugared, brandied beverage, according to the dicta of connoisseurs. You are universally sneered at, and said to have no good in you. But console yourself, you are universally drunken—you are the wine of the world—you are the liquor in whose bubbles lies the greatest amount of the sparkle of good spirits. May I die but I will not be ashamed to proclaim my love for you! You have given me much pleasure, and never any pain—you have stood by me in many hard moments, and cheered me in many dull ones—you have whipped up many flagging thoughts, and dissipated many that were gloomy—you have made me hope, ay, and forget. Ought a man to disown such a friend?

WILLIAM THACKERAY
"Barmecide Banquets"

The Count Pours

"Now," the count brought up a bottle. "I think this is cool."

I brought a towel and he wiped the bottle dry and held it up. "I like to drink champagne from magnums. The wine is better but it would have been too hard to cool." He held the bottle, looking at it. I put out the glasses.

"I say. You might open it," Brett suggested.

"Yes, my dear. Now I'll open it."

It was amazing champagne.

"I say that is wine." Brett held up her glass. "We ought to toast something. 'Here's to royalty.' "

"This wine is too good for toast-drinking, my dear. You don't want to mix emotions up with a wine like that. You lose the taste."

Brett's glass was empty.

"You ought to write a book on wines, count," I said.

"Mr. Barnes," answered the count, "all I want out of wines is to enjoy them."

ERNEST HEMINGWAY
The Sun Also Rises

New Year's Eve

Notwithstanding that this melancholy was eating into my soul, we were preparing to welcome the New Year with unwonted solemnity and were waiting with considerable impatience for midnight.

The fact was, we had saved up two bottles of champagne, champagne of the real sort, with the label "Veuve Clicquot" on the bottle. I had won this treasure that autumn in a bet at a christening party. It sometimes happens that during an arithmetic lesson, when the very atmosphere seems heavy with tedium, a butterfly will flutter into the classroom from out-of-doors. Then the urchins will all crane their necks and follow its flight with curiosity, as if they saw before them something strange and new and not simply a butterfly. We were amused in just such a way by this ordinary champagne which had dropped by chance into the midst of our dull life at the station. We said not a word and kept looking first at the clock and then at the bottles.

When the hands pointed to five minutes to twelve I slowly began to uncork one of the bottles. Whether I was weak from the effects of the vodka or whether the bottle was moist, I know not; I only remember that when the cork flew up to the ceiling with a pop the bottle slipped from my hands and fell to the floor. Not more than half a glassful of wine was spilled, for I was able to catch the bottle and to stop its fizzing mouth with my finger.

"Well, a happy New Year!" I cried, pouring out two glasses. "Drink!"

My wife took the glass and stared at me with startled eyes. Her face had grown pale and was stamped with horror.

"Did you drop the bottle?" she asked.

"Yes; what of it?"

"That is bad," she said, setting down her glass. "It is a bad omen. It means that some disaster will befall us this year."

"What a peasant you are!" I sighed. "You are an intelligent woman, but you rave like an old nurse. Drink!"

"God grant I may be raving, but—something will surely happen. You'll see."

She did not finish her glass but went off to one side and lost herself in thought. I made a few time-honoured remarks on the subject of superstition, drank half the bottle, walked back and forth across the room, and went out.

ANTON CHEKHOV
"Champagne"

Well, Just a Glass

"Now, J., for a glass of champagne—take it out of the pail—nay, man! not with both hands round the middle, unless you like it warm—by the neck, so," showing him how to do it, and pouring him out a glass of still champagne. "This won't do," said Jorrocks, holding it up to the candle; "*garsoon! garsoon!*—no good—no bon— no fizzay, no fizzay," giving the bottom of the bottle a slap with his hand to rouse it. "Oh, but this is still champagne," explained the Yorkshireman, "and far the best." "I don't think so," retorted Mr. Jorrocks, emptying the glass into his water-stand. "Well, then, have a bottle of the other," rejoined the Yorkshireman, ordering one. "And who's to pay for it?" inquired Mr. Jorrocks. "Oh, never mind that—care killed the cat—give a loose to pleasure for once, for it's a poor heart that never rejoices. Here it comes, and 'may you never know what it is to want,' as the beggar boys say. Now, let's see you treat it like a philosopher—the wire is off, so you've nothing to do but cut the string, and press the cork on one side with your thumb. Nay! you've cut both sides;" fizz-pop-bang, and away went the cork close past the ear of an old deaf general, and bounded against the wall. "Come, there's no mischief done, so pour out the wine. Your good health, old boy, may you live for a thousand years, and I be there to count them! Now, that's what I call good," observed the Yorkshireman, holding up his glass, "see how it dulls the glass, even to the rim—champagne isn't worth a copper unless it's iced— is it, Colonel?" "Vy, I don't know—I carn't say I like it so werry cold; it makes my teeth chatter, and cools my courage as it gets below—champagne certainly gives one werry gentlemanly ideas, but for a continuance I don't know but I should prefer mild hale."

ROBERT SMITH SURTEES
Jorrock's Jaunts and Jollities

Drink Up

To the Mall and the Park,
Where we love till 'tis dark,
Then sparkling Champagne
Puts an end to their reign;
It quickly recovers
Poor languishing lovers,
Makes us frolic and gay, and drowns all sorrow;
But alas we relapse again on the morrow.

SIR GEORGE ETHEREGE
The Man of Mode
1676

Drawing the Line

It is said that dining one night at Potsdam with Wilhelm II Bismarck was served German "champagne" or Sekt. He tasted it—and put down his glass. The kaiser looked at him enquiringly. "Your Majesty," said Bismarck, "I cannot drink German champagne." Wilhelm explained that he had decided to serve Sekt rather than the Chancellor's beloved Heidsieck, not only for reasons of economy, but as a patriotic gesture. "Your Majesty," said Bismarck simply, "I am extremely sorry; my patriotism stops short of my stomach."

PATRICK FORBES
Champagne

Old Veuve

They were known at the house of the turtle and the attractive Old Veuve: a champagne of a sobered sweetness, of a great year, a great age, counting up to the extremer maturity attained by wines of stilly depths; and their worthy comrade, despite the wanton sparkles, for the promoting of the state of reverential wonderment in rapture, which an ancient wine will lead to, well you wot. The silly girly sugary crudity has given way to womanly suavity, matronly composure, with yet the sparkles; they ascend; but hue and flavour tell of a soul that has come to a lodgement there. It conducts the youthful man to temples of dusky thought: philosophers partaking of it are drawn by the the arms of garlanded nymphs about their necks into the fathomless of inquiries. It presents us with a sphere, for the pursuit of the thing we covet most. It bubbles over mellowness; it has, in the marriage with Time, extracted a spice of individuality from the saccharine: by miracle, one would say, were it not for our knowledge of the right noble issue of Time when he and good things unite. There should be somewhere legends of him and the wine-flask.

GEORGE MEREDITH
One of Our Conquerors

Champagne Charlie

The way I gained my title's
By a hobby which I've got
Of never letting others pay
However long the shot;
Whoever drinks at my expense
Are treated all the same,
From Dukes and Lords, to cabmen down,
I make them drink Champagne.

CHORUS:
For Champagne Charlie is my name
Champagne Charlie is my name,
Good for any game at night, my boys,
Good for any game at night, my boys,
For Champagne Charlie is my name,
Champagne Charlie is my name,
Good for any game at night, my boys,
Who'll come and join me in a spree?

From Coffee and from Supper Rooms,
From Poplar to Pall Mall,

The girls on seeing me, exclaim
"Oh, what a Champagne Swell!"
The notion 'tis of everyone
If 'twere not for my name,
And causing so much to be drunk,
They'd never make Champagne.

Some epicures like Burgundy,
Hock, Claret, and Moselle,
But Moët's vintage only
Satisfies this Champagne swell.
What matter if to bed I go
Dull head and muddled thick,
A bottle in the morning
Sets me right then very quick.

Perhaps you fancy what I say
Is nothing else but chaff,
And only done, like other songs
To merely raise a laugh.
To prove that I am not in jest,
Each man a bottle of Cham.
I'll stand fizz round, yes that I will,
And stand it like a lamb.

GEORGE LEYBOURNE

BORDEAUX

Praise Indeed

Of cheap wines, the first that deserve the attention of the consumer
are those of Bordeaux. They are, as a class, pure, light, and exhilarating; they are of moderate alcoholic strength, averaging under 20°
per cent.; they are pefectly fermented, and free from sugar and
other materials likely to undergo imperfect digestion and provoke
gout or headache; and they are admirably well adapted for children,
for literary persons, and for all whose occupations are chiefly carried on indoors, and which tax the brain more than the muscles.

ROBERT DRUITT
Report on the Cheap Wines

The True Aristocracy

I have learned to esteem the 'aristocracy of the cork' more highly than any other. It plays, in our modern world, a modest, but clearly defined, part. Since the burning of the Tuileries the hereditary nobility of France has lost its function. But the great wine-cellars of Bordeaux are eternal, and the vintages of my native land have a right to ennoble the families who serve them.

FRANÇOIS MAURIAC

The First Day at Mouton

I arrived in Mouton one morning in November 1922. I was twenty years old, and my father had given me full administrative rights. The journey from Paris to Pauillac had been very long and uncomfortable. At Mouton I found there was neither running water, electricity, nor telephone—only candle light, water pitchers, oil lamps, hand pumps, and carriages—1922 was still exasperatingly nineteenth century. However, touched by the charm of the land, I chose to be patient. I am today rewarded.

During my first night in Mouton a big piece of plaster fell from the ceiling on to my bed. At four in the morning I was awakened by the sounds of the oxen going to the fields. During breakfast I looked out of the window and saw a large bonfire in the courtyard. I inquired the reason for it. The accountant was burning the account books. A little later a breathless old gentleman burst into my room—the bailiff. He was elegantly dressed, a little bent with age, *ancien régime*, asthmatical, red in the face: 'Sir,' he said, 'the *maître de chai* (the steward) has just called me a thief.'

Someone brought me up from the kitchen a pan of hot water for shaving.

Later I walked out into the courtyard. A pig squealed, hens cackled, a cow looked at me sideways. Through the linen hung up to dry, I could see the steam rising from the manure-heap. Was it really in these anomalous buildings that one of the best wines in the world was produced? If the well-kept vineyards had not come up like sea waves to the walls of the houses one would have thought one was merely in some undistinguished farm.

BARON PHILIPPE DE ROTHSCHILD

A Gentleman

When Mr. Julius Ricardo spoke of a gentleman—and the word was perhaps a thought too frequent upon his tongue—he meant a man who added to other fastidious qualities a sound knowledge of red wine. He could not eliminate that item from his definition. No! A gentleman must have the great vintage years and the seven growths tabled in their order upon his mind as legibly as Calais was tabled on the heart of the Tudor Queen. He must be able to explain by a glance at the soil why a vineyard upon this side of the road produces a more desirable beverage than the vineyard fifty yards away upon the other. He must be able to distinguish at a first sip the virility of a Château Latour from the feminine fragrance of a Château Lafite. And even then he must reckon that he had only learnt a Child's First Steps. He could not consider himself properly equipped until he was competent to challenge upon any particular occasion the justice of the accepted classifications. Even a tradesman might contend that a Mouton Rothschild was unfairly graded amongst the second growths. But the being Mr. Ricardo had in mind must be qualified to go much farther than that. It is probable indeed that if Mr. Ricardo were suddenly called upon to define a gentleman briefly, he would answer: "A gentleman is one who has a palate delicate enough and a social position sufficiently assured to justify him in declaring that bottle of a good bourgeois growth may possibly transcend a bottle of the first *cru*."

A. E. W. MASON
The Prisoner in the Opal

Château Ducru Beaucalliou, 1918

This senatorial stuff was harvested
   By wives and grandfathers and children, when
   Upon the Western Front the last young men
In France were being pricked to join the dead.

Emotion is the enemy of taste:
   Dead harvesters do not affect the wine:
   'Sixteen, for instance, managed to combine
Carnage and vintage in one classic waste.

What right has anybody got to drink it
Who wasn't there?
                                     Well, it is at its prime—
          Polleny, firm, remarkable. What's more,
          Henceforth it will be dying all the time.
      I suck and swallow. Strange indeed I think it
          That this is what the grapes were gathered for.

                                                    PETER DICKINSON

The Origins of Château Palmer

[General Palmer's] fortune was sufficiently large for all his wants;
but, unfortunately, as it turned out, the House of Commons voted
to him, as the representative of his father, £100,000, which he was
desirous of laying out to advantage. A fine opportunity, as he imagined, had presented itself to him for, in travelling in the diligence
from Lyons to Paris—a journey then requiring three days—he met a
charming widow, who told a tale that had not only a wonderful
effect upon his susceptible heart, but upon his amply-filled purse.
She said her husband, who had been the proprietor of one of the
finest estates in the neighbourhood of Bordeaux, was just dead, and
that she was on her way to Paris to sell the property, that it might
be divided, according to the laws of France, amongst the family.
Owing, however, to the absolute necessity of forcing a sale, that
which was worth an enormous sum would realize one quarter only
of its value. She described the property as one admirably fitted for
the production of wine; that it was in fact the next estate to the
Château Lafite, and would prove a fortune to any capitalist. The
fascinations of this lady, and the temptation of enormous gain to the
speculator, impelled the gallant general to offer his services to relieve her from her embarrassment; so by the time the diligence
arrived in Paris he had become the proprietor of a fine domain,
which was soon irrevocably fixed on him by the lady's notary, in
return for a large sum of money: and, had the general proved a man
of business, he would no doubt have been amply repaid, and his
investment might have become the source of great wealth.

   Palmer, however, conscious of his inaptitude for business,
looked around him for an active agent, and believed he had found
one in a Mr. Gray, a man of captivating manners and good connex-
ions, but almost as useless a person as the general himself. Fully
confident in his own abilities, Gray had already been concerned in

many speculations; but not one of them had ever succeeded, and all had led to the demolition of large fortunes. Plausible in his address, and possessing many of those superficial qualities that please the multitude, he appeared to be able to secure for the claret—which was the production of the estate—a large clientele. Palmer's claret, under auspices, began to be talked of in the clubs; and the bon vivant was anxious to secure a quantity of this highly-prized wine.

The patronage of the Prince Regent, being considered essential, was solicited, and the prince, with his egotistical good nature, and from a kindly feeling for Palmer, gave a dinner at Carlton House, when a fair trial was to be given to his claret. A select circle of gastronomes was to be present, amongst whom was Lord Yarmouth, well known in those days by the appellation of 'Red-herrings,' from his rubicund whiskers, hair, and face, and from the town of Yarmouth deriving its principal support from the importation from Holland of that fish; Sir Benjamin Bloomfield, Sir William Knighton, and Sir Thomas Tyrwhitt, were also of the party. The wine was produced, and was found excellent, and the spirits of the party ran high; the light wine animating them without intoxication. The Prince was delighted, and, as usual upon such occasions, told some of his best stories, quoted Shakespeare, and was particularly happy upon the bouquet of the wine as suited 'to the holy Palmer's kiss.'

Lord Yarmouth alone sat in moody silence, and, on being questioned as to the cause, replied that whenever he dined at his Royal Highness's table, he drank a claret which he much preferred—that which was furnished by Carbonell. The prince immediately ordered a bottle of this wine; and to give them an opportunity of testing the difference, he desired that some anchovy sandwiches should be served up. Carbonell's wine was placed upon the table: it was a claret made expressly for the London market, well-dashed with Hermitage, and infinitely more to the taste of the Englishmen than the delicately-flavoured wine they had been drinking. The banquet terminated in the prince declaring his own wine superior to that of Palmer's, and suggesting that he should try some experiments on his estate to obtain a better wine. Palmer came from Carlton House much mortified. On Sir Thomas Tyrwhitt attempting to console him, and saying that it was the anchovies that had spoiled the taste of the connoisseurs, the general said, loudly enough to be heard by Lord Yarmouth, 'No; it was the confounded red herrings.' A duel was very nearly the consequence.

General Palmer, feeling it his duty to follow the advice of the prince, rooted out his old vines, planted new ones, and tried all sorts of experiments at an immense cost, but with little or no result. He and his agent, in consequence, got themselves into all sorts of difficulties, mortgaged the property, borrowed largely and were at last obliged to have recourse to usurers, to life assurances, and every sort of expedient, to raise money. The theatre at Bath was sold, the Reform of Parliament robbed him of his seat, and at last he and his agent became ruined men. A subscription would have been raised to relieve him, but he preferred ending his days in poverty to living upon the bounty of his friends. He sold his commission, and was plunged into the deepest distress; while the accumulation of debt to the usurers became so heavy, that he was compelled to pass through the Insolvent Court.

REES HOWELL GRONOW
Reminiscences

No Vin de Pays, Please

Upon the principle, I suppose, of the nearer the church, the further from God, Bordeaux is by no means a good place for good ordinary wine; on the contrary, the stuff they give you for every-day tipple is positively poor, and very flavourless. In southern Burgundy, the most ordinary of the wines is capital. At Mâcon, for a quarter of a handful of sous they give you nectar; at the little town of Tain, where the Rhône sweeps gloriously round the great Hermitage rock, they give you something better than nectar for less. But the ordinary Bordeaux wine is very ordinary indeed; not quite so red-inky, perhaps, as the *Vin de Surenne*, which, Brillat Savarin says, requires three men to swallow a glassfull—the man who drinks, and the friends who uphold him on either side, and coax, and encourage him; but still meagre and starveling, as if it had been strained through something which took the virtue out of it. Of course, the best of wine can be had by the simple process of paying for it, but I am talking of the ordinary work-a-day tipple of the place.

ANGUS B. REACH
Claret and Olives

Trooping the Colors

Another St. Julien wine, well-known in England, is La Rose, the celebrity of which dates back to the middle of the last century, when the owner of the vineyard was in the habit of hoisting the flag of the particular nation which he considered his wine most likely to suit. Thus, when it was thin and low in price the German colours were run up; when full of body and correspondingly dear, the British standard was unfurled; while, when the wine proved to be of an intermediate character, the Dutch flag was seen flying from the square tower of the château.

HENRY VIZETELLY
Glances Back Through Seventy Years

A Bordeaux Dinner

The main purpose of our visit was rapidly approaching, the fiftieth anniversary dinner of the Bordeaux Club.* David and Margot Pollock, who were already staying in the château [Latour], had arranged to go out for dinner in order to leave the room free for us. It was a terribly nice gesture and I had imagined that they would be having dinner in the little restaurant in Pauillac, but not a bit of it, they had been bidden to dine at Château Mouton Rothschild by Philippe and Pauline de Rothschild.

Our apéritif before dinner was a magnum of Taittinger Comtes de Champagne 1959, a fine wine and just right for the occasion.

The decoration and furnishing of the dining room was exactly right too for a dinner such as ours. The period is of the 1880's and it has been beautifully arranged by no less a person than John Fowler. The walls are covered by striped terra cotta paper in two deep shades and there are magnificent matching curtains over the windows.

Ch. Latour is run by a very nice couple, M. and Madame Robert Verge. Robert served as a steward on the French Line for most of his life and his wife is a superlative cook, as any visitor to the château quickly finds out.

The white china and candlesticks are Crown Derby and are

---

* The Bordeaux Club was started in 1949 obviously by enthusiasts for Bordeaux wines (later they slipped and allowed a few white wines in from Burgundy at their dinners), the three principal founders being Harry Waugh, Allan Sichel and the famous historian, Fellow of Christ College, Cambridge, Professor J. H. Plumb. Membership has changed but there is still a nucleus of wine merchants and University dons from both Oxford and Cambridge. The meetings have been taking place about three times a year in London, Oxford and Cambridge respectively, but the fiftieth meeting was planned to be celebrated in Bordeaux. At this meeting Allan Sichel, one of the founder members, happened to be in that town at the time and was able to take the place of Maurice Platnauer, the only member not able to get to Bordeaux for the occasion.

especially attractive, with the tower of Latour as their device in gold. We began with a delicious consommé made of beef and many vegetables; this was followed by one of Madame's specialities, *omelette fourrée*, which has the very lightest of cheese filling.

In view of the splendour of the wines, Margot Pollock had ordered the most simple food possible to set them off, and this omelette was exactly right at the beginning of such a *grand diner*.

There was one exception, however, and that was inevitable because this is the season for *ceps* and everybody in Bordeaux simply has to eat them. So we had *ceps aux tomates*. Cooked with tomato, diced garlic and so on, they were quite delicious.

By this time the first wine was on the table, a magnum of Ch. Latour 1929, decanted only half-an-hour beforehand. What a bouquet, what a perfume! This magnum was a dream, a really great 1929, at its very best. Allan Sichel, who in the past has often been critical of the 1929's (my own favourite vintage), thought that considering its power and strength, it would keep and be even better in ten years' time.

The gigot, so beautifully cooked, came from a lamb fattened in the Marais de Pauillac, *pré salé* in fact. The low lying meadows between the vines and the vast river give a specially good flavour to the meat, consequently, the district of the Médoc is noted for its *agneau pré salé*.

By this time we were conscious of the presence of M. Metté. M. Metté, the huge *maître de chai* Ch. Latour, was taking such an interest in the proceedings, that he had stationed himself in the kitchen for the evening to watch the course of the meal so that he could decant his precious bottles at exactly the right moment. His task was carried out of perfection.

Now the 1924 Ch. Latour, also from a magnum, appeared alongside the 1929. Being such a fan of the 1929's I did not really expect anything to be much better, but I was utterly confounded; the 1924 was in fact an even greater wine than the 1929, certainly with more *finesse*. My notes say, deep in colour with a perfumed bouquet and a simply gorgeous flavour. It was full of natural sugar and that added tremendously to its charm; what a wine!

The 1924 had also been decanted about thirty minutes before being served, so it grew and glorified throughout the meal.

Almost incredibly these two quite outstanding magnums were only leading up to the *pièce de résistance* of the evening, for with the cheese there arrived the precious bottle of 1865, a wine virtually 100 years old!

David Pollock had tried a bottle of this vintage only a month or so beforehand, and had found it so outstanding that he thought we should have one for our dinner.

With these very ancient wines, only one bottle among a number turns out to be even drinkable, so I am sure none of us expected very much; we only hoped! Jack's glass was filled first and he gasped! This 1865 had an astonishingly deep colour and such a bouquet. A great big fellow, full of fruit and absolutely fabulous for a centenarian. What a culmination to our fiftieth dinner!

I can only hope that the *maître de chai* who lovingly laid this bottle in its bin under the château almost a hundred years ago, could have had some premonition of the pleasure it was to give so very many decades later. Frankly it tasted like quite a young wine and was nothing more nor less than a miracle.

At this point M. Metté, who had decanted it only five minutes before, was called in to receive our thanks for his care and attention. It was easy to see from his beaming face how pleased and proud he was.

We had not finished yet because with the sweet, *crème renversée*, we drank an excellent bottle of Château d'Yquem 1945. Visiting the château soon after the war I remember the *maître de chai* telling me his 1945 was considered to be the best vintage produced at Château d'Yquem since the great year of 1869. One does not know, of course, but this 1945 was certainly reaching for the stars.

Then with our coffee we had the Martell 1914, landed in Bristol very soon afterwards and matured there. It was my one ewe lamb that I had been saving up for a very great occasion. To my sorrow it passed almost unnoticed; it was magnificent but by this time my colleagues had run out of praise. I enjoyed it anyway!

HARRY WAUGH
Bacchus on the Wing

Maître de Chai: Latour

Large, elderly, stiff, remote,
He moves like a narrow-boat
  Down the long canals between
His casks in regular line.
He does not talk about wine
  In wine-talk (you know what I mean—

The mysterious jargon in use
Among those who are fond of this juice).
  Indeed, he seems almost perverse
The way he tends to compare
One year with another year
  By calling it 'Better' or 'Worse.'

His hairy fingers stroke
The close-grained staves of oak
  Where a dribbling indigo stain
Covers the round of the cask.
'Is that fermentation?' I ask.
  He grunts and tries to explain

That the seasons tug like a tide
On the raw new wine. When, outside,
  The vines are in trivial flower
It works and moves to that pull.
And again, when the grapes are full,
  It knows, he remarks, its hour.

I feel the hair on my nape
Prickle, to think of the grape
  Being mashed, fermented, and run
Into barrels, and fined, and racked—
Being ten-times-processed, in fact—
  But moving still when the sun

Moves, here, in the wood, in the dark.
No wonder his language is stark:
  When phenomena such as these
Are part of his everyday
Problems down in the *chai*
  He needn't *make* mysteries.

PETER DICKINSON

Press, Don't Eat

If ever you want to see a homily, not read, but grown by nature, against trusting to appearances, go to Médoc and study the vines. Walk and gaze, until you come to the most shabby, stunted, weazened, scrubby, dwarfish, expanse of snobbish bushes, ignominiously bound neck and crop to the espaliers like a man on the rack—these utterly poor, starved, and meagre-looking growths, allowing, as they do, the gravelly soil to show in bald patches of grey shingle through the straggling branches—these contemptible-looking shrubs, like paralysed and withered raspberries, it is which produce the most priceless, and the most inimitably flavoured wines. Such are the vines which grow Château Margaux at half a sovereign the bottle. The grapes themselves are equally unpromising. If you saw a bunch in Covent Garden you would turn from them with the notion that the fruiterer was trying to do his customer, with over-ripe black currants. Lance's soul would take no joy in them, and no sculptor in his senses would place such meagre bunches in the hands and over the open mouths of his Nymphs, his Bacchantes, or his Fauns. Take heed, then, by the lesson, and beware of judging of the nature of either men or grapes by their looks.

ANGUS B. REACH
Claret and Olives

Thomas Jefferson Buys Nothing But the Best

Making a tour round the sea-ports of this country on matters of business, and meeting at this place with Capt. Gregory, just sailing for Portsmouth, I cannot deny myself the pleasure of asking you to participate of a parcel of wine I have been choosing for myself. I do it the rather as it will furnish you a specimen of what is the very best Bordeaux wine. It is of the vineyard of Obrion, one of the four established as the very best, and it is of the vintage of 1784, the only very fine one since the year 1779. Six dozen bottles of it will be packed separately addressed to you . . .

Letter to Francis Eppes
1787

I received your favor of Dec. 15. two days after I had written my letter of the 7th. inst. and at the same time with one from Callow Carmichael & co. informing me that your vessel would sail from Havre about the 19th. instant. The shortness of warning not admitting time to order claret for you from Bordeaux early enough to go either by the Bowman or by your next ship, I send you two hampers from my own cellar, containing 124 bottles. I am afraid it will not get to Havre in time for the Bowman. You say you had tasted at Mr. Eppes's some wine I had sent him, which was good, but not equal to what you have seen. I have sent to him twice; and what you say would correspond to the first batch. The second was of Chateau Margau of the year 1784, bought by myself on the spot, and a part of the very purchase from which I now send you. It is of the best vintage which has happened in nine years, and is of one of the four vineyards which are admitted to possess exclusively the first reputation. I may safely assure you therefore that, according to the taste of this country and of England there cannot be a bottle of better Bordeaux produced in France. It cost me at Bordeaux three livres a bottle, ready bottled and packed. This is very dear; but you say you do not limit me in price.

Letter to Alexander Donald
1788

'Tis the Last Glass of Claret

'Tis the last glass of claret
    Left sparkling alone;
All its rosy companions
    Are cleaned out and gone.
No wine of her kindred,
    No red port is nigh
To reflect back her blushes,
    And gladden my eye.

I'll not leave thee, thou lone one,
    This desert to crown:
As the bowls are all empty,
    Thou too shalt float down.
Thus kindly I drink up
    Each drop of pure red,
And fling the bright goblet
    Clean over my head.

So soon may Dame Fortune
  Fling me o'er her head,
When I quit brimming glasses,
  And bundle to bed.
When champagne is exhausted,
  And Burgundy's gone,
Who would leave even claret
  To perish alone?

WILLIAM MAGINN

BURGUNDY

Chambertin Clos de Bèze 1904

I rejoiced in the Burgundy. How can I describe it? The Pathetic Fallacy resounds in all our praise of wine. For centuries every language has been strained to define its beauty, and has produced only wild conceits or the stock epithets of the trade. This Burgundy seemed to me, then, serene and triumphant, a reminder that the world was an older and better place than Rex knew, that mankind in its long passion had learned another wisdom than his. By chance I met this same wine again, lunching with my wine merchant in St. James's Street, in the first autumn of the war; it had softened and faded in the intervening years, but it still spoke in the pure, authentic accent of its prime and, that day, as at Paillard's with Rex Mottram years before, it whispered faintly, but in the same lapidary phrase, the same words of hope.

EVELYN WAUGH
Brideshead Revisited

What's in a Name?

I shall never forget being given a Corton Charlemagne of 1893, shipped by Louis Latour, many years ago, when I was not only quite a young man but a newcomer to the City. My host was one of the best known among the wine-merchants of pre-whisky days, almost pre-railway days, and he asked me: "Well, young fellow, my lad, how do you like this Chablis?" Looking at the bottle which stood starkly before me with its name across a blameless white label, I hesitatingly replied: "You mean Corton, Sir?" "Tut, tut," snorted the old gentleman, "don't try to be so clever, and don't fuss us with all manner of French names. You'd better remember that in this country all white Burgundies are called Chablis."

ANDRÉ L. SIMON
Vintagewise

No Laughing Matter

The true Burgundian takes life seriously; food, wine and architecture are three things that he cannot joke about; the true Burgundian would weep over an *escargot* and commit suicide over a fish. And, if you ever want to shuffle off this mortal coil, I can suggest no better way than to go into a Dijon restaurant, order a bottle of Clos Vougeot 1890 and, when you taste it, make a wry face and say *"le gout du cuit."* If the waiter doesn't get you, the *patron* will; and a crime of this sort, in Burgundy, is considered justifiable homicide.

FRANK SCHOONMAKER
Come with Me Through France

Sounds Good

Burgundy is pre-eminently a full-bodied wine; but its body is aromatic, not alcoholic. Of course, like all great artists, I am drawing from the live model. I write with a bottle before me, which I am sacrificing for my own inspiration and my readers' profit; and the alcoholic strength of the generous liquid is only 22 or thereabouts, whereas a bottle of Cape Port sent me by a patient (of course, being undrinkable, it shall be given to the poor) is quite 36. One-eighth of a bottle is as much as a man need drink with the most savoury parts of his dinner; one-fourth of a bottle is quite a good dose for a moderate man. It makes one feel decidedly warmer and more genial; it is a thorough exhilarant, and if taken too freely produces a tightness and uneasiness in the head. But if good, it does not produce any other ill-effect; neither does it do so if other wines be taken before and after it, as people ought to do, for to drink Burgundy throughout a dinner is like trumpets throughout a sonata or an apple tart all quince. But if too new, or in a state of fermentescibility or acidity, it will be felt in every joint in the body.

ROBERT DRUITT
Report on the Cheap Wines

For a Thirtieth Birthday, with a Bottle of Burgundy

Drop by
Drop it
Empties
Now not
Even as
Our own
Tearful
Vintage
Gathering
Itself with
Such slowness
Gradually might
Widen in the bottom
Of some oblate vessel
But as when the pouring
Bottle now nearly half of
Its old wine spent delivers
The rest up in sobs rapidly
Tears years and wine expire
As tosspot Time sends after
His cellarer once more alas
Then let the darkling drops
Wept in a decent year along
The golden slopes elude for
A moment or so his horribly
Steady pouring hand and run
Into sparkling glasses still
Unshattered yes and undimmed

JOHN HOLLANDER

A Word of Caution

How good the Burgundy smacks after it! I always drink Burgundy at this house, and that not of the best. It is my firm opinion that a third-rate Burgundy, and a third-rate claret—Beaune and Larose, for instance, are *better* than the best. The Bordeaux enlivens, the Burgundy invigorates; stronger drink only inflames; and where a bottle of good Beaune only causes a man to feel a certain manly warmth of benevolence—a glow something like that produced by sunshine and gentle exercise—a bottle of Chambertin will set all your frame in a fever, swell the extremities, and cause the pulses to throb. Chambertin should *never* be handed round more than twice; and I recollect to this moment the headache I had after drinking a bottle and a half of Romanée-Gélée, for which this house is famous. Somebody else *paid* for the—(no other than you, O Gustavus! with whom I hope to have many a tall dinner on the same charges)—but 'twas in our hot youth, ere experience had taught us that moderation was happiness, and had shown us that it is absurd to be guzzling wine at fifteen francs a bottle.

WILLIAM THACKERAY
"Memorials of Gormandising"

Up from the Cellar

Silence is a great part of the life the Serein here encloses. A peacefulness so profound that one wants to retard every slow moment and see it from both sides. . . .
The wine stacked in bins in the cellar, to lie there cool and obscure, for years to come—the act of placing it has a ritual gravity. And brought upstairs in its little basket, like a baby in a bassinette, carefully horizontal, a bottle of Musigny or Corton-Grancey has the full righteousness of colour, bouquet, and *goût* that make it as perfect in its own realm as an ode by Keats. There is no tariff in these matters. Perfection costs whatever you have to pay for it. Indeed the exhalation rising from a wine like Musigny, the ghost of the grape rising in the clear half-empty crater of those vast goblets, is so divine that it would seem the supreme act of connoisseurship simply to relish it in the nostrils and never taste it at all. Nor is it wise to taste rich Burgundies too continuously; the Subscriber in Waterbury who reproached me for an interest in such matters may console himself with the linguistic reflection that *goût* is easily transformed into gout.

CHRISTOPHER MORLEY
"An Old House in Burgundy"

A Good Bottle

The average youth of twenty may expect to live for some thirty-six years. But if he was an infantry subaltern marching up into the Somme battle front in the summer of 1916, his expectation of life was thirteen days and a bit. Some men took this contracted horizon in one way, and some in another. One virgin youth would think: "Only a fortnight? Wouldn't do to chuck it in the straight." Another would think: "Only a fortnight? And life scarcely tasted! I must gather a rose while I can."

Phil Gresson thought that he was, on the whole, for the rose. So he got a night's leave from Daours, where his company lay for two days on its way to the mincing machine at Pozières. Then he borrowed the winking medical officer's horse and trotted off into Amiens, pondering what sort of wine to have with his dinner at Gobert's famed restaurant. Burgundy, he concluded: Burgundy was the winiest wine, the central, essential, and typical wine, the soul and greatest common measure of all the kindly wines of the earth, the wine that ought to be allowed to survive if it were ever decreed that, after thirteen days and a bit, only one single wine was to be left alive to do the entire work of the whole heart-gladdening lot. He thought it all out very sagely.

Gobert's was full: Gresson just bagged the last single table. Soon the rising buzz of talk drew its light screen of sound in front of the endless slow thud of the guns in the east. Soon, too, the good Burgundy did its kind office, and Phil's friendly soul was no longer alone: all the voices at the other tables had melted into one mellow voice: he recognized it as the genial voice of the whole of mankind, at its admirable best—not stiff, or cold, or forbidding, as some voices seemed at some times. It set him all a-swim in a delicious reverie about the poignant beauty of this extreme brevity that had come upon life. Thirteen days and a bit—and then all love, all liking, all delight to lie drowned forever at the bottom of an endless night. Lovely, lovely. The individual life just a mere wisp of an eddy formed and re-formed on the face of a stream, and then smoothed away. Oh! it was good Burgundy. And Phil, a modest and a sober youth, drank more of it than he had ever drunk of any wine at a sitting.

C. E. MONTAGUE
"Judith"

Burgundy

Praise now the ancient Duchy of the Vine
Where the warm tide of summer sunlight spills
On vineyards ranged along the Golden Hills,
Upbrimming every long and leafy line.

In grapes of Chambertin and Clos de Bèze,
Richebourg, La Romanée, lie darkly curled
The purple kings of all the vinous world;
Till from the dusky fruit in autumn days

That juice is crushed which slowly, subtly grows,
Through hidden workings, whispered fermentations,
Like ghostly dancers mixed in strange mutations,
To essence of the ruby and the rose.

Be patient then, while generous years devise
Maturity and riches to the wine,
Till, to perfection come, it darkly shine
Upon the banquets of the truly wise.

MARTIN ARMSTRONG

PORT

The Naked Mahogany

"Beautiful white damask and a green cloth are indispensable." Ah, my dear Lionel, on this head I exclaim, let me see the old mahogany back again, with the crystal, and the wine quivering and gleaming in it. I am sorry for the day when the odious fashion of leaving the cloth down was brought from across the water. They leave the cloth on a French table because it is necessary to disguise it; it is often a mere set of planks on tressels, the meanness of which they disguise as they disguise the poverty of their meat. Let us see the naked mahogany; it means, I think, not only a good dinner, but *a good drink after dinner*. In houses where they leave the cloth down you know they are going to shirk their wine. And what is a dinner without a subsequent drink? A mockery—an incomplete enjoyment at least. . . .

This I honestly say as a diner-out in the world. If I accept an invitation to a house where the dessert-cloth practice is maintained (it must be, I fear, in large dinners of *apparat* now, but I mean in common *réunions* of ten or fourteen)—if I accept a dessert-cloth invitation, and a mahogany invitation subsequently comes, I fling over dessert-cloth. To ask you to a dinner without a drink is to ask you to half a dinner.

WILLIAM THACKERAY
"Barmecide Banquets"

Judicious Words

For Port—*red* Port, as one of its earliest celebrants after the Methuen treaty no less justly than emphatically calls it, White Port being a mere albino—is incomparable when good. It is not a wine-of-all-work like Sherry—Mr. Pendennis was right when he declined to drink it *with* his dinner. It has not the almost feminine grace and charm of Claret; the transcendental qualities of Burgundy and Madeira; the immediate inspiration of Champagne; the rather unequal and sometimes palling attractions of Sauternes and Moselle and Hock. But it strengthens while it gladdens as no other wine can do; and there is something about it which must have been created in pre-established harmony with the best English character.

GEORGE SAINTSBURY
Notes on a Cellar-Book

A Question

"To which University," said a lady, some time since, to the late sagacious Dr. Warren, "shall I send my son?" "Madam," replied he, "they drink, I believe, near the same quantity of port in each of them."

The Times
1798

No Hurry

In the old graces and ritual of the table such as are observed in the common-rooms of Oxford and the combination-rooms of Cambridge, Port bears an important role. After dinner is concluded with a savoury, the table is cleared, the cloth is deftly removed, dishes of fruit, biscuits and nuts are laid out on the bare table where each one can help himself, and each diner is furnished with a Port glass, a Sherry glass, and a fruit plate, fork, and silver knife. A decanter of Port and one of Madeira or Sherry are placed by the Senior Fellow at the head of the table, and the servant retires, only to reappear if fresh supplies of wine are required. The Senior Fellow first fills the glass of the gentleman at his right hand, next serves himself, and then the gentleman at his left. The decanters are then slid around the polished table on padded coasters, clockwise or "with the sun," because Port will take offence at being circulated "against the sun," and go sour on you. When the head of the table judges that it is time, he starts the decanters around a second time, and sometimes there is a third round of a light sherry for "mouth-wash" after an unusually rich and fruity Vintage Port. A short glass from the bottom of the decanter is called a "buzz," and entitles the victim to another full glass, provided he has put the "buzz" away by the time the servant brings a new decanter. When everyone who wants it has had a second glass, the head of the table rings for coffee and cigarettes. Up to that point smoking is absolutely prohibited; and when I first knew Oxford, smoking was never allowed at any time in the same room where Port was drunk. One had to adjourn to another room after dinner if one wished to smoke.

In America few can afford servants with the technique of rolling up a tablecloth and whisking it over the heads of the diners, but we can see that Port is handed around "with the sun," and a little restraint in the matter of smoking will be amply repaid by full enjoyment of the delicious grapy bouquet and rich, full flavour of the Noblest of Wines.

SAMUEL ELIOT MORISON

Gladstone and Port

I went to Cambridge because of my interest in mathematics. My first experience of the place was in December 1889 . . . I was invited to dine with the Master, who had been Headmaster of Harrow in my father's time. . . . I was alarmed by so formidable a social occasion, but less alarmed than I had been a few months earlier when I was left *tête-à-tête* with Mr. Gladstone. He came to stay at Pembroke Lodge, and nobody was asked to meet him. As I was the only male in the household, he and I were left alone together at the dinner table after the ladies retired. He made only one remark: "This is very good port they have given me, but why have they given it me in a claret glass?" I did not know the answer, and wished the earth would swallow me up. Since then I have never again felt the full agony of terror.

The Autobiography of Bertrand Russell

Mr. Tulkinghorn's Port

Mr. Tulkinghorn sits at one of the open windows, enjoying a bottle of old port. Though a hard-grained man, close, dry, and silent, he can enjoy old wine with the best. He has a priceless bin of port in some artful cellar under the Fields, which is one of his many secrets. When he dines alone in chambers, as he has dined to-day, and has his bit of fish and his steak or chicken brought in from the coffee-house, he descends with a candle to the echoing regions below the deserted mansion, and, heralded by a remote reverberation of thundering doors, comes gravely back, encircled by an earthy atmosphere, and carrying a bottle from which he pours a radiant nectar, two score and ten years old, that blushes in the glass to find itself so famous, and fills the whole room with the fragrance of southern grapes.

Mr. Tulkinghorn, sitting in the twilight by the open window, enjoys his wine. As if it whispered to him of its fifty years of silence and seclusion, it shuts him up the closer. More impenetrable than ever, he sits, and drinks, and mellows as it were, in secrecy.

CHARLES DICKENS
Bleak House

A Compliment

That the host should praise his own wine is not only lawful but desirable: so that it deserve the praise, that will put the guests in the right frame of mind. Yet it is dangerous at times. A relative of mine, justly famous for fierce economy at the Treasury and for luxuriousness in private life, once found himself obliged to entertain semi-officially some awful body of currency experts. Not content with the wines at his club, and availing himself of the system of corkage, he sent his own wines—of course, well in advance of the event—to the club. The financial Philistines absorbed incomparable wines without a word or look of appreciation, and the host "endured an hour and saw injustice done"; till his Port was on the table. It was of the 1834 vintage, which ranks historically with the wine of other classic years of the nineteenth century, "Waterloo," "Twenty," the supreme "Forty-seven," 1851, 1854, 1863, 1868. . . . "And what," said he to a miserable, mentally side-whiskered monetary expert, "do you think of my '34 Port?" "Very nice; indeed, better than some I pay 36 for."

T. EARLE WELBY
The Cellar Key

Panic in the Pantry

"I've put out the plates like you said, Mr. Bunter," announced that lady with meek self-righteousness. Bunter frowned. She had something rolled in the corner of her apron and was rubbing at it as she spoke. He felt that it would take a long time to teach Mrs. Ruddle a good servant's-hall manner.

"And I've found the other vegetable-dish—only it's broke."

"Very good. You can take these glasses out and wash them. There don't seem to be any decanters."

"Never you mind that, Mr. Bunter. I'll soon 'ave them bottles clean."

"Bottles?" said Bunter. "What bottles?" A frightful suspicion shot through his brain. "What have you got there?"

"Why," said Mrs. Ruddle, "one o' them dirty old bottles you brought along with you." She displayed her booty in triumph. "Sech a state as they're in. All over whitewash."

Bunter's world reeled about him and he clutched at the corner of the settle.

"My God!"

"You couldn't put a thing like that on the table, could you now?"

"Woman!" cried Bunter, and snatched the bottle from her, "that's the Cockburn '96!"

"Ow, is it?" said Mrs. Ruddle, mystified. "There now! I thought it was summink to drink."

Bunter controlled himself with difficulty. The cases had been left in the pantry for safety. The police were in and out of the cellar, but by all the laws of England, a man's pantry was his own. He said in a trembling voice:

"You have not, I trust, handled any of the other bottles?"

"Only to unpack 'em and set 'em right side up," Mrs. Ruddle assured him cheerfully. "Them cases'll come in 'andy for kindling."

"Gawdstrewth!" cried Bunter. The mask came off him all in one piece, and nature, red in tooth and claw, leapt like a tiger from ambush. "Gawdstrewth, would you believe it? All his lordship's vintage port!" He lifted shaking hands to heaven. "You lousy old nosey-parking bitch! You ignorant, interfering old bizzom! Who told you to go poking your long nose into my pantry?"

"Really, Mr. Bunter!" said Mrs. Ruddle.

"Go it," said Crutchley, with relish. " 'Ere's someone at the front door."

" 'Op it out of here!" stormed Bunter, unheeding, "before I take the skin off you!"

"Well, I'm sure! 'Ow was I to know?"

"Get out!"

Mrs. Ruddle retired, but with dignity.

"Sech manners!"

"Put yer flat foot right into it that time, Ma," observed Crutchley. He grinned. Mrs. Ruddle turned in the doorway.

"People can do their own dirty work after this," she remarked, witheringly, and departed.

Bunter took up the violated bottle of port and cradled it mournfully in his arm.

"All the port! all the port! Two and a half dozen, all shook up to blazes! And his lordship bringing it down in the back of the car, driving as tender and careful as if it was a baby in arms."

"Well," said Crutchley, "that's a miracle, judgin' by the way he went into Pagford this afternoon. Nearly blew me and the old taxi off the road."

"Not a drop fit to drink for a fortnight!—And him looking forward to his glass after dinner!"

"Well," said Crutchley again, with the philosophy we keep for other men's misfortunes, "he's unlucky, that's all."

Bunter uttered a Cassandra-like cry:

"There's a curse upon this house!"

DOROTHY L. SAYERS
Busman's Honeymoon

Advice

First and foremost then, Gentlefolks, learn from my song,
Not to lock up your wine, or malt-liquor, too long!
  Though Port should have age,
  Yet I don't think it sage
To entomb it, as some of your *connoisseurs* do,
Till it's losing in flavour, and body, and hue;
—I question if keeping it does it much good
After ten years in bottle and three in the wood.

R. H. BARHAM
The Ingoldsby Legends

Careful, Now

Port is the wine proper to the heavy drinker, and it may be admitted that whereas champagne, claret, burgundy, and hock are all entirely beneficial and indeed, in a well-ordered constitution, essential to the digestion of food, port, and the very finest port at that, can be slightly deleterious. Its charm insidiously invites excess, and excess of port, though not in itself harmful, sometimes discloses latent infirmities. The heavy port drinker must be prepared to make some sacrifice of personal beauty and agility. Its martyrs are usually well content with the bargain, and in consolation it may be remarked that a red nose never lost a friend worth holding, and that by universal testimony the sharpest attacks of gout are preceded by a period of peculiar mental lucidity. . . . No one, I think, ever contracted gout by port-drinking. What can be said is that those who are naturally gouty may find their weakness aggravated by port. Port is not for the very young, the vain, and the active. It is the comfort of age, the companion of the scholar and philosopher. Those qualities of British university scholarship—alternations of mellow appreciation and acid criticism—may be plausibly derived from the habits of our Senior Common-rooms.

EVELYN WAUGH

A Conscious Ritual

During my several visits to Oporto, I succumbed to the enticements of the port shippers, in their lodges, their homes, and their Factory

House. The lodges are the men's province: it is delightful to watch some of these devout connoisseurs, lifting an empty glass, holding it up to the window to see that it is crystal clear, half filling it with wine, and then allowing their face muscles to relax from a frown of interrogation to a satisfied smile. Lunch in any of the lodges is a conscious ritual; the enjoyment of the port that follows is serious, and it excites serious conversation. The golden light over the river becomes more golden still, and there is a stateliness of manner in the host's movements as he sends the decanter on its journey around the table, the second and third time. This is no mere tippling for tippling's sake: one is in the company of poets, listening to ancestral voices that whisper to them of the dedication in their task, as well as of the realistic business of selling their wine.

HECTOR BOLITHO
The Wine of the Douro

Doing It the Hard Way

The simplest way to catch a salmon is to net it, but this is not sport—English sport, anyway. English sport insists that the method employed must be one that makes the capture as difficult as possible for the fisherman while affording the maximum chance of escape to the fish when hooked. The quickest means of destroying a fox that raids your hen-coops is to shoot it, but the English sense of sport requires of you, under pain of social ostracism little short of excommunication, to hunt it in the company of scarlet-apparelled horsemen with a pack of hounds, and even that licence is only accorded during a very few months of the year. Fly-fishing and fox-hunting are very serious matters, national institutions that are part of the English tradition—like the Monarchy or Party Government, the Bible and the Established Church—which we are sent to Public Schools to learn to appreciate and uphold. Port, too, is a national institution in England, albeit not a very venerable one, which is apparently considered as a province bordering on the realm of sport, like coursing or cock-fighting, and as such susceptible to very much the same conditions and generally prevailing ideals. The object in this case is to prevent a wine that would naturally be quite drinkable within ten years, and at its best in fifteen, reaching maturity before the lapse of three decades or attaining its prime much under half a century. The goal is not to enjoy a fine wine as quickly and effortlessly as possible, but by dint of family altruism and Spartan *esprit-de-corps* to retard as long as may be that crowning moment when, "fulgent by clarity," the slowly crusted and cob-webbed bottles of beeswing, that represent the wine's slow and dogged victory over exceedingly arduous artificial obstacles, shall at last be ready to drink in a state nearer to wine than brandy. The added alcohol which has been put in at the beginning must first be given time to work itself out, just as the fox must have a fair start, the salmon be played patiently and laboriously before it is brought to land. This chivalrous ritual has the further advantage of rendering a wine that would be otherwise cheap and wholesome both dear and gouty. With Port it is the spirit of the cult of the wine which matters far more than the wine's actual relative quality or intrinsic worth. The Oporto game is played partly in Portuguese Wine-Lodges, where the fanciers' eliminatory trials take place, and partly in the cellars of English country-houses (some base publicans and plebeian professionals deliberately reduce the duration of the contest, cutting down the earlier stages of development by expert training of the wine into condition at the London Docks) where the grim struggle is fought to a sporting finish in a couple of generations or so, though the gamest and biggest wines (such as the "wine aged ninety" of Dr. Middleton's predilection, which Sir Willoughby Patterne's grandfather had inherited) see out father, son, and grandson, each of whom dies in peace of mind knowing he leaves a fair field to his successor after having played out his life in the straight game as a clean amateur sportsman and an honourable English gentleman. A properly matured Port is rightly considered unequalled as the test of the pretensions of a county family to proper pride, patient manly endurance, Christian self-denial, and true British tenacity.

P. MORTON SHAND
A Book of Other Wines Than French

A Young Expert

Brought up, as I was, in the north of Ireland, I soon learnt, however, to appreciate Port. I well remember people being pointed out to me as 'two bottle men.' At many houses Port was consumed at table as we drink Claret to-day. The raw climate, the continual hunting, and many other reasons may have made this possible. It took me, however, a certain time to appreciate and distinguish different kinds of Port. My father was most impatient at my early lack of appreciation of some of the treasures of his cellar. At the age of sixteen I was expected to know something of Port, although, in fact, I knew nothing at all. The only way to placate my father, who was very irritable if one failed to recognize some wonder in a bottle, was to ask the butler when pouring out my glass to whisper confidentially its year. Then, after sniffing it for some time, and holding it up to the light, I would taste it, and after a decent pause remark: 'Well, I don't want to make a dreadful mistake, but it really tastes to me like your wonderful '68.' My delighted father would then slap me on the back and shower praises on me, which I received with the modest smile of the true hypocrite.

GERALD HAMILTON
"The Birth of a Gourmet"

Too Much Port

As I was poor, I couldn't habitually make an alcoholic fool of myself, but love will find out a way; not very long afterwards a chance appeared by which I could gratify my inclination towards wine, and that in the silliest manner. None of this is much to my credit, I know; but others may learn from my follies. Anyway, it is all a long time ago and, as Clytemnestra says in the *Agamemnon*, bashfulness dies in anybody after a while. Very well then, at this period there was a young woman of Somerville who was distinguished from her colleagues in that she was good looking, well dressed, did not squawk, and did not walk like a hen. I had been engaged to her and she had told me she wanted no more of me; and she stuck to it. This inconceivable piece of bad taste and bad judgment had shattered my balance. I took the right way out for an Edwardian young man of spirit; I decided to drink myself to death to bring home to her her wickedness. But how should I do this on a very small budget? Here a kind (as I thought it) fate intervened. The Fellows of St. John's observed a most disquieting symptom in the cellars. A large amount of port bought and laid down by a long-dead President was going off. It had been carelessly corked. It was a great vintage; I am no longer sure which, but I think it was 1878; there were several hundred bottles. Now, the Fellows of my day were important, solid men, devoted to duty, but they quailed before the duty of drinking some five hundred bottles of vintage port in five months—for that was what seemed to be necessary. All that could be done, therefore, was to cancel the arrangement by which this splendid wine was reserved to the Senior Common Room and allow it to the Junior Common Room—in other words, to let the undergraduates buy it. But there would have to be a limitation of some kind. The dons were (they felt) men of the world; they might be forced to put this nectar in the hands of young men, but they were not such recluses as to fail to understand that these young men must be prevented from abusing their good fortune. A deterrent price, in these worthy men's decision, was 5s. 6d. a bottle. Now may Mr Croft, Mr Cockburn, Mr Taylor, Mr Fladgate, Mr Dow, Mr Warre, Mr Graham, Mr Offley, and Senhor Fonseca, if they are still with us, or their ghosts if they are not, forgive what followed, if they will. I was not the worst offender; I did indeed notice that what I drank was rather different from Public House Ruby; but my mind was not paying attention. I was spiting young Katherine, and I drank so much that I was soon boasting (young fools boast even more foolishly than old fools) that I could drink two bottles of port and get to bed. So I did, though in what state is another matter.

After this St Martin's summer was over, I had not caused any change of mind in the young woman; all I had done was so hideously to strain my liver that I can no longer drink port at all. After one glass, I know I shall be ill in the night.

RAYMOND POSTGATE
"Oinoposiai"

Port

In Vintage Port of noble year
What multifarious joys appear—
A liquid ruby; a bouquet
Like odours of a tropic day,
So ripe you'd almost say it *glows*
In the portals of the nose;
A palate luscious yet serene,
The right essential Hippocrene,
Blandness combined with potency;
A finish dry, yet not too dry,
With just a hint of cedarwood
To spice the ripe fruit's nectarous blood.

Certain pundits, here unnamed,
Have unequivocally claimed
That '63 and '68
Could turn the hinges of Heaven's Gate:
Some have held that '87
Rose to not so far from Heaven,
While others resolutely stated
That '87 was overrated,
'90 caught it up and beat it.
But if we gathered and repeated
All that has been written, said,
Argued, thought, upon this head,
And set ourselves to celebrate
Younger wines by name and date,
We should drift—a fact that shocks
By its glaring paradox—
On and on in such a sort
As never to get home to Port.

MARTIN ARMSTRONG

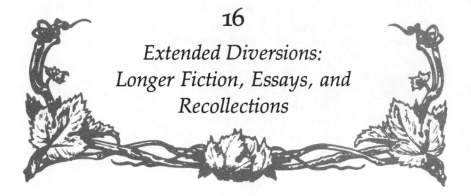

16

Extended Diversions:
Longer Fiction, Essays, and
Recollections

This section is made up of longer pieces about wine, including short stories, excerpts from novels, humorous essays, observations, and recollections. Some of the selections, such as those by Roald Dahl, Stephen Potter, George Meredith and Art Buchwald are well known, and belong in any collection of wine writing. Others, such as the stories by Bruce Todd, Marcel Aymé and Stanley Ellin are less familiar, but no less entertaining.

The other selections include a varied collection of fact and fiction. G. B. Stern's recollection of an interminable afternoon in Sauternes is a welcome antidote to the usual travelers' reminiscences of wonderful bottles. "Adam Smith" describes an unusual method of acquiring fine wines. Fake wines and mislabeled bottles are often the subject of humorous essays—but an interesting contrast is provided by Robert Keeling's dramatic courtroom account of the legal action taken against a firm in England for selling Spanish sparkling wine as "champagne." Colette recalls being introduced to good wines as a child by her mother, who would "contemplate the glory of the great French vineyards in my cheeks." There is not yet much available in literature about the wines of California, so I am pleased to include an excerpt from Idwal Jones' novel *The Vineyard*, set in California at the turn of the century. (Robert Louis Stevenson's description of his visit to the Napa Valley can be found elsewhere in this book.)

One novel that revolves around food and wine is *Gluttony*, by

342

Eugène Sue. The big meal of the book, so to speak, features a different wine with every course. The 1807 Madeira has traveled from Rio
and Calcutta five times, which may be excessive even for Madeira;
then we learn that the 1834 Sauternes has been three times to the
Indies, and even the 1834 Margaux has been to the Indies and
back—surely the best-traveled wines since Napoleon's ever-present
Chambertin. The meal continues with Clos Vougeot 1817 ("Pour out
this wine with emotion, drink it with religion"); Côte Rôtie 1829,
Johannisberg 1729 ("approach it with veneration . . . drink it with
compunction"); then champagne and port. A remarkable collection
of wines, but less fun to read about, I think, than the selections that
follow.

Winesmanship

STEPHEN POTTER

DEFINITIONS.

Winesmanship was once listed as a department of Clubmanship.
But although it is itself only a province, though a vast one, of the
area roughly defined as the Gracious Living Gambit of Lifeman-
ship, Winesmanship may play a big part, sooner or later, in the
lives of all of us.

A schoolboy definition of Winesmanship is "How to talk about
wine without knowing a hock from a Horse's Neck." But in fact
Winesmanship is itself a philosophy if not an ethic, and can be
used in Young Manship, in Jobmanship, even in wooing.

WINESMANSHIP BASIC.

A few phrases and a ploy or two, to get our bearings. Consider the
simplest approach first. If you are taking a girl, or even a former
headmaster, out to lunch at a restaurant, it is WRONG to do what
everybody else does—namely to hold the wine list just out of sight,
look for the second cheapest claret on the list, and say "Number 22,
please." Never say the number anyhow, because it suggests that
you are unable to pronounce the name of the wine you are ordering. Nominate the wine in English French, and make at the same
time some comment which shows at least that you have heard of it
before. Say, for instance:

"They vary, of course, but you seldom get a complete dud."

Or simply:

"I wonder . . ."

A useful thing is to look at the wine list before the waiter comes and say "Amazing. Nothing here you can be sure of. Yet the food is quite good. But I've got an idea."

Then, when the waiter comes, say to him "Look. You've got a Château-Neon '45 somewhere secreted about the place, I know. Can you let us have a bottle?"

(You know he's got it because you have in fact read it off the wine list, cheapest but one.)

When the waiter leaves you can say, "They keep a little câche for favoured customers."

With a little trouble a really impressive effect, suitable for average city-man guest, can be made by arriving fifteen minutes early, choosing some cheap ordinaire, and getting waiter to warm and decant it. When guest comes say, "I know you'll like this. Should be all right. I got them to get it going at nine o'clock this morning. Not expensive but a perfectly honest wine—and a *good* wine if it's allowed to breathe for three or four hours."

For Home Winesmanship, remember that your mainstay is hypnotic suggestion. Suggest that some rubbishy sherry, nine bob, is your special pride, and has a tremendously individual taste. Insist on getting it yourself "from the cellar." Take about four minutes uncorking it. Say, "I think decanting destroys it," if you have forgotten, or are too bored, to decant it. Keep staring at the bottle before you pour it. When you have drawn the cork, look particularly hard at the cork, and, of course, smell it.

For the first sip of the wine, here are some comments for Student Winesmen. Remember, if the wine is claret, 1920 St. Emilion Château Cheval-Blanc, that strangely enough absolutely everybody is supposed to know whether it is a claret or a burgundy. Remember also that practically absolutely everybody is supposed to recognise instantly the year. Practically almost absolutely everybody should be able to say "St. Emilion." The only tiny shade of doubt which can enter your comment is about its being Château Cheval-Blanc.

Don't say too much about the wine being "sound" or "pleasant"; people will think you have simply been mugging up a wine-merchant's catalogue. It is a little better to talk in broken sentences and say, "It has . . . don't you think?" Or "It's a little bit cornery," or something equally random like "Too many tramlines." I use this last phrase because it passes the test of the *boldly meaningless*.

An essential point to remember is that everybody is supposed to take it for granted that every wine has its *optimum year* up to which it progresses, and beyond which it falls about all over the place. E.g., you can give interest to your bottle of four-and-six-penny grocer's port by telling your guest that you "wish he had been able to drink it with you when it was at the top of its form in forty-nine." Alternatively you can say, "I'm beginning to like this. I believe it's just on the brink." Or I rather like saying, "I drink this now for sentimental reasons only . . . just a pleasant residue, an essence of sugar and water—but still with a hint of former glories. Keep it in your mouth for a minute or two . . . see what I mean?" Under this treatment, the definitive flavour of carbolic which has been surprising your guest will seem to him to acquire an interest if not a grace.

Alternatively you may admit, frankly, that your four-and-six-penny is a failure. "They were right," you say. "The Twenty-fours should have been wonderful. Perfect grapes, perfect weather, and the *vestre*—the Dordogne wind. But for some reason or other they mostly sulked. Taste it and tell me what you think. You may like it."

Or if your four-and-sixpenny is only two years old and unbearably acid you can say, "Let it rest in your mouth. Now swallow. There! Do you get it? That 'squeeze of the lemon,' as it's called . . ."

Then, if there is no hope whatever of persuading Guest that what he is drinking has any merit whatever, you can talk of your bottle as an Academic Interest treat.

"Superb wine, but it has its periods of recession. Like a foot which goes to sleep, has pins and needles, and then recovers. I think that was André's * explanation. At the moment it's BANG in the middle of one of its WORST OFF-COLOUR PERIODS."

Watch your friend drink this wine, and if he shudders after it, and makes what we winesmen call "the medicine face," you can say . . . "Yes! You've got it? Let it linger a moment."

"Why?" says Guest.

"Do you notice the after-sharpness, the point of asperity in the farewell, the hint of malevolence, even, in the *au revoir*?" If he says "Yes," as he will, be pleased.

NOTE ON TASTINGSHIP.

Many Yeovil Lifemen are so completely ignorant of wine of all kinds that in our small pamphlet AC/81 we have had to tell them that the red wines are red in colour and, confusing point, the white

---

* André Simon, completely O.K. wine name.

yellow. It may not be out of place if I remind general readers here, too, that *method of drinking* is an essential accompaniment to *method of comment.*

Before drinking or, rather, sipping the wine, you smell it for bouquet. *Not* with a noisy sniff but *silently and delicately,* perhaps making a funnel of your hands to concentrate the essence. G. Gibbs used to create some effect by smelling the stem of the glass as well, but there is no real point in this. A good general rule is to state that the bouquet is better than the taste, and vice versa.

In sipping, do not merely sip. Take a mouthful and chew it, making as much noise as you can. Having thus attracted attention, you can perform some of the evolutions favoured by that grand old Winesman Bath-Meriton. The most ordinary method he used was to lean his head forward so that his rather protuberant ears were extended like the wings of a monoplane and drink the wine from the far side of his glass. To get the bouquet he would smell it first with the left nostril, closing the other with his forefinger, and then with the right. He would also hold it up to the light and then shine a small pocket torch containing what really looked like a miniature fog lamp through from the other side! He would dip the end of his handkerchief in the wine and then hold the dipped end up to the light. And then, when it actually came to the tasting, he would sip from the *far* side of the glass. Gattling-Fenn once said, "Why not simply turn the glass the other way round?"

WINESMANSHIP ADVANCED.

The average guest, who knows no more about wine than the Winesman himself, can be easily impressed by such methods. But there are men who genuinely know something of this subject, and they are a very different problem.

I used to advise a simple and direct approach with such people, including an anglicising of the simplest French words (e.g., call the Haut-Brion the High Brion). Gattling-Fenn at his first Saintsbury Club dinner realised that it was 1,000 to 1 the man on his left knew more about wine than he did. So he said (of an old burgundy), using the recommended Ordinary Approach:

"Like it?"

EXPERT: Yes.

GATTLING: It's good.

EXPERT: Yes, but you know what's happened?

GATTLING: Yes—in a way. What?

EXPERT: It's been poured through the same strainer that they used for the Madeira.

Gattling broke into a hearty laugh at this, which quickly froze as he realised from the puzzled faces round him that the expert was speaking seriously.

No—the only method with the true specialist is what we call Humble Studentship, mixed in with perhaps *two* carefully memorised genuine advanced facts.

There are however lesser specialists, semiamateurs, perhaps trying a little amateur winesmanship on their own, for whom we recommend the following advanced methods.

1. *Beaded-bubbleship*. This obscurely titled ploy is merely the art of speaking and especially writing about wine as if it was one of the O.K. Literary Things. Be vague by being literary. Talk of the "imperial decay" of your invalid port. "Its gracious withdrawal from perfection, keeping a hint of former majesty withal, as it hovers between oblivion and the divine *untergang* of infinite recession."

Smiling references to invented female literary characters are allowed here. "The sort of wine Miss Mitford's Emily would have offered Parson Square, sitting in the window-seat behind the chintz curtains."

2. *Percentageship* is, of course, the opposite method, and designed to throw a different kind of haze, the figure fog, over the wine conversation. Remarks like "The consumption of 'treated' vermouth rose from 47.5 in 1924 to 58.9 in 1926 . . ." will impart a considerable degree of paralysis to any wine conversation. So will long lists of prices, or imaginary percentages of glucosity in contrasted champagnes, or remarks about the progress in the quality of cork trees, or the life-cycle of *Vinoferous demoliens*, little-known parasite now causing panic in the Haut-Baste.

It is always possible, if a wine completely stumps you, to talk in general terms about winemanly subjects.

If it is a warm summer day, remark that "dear old Cunoisier will be getting worried about the fermentation of his musts."

But if in real difficulties, remember that there are moments when the pickaxe is a more useful instrument than the most delicate surgeon's forceps. And I shall always remember Odoreida thrusting aside sixteen founder members of the Wine and Food Society with a "Well, let's have a real drink," and throwing together a mixture which left them breathless. "Popskull, they called it in Nevada," he said, and poured two parts of vodka into one of sherry and three of rum, adding a slice cut from the disc of a sunflower.

from One-Upmanship

Earliest Wine Memories

COLETTE

I was very well brought up. As a first proof of so categorical a statement, I shall simply say that I was no more than three years old when my father poured out my first full liqueur glass of an amber-colored wine which was sent up to him from the Midi, where he was born: the muscat of Frontignan.

The sun breaking from behind clouds, a shock of sensuous pleasure, an illumination of my newborn tastebuds! This initiation ceremony rendered me worthy of wine for all time. A little later I learned to empty my goblet of mulled wine, scented with cinnamon and lemon, as I ate a dinner of boiled chestnuts. At an age when I could still scarcely read, I was spelling out, drop by drop, old light clarets and dazzling Yquems. Champagne appeared in its turn, a murmur of foam, leaping pearls of air providing an accompaniment to birthday and First Communion banquets, complementing the gray truffles from La Puisaye. . . . Good lessons, from which I graduated to a familiar and discreet use of wine, not gulped down greedily but measured out into narrow glasses, assimilated mouthful by spaced-out, meditative mouthful.

It was between my eleventh and fifteenth years that this admirable educational program was perfected. My mother was afraid that I was outgrowing my strength and was in danger of a "decline." One by one, she unearthed, from their bed of dry sand, certain bottles that had been aging beneath our house in a cellar—which is, thanks be to God, still intact—hewn out of fine, solid granite. I feel envious, when I think back, of the privileged little urchin I was in those days. As an accompaniment to my modest fill-in meals—a chop, a leg of cold chicken, or one of those hard cheeses, "baked" in the embers of a wood fire and so brittle that one blow of the fist would shatter them into pieces like a pane of glass—I drank Château Lafites, Chambertins, and Cortons which had escaped capture by the "Prussians" in 1870. Certain of these wines were already fading, pale and scented still like a dead rose; they lay on a sediment of tannin that darkened their bottles, but most of them retained their aristocratic ardor and their invigorating powers. The good old days!

I drained that paternal cellar, goblet by goblet, delicately. . . . My mother would recork the opened bottle and contemplate the glory of the great French vineyards in my cheeks.

Happy those children who are not made to blow out their stomachs with great glasses of red-tinted water during their meals! Wise those parents who measure out to their progeny a tiny glass of pure wine—and I mean "pure" in the noble sense of the word—and teach them: "Away from the meal table, you have the pump, the faucet, the spring, and the filter at your disposal. Water is for quenching the thirst. Wine, according to its quality and the soil where it was grown, is a necessary tonic, a luxury, and a fitting tribute to good food." And is it not also a source of nourishment in itself? Yes, those were the days, when a few true natives of my Burgundy village, gathered around a flagon swathed in dust and spiders' webs, kissing the tips of their fingers from their lips, exclaimed—already—"a nectar!" Don't you agree that in talking to you about wine I am describing a province I know something about? It is no small thing to conceive a contempt, so early in life, not only for those who drink no wine at all but also for those who drink too much.

The vine and the wine it produces are two great mysteries. Alone in the vegetable kingdom, the vine makes the true savor of the earth intelligible to man. With what fidelity it makes the translation! It senses, then expresses, in its clusters of fruit the secrets of the soil. The flint, through the vine, tells us that it is living, fusible, a giver of nourishment. Only in wine does the ungrateful chalk pour out its golden tears. A vine, transported across mountains and over seas, will struggle to keep its personality, and sometimes triumphs over the powerful chemistries of the mineral world. Harvested near Algiers, a white wine will still remember without fail, year after year, the noble Bordeaux graft that gave it exactly the right hint of sweetness, lightened its body, and endowed it with gaiety. And it is far-off Jerez that gives its warmth and color to the dry and cordial wine that ripens at Château Chalon, on the summit of a narrow, rocky plateau.

From the ripened cluster brandished by its tormented stem, heavy with transparent but deeply troubled agate, or dusted with silver-blue, the eye moves upward to contemplate the naked wood, the ligneous serpent wedged between two rocks: on what, in heaven's name, does it feed, this young tree growing here in the South, unaware that such a thing as rain exists, clinging to the rock by a single hank of hemplike roots? The dews by night and the sun by day suffice for it—the fire of one heavenly body, the essence sweated by another—these miracles . . .

What cloudless day, what gentle and belated rain decides that a year, one year among all the others, shall be a great year for wine?

Human solicitude can do almost nothing, it is a matter in which celestial sorcery is everything, the course the planets take, the spots on the sun.

Simply to recite our provinces and their towns by name is to sing the praises of our venerated vineyards. It is profitable both to the spirit and the body—believe me—to taste a wine in its own home, in the landscape that it enriches. Such a pilgrimage, well understood, has surprises in store for you that you little suspect. A very young wine, tasted in the blue light of its storage shed—a half bottle of Anjou, opened under a barrel vault dusted with pale light by a violent and stormy summer afternoon—moving relics discovered in an old stillroom unaware of the treasures it contains, or else forgetful of them . . . I once fled from such a stillroom, in the Franche-Comté, as though I had been stealing from a museum. . . . Another time, among the furniture being auctioned off on a tiny village square, between the commode, the iron bedstead, and some empty bottles, there were six full bottles being sold: it was then, as an adolescent, that I had my first encounter with an ardent and imperious prince, and a treacherous one, like all great seducers: the wine of Jurançon. Those six bottles made me more curious about the region that produced them than any geography teacher ever could have done. Though I admit that at such a price geography lessons would not be within the reach of everyone. And that triumphant wine, another day, drunk in an inn so dark that we never knew the color of the liquid they poured into our glasses . . . Just so does a woman keep the memory of a journey, of how she was surprised one night, of an unknown man, a man without a face, who made himself known to her only by his kiss . . .

The present snobbery about food is producing a crop of hostelries and country inns the like of which has never been seen before. Wine is revered in these places. Can wisdom be born again from a faith so unenlightened, a faith professed by mouths already, alas, armored with cocktails, with venomous apéritifs, with harsh and numbing spirits? Let us hope that it can. As old age approaches, I offer, as my contribution, the example of a stomach without remorse or damage, a very well-disposed liver, and a still sensitive palate, all preserved by good and honest wine. Therefore, wine, fill up this glass I now hold out to you! A delicate and simple glass, a light bubble in which there play the sanguine fires of a great Burgundian ancestor, the topaz of Yquem, and the balas ruby, sometimes with a paler purple tinge, of the Bordeaux with its scent of violets . . .

There comes a time of life when one begins to prize young

wine. On a Southern shore there is a string of round, wicker-covered demijohns always kept in store for me. One grape harvest fills them to the brim, then the next grape harvest, finding them empty once more, in its turn fills them up again. Perhaps you have a hoard of fine old wines in your cellar, but do not disdain these wines because they give such quick returns: they are clear, dry, various, they flow easily from the throat down to the kidneys and scarcely pause a moment there. Even when it is of a warmer constitution, down there, if the day is a really hot one, we think nothing of drinking down a good pint of this particular wine, for it refreshes you and leaves a double taste behind, of muscat and of cedarwood.

from Prisons et Paradis

The Greatest Wine in the World

BRUCE TODD

It was towards the end of dinner, one of those beautifully designed little dinners with which Charles Cullam sometimes delights a few of his friends. The fare was simple, but perfectly cooked, and with it was a series of wines which started with a cool exquisite Macharnudo and culminated in a magnum of Château Lafite 1875. Then an old Armagnac brandy was put before us, and soon afterwards a discussion started about the best bottle of wine that each of us had ever drunk. I remember André Renoir surprised us by saying that the best wine he ever had was given to him at an Edinburgh club— a Margaux 1858, I think it was. Bernard Sears remembered as the bottle of his life a Latour 1870 he had drunk at the house of some friends of mine in the Rue Fondaudège at Bordeaux. Then Charles was asked. He smiled.

"I know that none of you will believe it, but the best bottle of wine I ever drank was a Château Beaugency. What the vintage was we never knew; it was pre-phylloxera, that was all we could be sure of."

There was a moment's silence. Charles Cullam was reputed to be about the best judge of claret in England. Was it possible that the best wine he ever drank was something that no one had ever heard of, and whose vintage even he did not know?

"*Beaugency*, did you say, Charles? Château *Beaugency?*"

"Where and what . . . ?"

"It is only one of Charles' leg-pulls."

But Charles was not leg-pulling.

"I knew you would not believe me," he said, "but actually it is a fact. The Château Beaugency was far and away the best bottle of wine I have ever drunk or ever hope to drink. And if you asked Georges Lafont or Desmond Byrne" (they are two of the greatest of Bordeaux's wine-shippers) "they would say just the same. If you would like to hear the story"—he glanced round the table—"I will try not to be too long-winded."

Then he took a sip of his brandy.

It was during the vintage in 1924 (said Charles)—a good one, as you have just seen! I was out in Bordeaux where I had not been since the War. I knew there were a lot of changes among my friends there, for several had been killed in the War and several had died, and there were quite a number of young lads who had stepped into their fathers' or their uncles' shoes. However, old Georges Lafont was still the head of Lafont's, as he had been for over thirty years. And Desmond Byrne was there too, of course. I expect most of you know him? He has lived in Bordeaux ever since he came down from Cambridge, but he is pretty Irish still.

I had a very good time and made a lot of new friends among the younger generation. By the middle of September the vintage was nearly over and late one afternoon we three, old Lafont, Desmond and I, were driving back to Bordeaux from Pauillac, where we had spent a day among the vines and the press-houses. In every village we passed there were big doors open to the street, and in the semi-darkness within you could see the great oak vats and the gleam of the steel press-screws. Everywhere, too, there was the smell of the new must, and the cobbles and the walls were splashed purple with it.

As we were coming up the hill out of Listrac, I noticed a fine old château in a nest of trees away to our right.

"That is Beaugency," Desmond told me. "Belongs to an old fellow called Jauréguy, a very good chap but not a wine man at all. He farms his land and has no vines. It is a beautiful place though . . . I wonder if you would like to see it? I expect he would be at home."

We were just approaching a gateway and Desmond tapped the glass in front of him and spoke to the chauffeur. We turned through the gate and drove up a straight avenue of chestnut trees till we emerged from the green gloom into the forecourt of the château. Old Jauréguy was at home and delighted to see us. His wife was away, he said, and he was alone. He insisted that we should stay to supper with him, and, having no other plans for the evening we were very pleased.

The arrival of unexpected guests seems to act like a spur upon a French cook, and we could not have had a better supper if we had been invited days before. A lovely white wine was served with the omelette and old Jauréguy turned to me with solemn face and said: "I must apologize for the wine, Monsieur Cullam, but, as my friends here will have told you, I am no vigneron, but a farmer. This wine that you are drinking is dreadful, I know, but as it comes from Monsieur Byrne's own vineyards I make him drink it whenever he comes here."

We all laughed and the meal went on very pleasantly. He was most entertaining, was old Jauréguy. He was a Basque, he told us, and came from the Landes country further south. His grandfather had kept sheep in the marshes near Marsanne, and his father as a boy used to go out on stilts to mind the flock. Then came the Planting of the Pines. The whole coast for two hundred miles from the Point of the Médoc nearly to Biarritz was changed within a decade or so. On the bare sand-dunes and the inland marshes the great pine forest began to grow. Soon the shepherd of the Landes, with his pipe and his stilts, vanished from the scene, and in his place came the woodman and the "gommeur." Where a little wool and mutton had once been the only products of the land, now gum by the ton was sold to the paint and varnish makers, and timber by the hundred tons was shipped to Cardiff for the South Wales coalpits. There was money to be made, of course. The government promoted the scheme and some people did well who had seen what was coming. Among these was Jauréguy *père*. He borrowed money, bought marshland and re-sold to the Government at a profit. Then with the capital he made he launched out into the gum business and made a fortune. At the time of the Franco-Prussian War Jauréguy *père* had his business headquarters in Bordeaux and soon afterwards he bought the château at Listrac from the widow of a Monsieur Ducrocq.

"Old Ducrocq was an unusual man by all accounts," went on Jauréguy. "Farming and gardening were his passions, and he made a lot of improvements to the place which were very up to date for those days. Generally speaking though, he was conservative in his methods. He preferred to do everything on a small scale, but to aim always at perfection. His strain of Faverolles, for instance, was known all over France, though he never hatched more than a hundred birds a season. And you have heard of the Beaugency-

Cantaloup melon, I expect? That was developed by him in the gardens here, though I must say it was my father who made it known commercially long afterwards. Ducrocq was not keen on what nowadays we call 'publicity.' His widow once told my mother that it was a kind of religion with him: it was his duty to God, he felt, to make the best use of all God's gifts. He was well qualified too, for he had real genius. He was artist and scientist and man of piety all at once—and very remarkable in all of these capacities.

"There was a vineyard, too, in his time. Quite tiny, of course, for in this, as in everything, he liked to concentrate all his attention upon a small area. The wine he made was excellent, but it was never sold, as he made only enough to supply his own table and to give some away to friends.

"My father was not a wine man, and would have rooted up the vines when he came into possession. But old Madame Ducrocq begged him to keep them and at length he promised that he would. A few years afterwards the phylloxera plague spread through the Médoc and the little vineyard here was completely destroyed by it. A lot of neighbours were experimenting with grafted vine-stocks, but my father would have none of it. The vines had died of themselves, and he was absolved from his promise, so that was the end of the matter."

This was all very interesting. And then he said something that interested me still more.

"I remember another person," he said, "who begged my father to preserve the vineyard when he took the place. Did you ever hear of Baron de Brane?" Of course we had, every vigneron in the Médoc must have heard of the man who created the vineyards of Mouton-Rothschild and Brane-Cantenac. Jauréguy was certainly no wine man to have even asked the question.

"The Baron had been an old friend of Ducrocq's and he told my father that it would be a 'crime' to destroy the vines. 'This little vineyard is the jewel of all the Médoc,' he said."

This was praise indeed from a man like Baron de Brane.

Was there any of the wine left, Lafont asked? Jauréguy shook his head.

"No; I am afraid it has all gone now. My wife and I prefer white wine. It was the curé who used to like it, and I had it put aside for when he dined with us. But some time ago I had to buy another red wine and now he is always lamenting that it is nothing like the old stuff. If you like though, I will go down to the cellar and see what I can find."

Our host was absent for a little while but he returned smiling.

"You are in luck," he said, "I was right down to the end of it, as I thought; but there was just one bottle left and I have it here, decanted. I think under the circumstances we should give it the place of honour at the end of our meal, and we will let it breathe a little while on the sideboard."

It was with a cheese soufflé, I remember, that the Beaugency wine was eventually served.

"Well, gentlemen," said Jauréguy, as he took up the decanter, "this is the last bottle of Château Beaugency in existence and I think old Ducrocq would have been glad to see it make its farewell before such appreciative company!"

Certainly its merits, if it had any, would not be lost on Lafont and Desmond, for they were as good judges of claret as any two men alive.

The wine was poured and we took up our glasses. I looked at it rather casually, but I saw that it had all the colour that an old wine should have. Then I held it to my nose . . . Not a flaw! I inhaled again, more slowly and deeply . . . everything was there and in exquisite proportion. I put it to my lips, and, as the flavour gradually revealed itself, an incongruous thought came into my mind; it was as if I had picked up a Poker hand and found myself looking at a Royal Straight Flush!

There had been an unusual silence and I looked across at Lafont.

"Marvellous . . . Quite incredible," he said at last. "Let me taste it again . . . Yes . . . It is perfect—absolutely perfect. I think it is among the best wines I ever tasted. Don't you agree, Desmond? . . . Let me taste it again . . . But *perfect!* . . . Do you know," he said—and there was a kind of awe in his voice—"do you know, I am quite sure now that this is the best bottle of wine I ever tasted in my life."

We all agreed with that, and there was a reverent silence as we sipped this miracle of a wine. When the bottle was finished at last, old Lafont said quietly:

"Thank God for His many gifts and blessings." And we all murmured "Amen."

We begged to see where the vineyard had been, and Jauréguy said "Come along then; it is near the house and I will show it to you."

It was nearly dusk but he led us across a lawn and then along a path that sloped down a plantation of pine trees. Halfway through this another path crossed at right angles and at the intersection there stood a stone cross with the simple legend carved upon its base, "Deo Optimo Maximo, 1850."

"We are at the centre of the old vineyard," said Jauréguy. "These pine trees were planted when the phylloxera destroyed the vines."

So this was where those incomparable vines had grown! Two acres of pine-trees now stood where once had been the finest vineyard in the world.

We stood beside that cross and it was as if we were at a graveside. Jauréguy felt what we were thinking. "Yes," he said, "I have often felt it was a pity. But my father was an obstinate old fellow, and of course he had a sort of affection for the pine trees that had made his fortune . . . And they give good gum, you know. Look at these!" He pointed to the little cups full of golden liquid that were fastened to each tree. "I might have felled the trees after my father died, but what was the use? Good wine never came from land where the pines have grown, so it will never make a vineyard again . . . No. I think I will let them grow old with me now, and I am afraid, gentlemen, you will never again taste the wine of Château Beaugency!"

He smiled. It was a rather apologetic smile, I thought.

Then we went back to the château and soon afterwards we were on the Bordeaux road again.

That is about all the story, I think (Charles said). As I told you, we could not trace the vintage date, as it was only printed on the seal over the cork, and Jauréguy forgot to look before he broke the wax. But the bottle had a label—in itself an unusual thing for those days. I remember it simply bore the name, "Château Beaugency," with a coat-of-arms, and then the words: *Mis en bouteille au Château—par les mains dévouées de Gaston Ducrocq.*

A Vineyard Confrontation

IDWAL JONES

They had come to the field she and Hector had just planted. Giorgio stopped short.

"What's been going on here?" He looked at the trellis vines. He froze, then slowly touched a rootling with his cane. "What's this?"

"Zinfandel."

"What!" He shouted in anger, eyes blazing, his thin mouth atwitch, one eyebrow up in a straight line. "Zinfandel! Why didn't he plant what I told him? He could have put down Grenache here, or Mission, and got twice as much for the yield. Zinfandel!"

He wheeled about, blowing hard, his cane vibrant. He looked at the winery. No trace of Hector and Carola, and the girl was thankful.

"Why not Grenache?"

"Everybody plants Grenache," she said. "Mission grows coarse, and ranky. It would be a pity to waste this good field on it." She looked at him defiantly, her smile set hard. "He put down Zinfandel because he wanted something very good, almost fine, and a good run of it. It'll do very well on this iron. And down there, we found some sound old stock to graft on." She came out with it. "Mantuos. Bual's Mantuos."

Giorgio's head went back with a jolt. It was an artistic head, under a velour hat. It reminded her of a faun's head she had seen in a book at school. His eyes still glared. His mouth went slack, and his hand beat helplessly on the knob of his cane.

"Where is he?" he shouted. "Where is Hector? By God, this place is certainly going to hell!"

He champed his jaw and fixed her with the gaze of a basilisk. "Some of your work, I guess! You been telling him what to do?"

She couldn't help but admire that splendid, fiery old head. He loathed her. But she had a way of looking upon rage as something impersonal, like lightning, or a hailstorm. It could never last. His eyes trailed from her to stare down the slope.

"I thought the last of those damned Mantuos were plowed up long ago. They should have been burnt up, every bloody one of them!"

"They were sound," Alda said. "It wouldn't have been saving to waste them. We had some on our farm, older ones, and the black-rot never touched them."

"What farm?"

"Oxhill. I'm Abel Pendle's daughter. I never worked anywhere else until I came here."

His jaw slid.

"And so," he intoned with dry sarcasm, "you've had to come to Montino and Hector Regola to work—is that it?"

She could have cried with vexation. She was near choking, her chest heaved, and she breathed deeply in a tense effort to control herself. Waves of homesickness swept over her. Her eyes filmed. This was her father's enemy, and she had not her father to lean against. He would have defended her, conquering him. This was his old fighting ground; he had come to the valley before the Regolas. She looked away. She had a sense of nearness to home. She saw the winding highway, the crown of Mount St. Helena, the steam, like ostrich plumes, above the Calistoga geysers. All this her father had seen and known and loved before his enemy ever came upon the slope.

"What if I had?" she asked. "Montino's a better vineyard than when you had it. What do you know about vines except to kill them if they don't make you richer? You killed the Mantuos. You killed the White Pendle—after you had put your own name on it—and you stamped it out forever! A murder of Herod's! You murdered it to plant cheap trash in its place. To make a miserable champagne that brought shame to the farm that grew the Regolberg!

"You're still killing. You are still trying to kill Montino, and you're strangling your son who strives to do his utmost because he is proud of his vineyard—and what its name once meant! Go ahead and finish your killing! Try and uproot the Zinfandel, if you dare! I made him plant them. But I'll fight for the vineyard if nobody else will!"

Alda turned to leave. She heard a deep intake of breath; then another one.

"You stay right here!"

The command snapped at her. She faced about. Giorgio looked suddenly old, old and tired. He moved to a wheelbarrow near the vines and sat down. He removed his hat, and stared at the ground. He took out his cigar case, his eyebrows drooped in fatigue, chose a twisted, black spike of a Toscano, and fitting it carefully to his mouth, lit it. He smoked deliberately, looked at the ash after a long-drawn puff, then pointed to an upturned keg near the wheelbarrow.

"Sit down a while."

She obeyed. The sun was warm upon them. Save for the butterflies that flitted in the light vapor, order was the only beauty on the tract still dormant on the edge of spring. The upright stakes, the cane-bearing trellis wires, taut from post to post, the gnarled roots, like arms lifted to the sun, wheeled to pattern from this knoll. Beyond were the patches of Cabernet, Herbemont, Gamay, Refosco and Pinot, on their undulating fields. On that jumble of crests and dips the sun could not be impartial. It would linger an hour there, pass over lightly here; with the sky shifting to a different mood in a brief traversal. Even at night subtle influences moved about them, some twin vine awakening at a breath of mist, or the light of a strange star, to sleep again unaware of its interior change, that it was set apart from its twin, and in a sense they were twins no longer.

"Your hands," he said.

Alda showed them. She had kept her roughened, nicked hands closed at table, so that Carola, who had beautiful hands, would not see them.

"You tend those vines." He cleared his throat. "You've got the right hands, and you've got the right head. You think what you damn please, too. And that's all right. I've been wrong about a few things. I was wrong about the Zinfandel."

Elation swept through her, she was glad for Hector's sake. Then she was full of pity.

"I hope, Mr. Regola—I hope you won't think that I wanted to—"

"I do!"

With cigar raked skyward, his head wagging, his eyes gleamed with an unholy joy. He looked at her with something akin to pride.

"I do! You wanted to fight Giorgio Regola—and you did!" He chuckled. "You gave me the axe a couple of times, and you gave it fast!"

He waved his stick over Montino. "I always had good fights here. I fought to keep the place alive. We didn't make wines for love in those days. We were out for all the tin there was in it. All of us, except fellows like Crabb, Haraszthy, and Abel Pendle.

"I fought Bual, too, my partner, when he kept on growing those vines of his. I tore 'em up. And I tore up the Regolberg. I let nothing stand in my way, I didn't.

"They fought, too. They were all damn good fighters, never gave in. They knew better than to give in. They were all in cahoots with something beyond me. I don't say I understood them. I'm not sure I understand Hector either, at times."

Alda interposed for him. "He only wants to be left alone in his own vineyard."

"He doesn't want that badly enough to fight for it."

"He fights in his own way."

"Well, it isn't my way! I've always fought for Montino because I like the old place. I often got near licked, too," he chuckled, "but since nobody knew that but me, I won out. Except this time. And all over a parcel of twigs not yet sprouting!"

The grim humor of it struck him, and he laughed harshly.

"Those Zinfandels whipsawed me—after forty years. Pendle of Oxhill's girl swung that trick. Oh, well, I had a good time fighting. I don't say that if I started all over again I'd be different. I haven't changed any. But when a man's eighty, nobody fights him any more. They give in to him, as if he were a sage, even when he's mulish wrong.

"I'd think more of them if they'd just knock him down!"

Giorgio tossed the end of his cigar into a furrow. He laughed, then looked at her quizzically.

"Tell me one thing. What brought you here?"

"Well, I've got a boy, and—"

He nodded. The wheelbarrow was already in cool shade, for the afternoon was far advanced. Sometimes it was Alda who talked; more often it was Giorgio, who had gone back to the beginning of things.

from The Vineyard

The Wine of Paris

MARCEL AYMÉ

In a village in the Arbois country there lived a wine-grower named Félicien Guérillot who did not like wine. Yet he came of sound stock. His father and his grandfather, also wine-growers, had both been carried off by cirrhosis of the liver at the age of fifty or thereabouts, and none of his forebears on his mother's side had ever done injustice to a bottle. This strange and shameful weakness weighed heavily upon Félicien. He grew the best wines in the district, besides possessing the best cellar. Léontine Guérillot, his wife, was a woman of a gentle and submissive nature, neither prettier nor better shaped than is desirable for the peace of mind of an honest man. Félicien would have been the happiest of wine-growers had he not had an aversion for wine that appeared to be insurmountable. Vainly had he striven with the utmost zeal and resolution to overcome the failing. Vainly had he tested all vintages in the hope of finding one that would yield him the key to the unknown paradise. Besides sampling all the wines of Burgundy and Bordeaux, those of the Loire and the Rhône, and the champagnes and the wines of Alsace, and the straw-coloured wines, and red, white and *rosé*, and Algerian wines and the roughest and thinnest of table-wines, he had not neglected the Rhine wines, or the Tokays, or the wines of Spain and Italy, Cyprus and Portugal. But each of his experiments had ended in disillusion. With every wine it was the same as with that of his own country. Even in the driest, thirstiest season of the year he could not swallow a mouthful without having the sensation, horrible to relate, of gulping down cod-liver oil.

Léontine alone knew her husband's dreadful secret and helped him to conceal it. Félicien could never have brought himself to admit in public that he did not like wine. It would have been as bad as to say that he did not like his own children, even worse, for it may happen anywhere that a father comes to detest his son, but there has never been anyone in the Arbois country who did not like wine. Such a thing is Heaven's retribution for who shall say what sin, an aberration on the part of Nature, a monstrous deformity that any right-thinking and well-drinking man will refuse to contemplate. One may dislike carrots, spinach, beetroot or the skin on hot milk. But not wine. It is like hating the air one breathes, since each is equally indispensable. So it was not from any foolish sense of pride, but out of respect for human dignity, that Félicien Guérillot . . .

Well, now, there is a story about wine that seemed to be starting quite nicely. But it has suddenly begun to weary me. It does not belong to the age we live in, and I feel uncomfortable with it. Besides which, I am too old for cod-liver oil. So I shall drop that story, although all kinds of things might have happened to Félicien, amusing, cruel, stirring and pathetic. I can see him, for example, simulating a slight alcoholic tremor in order to mislead his neighbors, all of whom, deceived and at the same time amazed, would be filled with esteem for him, and one would say to the others, speaking for all:

'Do you see that? Here's Félicien getting the shakes already, and not yet thirty, taking after his father, Achille Guérillot, now there was a drinker for you! You remember him, eh, Achille Guérillot? He wasn't a one to suck acid-drops as plenty of us know, but never drunk, mind, always under control—a real wine-grower, in fact, a real drinker, a real man. Yes, that was his father, Achille Guérillot, a proper drinker, no denying it, what I call a real drinker, or a real man if you'd rather put it that way. And do you remember how father Guérillot—Achille, I mean, I'm not going back to the old man, Guérillot Auguste, although mark you he was a good drinker too, but it's Achille I'm talking about, Guérillot Achille, who's been dead these fifteen years, come to think of it, that very hot year, the year the fleas were hopping about on people the way they do on cattle—but it was, I tell you, it was the year the girl Claudette got the gendarmes drunk the time they came here about that business of Panouillot's mare. And talking of Jules Panouillot, there was another drinker who could have shown them a thing or two if he was alive today. Why, him and Achille, they were like brothers, and they got up to some capers together, I can tell you. There was the time they dressed up as devils to scare the curé's maid-servant. But if I was to start on that story now I'd have you laughing till you choked and it'd cost you a bottle apiece. To come back to father Guérillot (Achille), it's not hard to reckon how old he was when he started getting the shakes because he was born two days after my own father, and I know that because they were conscripted together, I remember my father telling us one day when we were chatting about one thing and another the way we are today, but mark you that was ten years ago. Yes, it must be at least ten years because my great-uncle, Glod'Pierre, was still alive, he'd come from Aiglepierre to visit us in Tantiet-le-jambe's pony-trap (there was another solid drinker for you and after the skirts in a flash); well, it was all of ten years ago and maybe eleven, ten or eleven it doesn't matter which, it's only the facts that matter. So there were the three of us you see, me and my father and my great-uncle and a bottle on the table—oh, nothing special in the way of a bottle, just a little wine that I remember my old man used to make out of a corner of the vineyard that sometimes yielded and sometimes didn't, but a nice little wine all the same, fresh and round, with a taste of the pebbles on the Labbé slope. Well, there we were, chatting about this and that, anything that came into our heads, and all of a sudden my Uncle Glod'Pierre—I call him my uncle, but he was my great-uncle really—my Uncle Glod'Pierre, he said, "And what's become of that fellow you did your service with, what was his name?" (My uncle didn't come from round here, you must remember. I keep on calling him my uncle . . .) "What was the fellow called?" says my uncle . . . "Do you mean, Antoine Bougalet?" says my father . . . "No, that's not it. He was called—" "Clovis Rouillot?" "No, no, the name was—" "Adrien Bouchat?" . . . "No, no, no, no. His name was—now I've got it—Achille! Achille—that was his name!" . . . "Ah, you mean Achille Guérillot," my father said. "Well, so far as I know he isn't doing so badly and anyway he isn't complaining. He's lying quiet as quiet alongside his parents in the cemetery. Poor Achille," my father said, "he had a bad time dying. He died the day before his fifty-second birthday, and that I know for certain because it was the day after my own fifty-second birthday and I came into the world two days before him. The poor old fellow, he started to get the shakes, I remember, two years before he died." . . . That's what my father said. Two years, he said. And two from fifty-two leaves fifty. So you see Achille was fifty when he started to get the shakes and here's this son of his starting when he's barely thirty. And let me tell you something. Félicien's a man who knows how to drink. . . .'

Secure in his reputation as a drinker, Félicien might develop political ambitions and find himself compelled by the necessities of his electoral campaign to drink in public. I can see a fine theme here for a good, boozy novel, bursting with fearless realism and devilish profound psychology, but the very thought of it makes me tired. I am too immersed in the present. There are certain lateral trends which have started all kinds of contemporary gimmicks fizzing at the back of my head. I simply haven't the heart to write about sun-bathed terraces and merry little wines. In consequence of which, I will now tell a sad story about wine. It happens in Paris, and the name of the hero is Duvilé.

There lived in Paris, in January in the year 1945, a certain Étienne Duvilé, aged thirty-seven or eight, who adored wine. Alas, he had none. Wine cost 200 francs a bottle, and Duvilé was not rich. A clerk in the Government service, he asked nothing better than to be bribed, but his was an unrewarding post where there was nothing to sell. On the other hand he had a wife, two children and a father-in-law aged seventy-two, a bad-tempered, self-indulgent old party who made a favour of the 1500 francs monthly pension which he contributed to the household budget, and would have eaten enough for half a dozen fathers-in-law if he hadn't been rationed. And pork cost 300 francs a kilo, eggs 21 francs apiece and wine, I repeat, 200 francs a bottle. On top of which the weather was bitterly cold, four degrees below freezing in the apartment, and not a stick of wood or a lump of coal. The family's only resource was to plug in the electric iron, which was passed from hand to hand at mealtimes and during their hours of leisure. When the father-in-law got hold of it he would never let go until it was taken from him by force, and the same thing happened with bread, potatoes, greens and meat, when there was any. Bitter disputes, violent and often sordid, arose between him and Duvilé. The old man would complain that he did not get the comforts to which his 1500 francs entitled him, where-upon Duvilé would invite him to go and live elsewhere and his wife would come to her father's support, calling her husband un-kind names. The two men had had difficulty enough in putting up with one another even in easier times, before the war, but in those days their mutual antipathy had found a noble and abundant outlet in politics. One was a republican-socialist and the other a socialist-republican, and the gulf represented by this clash in their political views had been large enough to swallow up all other quarrels. But now that wine had failed them, disputation in this field had ceased to be possible. The fact is that before the war wine and politics went together, each waxing and thriving upon the other. Wine drove men to politics and politics drove them to wine, generously, symbiotically, and thunderously. But in the year 1945, lacking the sustenance of wine, politics stayed buried in the newspaper. Grievances, challenges, war-cries and anathemas were squalidly concerned with matters of food and fuel. Like so many others, the Duvilé household lived in a state of constant hankering after things to eat and drink. The children's daydreams, and those of their mother and grandfather, were stuffed with sausage and pâté, poultry, chocolate and pastries. And Duvilé thought about wine. He thought of it with a sensual fervour that was sometimes acute, and at such moments felt his very soul rise strangled to his parched throat. Being by nature reserved, he said nothing to anyone of this yearning for wine that so tormented him, but in moments of solitude he lost himself in visions of bottles, casks, litres of red wine, and without emerging from his dream, taking a step backward, as it were, and contemplating this red abundance, he felt rising to his lips the despairing cry of the dying man who yet clutches at life.

On a Saturday night, with the need for wine burning within him, he got into bed bside his wife, slept badly and dreamed the following dream: Towards nine o'clock in the morning, in a dim half-light, he left his house to catch the métro. The entrance to the station was deserted. The ticket-collector at the barrier was a woman who turned out to be his wife. After punching his ticket she said to him casually, 'Our children are dead.' So intense was his grief that he nearly cried aloud, but he controlled himself and reflected, 'After all, I might not have known of it until later. I shall go to the party just the same.' He went down the stone circular staircase leading to the bowels of the métro and forgot his children. As he reached the third landing a patch of darkness formed in front of him, causing him to stray into a sort of tunnel with walls made jagged with artificial rocks. A café waiter whom he knew by sight was standing by a narrow door which he opened for him. Duvilé passed through and found himself in a large, unevenly lighted room. Drifts of shadow partly obscured the walls, one of which, in process of demolition, allowed the passage of a stream of dubious daylight which caused him a sense of acute anguish. In the middle of the room stood a table loaded with cakes and sandwiches. Two fountains of wine, white and red, played into successive basins, one below the other. Duvilé's astonishment did not cause him to lose his head. He calmly drank as an apéritif a glass of white wine that had no taste, and then ate several sandwiches, including one of cheese, in the hope that they would bring out the flavour of the red wine. Neither the consistency nor the taste of the sandwiches matched their appearance, and in his disappointment he began to suspect that he was the victim of a dream. To prevent himself waking up he ran to the red-wine fountain and, bending over the basin, drank like an animal. But despite his efforts and the long gulps he took he absorbed very little liquid, so little indeed that its taste still remained uncertain. In his distress he straightened himself and glanced behind him. On the other side of the table, seated in enormous armchairs, three plump, full-bellied men with large, presidential faces were watching him with malicious smiles. Duvilé wanted to run away, but he found that he was wearing no shoes. He smiled obsequiously back at them and felt no shame in doing so. One of the three men arose and addressed him without opening his mouth, his thoughts imprinting themselves upon Duvilé's mind without the trickery of words. 'We live in the depths, far below the world that suffers and runs risks. We constantly increase our happiness by thinking of the sufferings of others. We play at being poor, at being hungry and cold and frightened, and we find the game delightful. But nothing is as good as reality. That is why I have brought you here, so that . . .' At this point the words, or rather the thoughts, of the happy man became confused and ceased to be comprehensible. Then he resumed in a huge and crushing voice that was still silent: 'Impostor! You are wearing a gold wedding-ring and a gold watch which you received on the occasion of your first communion. Give them to me!' The three happy men, each having donned an officer's cap, abruptly left their places, and Duvilé, who now had shoes on his feet, ran to the far end of the room. When it seemed that he was certain to be caught he thrust his hand into the pocket of his overcoat and fished out his wife, behind whom he sought to hide. But he was already cut off from his pursuers by a mist marked with squares along which he hurried until this criss-cross took the form of a barred pigeon-hole, behind which he found his wife selling métro tickets, bread-coupons and cleaning-pads of wire gauze. Without stopping at the pigeon-hole he ran down a sloping corridor, reflecting with extreme anxiety that his wife would be waiting for him on the platform. The corridor was several miles long, but he reached the end without having to run along it, simply by arranging figures in his head. On the platform he again suspected that he was dreaming, because beneath the vaulted roof there were several zones of light of differing degrees of intensity and having no connection between them. It was in one of these breaks in continuity that he discovered his wife. Colourless and hard to see, she was wearing an extravagant feathered hat which caused him great concern. He looked about him a number of times, fearing to find his departmental chief among the passengers. 'You must look after father,' she said to him. 'He's in his basket.' Duvilé saw his father-in-law, a few paces behind his wife, standing with both legs in one of the four compartments of a wicker bottle-carrier. Standing very erect, his arms tight at his sides, the old man was wearing the red cap of the *Chasseurs d'Afrique*. Followed by his wife, Duvilé picked up the basket without any conscious effort and carried it to the edge of the platform, where he set it down. The string of métro coaches which the three of them thus stood awaiting had become for him an immense hope filling him with anxious joy. At length he heard the subterranean rumbling which heralded their approach, but what emerged from the tunnel was only a miniature train, a child's toy such as may be bought in a cardboard box. A feeling of violent disappointment, commensurate with his hope, rent his heart. So extreme was his anguish that he thought himself dying and awoke with groans.

Duvilé did not get to sleep again, but lay until daybreak pondering over his dream. As his thoughts dwelt upon it, details re-emerged from the depths of his consciousness and were brought into sharp relief. For him the culminating episode was his entry into that cellar of the happy life. The thought of it obsessed him throughout the Sunday morning. He replied absently to his wife and children, sought to be alone, and often paused and stayed motionless, in the midst of some activity, while he listened to the sound of a fountain, the splash of wine from a basin to the one below. As happened every Sunday morning, at about eleven he went out by himself to do the household shopping. Three days previously it had been announced that a new issue of wine was shortly to take place, and their provision merchant believed that it would be coming very soon. Duvilé had a strong feeling that it would come today. But contrary to his expectation it had not arrived, and he was as deeply disappointed as he had been when the child's train pulled into the métro station. His wife, when he returned home, asked him if he did not think he had caught 'flu, so haggard was his appearance. He was irritable and taciturn during the meal. The fountains of wine sang a sad and piercing song in his head. He ate without appetite and drank nothing at all. There was nothing on the table but a jug of water, revolting in its limpidity.

They were half-way through their meal, and Duvilé was still

brooding over his dream, when suddenly the recollection of the straw bottle-carrier caused him to raise his eyes to glance at his father-in-law. A light of curiosity, of sudden astonishment, illuminated his apathetic gaze. It occurred to him abruptly that the old man had an interesting shape. His slender torso, his narrow, sloping shoulders and thin neck surmounted by a small head with a rubicund, bald crown, all this gave food for thought. 'I'm not dreaming now,' said Duvilé to himself. 'He really does look like a bottle of claret.' The notion seemed to him preposterous and he tried to turn his thoughts elsewhere, but despite himself he found his eyes constantly returning to glance furtively at his father-in-law. The resemblance became more and more striking. With his rosy cranium one could have sworn that he was a capped wine bottle.

In order to escape his obsession Duvilé went out for the afternoon, but when he again saw his father-in-law, at supper that evening, the likeness leapt to his eyes with a vividness that caused his heart to thump. The fixity of his gaze finally struck the old man, who was annoyed by it.

'There must be something very queer about me if you can't take your eyes off me. But I suppose it's because you think I'm eating too much. You think fifteen-hundred a month isn't enough to pay for a mess of cabbage-stalks, old potatoes and frozen carrots—ha!'

Duvilé blushed deeply and stammered humble apologies. He was accustomed to retort savagely to utterances of this kind, and his change of tone surprised everyone. When the meal was over and the children, playing near their grandfather, occasionally bumped against him, he intervened with a solicitude which was no less unusual.

'Be careful what you're doing,' he said sharply. 'You mustn't shake him like that. He must be kept quite still.'

He passed a bad night, his slumber oppressed by nightmares, in which, however, no wine figured and no father-in-law. Next morning, for the first time in his life, he felt bored and irritated at the thought of having to go to the office. As a rule he went readily enough: indeed, like many other men who would blush to admit it, he preferred the atmosphere of his place of work to that of the domestic hearth. But that morning he would have liked to stay at home. Family life had suddenly acquired for him an inexplicable charm. As he stood in the lobby, about to leave, he heard a thud followed by a groan. Without even troubling to ask where the sound came from he rushed into his father-in-law's room and found him lying face down on the floor. The old man had stumbled and in falling had struck his head against the edge of the chest of drawers. Trembling with anxiety, Duvilé picked him up and helped him into the bathroom. Blood was trickling from a small cut over one eyebrow. For some moments Duvilé stood motionless, staring wide-eyed at the precious red liquid flowing as though from a fountain. It took the arrival of his wife to arouse him from his state of rapt contemplation, and while she was busying herself with the wound he murmured:

'Fortunately it's near the cork. That isn't so serious.'

From that day on Étienne Duvilé went to work only with the utmost reluctance. The anxious hours he spent at the office seemed to drag interminably, for he was tormented by the fear lest in his absence his father-in-law should get broken. In the evening he would run for the métro and burst breathlessly into the apartment crying, 'Is Grandfather all right?'; and upon being assured that he was he would hasten to the old man's side and overwhelm him with tokens of solicitude, urging him to take a more comfortable armchair, fetching a cushion, watching over his movements, begging him to take care as he passed through a doorway—in short, sparing no pains to ensure him a shock-free and well-padded existence. Touched by the change in him, his father-in-law responded with amicable gestures of his own, so that an atmosphere of affectionate harmony now prevailed in the home. Nevertheless the old man had vague misgivings when he found his son-in-law hovering round him with a corkscrew.

'Étienne, what the devil are you doing with that thing?' he asked. 'You can't have any use for it.'

'True, true,' said Duvilé with a sigh. 'It's too small.'

With a sense of frustration he returned the corkscrew to the kitchen drawer.

One day when he was on his way home to lunch Duvilé ran into an old army comrade with whom he had gone through the retreat of 1940. There are memorable bottles in the lives of all old soldiers. In the course of their reminiscences his friend asked him if he remembered how they had sheltered for a time in an abandoned wine-cellar. 'Remember Sergeant Moreau opening the bottles? One whack with a poker and he took the neck off just level with the shoulders, neat as anything.' His head filled with these recollections, Duvilé went on home. A light of secret rejoicing irradiated his countenance and his eyes bulged slightly.

'Is Grandfather all right?'

'Peep-bo!' answered the old gentleman in person, putting his head round the door.

They both laughed heartily and went to the luncheon-table. When his father-in-law was seated Duvilé approached him with the poker in his hand.

'Don't move,' he said, putting a finger under his chin.

The old man chuckled amiably. Taking a pace backwards to allow himself freedom of movement, Duvilé caught him a hefty whack on the side of the neck. The shock was severe but not fatal. The victim uttered a yell. Mme Duvilé and the children sought to intervene with cries and supplications. But Duvilé was seeing red wine. Luckily a neighbour, alarmed by the commotion, burst into the room. Thinking that a bottle of burgundy had entered, Duvilé turned to concentrate upon him, for he was particularly fond of burgundy. But here he met with a vigorous resistance which soon caused him to give up the attempt. Escaping from the apartment he dashed downstairs, still grasping the poker. And in the street a wonderful sight met his eyes. Dozens and dozens of bottles of every conceivable vintage were parading up and down the pavement, some singly and others in groups and pairs. For a moment he stood gazing with affection at the charming spectacle of a vigorous, mature burgundy escorting a slender, long-necked bottle of Alsatian wine. Then he noticed a beggar whose dusty aspect appealed to him, and, rushing at him, he knocked him cold with a single blow of the poker. He was overpowered by two passing American soldiers and taken to the police station, where he showed a lively desire to drink the duty sergeant.

The latest news of Duvilé is that he is in a mental home, and since the doctors have put him on *eau de Vittel* it does not look to me as though he will be ready to come out very soon. Fortunately for him, I am on the friendliest terms with his wife and father-in-law, and I hope soon to persuade them to send him into the Arbois country, to stay with a wine-grower named Félicien Guérillot, who, after numerous adventures that deserve to be recounted, has finally developed such a taste for wine that he has genuinely got the shakes.

It Puckers Your Mouth

ART BUCHWALD

"There are not in this world any lords of higher lineage than the great wines of Médoc, which form the first nobility of the vintages of France, whether they be Margaux, Saint-Julien, Saint-Estèphe, Pauillac, or Moulis. They rival each other in their incomparable elegance and in their rich, ruby-red color."

That is what they would have told you if you had gone to Bordeaux for the harvesting of the 1959 grapes. As a guest of Alexis Lichine, proprietor of the Château Prieuré-Lichine and Lascombes, I spent a few days in the Médoc, watching one of the great vintages being brought in. The sight was one to make the heart beat faster. The dry French summer and fall, which had played havoc with vegetables and dairy products, had been a boon to the grapes. Not only was it a great year in quality, but in quantity as well.

In one of those inexplicable French economic explanations we were told that the price of wine would not go down because it had been a successful year. The previous years, 1956, 1957, 1958, were bitter and cold years for the wine growers, and very little wine was made. The shortage sent the price up. This is reasonable. But last year, with wine in quantity, the price still went up.

I made the mistake of asking one of the growers why.

"Because," he said, as if talking to a child, "it is a great year and everybody wants it."

So much for the economics of wine.

M. Lichine promised to take me on a tour of the Médoc and we started, quite naturally, with his own Château Lascombes. He told me that in the course of the tour I would be asked to taste some wines and he didn't want me to disgrace him.

I practiced by tasting some wine from one of his vats. It tasted good, and I swallowed it.

"No, no, no," he said. "Don't swallow it. Swish it around in your mouth."

"Clockwise or counterclockwise?"

"Clockwise. Counterclockwise is for Burgundy. And then spit it on the floor."

I practiced a few times until I got it right.

"Now say something," he said.

"It sure puckers the inside of your mouth."

"No, that's not what you're supposed to say," M. Lichine cried. "You're supposed to say something beautiful like, 'How full and generous. It will fulfill its promise.' "

"Okay, but it still puckers the inside of your mouth."

Our first stop was Château Margaux, one of the four greatest wine châteaux in France. We visited the chai, the long shed where the grapes are put in vats and barrels. The master of the chai asked me if I wanted to taste some. I nodded, and he gave me a glass.

I swished it around and spat it out. Lichine looked pleased at his pupil. "It has a texture all its own," I said. "It tastes like cotton."

Lichine kicked me in the leg. "What he means," he said to the master, "is that it tastes like velvet."

After we were shown around the Château (I discovered that no one in Bordeaux presses wine in their bare feet any more) Lichine took me to the Château Latour, another of the four greatest vineyards in France.

I tasted the Latour wine and said, "A great wine. It has such a rich, soft flavor."

Lichine smiled.

"Could I have some water?" I asked of the owner, Count Hubert de Beaumont.

Lichine's face dropped.

"Water?" The count looked puzzled. "Do you want to wash your hands?"

Before I could say I wanted to drink the water, Lichine dragged me away.

"Never, never, never ask for water in Bordeaux," he admonished me.

"But I tell you my mouth is all puckered up. My cheeks are stuck to my teeth."

Lichine would have none of it. The last château we visited belonged to Philippe de Rothschild, owner of the Mouton-Rothschild vineyards. M. Rothschild, a gracious host, showed us through his caves and invited us to have a glass of champagne with him in his house, one of the most beautiful in France.

We went upstairs and a servant served us each a bubbling glass. Lichine toasted his host and we each sipped some. Then as Lichine looked on in horror, I swished it around in my mouth.

He screamed, "No!"

But it was too late. I spat it on the floor.

But Then, How It Was Sweet!

G.B. STERN

Still firmly entangled in the web of M. Calvet's benevolent efficiency, we drove on the morning of September 23rd [1926] to the

Hôtel de Lion d'Or, at Langon, in the Sauternes district. He had given us a card with, quite simply, the name of an unknown man on it, the name of the hotel, and the time of day that we were to arrive there. Trustfully we delivered this card, not quite knowing what was to happen to us. They seemed a little fogged, too, at the hotel, but they showed us into a private room, with the table all ready for three. Then they left us alone.

We waited—it seemed for hours—growing hungrier every minute. We could not order the lunch, for we did not know whether M. Calvet had ordered it for us—we dared not run counter to the arrangements of M. Calvet, you see!—or whether we were the guests of the unknown name on the card. On the other hand, the hotel might be waiting for us to order our own lunch, and do it quickly, so as not to keep the unknown name waiting, when it arrived to take us round the châteaux. Finally, it occurred to us that neither the room nor the table nor the knives and forks might be meant for us at all.

At last, desperately, I went into the kitchen and made further inquiries. A very good-looking waiting-maid, tall and strong like Diana, suddenly pushed her way forward, laughing, and affirming that she knew all about it. It was she who had taken the message; and yes, please, we were to lunch at once. We would be called for at one-thirty. Much relieved, I returned to the dining-room, but we still did not know if we were to be allowed to order our own lunch. Apparently not, for she arrived with the hors-d'œuvres and a menu already written. Doubtfully she inquired whether "our chauffeur" would eat with us or not? We looked at Humphrey. He seemed fairly neat and clean, and we decided that we might show thus much condescension, and put up with him for once, making it clear that we were not thereby creating a precedent. . . . So the girl laid another place at the table.

Presently she brought in two bottles of wine. We had reached that stage of sophistication where we were really not quite happy when faced with the wine of another's choice. "Did M. Calvet—?" I asked, doubtfully. No, not M. Calvet; the unknown gentleman, whose name was on the card, he had chosen our wines for us. She poured out the Cheval Blanc, a Graves Saint-Émilion of 1923, and then left us to it.

It was hopelessly sweet, of course, sweeter even than our apprehensions. The awful feeling of helplessness increased. *Where* was our host? *Who* was our host? Sweet wine, and nobody to kick for it! We left most of it, and hoped for relief from the next bottle. The food itself was good.

With the *poulet en cocotte* the second bottle was opened for us—
Sauternes, Sigalas-Rabaud, 1922.

Perhaps the best way of describing it would be to state that by
force of its sweeter sweetness, it made the first wine seem quite
dry; in fact, that was its principal merit, that whenever we took a
sip of the Sigalas-Rabaud, and then, quickly on top of it, the Cheval
Blanc, we could find real enjoyment in the Cheval Blanc.

Mind you, I believe the Rabaud was an excellent wine, rich and
round and lusciously golden. It is classified as a first growth of
Sauternes. And now, not for the first time, I was beginning to feel a
little worried about Château Yquem. A bottle of old Château
Yquem had first aroused my interest in wine, and Johnny's, about
seven years ago. We had not drunk it often since then, usually only
as a dessert wine, but we had kept our illusions about it; and
strangely enough, Rosemary, too, had begun her education on Château Yquem.

. . . The sort of actor-manager you had fallen in love with while
still at school. . . . "You won't like him so much in ten years' time,
my child!" Indignant repudiation—but they were right; oh, they
were right! I didn't. I don't. The sort of poetry, passionate, erotic,
pierrotic—Stephen Phillips's *Paolo and Francesca,* for instance—
which in your early youth had flushed the world rose-red for you,
and clanged in your ear with a sound of silver clarions: "Have you
tried re-reading it lately?" "No—but"—confidently—"I will!" and I
did. It was awful.

So that I wondered a little uneasily about Château Yquem. . . .

Meanwhile the affable chambermaid was chatting to Rosemary
about the wines. "They are good—yes? M. Garosse"—M. Garosse
was the unknown gentleman—"M. Garosse was puzzled at first, not
knowing the company, which wines to choose; and then he said:
'Puisqu'il y a des dames . . .' "

"*Puisqu'il y a des dames.*"

Because of the ladies!

It did not need the rolling eyes of hatred which Humphrey and
Johnny both turned upon us for Rosemary and myself to explode
into fury. We just waited until the chambermaid departed.
"*Puisqu'il y a des dames*—" the old story, the old idiot fallacy that the
ladies preferred sweet wine. Why should we prefer sweet wine?
Has not a woman eyes, organs, dimensions, senses, affections, pas-
sions, even as a man has? And have we not palates, intelligence,
taste, subtlety, and a fastidious discrimination—even as a man has?
But there is a masculine type who will always classify the ladies—
God bless 'em!—as a form of kittle-cattle who must be humoured

and indulged, given compliments, lies, and sweetmeats, relegated to the drawing-room to gossip or to fuss, to read pretty novels or to show off their frocks to an envious rival in frocks; and that sums up the ladies, God bless 'em! So let's open a bottle of Sauternes, Sigalas-Rabaud 1922. . . . That'll please 'em. And so to the serious business of life.

—By this time, when we had exhausted ourselves in repudiating our responsibility for the sweet wine, a responsibility which obviously rested entirely with M. Garosse's too easy conviction that all he heard about ladies was true, we were informed that M. Garosse's chauffeur was waiting to take us round the châteaux. Perhaps M. Garosse himself was a legend, for we never saw him. He remained a mysterious presence, dimly moving in the background, ordering our lives for that one day alone; and behind him M. Calvet moved; and behind M. Calvet? Was there anything still more virile and godlike and competent? I believe not.

At all events, the chauffeur, a nice plump sloe-eyed little man, having received his orders that we should be shown the vineyards of Sauternes, had determined that he would not be accused of a lack of zeal in performance of his duty. We *were* shown the vineyards of Sauternes, and the châteaux of Sauternes, and the cellars of Sauternes.

I must mention here that this day of September 23rd was the hottest which had yet blazed down upon us on all the tour. It was hotter even than at Hermitage. I must mention, too, that as the chauffeur placed himself in front of our car, in order to guide Humphrey, who was driving, Johnny, Rosemary, and I were squeezed in behind. It was our fault that we had too many cloaks with us that day. It had been the sort of hot day which begins in mist, and might equally well have resulted in cold. I must mention, too, that we had finished those two bottles of Sauternes, because, thinking ourselves the guests of M. Garosse, backed by M. Calvet, backed by Jehovah, we were neither brave enough nor impolite enough to leave any! The affable chambermaid would doubtless have reported our actions and reactions. So that we set off for Château Yquem, that grand first growth of Sauternes, feeling already hot, sweet, and sticky; also with an uneasy longing upon us to turn our backs on the sort of afternoon that this was bound to be, and go and lie down somewhere, in a quiet, dim, and shadowy limbo.

Nevertheless, the first sight of Château Yquem brought its rewarding thrill, for this was really a château, not just a house; a beautiful old castle, with towers and big ceremonial gates, and an incredibly deep and ancient well in the central courtyard. While we were looking fearfully down the black hole of the well, through an archway at the far end of the courtyard appeared one of the smallest men I have ever seen, with enormous fierce white moustaches, and kind, childlike blue eyes. He looked like the Generalissimo of the Gnome Army. This was M. Daret, the steward at Château Yquem. Delightfully hospitable and witty he proved to be, and not at all averse from a certain quaint notoriety which his personality had earned for him among visitors to the romantic château. He made us sign our names in the visitors' book, where King Alphonso and Mr. Winston Churchill—these two especially—had already signed theirs; and then he invited us to sample the wine of three different years from the wood, '23, '24, '25.

Feeling rather faint and heavy, we straggled outside into the sunshine again, and down the steep bank which led to the vine-yards. There the *vendangeuses* were already picking; they were very coy with Johnny when he tried to photograph them at their pictur-esque job, and dodged and scuffled round the vines, pretending that they were not worthy of the honour. Meanwhile the General of the Gnome Army showed us the dried grapes left hanging on their stalks, to grow sweeter and sweeter, and rotten-sweet, until they were like raisins with just one single drop of juice left in each centre.

The picking that was going on now was called the *trie*; that is to say, a sort of decimation, for only about every tenth grape had hung long enough to be ready. They have to be left until a sort of fungus, called Botrytis, produces the grey mould on them which is the very essence of Sauternes.

As we drove away from Château Yquem, I noticed, though my sense of beauty was rapidly becoming submerged and sleepy, that at the end of each row of vines a rose-bush grew and was in bloom.

The chauffeur told us, with vicarious pride, that the wines of Sauternes, *vins liquoreux*, sweet and rich and golden, gracious, mel-low, and swooning, would never have existed but for an accident and M. Garosse's grandfather. It was in 1847, ten years after our good Queen Victoria came to the throne, that M. Garosse's grand-father noticed that a portion of his vineyard had been left too long unharvested, and that the grapes lay shrivelled and rotten, most of them, on the ground. Perhaps the weather had been unfavourable, or perhaps he had been away, and . . . At all events, there the grapes lay useless, which had hitherto been plucked at their normal season, and made into ordinary wine; good, plain, inconspicuous white wine; dry, perhaps; dry, not sweet. M. Garosse's grandfather could not bear waste. Sharply he ordered even these grapes to be gathered up and pressed out. That barrel could be set aside for the last among his labourers. And that barrel, *Messieurs et Mesdames*, that marvel of a wine, sweet, rich, and golden, was tasted by the Emperor of all the Russias on his tour through Europe, and he bought it for a fabulous sum! So that the haphazard discovery established a precedent; year after year all the owners of the vineyards of Sauternes allowed their grapes to grow, not only ripe, but rotten.

And we, uttering lip-service to this marvellous discovery, this joy, this miracle, this boon of mankind, swore softly, meanwhile, in our souls, at M. Garosse's grandfather, and at the Emperor of all the Russias, and at that fatal year 1847, in which vineyards which might have produced wine fit for gentlemen to drink—ay, and even for ladies, God bless 'em!—produced instead this clinging, highly perfumed, luscious, and full-blooded horror known as the great wine of Sauternes!

I think that after this we must have all been too sullen with warmth and sweetness to put up any resistance to the will of the chauffeur of M. Garosse. I could not count how many châteaux we visited in that smiling region, nor how many sweet wines we sampled. There was Château Vignan, Château Filhot, Château Latour Blanche. . . . I believe, to the eternal credit of three of us, at least, that Rosemary and I still succeeded in paying the recurring Simon the Cellarer his meed of compliment, as we sampled his 1924 and 1925 of sticky new wine; and that Johnny still succeeded each time in twisting his face into something of a connoisseur's expression as he held his glass up to the light and drank. As for Humphrey, we missed him from these performances somewhere round about the fourth château after Château Yquem. . . . And found him sitting by the car, pretending to examine something in its inside, and asserting cantankerously that as far as Sauternes went: "I'm sunk!"

The rays of the sun grew ever hotter, our cloaks heavier, our skins stickier, and the chauffeur of M. Garosse ever more cheerful and implacable.

"Next," he cried merrily, "we will visit Château Rieussec. They will let us taste their wine. It is of a very good quality. After that, Château d'Arche. You can see it from here if you stand up!" And obediently we tried to stand up.

The nightmare reached its epitome at Latour Blanche, where, just in front of the entrance to the cellars of that noble beverage, Humphrey was unable to start up the car. Something had gone wrong. There was no doubt but that here we were to remain for ever, stuck fast in the very heart and core of Sauternes; and waves of warm, sickly hopelessness flowed over us as again and again he cranked up the engine, and in vain. Presently, we imagined, the hospitable Simon the Cellarer and his wife would step out, seeing our plight, and beg us to come in and sit down, and eat and drink with them, and remain the night; and we should be given Sauternes for tea and for dinner and for breakfast and for ever. . . . We talked, in low, subdued voices, about the niceness of vinegar and sharp apples and olives and anchovies, and tried to keep up our spirits in that way, as we sat stuck together like three pear-drops at the back of the car which would not go.

And in about half an hour it did go, and we drove away from Château Latour Blanche, and away from Sauternes, and back to Langon, where, with many thanks and an adequate tip, we dropped M. Garosse's chauffeur; and then we drove away from Langon, and still farther away from Sauternes, along the road to Saint-Émilion. And the sun was setting, and there was a tang of autumn coolness in the air, and plenty of room in the car; and the scenery was unexpectedly exhilarating, and the plum-coloured bloom of evening lay upon the hills; and we were going towards a dinner at Libourne where we could choose the wine ourselves—dry wine, *vin sec,* not *demi-sec,* but *sec, sec, sec!*

from Bouquet

The Boom in the Bottle

"ADAM SMITH"

I do not have a very good record at turning one dollar into three in the commodity markets, but now I have a commodity that looks like it is really ready to move. No downside risk, either. You don't necessarily get to pocket a lot of money by going long on this commodity if I am right, but you do get points for taste and status and you can make yourself feel good, and all that psychic income has to count for something. My research tells me that the top French wines have nowhere to go but up. Now in our affluent papered economy, everything goes up: rents go up, co-ops go up, beef goes up, Picasso sketches go up. It all has to do with the Phillips curve, the unemployment rate, the money in circulation, the Stage Door Delicatessen going public, and the fact that there is so much *paper* around that *things* look better every day. But if my dire predictions come true, the classic French wines will remove themselves from ordinary dinners and come to rest somewhere between the expense-account crowd and Parke-Bernet.

By way of warning, I should tell you that my last commodity venture was not successful. The theory was right, but the timing was wrong. The theory was that the world was just about out of cocoa, and when the world is out of something and everybody still wants it, the price goes up. Cocoa was at 24 cents and we figured that it could go to 40 cents, given a few capsid flies eating the bushes in Ghana and Nigeria, some torrential rain, and a little outbreak of Black Pod to get rid of any cocoa brave enough to grow. No sooner did we put our money where our theory was than cocoa went to 21 cents, giving a severe drubbing to those of us on thin margins. After the buyers from Hershey, Nestlé, and M & M had taken all our contracts away, the capsid flies descended on the cocoa, it started raining and never stopped, and in Ghana Black Pod became a household word like Spiro T. Agnew. And if you will glance at the financial section, you will see that cocoa is indeed at 40 cents. You can't win them all.

A while back I was having dinner with a friend of mine and I asked him what he was buying.

"We are buying," he said, "Lafite Rothschild 1964."

I told him it was nice he was giving a dinner party, but seriously, was the computer-leasing fad over and what was he buying.

"We are buying Lafite Rothschild 1964," he said. "It's already gone from $40 a case to $135 a case, and there isn't going to be any more."

There isn't going to be any more. Those are words to excite latent greed.

"How much have you bought?" I asked.

"We bought the floating supply and promised to maintain an orderly market," said my friend. "I just wrote out a check for $483,000."

Now those two phrases, *we bought the floating supply*, and *there isn't going to be any more*, are enough to get anyone going.

"Why isn't there going to be any more?" I asked.

"The acreage of the Château-bottled wines is fixed," said my friend, "and there are more people in the world all the time, and there is more money in the world all the time. Textbook case. A couple of bad vintages make the supply even tighter, and 1968 is a disaster."

"There's a dock strike coming up, and all the wages in France are going up since the May troubles," I added.

"Right," said my friend. "But consider this. Most of the wine in America is drunk too young. It takes a good Burgundy a couple of years to get going, and a Château-bottled Bordeaux may not be ready to drink for ten years. But liquor stores have to turn over their inventory—it costs them 12 per cent a year just to keep the wines—so they push the stuff right out. If you wait to serve the wine when it's ready to drink, the price will not only be sky-high, there may not be any at all. It's a depleting asset."

I now have to insert a couple of footnotes, just to be honest. First of all, if your greed is now in high gear and you are thinking of making a killing from my hot tip here, forget it. Wine is alcohol, and the laws about alcohol and selling it are very strict in this country, and involve lots of red tape. So unless you have a license, you can't resell spirits in any form. This hot tip only does you any good if you happen to like wine, and if you are going to serve it at dinner sometime, and if you can keep your guests away from the gin bottle long enough to be sure they appreciate the good stuff. If you are going to give them an hour of heavy-handed martinis first, you might as well give them Old Catawba, Thunderbird, or Shapiro's Best. I am not knocking our native products, but that is not the commodity under discussion.

The kind of killing you make here is from sopping up the float at $5.75 a bottle, and then, in three or five or seven years, when the wine is properly matured, you serve it to your friends, who are properly appreciative because a) it doesn't taste like anything else they've tasted, and b) it costs $30 a bottle at the local retailer. You do have to store the wine yourself, however, in the meantime. My friend who bought the float in the '64 Lafite says there isn't any-place in New York that stores the wine properly. That wine is *alive* inside the bottle, quietly getting serene, and if it's too hot or too cold or the vibration from the subway joggles it, the wine goes belly-up and doesn't get serene. So my Lafite friend built himself a wine cellar in the basement of his Park Avenue apartment building, put Styrofoam in the walls to cushion it (the IRT is only a block away), installed special air conditioning to keep the place at a constant 60°, and hooked up a special alarm. If the main power ever fails, the alarm goes off and the building superintendent rushes down, seals the place, and throws on the emergency air conditioning.

My own procedure, before this greed mobilized my anxieties, was to trot down to the local wine store and say, "Eight for dinner, roast lamb, what have we got for $3.99?" Or almost. I say almost, because now you have to sit through the medical part of this footnote.

I got hooked on wine as an Oxford student. Oxford had, so help me, a wine team, which started as a club, and every month the wine merchants would donate a couple of cases to be tasted, on the theory that if you got the young bloods in their student years, they would remember the merchant with gratitude and order three thousand cases, when they went to the city and got rich or when the Title in the family fell upon them. We all ambled around the tables, sipping carefully, chewing bread crusts in between wines, and spitting the wine out into sawdust boxes. The climax each year was the Big Game with Cambridge. Ten unlabeled bottles on each side of the table, and you got 4 points for identifying the Château, 3 points for the vintage, 2 points for the district, and 1 point for the overall type, i.e., Burgundy, Bordeaux and so on.

I was only a raunchy American, and the young bloods were much given to the wine merchant–Roald Dahl vocabulary. They would swirl the wine a bit, hold it to the light, sip it, and come up with something like: "A good nose, and splendid body, but I find it perhaps lacking in finesse. It is a Clos Vougeot, but *not from the upper part of the slope*—closer to the road, where the shade comes earlier in the afternoon."

I didn't have much of a palate, but I did find one private help to identification. Some of the white wines made me feel like I was getting a cold, a kind of sogginess under the eyes. The day of the Big Game I was sitting on the bench, second-string Burgundy, and one of our stalwart linebackers showed up with so bad a cold that they had to use me. Cambridge beat us, 104–81, but two of the wines were my soggy-eyeball vintages and I got to score, saving the Stars and Stripes from total disgrace. ("Your American," the Cambridge captain said to our captain after the game, "did all right on the white Burgundies. Why is he crying?")

Now we fade out, and when we fade back in again it is a full decade later and the doctor is telling me that, due to a stomach ailment, I can't drink anything at all. After a month or two, as bad patients do, I began fudging, but I found I did have to be careful. If I went out to dinner and had even one glass of a red wine too young, I doubled over and had to pretend I had dropped my napkin on the floor and was retrieving it. If the white wine was a real soggy-eyeball vintage, I practically had to carry Dristan. And pretty soon, with those terrible penalties for guessing wrong, I could actually sort out the stomach-cramp vintages from the others with only a sip or two. B. F. Skinner and all the other behaviorist types would love it: rewards for being right, penalties for being wrong, and you speed the learning terrifically.

A little research and some consultation with my patient physician revealed that malic acid was the villain in the eyeball business, and tannin in the reds. Now you do need the malic acid or you have no sharpness to white wines, and all good red wines have tannin. The tannin holds the wine together and gives it long life and body, but you do have to give it time to quiet down, and that time is part of what makes good wines so expensive. In short, I did not have a really educated palate. I had just inflicted myself with the physical inability to drink anything but smooth and expensive wines. . . .

One day in London I had lunch with Hugh Johnson, author of a book called *Wine,* and a former tailback on the Oxford U. wine team. We had a bottle of Musigny Comte Georges de Vogüé 1959 Vieilles Vignes and it was all the best things in the wine vocabulary: splendid, magnificent, real symphonic structure. A bottle like that can cheer you up for two days.

So, back in New York, I tried collecting some. I managed to acquire all of seven bottles before I was told *there isn't any more.* Then my office phone rang one day and it was the eminent tape-trader, The Great Winfield, who hears all the hot stories and then watches their action.

"My informants tell me," he said, "that you have been scuttling around trying to buy something, Musigny something, and it's not even in the Pink Sheets."

The Pink Sheets carry all the over-the-counter quotations.

"It's not in the Pink Sheets," I said. "It's a wine. Send your spies to find a new computer-leasing outfit, and stay out of this. I haven't completed my position. In fact, I have only seven bottles."

"Wait a minute," he said. "Is wine going up?"

"Take Lafite Rothschild 1961," I said. "You could have bought it for $40 a case at the issue. It would have to sell for $270 to $300 now, and it looks higher." I told him the rest of the anxiety-mobilizing story. That was a mistake.

"Now let me get just one thing straight," said The Great Winfield. "The market is thin. A couple of bad crops, and the price goes through the roof. Do wine bushes, or vines, or whatever the hell they are—don't they get diseases? Like Black Pod?"

Black Pod was a factor in the Cocoa Caper, but vines don't get Black Pod.

"I'm sure there's some disease they could catch," said The

Great Winfield, "but maybe we don't need it. Let's just run down a few of the factors here. If this Musigny is doing so well, why don't they plant more?"

"The area is limited by law," I said. "You could plant more vines, but you couldn't call them by the same name as the estate. And it takes four years to grow a grape. . . ."

"I like it," he said, "I like it. Now, about the competition. The price goes up too much on these French bottles, we start drinking the substitutes. California—what about California?"

I told him there was no reason California wines couldn't be almost the equal of the Château bottlings. But most California production is mass production, blended and aimed at a mass market. No fancy names, just Thunderbird and Hearty Burgundy and so on. And while some California growers do produce some premium wines, most of these wines never leave California, and the labor cost is so high that they, too, would be expensive. And even the best California reds should sit longer than people let them sit.

"You're sure there's nothing that could get into our market," said The Great Winfield. "Nobody could blend a wine and pass it off."

The Italians are still recovering from a wine scandal that had shoe polish and oxblood and all sorts of things in one popular wine, and the good vintners of Geisenheim in Germany managed to produce wine without any grape juice at all, just acids and chemicals. There can be good wines from Italy and Germany and lots of other places, but in the expense-account restaurants, nothing is going to replace the top French Château bottlings.

"I like it," said The Great Winfield. "It feels right."

I should have kept quiet, because I noticed a bid in a trade paper. Usually the bids and offers off the board say something like:

We offer, subject to prior sale and price change
5000 Shares
Weequaahic Bank & Trust 2.20 prior preferred

---

that sort of thing. And here is an ad with a bid:

We are bidding for
*   Musigny Comte Georges de Vogüé 1959 Vieilles*
Vignes (French Red Burgundy Wine)
* $120 a case*

Even before I could call up and complain, The Great Winfield's assistant was on the phone.

"We thought you would like to know," he said, "that your Musigny Comte Georges de Vogüé just traded at 17. Currently it is 17–18, on a workout. The offering side seems to be light."

"Thanks a lot," I said. "I have all of seven bottles and I plan to drink them, and now I'll never get any more."

"The Great Winfield," said his assistant, "would appreciate it if you did not plug in John Hartwell, Fred Carr, Rodney White, Dave Meid, Roland Grimm, the banks, or any of your gunslinger friends just yet. That is too much buying power for this market. The offering side is light, and we drank two bottles of the stuff last night so now it's even lighter."

Three days later the same gentleman called again.

"Musigny Comte Georges de Vogüé," he said, "just traded at 24½ and is now 25–27. You might like to know that a Romanée-Conti 1959 went for over $40 in New Orleans the other day. That's making it easy for us. The chart on your Musigny—"

"The *chart!*" I said.

"The chart on your Musigny shows a breakout at 27, with 40 the next stop," said the voice, unruffled. "It has come off the base beautifully, and the 40 resistance level may not be a top."

The next phone call was from a hedge fund manager of my acquaintance.

"What took you so long?" he said.

"What took me so long to what?" I said.

"To go long on some wine. I've been long for three years. It's one of my best positions. Bamberger's, or Macy's, or one of them was having a closeout sale and I got this stuff at 7 when it was already 10–11 in the open market."

"What have you got?" I said.

"Only the big blues. Lessee, I got 500 La Tâche 1959, 500 Romanée-Conti 1950, 200 Margaux 1961, 200 Lafite 1961, 400 Latour 1957, 271 Richebourg—"

"271?"

"I been drinking that one. What have you got?"

"I have seven bottles of Musigny Comte Georges de Vogüé 1959," I said.

"I hear that's hot," said the hedge fund manager. "The chart says 40, but I'm not going to chase it. My basement's full anyway, and now I have to get the contractor in to insulate the steam pipes down there. You have to be careful with this stuff, you know. I don't let the kids down there. They might run around and joggle it."

A sympathetic underwriter called with some good news.

"I hear you are trying to fill out a block of Musigny," he said. "We were talking to Abdulla Zilkha in Paris this morning—"

"Abdulla *Zilkha?*" I said. Abdulla Zilkha is a merchant banker in Paris, Zurich, London, and other places.

"Right, Abdulla Zilkha. He has just been made a member of the Chevaliers du Tastevin, and he says if you'll send him the name of your dealer, he'll see what he can do with Comte Georges de Vogüé."

This is an unfinished story, but you will be able to check what happens yourself. The big blues will have big moves, but there are some good wines just behind the big blues that the expense-account crowd will not feel so comfortable with. I have found the name of a vineyard just across from the Comte de Vogüé, and it's not on any of the winelists.

In fact, all kinds of new funds are so easy to bring out these days that I am thinking of starting Adam Smith's Wine Fund, with top Establishment figures as the portfolio managers and dividends paid in vintages ready to drink. We have already spotted a California sleeper and some promising stuff in the direction of the village of Monthelie.

But I still have only six bottles of Musigny Comte Georges de Vogüé 1959. Six. I forgot to add, the first thing you have to buy when you are building a wine cellar is a padlock.

The Last Bottle in the World

STANLEY ELLIN

It was a bad moment. This café on the rue de Rivoli near the Meurice had looked tempting, I had taken a chair at one of its sidewalk tables, and then, glancing casually across at the next table, had found myself staring into the eyes of a young woman who was looking at me with startled recognition. It was Madame Sophia Kassoulas. Suddenly, the past towered over me like a monstrous genie released from a bottle. The shock was so great that I could actually feel the blood draining from my face.

Madame Kassoulas was instantly at my side.

"Monsieur Drummond, what is it? You look so ill. Is there anything I can do?"

"No, no. A drink, that's all. Cognac, please."

She ordered me one, then sat down to solicitously undo the buttons of my jacket. "Oh, you men. The way you dress in this summer heat."

This might have been pleasant under other conditions, but I realized with embarrassment that the picture we offered the other patrons of the café must certainly be that of a pitiful, white-haired old grandpa being attended to by his soft-hearted granddaughter.

"Madame, I assure you—"

She pressed a finger firmly against my lips. "Please. Not another word until you've had your cognac and feel like yourself again. Not one little word."

I yielded the point. Besides, turnabout was fair play. During that nightmarish scene six months before, when we were last in each other's company, she had been the one to show weakness and I had been the one to apply the restoratives. Meeting me now, the woman must have been as hard hit by cruel memory as I was. I had to admire her for bearing up so well under the blow.

My cognac was brought to me, and even *in extremis*, so to speak, I automatically held it up to the sunlight to see its color. Madame Kassoulas' lips quirked in a faint smile.

"Dear Monsieur Drummond," she murmured. "Always the connoisseur."

Which, indeed, I was. And which, I saw on grim reflection, was how the whole thing had started on a sunny Parisian day like this the year before. . . .

That was the day a man named Max de Marechal sought me out in the offices of my company, Broulet and Drummond, wine merchants, on the rue de Berri. I vaguely knew of De Marechal as the editor of a glossy little magazine, *La Cave*, published solely for the enlightenment of wine connoisseurs. Not a trade publication, but a sort of house organ for La Société de la Cave, a select little circle of amateur wine fanciers. Since I generally approved the magazine's judgments, I was pleased to meet its editor.

Face to face with him, however, I found myself disliking him intensely. In his middle forties, he was one of those dapper, florid types who resemble superannuated leading men. And there was a feverish volatility about him which put me on edge. I tend to be low-geared and phlegmatic myself. People who are always bouncing about on top of their emotions like a Ping-Pong ball on a jet of water make me acutely uncomfortable.

The purpose of his visit, he said, was to obtain an interview from me. In preparation for a series of articles to be run in his magazine he was asking various authorities on wine to express their opinions about the greatest vintage they had ever sampled. This way, perhaps, a consensus could be made and placed on record. If—

"If," I cut in, "you ever get agreement on the greatest vintage. Ask a dozen experts about it, and you'll get a dozen different opinions."

"It did look like that at the start. By now, however, I have found some small agreement on the supremacy of two vintages."

"Which two?"

"Both are Burgundies. One is the Richebourg 1923. The other is the Romanée-Conti 1934. And both, of course, indisputably rank among the noblest wines."

"Indisputably."

"Would one of these be your own choice as the vintage without peer?"

"I refuse to make any choice, Monsieur de Marechal. When it comes to wines like these, comparisons are not merely odious, they are impossible."

"Then you do not believe any one vintage stands by itself beyond comparison?"

"No, it's possible there is one. I've never tasted it, but the descriptions written of it praise it without restraint. A Burgundy, of course, from an estate which never again produced anything like it. A very small estate. Have you any idea which vintage I'm referring to?"

"I believe I do." De Marechal's eyes gleamed with fervor. "The glorious Nuits Saint-Oen 1929. Am I right?"

"You are."

He shrugged helplessly. "But what good is knowing about it when I've never yet met anyone who has actually tasted it? I want my series of articles to be backed by living authorities. Those I've questioned all know about this legendary Saint-Oen, but not one has even seen a bottle of it. What a disaster when all that remains of such a vintage—possibly the greatest of all—should only be a legend. If there were only one wretched bottle left on the face of the earth—"

"Why are you so sure there isn't?" I said.

"Why?" De Marechal gave me a pitying smile. "Because, my dear Drummond, there can't be. I was at the Saint-Oen estate myself not long ago. The *vigneron's* records there attest that only forty dozen cases of the 1929 were produced altogether. Consider. A scant forty dozen cases spread over all the years from then to now, and with thousands of connoisseurs thirsting for them. I assure you, the last bottle was emptied a generation ago."

I had not intended to come out with it, but that superior smile of his got under my skin.

"I'm afraid your calculations are a bit off, my dear De Marechal." It was going to be a pleasure setting him back on his heels. "You see, a bottle of Nuits Saint-Oen 1929 is, at this very moment, resting in my company's cellars."

The revelation jarred him as hard as I thought it would. His jaw fell. He gaped at me in speechless wonderment. Then his face darkened with suspicion.

"You're joking," he said. "You must be. You just told me you've never tasted the vintage. Now you tell me—"

"Only the truth. After my partner's death last year I found the bottle among his private stock."

"And you haven't been tempted to open it?"

"I resist the temptation. The wine is dangerously old. It would be extremely painful to open it and find it has already died."

"Ah, no!" De Marechal clapped a hand to his brow. "You're an American, monsieur, that's your trouble. Only an American could talk this way, someone who's inherited the obscene Puritan pleasure in self-denial. And for the last existing bottle of Nuits Saint-Oen 1929 to have such an owner! It won't do. It absolutely will not do. Monsieur Drummond, we must come to terms. What price do you ask for this Saint-Oen?"

"None. It is not for sale."

"It must be for sale!" De Marechal said explosively. With an effort he got himself under control. "Look, I'll be frank with you. I am not a rich man. You could get at least a thousand francs—possibly as much as two thousand—for that bottle of wine, and I'm in no position to lay out that kind of money. But I am close to someone who can meet any terms you set. Monsieur Kyros Kassoulas. Perhaps you know of him?"

Since Kyros Kassoulas was one of the richest men on the Continent, someone other magnates approached with their hats off, it would be hard not to know of him, despite his well-publicized efforts to live in close seclusion.

"Of course," I said.

"And do you know of the one great interest in his life?"

"I can't say I do. According to the newspapers, he seems to be quite the man of mystery."

"A phrase concocted by journalists to describe anyone of such wealth who chooses to be reticent about his private affairs. Not that there is anything scandalous about them. You see, Monsieur Kassoulas is a fanatic connoisseur of wines." De Marechal gave me a meaningful wink. "That's how I interested him in founding our Société de la Cave and in establishing its magazine."

"And in making you its editor."

"So he did," said De Marechal calmly. "Naturally, I'm grateful to him for that. He, in turn, is grateful to me for giving him sound instruction on the great vintages. Strictly between us, he was a sad case when I first met him. A man without any appetite for vice, without any capacity to enjoy literature or music or art, he was being driven to distraction by the emptiness of his life. I filled that emptiness the day I pointed out to him that he must cultivate his extraordinarily true palate for fine wine. The exploration of the worthier vintages since then has been for him a journey through a wonderland. By now, as I have said, he is a fanatic connoisseur. He would know without being told that your bottle of Nuits Saint-Oen 1929 is to other wines what the Mona Lisa is to other paintings. Do you see what that means to you in a business way? He's a tough man to bargain with, but in the end he'll pay two thousand francs for that bottle. You have my word on it."

I shook my head. "I can only repeat, Monsieur de Marechal, the wine is not for sale. There is no price on it."

"And I insist you set a price on it!"

That was too much.

"All right," I said, "then the price is one hundred thousand francs. And without any guarantee the wine isn't dead. One hundred thousand francs exactly."

"Ah," De Marechal said furiously, "so you really don't intend to sell it! But to play dog in the manger!"

Suddenly he went rigid. His features contorted, his hands clutched convulsively at his chest. As crimson with passion as his face had been the moment before, it was now ghastly pale and bloodless. He lowered himself heavily into a chair.

"My heart," he gasped in agonized explanation. "It's all right. I have pills—"

The pill he slipped under his tongue was nitroglycerin, I was sure. I had once seen my late partner Broulet undergo a seizure like this.

"I'll call a doctor," I said, but when I went to the phone De Marechal made a violent gesture of protest.

"No, don't bother. I'm used to this. It's an old story with me."

He was, in fact, looking better now.

"If it's an old story, you should know better," I told him. "For a man with a heart condition, you allow yourself to become much too emotional."

"Do I? And how would you feel, my friend, if you saw a legendary vintage suddenly appear before you and then found it remained just out of reach? No, forgive me for that. It's your privilege not to sell your goods if you don't choose to."

"It is."

"But one small favor. Would you, at least, allow me to see the bottle of Saint-Oen? I'm not questioning its existence. It's only that the pleasure of viewing it, of holding it in my hands—"

It was a small enough favor to grant him. The cellars of Broulet and Drummond were near the Halles au Vin, a short trip by car from the office. There I conducted him through the cool, stony labyrinth bordering the Seine, led him to the Nuits Saint-Oen racks, where, apart from all the lesser vintages of later years, the one remaining bottle of 1929 rested in solitary grandeur. I carefully took it down and handed it to De Marechal, who received it with reverence.

He examined the label with an expert eye, delicately ran a fingertip over the cork. "The cork is in good condition."

"What of it? That can't save the wine if its time has already come."

"Naturally. But it's an encouraging sign." He held the bottle up to peer through it. "And there seems to be only a normal sediment. Bear in mind, Monsieur Drummond, that some great Burgundies have lived for fifty years. Some even longer."

He surrendered the bottle to me with reluctance. His eyes remained fixed on it so intensely as I replaced it in the rack that he looked like a man under hypnosis. I had to nudge him out of the spell before I could lead him upstairs to the sunlit outer world. We parted there.

"I'll keep in touch with you," he said as we shook hands. "Perhaps we can get together for lunch later this week."

"I'm sorry," I said without regret, "but later this week I'm leaving for New York to look in on my office there."

"Too bad. But of course you'll let me know as soon as you return to Paris."

"Of course," I lied.

However, there was no putting off Max de Marechal now that he had that vision of the Nuits Saint-Oen 1929 before his eyes. He must have bribed one of the help in my Paris office to tell him when I was back from the States, because no sooner was I again at my desk on the rue de Berri than he was on the phone. He greeted me with fervor. What luck he had timed his call so perfectly! My luck, as well as his. Why? Because La Société de la Cave was to have a dinner the coming weekend, a positive orgy of wine-sampling, and its presiding officer, Kyros Kassoulas himself, had requested my presence at it!

My first impulse was to refuse the invitation. For one thing, I knew its motive. Kassoulas had been told about the Nuits Saint-Oen 1929 and wanted to get me where he could personally bargain for it without losing face. For another thing, these wine-tasting sessions held by various societies of connoisseurs were not for me. Sampling a rare and excellent vintage is certainly among life's most rewarding experiences, but, for some reason I could never fathom, doing it in the company of one's fellow *aficionados* seems to bring out all the fakery hidden away in the soul of even the most honest citizen. And to sit there, watching ordinarily sensible men vie with each other in their portrayals of ecstasy over a glass of wine, rolling their eyes, flaring their nostrils, straining to find the most incongruous adjectives with which to describe it, has always been a trial to me.

Weighed against all this was simple curiosity. Kyros Kassoulas was a remote and awesome figure, and here I was being handed the chance to actually meet him. In the end, curiosity won. I attended the dinner, I met Kassoulas there, and I quickly realized, with gratification, that we were striking it off perfectly.

It was easy to understand why. As De Marechal had put it, Kyros Kassoulas was a fanatic on wines, a man with a singleminded interest in their qualities, their history, and their lore; and I could offer him more information on the subject than anyone else he knew. More, he pointed out to me, than even the knowledgeable Max de Marechal.

As the dinner progressed, it intrigued me to observe that where everyone else in the room deferred to Kassoulas—especially De Marechal, a shameless sycophant—Kassoulas himself deferred to me. I enjoyed that. Before long I found myself really liking the man instead of merely being impressed by him.

He was impressive, of course. About fifty, short, and barrel-chested, with a swarthy, deeply lined face and almost simian ears, he was ugly in a way that some clever women would find fascinating. Somehow, he suggested an ancient idol roughhewn out of a block of mahogany. His habitual expression was a granite impassivity, relieved at times by a light of interest in those veiled, ever-watchful eyes. That light became intense when he finally touched on the matter of my bottle of Saint-Oen.

He had been told its price, he remarked with wry humor, and felt that a hundred thousand francs—twenty thousand hard American dollars—was, perhaps, a little excessive. Now, if I would settle for two thousand francs—

I smilingly shook my head.

"It's a handsome offer," Kassoulas said. "It happens to be more than I've paid for any half-dozen bottles of wine in my cellar."

"I won't dispute that, Monsieur Kassoulas."

"But you won't sell, either. What are the chances of the wine's being fit to drink?"

"Who can tell? The 1929 vintage at Saint-Oen was late to mature, so it may live longer than most. Or it may already be dead. That's why I won't open the bottle myself or sell anyone else the privilege of opening it. This way, it's a unique and magnificent treasure. Once its secret is out, it may simply be another bottle of wine gone bad."

To his credit, he understood that. And, when he invited me to be a guest at his estate near Saint-Cloud the next weekend, it was with the blunt assurance that it was only my company he sought, not the opportunity to further dicker for the bottle of Saint-Oen. In fact, said he, he would never again broach the matter. All he wanted was my word that if I ever decided to sell the bottle, he would be given first chance to make an offer for it. And to that I cheerfully agreed.

The weekend at his estate was a pleasant time for me, the first of many I spent there. It was an enormous place, but smoothly run by a host of efficient help under the authority of a burly, grizzled majordomo named Joseph. Joseph was evidently Kassoulas' devoted slave. It came as no surprise to learn he had been a sergeant in the Foreign Legion. He responded to orders as if his master was the colonel of his regiment.

What did come as a surprise was the lady of the house, Sophia Kassoulas. I don't know exactly what I expected Kassoulas' wife to be like, but certainly not a girl young enough to be his daughter, a gentle, timid creature whose voice was hardly more than a whisper. By today's standards, which require a young woman to be a lank-haired rack of bones, she was, perhaps, a little too voluptuous, a little too ripely curved, but I am an old-fashioned sort of man who believes women should be ripely curved. And if, like Sophia Kasoulas, they are pale, dark-eyed, blushing beauties, so much the better.

As time passed and I became more and more a friend of the family, I was able to draw from her the story of her marriage, now approaching its fifth anniversary. Sophia Kassoulas was a distant cousin of her husband. Born to poor parents in a mountain village of Greece, convent bred, she had met Kassoulas for the first time at a gathering of the family in Athens, and, hardly out of her girlhood, had married him soon afterward. She was, she assured me in that soft little voice, the most fortunate of women. Yes, to have been chosen by a man like Kyros to be his wife, surely the most fortunate of women.

But she said it as if she were desperately trying to convince herself of it. In fact, she seemed frightened to death of Kassoulas. When he addressed the most commonplace remark to her, she shrank away from him. It became a familiar scene, watching this happen, and watching him respond to it by then treating her with an icily polite disregard that only intimidated her the more.

It made an unhealthy situation in that household because, as I saw from the corner of my eye, the engaging Max de Marechal was always right there to soothe Madame's fears away. It struck me after a while how very often an evening at Saint-Cloud wound up with Kassoulas and myself holding a discussion over our brandy at one end of the room while Madame Kassoulas and Max de Marechal were head-to-head in conversation at the other end. There was nothing indecorous about those tête-à-têtes, but still I didn't like the look of them. The girl appeared to be as wide-eyed and ingenuous as a doe, and De Marechal bore all the earmarks of the trained predator.

Kassoulas himself was either unaware of this or remarkably indifferent to it. Certainly, his regard for De Marechal was genuine.

He mentioned it to me several times, and once, when De Marechal got himself dangerously heated up in an argument with me over the merits of some vintage or other, Kassoulas said to him with real concern, "Gently, Max, gently. Remember your heart. How many times has the doctor warned you against becoming overexcited?"— which, for Kassoulas, was an unusual show of feeling. Generally, like so many men of his type, he seemed wholly incapable of expressing any depth of emotion.

Indeed, the only time he ever let slip any show of his feelings about his troublesome marriage was once when I was inspecting his wine cellar with him and pointed out that a dozen Volnay-Caillerets 1955 he had just laid in were likely to prove extremely uneven. It had been a mistake to buy it. One never knew, in uncorking a bottle, whether or not he would find it sound.

Kassoulas shook his head.

"It was a calculated risk, Monsieur Drummond, not a mistake. I don't make mistakes." Then he gave an almost imperceptible little shrug. "Well, one perhaps. When a man marries a mere child—"

He cut it short at that. It was the first and last time he ever touched on the subject. What he wanted to talk about was wine, although sometimes under my prodding and because I was a good listener, he would recount stories about his past. My own life has been humdrum. It fascinated me to learn, in bits and pieces, about the life of Kyros Kassoulas, a Piraeus wharf rat who was a thief in his childhood, a smuggler in his youth, and a multimillionaire before he was thirty. It gave me the same sense of drama Kassoulas appeared to feel when I would recount to him stories about some of the great vintages which, like the Nuits Saint-Oen 1929, had been cranky and uncertain in the barrel until, by some miracle of nature, they had suddenly blossomed into their full greatness.

It was at such times that Max de Marechal himself was at his best. Watching him grow emotional in such discussions, I had to smile inwardly at the way he had once condescendingly described Kassoulas as a fanatic about wines. It was a description which fitted him even better. Whatever else might be false about Max de Marechal, his feelings about any great vintage were genuine.

During the months that passed, Kassoulas proved to be as good as his word. He had said he wouldn't again bargain with me for the precious bottle of Saint-Oen, and he didn't. We discussed the Saint-Oen often enough—it was an obsession with De Marechal— but no matter how much Kassoulas was tempted to renew the effort to buy it, he kept his word.

Then, one dismally cold and rainy day in early December, my secretary opened my office door to announce in awestruck tones that Monsieur Kyros Kassoulas was outside waiting to see me. This was a surprise. Although Sophia Kassoulas, who seemed to have no friends in the world apart from De Marechal and myself, had several times been persuaded to have lunch with me when she was in town to do shopping, her husband had never before deigned to visit me in my domain, and I was not expecting him now.

He came in accompanied by the ever-dapper De Marechal, who, I saw with increased mystification, was in a state of feverish excitement.

We had barely exchanged greetings when De Marechal leaped directly to the point.

"The bottle of Nuits Saint-Oen 1929, Monsieur Drummond," he said. "You'll remember you once set a price on it. One hundred thousand francs."

"Only because it won't be bought at any such price."

"Would you sell it for less?"

"I've already made clear I wouldn't."

"You drive a hard bargain, Monsieur Drummond. But you'll be pleased to know that Monsieur Kassoulas is now prepared to pay your price."

I turned incredulously to Kassoulas. Before I could recover my voice, he drew a check from his pocket and, impassive as ever, handed it to me. Involuntarily, I glanced at it. It was for one hundred thousand francs. It was worth, by the going rate of exchange, twenty thousand dollars.

"This is ridiculous," I finally managed to say. "I can't take it."

"But you must!" De Marechal said in alarm.

"I'm sorry. No wine is worth a fraction of this. Especially a wine that may be dead in the bottle."

"Ah," said Kassoulas lightly, "then perhaps that's what I'm paying for—the chance to see whether it is or not."

"If that's your reason—" I protested, and Kassoulas shook his head.

"It isn't. The truth is, my friend, this wine solves a difficult problem for me. A great occasion is coming soon, the fifth anniversary of my marriage, and I've been wondering how Madame and I could properly celebrate it. Then inspiration struck me. What better way of celebrating it than to open the Saint-Oen and discover it is still in the flush of perfect health, still in its flawless maturity? What could be more deeply moving and significant on such an occasion?"

"That makes it all the worse if the wine is dead," I pointed out.

The check was growing warm in my hand. I wanted to tear it up but couldn't bring myself to do it.

"No matter. The risk is all mine," said Kassoulas. "Of course, you'll be there to judge the wine for yourself. I insist on that. It will be a memorable experience, no matter how it goes. A small dinner with just the four of us at the table, and the Saint-Oen as climax to the occasion."

"The *pièce de résistance* must be an *entrecôte*," breathed De Marechal. "Beef, of course. It will suit the wine perfectly."

I had somehow been pushed past the point of no return. Slowly I folded the check for the hundred thousand francs and placed it in my wallet. After all, I was in the business of selling wine for a profit.

"When is this dinner to be held?" I asked. "Remember that the wine must stand a few days before it's decanted."

"Naturally, I'm allowing for that," said Kassoulas. "Today is Monday; the dinner will be held Saturday. That means more than enough time to prepare every detail perfectly. On Wednesday I'll see that the temperature of the dining room is properly adjusted, the table set, and the bottle of Saint-Oen placed upright on it for the sediment to clear properly. The room will then be locked to avoid any mishap. By Saturday the last of the sediment should have settled completely. But I don't plan to decant the wine. I intend to serve it directly from the bottle."

"Risky," I said.

"Not if it's poured with a steady hand. One like this." Kassoulas held out a stubby-fingered, powerful-looking hand which showed not a sign of tremor. "Yes, this supreme vintage deserves the honor of being poured from its own bottle, risky as that may be. Surely you now have evidence, Monsieur Drummond, that I'm a man to take any risk if it's worthwhile to me."

I had good cause to remember those concluding words at a meeting I had with Sophia Kassoulas later in the week. That day she phoned early in the morning to ask if I could meet her for lunch at an hour when we might have privacy in the restaurant, and, thinking this had something to do with her own plans for the anniversary dinner, I cheerfully accepted the invitation. All the cheerfulness was washed out of me as soon as I joined her at our table in a far corner of the dimly lit, almost deserted room. She was obviously terrified.

"Something is very wrong," I said to her. "What is it?"

"Everything," she said piteously. "And you're the only one I can turn to for help, Monsieur Drummond. You've always been so kind to me. Will you help me now?"

"Gladly. If you tell me what's wrong and what I can do about it."

"Yes, there's no way around that. You must be told everything." Madame Kassoulas drew a shuddering breath. "It can be told very simply. I had an affair with Max de Marechal. Now Kyros has found out about it."

My heart sank. The last thing in the world I wanted was to get involved in anything like this.

"Madame," I said unhappily, "this is a matter to be settled between you and your husband. You must see that it's not my business at all."

"Oh, please! If you only understand—"

"I don't see what there is to understand."

"A great deal. About Kyros, about me, about my marriage. I didn't want to marry Kyros, I didn't want to marry anybody. But my family arranged it, so what could I do? And it's been dreadful from the start. All I am to Kyros is a pretty little decoration for his house. He has no feeling for me. He cares more about that bottle of wine he bought from you than he does for me. Where I'm concerned, he's like stone. But Max—"

"I know," I said wearily. "You found that Max was different. Max cared very much for you. Or, at least, he told you he did."

"Yes, he told me he did," Madame Kassoulas said with defiance. "And whether he meant it or not, I needed that. A woman must have some man to tell her he cares for her, or she has nothing. But it was wicked of me to put Max in danger. And now that Kyros knows about us, Max is in terrible danger."

"What makes you think so? Has your husband made any threats?"

"No, he hasn't even said he knows about the affair. But he does. I can swear he does. It's in the way he's been behaving toward me these past few days, in the remarks he makes to me, as if he were enjoying a joke that only he understood. And it all seems to have something to do with that bottle of Saint-Oen locked up in the dining room. That's why I came to you for help. You know about these things."

"Madame, all I know is that the Saint-Oen is being made ready for your dinner party Saturday."

"Yes, that's what Kyros said. But the way he said it—" Madame Kassoulas leaned toward me intently. "Tell me one thing. Is it possible for a bottle of wine to be poisoned without its cork being drawn? Is there any way of doing that?"

"Oh, come now. Do you seriously believe for a moment that

your husband intends to poison Max?"

"You don't know Kyros the way I do. You don't know what he's capable of."

"Even murder?"

"Even murder, if he was sure he could get away with it. They tell a story in my family about how, when he was very young, he killed a man who had cheated him out of a little money. Only it was done so cleverly that the police never found out who the murderer was."

That was when I suddenly recalled Kassoulas' words about taking any risk if it were worthwhile to him, and felt a chill go through me. All too vividly, I had a mental picture of a hypodermic needle sliding through the cork in that bottle of Saint-Oen, of drops of deadly poison trickling into the wine. Then it struck me how wildly preposterous the picture was.

"Madame," I said, "I'll answer your question this way. Your husband does not intend to poison anyone at your dinner party unless he intends to poison us all, which I am sure he does not. Remember that I've also been invited to enjoy my share of the Saint-Oen."

"What if something were put into Max's glass alone?"

"It won't be. Your husband has too much respect for Max's palate for any such clumsy trick. If the wine is dead, Max will know it at once and won't drink it. If it's still good, he'd detect anything foreign in it with the first sip and and not touch the rest. Anyhow, why not discuss it with Max? He's the one most concerned."

"I did try to talk to him about it, but he only laughed at me. He said it was all in my imagination. I know why. He's so insanely eager to try that wine that he won't let anything stop him from doing it."

"I can appreciate his feelings about that." Even with my equanimity restored, I was anxious to get away from this unpleasant topic. "And he's right about your imagination. If you really want my advice, the best thing you can do is to behave with your husband as if nothing has happened and to steer clear of Monsieur de Marechal after this."

It was the only advice I could give her under the circumstances. I only hoped she wasn't too panic-stricken to follow it. Or too infatuated with Max de Marechal.

Knowing too much for my own comfort, I was ill at ease the evening of the party, so when I joined the company it was a relief to see that Madame Kassoulas had herself well in hand. As for Kassoulas, I could detect no change at all in his manner toward her or De Marechal. It was convincing evidence that Madame's guilty conscience had indeed been working overtime on her imagination, and that Kassoulas knew nothing at all about her *affaire*. He was hardly the man to take being cuckolded with composure, and he was wholly composed. As we sat down to dinner, it was plain that his only concern was about its menu, and, above all, about the bottle of Nuits Saint-Oen 1929 standing before him.

The bottle had been standing there three days, and everything that could be done to insure the condition of its contents had been done. The temperature of the room was moderate; it had not been allowed to vary once the bottle was brought into the room, and, as Max de Marechal assured me, he had checked this at regular intervals every day. And, I was sure, had taken time to stare rapturously at the bottle, marking off the hours until it would be opened.

Furthermore, since the table at which our little company sat down was of a size to seat eighteen or twenty, it mean long distances between our places, but it provided room for the bottle to stand in lonely splendor, clear of any careless hand that might upset it. It was noticeable that the servants waiting on us all gave it a wide berth. Joseph, the burly, hardbitten majordomo, who was supervising them with a dangerous look in his eye, must have put them in fear of death if they laid a hand near it.

Now Kassoulas had to undertake two dangerous procedures as preludes to the wine-tasting ritual. Ordinarily, a great vintage like the Nuits Saint-Oen 1929 stands until all its sediment has collected in the base of the bottle, and is then decanted. This business of transferring it from bottle to decanter not only insures that sediment and cork crumbs are left behind, but it also means that the wine is being properly aired. The older a wine, the more it needs to breathe the open air to rid itself of mustiness accumulated in the bottle.

But Kassoulas, in his determination to honor the Saint-Oen by serving it directly from its original bottle, had imposed on himself the delicate task of uncorking it at the table so skillfully that no bits of cork would filter into the liquid. Then, after the wine had stood open until the entrée was served, he would have to pour it with such control that none of the sediment in its base would roil up. It had taken three days for that sediment to settle. The least slip in uncorking the bottle or pouring from it, and it would be another three days before it was again fit to drink.

As soon as we were at the table, Kassoulas set to work on the first task. We all watched with bated breath as he grasped the neck of the bottle firmly and centered the point of the corkscrew in the cork. Then, with the concentration of a demolition expert defusing a live bomb, he slowly, very slowly, turned the corkscrew, bearing down so lightly that the corkscrew almost had to take hold by itself. His object was to penetrate deep enough to get a grip on the cork so that it could be drawn, yet not to pierce the cork through; it was the one sure way of keeping specks of cork from filtering into the wine.

It takes enormous strength to draw a cork which has not been pierced through from a bottle of wine which it has sealed for decades. The bottle must be kept upright and immobile, the pull must be straight up and steady without any of the twisting and turning that will tear a cork apart. The old-fashioned corkscrew which exerts no artificial leverage is the instrument for this, because it allows one to feel the exact working of the cork in the bottleneck.

The hand Kassoulas had round the bottle clamped it so hard that his knuckles gleamed white. His shoulders hunched, the muscles of his neck grew taut. Strong as he appeared to be, it seemed impossible for him to start the cork. But he would not give way, and in the end it was the cork that gave way. Slowly and smoothly it was pulled clear of the bottle-mouth, and for the first time since the wine had been drawn from its barrel long years before, it was now free to breathe the open air.

Kassoulas waved the cork back and forth under his nose, sampling its bouquet. He shrugged as he handed it to me.

"Impossible to tell anything this way," he said, and of course he was right. The fumes of fine Burgundy emanating from the cork meant nothing, since even dead wine may have a good bouquet.

De Marechal would not even bother to look at the cork.

"It's only the wine that matters," he said fervently. "Only the wine. And in an hour we'll know its secret for better or worse. It will seem like a long hour, I'm afraid."

I didn't agree with that at first. The dinner we were served was more than sufficient distraction for me. Its menu, in tribute to the Nuits Saint-Oen 1929, had been arranged the way a symphony conductor might arrange a short program of lighter composers in preparation for the playing of a Beethoven masterwork. Artichoke hearts in a butter sauce, *langouste* in mushrooms, and, to clear the palate, a lemon ice, unusually tart. Simple dishes flawlessly prepared.

And the wines Kassoulas had selected to go with them were, I was intrigued to note, obviously chosen as settings for his diamond. A sound Chablis, a respectable Muscadet. Both were good; neither was calculated to do more than draw a small nod of approval from the connoisseur. It was Kassoulas' way of telling us that nothing would be allowed to dim the glorious promise of that open bottle of Nuits Saint-Oen standing before us.

Then my nerves began to get the better of me. Old as I was at the game, I found myself more and more filled with tension, and as the dinner progressed, I found the bottle of Saint-Oen a magnet for my eyes. It soon became an agony, waiting until the entrée would be served and the Saint-Oen poured.

Who, I wondered, would be given the honor of testing the first few drops? Kassoulas, the host, was entitled to that honor, but as a mark of respect he could assign it to anyone he chose. I wasn't sure whether or not I wanted to be chosen. I was braced for the worst, but I knew that being the first at the table to discover the wine was dead would be like stepping from an airplane above the clouds without a parachute. Yet, to be the first to discover that this greatest of vintages had survived the years! Watching Max de Marechal, crimson with mounting excitement, sweating so that he had to constantly mop his brow, I suspected he was sharing my every thought.

The entrée was brought in at last, the *entrecôte* of beef that De Marechal had suggested. Only a salver of *petits pois* accompanied it. The *entrecôte* and peas were served. Then Kassoulas gestured at Joseph, and the majordomo cleared the room of the help. There must be no chance of disturbance while the wine was being poured, no possible distraction.

When the servants were gone and the massive doors of the dining room were closed behind them, Joseph returned to the table and took up his position near Kassoulas, ready for anything that might be required of him.

The time had come.

Kassoulas took hold of the bottle of Nuits Saint-Oen 1929. He lifted it slowly, with infinite care, making sure not to disturb the treacherous sediment. A ruby light flickered from it as he held it at arm's length, staring at it with brooding eyes.

"Monsieur Drummond, you were right," he said abruptly.

"I was?"I said, taken aback. "About what?"

"About your refusal to unlock the secret of this bottle. You once said that as long as the bottle kept its secret it was an extraordinary treasure, but that once it was opened it might prove to be nothing but another bottle of bad wine. A disaster. Worse than a disaster, a joke. That was the truth. And in the face of it, I now find I haven't the courage to learn whether or not what I am holding here is a treasure or a joke."

De Marechal almost writhed with impatience.

"It's too late for that!" he protested violently. "The bottle is already open!"

"But there's a solution to my dilemma," Kassoulas said to him. "Now watch it. Watch it very closely."

His arm moved, carrying the bottle clear of the table. The bottle slowly tilted. Stupefied, I saw wine spurt from it, pour over the polished boards of the floor. Drops of wine spattered Kassoulas' shoes, stained the cuffs of his trousers. The puddle on the floor grew larger. Trickles of it crept out in thin red strings between the boards.

It was an unearthly choking sound from De Marechal which tore me free of the spell I was in. A wild cry of anguish from Sophia Kassoulas.

"Max!" she screamed. "Kyros, stop! For God's sake, stop! Don't you see what you're doing to him?"

She had reason to be terrified. I was terrified myself when I saw De Marechal's condition. His face was ashen, his mouth gaped wide open, his eyes, fixed on the stream of wine relentlessly gushing out of the bottle in Kassoulas' unwavering hand were starting out of his head with horror.

Sophia Kassoulas ran to his side, but he feebly thrust her away and tried to struggle to his feet. His hands reached out in supplication to the fast-emptying bottle of Nuits Saint-Oen 1929.

"Joseph," Kassoulas said dispassionately, "see to Monsieur de Marechal. The doctor warned that he must not move during these attacks."

The iron grasp Joseph clamped on De Marechal's shoulder prevented him from moving, but I saw his pallid hand fumbling into a pocket, and at last regained my wits.

"In his pocket!" I pleaded. "He has pills!"

It was too late. De Marechal suddenly clutched at his chest in that familiar gesture of unbearable pain, then his entire body went limp, his head lolling back against the chair, his eyes turning up in his head to glare sightlessly at the ceiling. The last thing they must have seen was the stream of Nuits Saint-Oen 1929 become a trickle, the trickle become an ooze of sediment clotting on the floor in the middle of the vast puddle there.

Too late to do anything for De Marechal, but Sophia Kassoulas stood swaying on her feet ready to faint. Weak-kneed myself, I helped her to her chair, saw to it that she downed the remains of the Chablis in her glass.

The wine penetrated her stupor. She sat there breathing hard, staring at her husband until she found the strength to utter words.

"You knew it would kill him," she whispered. "That's why you bought the wine. That's why you wasted it all."

"Enough, Madame," Kassoulas said frigidly. "You don't know what you're saying. And you're embarrassing our guest with this emotionalism." He turned to me. "It's sad that our little party had to end this way, monsieur, but these things do happen. Poor Max. He invited disaster with his temperament. Now I think you had better go. The doctor must be called in to make an examination and fill out the necessary papers, and these medical matters can be distressing to witness. There's no need for you to be put out by them. I'll see you to the door."

I got away from there without knowing how. All I knew was that I had seen a murder committed and there was nothing I could do about it. Absolutely nothing. Merely to say aloud that what I had seen take place was murder would be enough to convict me of slander in any court. Kyros Kassoulas had planned and executed his revenge flawlessly, and all it would cost him, by my bitter calculations, were one hundred thousand francs and the loss of a faithless wife. It was unlikely that Sophia Kassoulas would spend another night in his house, even if she had to leave it with only the clothes on her back.

I never heard from Kassoulas again after that night. For that much, at least, I was grateful. . . .

Now, six months later, here I was at a café table on the rue de Rivoli with Sophia Kassoulas, a second witness to the murder and as helplessly bound to silence about it as I was. Considering the shock given me by our meeting, I had to admire her own composure as she hovered over me solicitously, saw to it that I took down a cognac and then another, chattered brightly about inconsequential things as if that could blot the recollection of the past from our minds.

She had changed since I had last seen her. Changed all for the better. The timid girl had become a lovely woman who glowed with self-assurance. The signs were easy to read. Somewhere, I was sure, she had found the right man for her, and this time not a brute like Kassoulas or a shoddy Casanova like Max de Marechal.

The second cognac made me feel almost myself again, and when I saw my Samaritan glance at the small, brilliantly jeweled watch on her wrist, I apologized for keeping her and thanked her for her kindness.

"Small kindness for such a friend," she said reproachfully. She rose and gathered up her gloves and purse. "But I did tell Kyros I would meet him at—"

"Kyros!"

"But of course. Kyros. My husband." Madame Kassoulas looked at me with puzzlement.

"Then you're still living with him?"

"Very happily." Then her face cleared. "You must forgive me for being so slow-witted. It took a moment to realize why you should ask such a question."

"Madame, I'm the one who should apologize. After all—"

"No, no, you had every right to ask it." Madame Kassoulas smiled at me. "But it's sometimes hard to remember I was ever unhappy with Kyros, the way everything changed so completely for me that night—

"But you were there, Monsieur Drummond. You saw for yourself how Kyros emptied the bottle of Saint-Oen on the floor, all because of me. What a revelation that was! What an awakening! And when it dawned on me that I really did mean more to him than even the last bottle of Nuits Saint-Oen 1929 in the whole world, when I found the courage to go to his room that night and tell him how this made me feel—oh, my dear Monsieur Drummond, it's been heaven for us ever since!"

The "Spanish Champagne" Case

ROBERT KEELING

One summer in the mid 1950s, an English student at Madrid University, hardly turned 21, found himself at the castle of Perelada, not far from Gerona, in the north-east of Spain, where he tasted the wines from the local vineyards. Most of them were still wines, but one was sparkling. He not only liked the sparkling wine but saw possibilities for its commercial exploitation in England. And so, towards the end of 1956, Champagne shippers in England slowly became aware of the presence of a usurper. To the long list of borrowed plumes another had been added. The long-suffering and still largely ignorant British public were being offered "Perelada Spanish Champagne."

No one successfully launches such a project without careful preparation, and "Spanish Champagne" was no exception. Discreet enquiries were made from the Customs and Excise authorities about the effect of the English law of merchandise marks; elaborate publicity material was devised; first class selling agents were sought and found. A company was formed, the Costa Brava Wine Co. Ltd, with a mixed English and Spanish board. But hardened though it was by years of "Spanish Sauternes" and "Spanish Graves," a considerable and influential part of the British wine trade found "Spanish Champagne" an affront. It was indeed the last straw. In the summer of 1957 the project was publicly attacked at a famous and fashionable wine tasting. "Perelada" replied through the wine trade press and invited anyone who did not like the new description either to hold his peace or to bring proceedings.

If the issue needed forcing, this was more than enough. Anxious consultation followed between the Association of Champagne Importers in Britain and their French counterparts, the growers and merchants in Reims and Epernay, who worked in this, as in all other communal purposes, through the *Comité interprofessionnel du vin de Champagne* (the C.I.V.C.) at Epernay.

Nor was this all. Frenchmen take seriously their national treasures; noble wines are one of the gifts of France to the civilized world, and of all wines Frenchmen count Champagne as the crown. The French Government had long since set up an organisation to control the use of French wine names within France and to seek, if possible, to protect them from abuse abroad. This organisation, called the *Institut National des Appellations d'Origine des Vins et eaux-de-vie* (the I.N.A.O.), joined the discussions with enthusiasm, and thereafter took a major part in the battle; for it was decided to accept Perelada's challenge and go to law.

But the law was no more simple and straightforward than it usually is. On the one hand lay the Merchandise Marks Acts. To invoke these meant mounting a so-called criminal action, with the possibility of the defence electing trial by jury. The advantages lay in a fairly quick procedure and an orthodox case, well marked by legal precedent and with apparently strong chances of success; albeit with the hazard of a jury. On the other hand lay the Chancery Division of the High Court and a civil action for "passing off." In the High Court, Champagne would be legally defined by a High Court judge, and a judgment in favour of Champagne would establish a resounding precedent, far outweighing the one word "guilty" which would be the result of a successful prosecution before a jury under the Merchandise Marks Acts. But the law in such an action was difficult and involved breaking new ground and establishing new principles.

In the event, the Champagne interests chose the criminal

courts, largely because the chances of success looked greater even though the prize was not so glittering; the defence, not unexpectedly, chose trial by jury rather than run the risk of a judgment of a magistrate; and so, after a preliminary skirmish before Mr Robey, the Clerkenwell magistrate, the case opened before a judge and jury in the notorious Court No. 1 at the Old Bailey on December 17, 1958.

One of the more remarkable features of any action of this kind, and one not generally known, is that the defence has to be told in advance the general line of the evidence the prosecution will call, who will be the prosecution's witnesses and what they will say. Champagne had mustered many well known names in the English trade to give evidence, including shippers, representatives of well known wholesale and retail houses, sommeliers, restaurateurs and writers. The defence, knowing the prosecution's witnesses in advance, had succeeded to a considerable extent in matching witness for witness. They too called wholesalers, retailers, barmen, writers and even a lady member of the public. Indeed the wine trade was deeply divided on this issue. Many whose trade had been built up on the imitation wines such as "Spanish Graves" and "Spanish Sauternes" feared that if the Champagne interests succeeded, a wholesale introduction of the system of *appellations contrôlées* would follow in England, with disastrous results for their business. Many, too, misunderstood the form of the action, and sympathised with this young man and his young company who were, they thought, being dragged like criminals by the Champagne interests to the Old Bailey. Many failed to understand that the prestige not only of Champagne but of the British wine trade was in the balance.

The jury were treated to the most prominent members of the bar of their day. Appearing for Champagne was Mr Geoffrey Lawrence Q.C. Facing him for Perelada was Mr Gerald Gardiner Q.C. The judge was Mr Justice McNair.

The case took six days, thirty witnesses were called (fifteen by each side), and the number of exhibits put to witnesses and shown to the jury reached fifty-nine; but the basic arguments were simple. The prosecution had to prove that, by calling their wine "Spanish Champagne," the Costa Brava Wine Company had applied a description to the wine which was either false or misleading. False in this context meant no more than "untrue." If the description was held to be false, then the defendants must be guilty. If it was not held to be false, then it was for consideration whether, though not false, it was misleading. Misleading meant, as the judge explained to the jury, a statement with a catch in it. He reminded them that often a misleading statement is more dangerous than a false one.

The prosecution said that "Spanish Champagne" was false because Champagne in England meant the sparkling wine from the French province and nothing else. It was, one witness said, as French as the Folies Bergères. Therefore because "Spanish Champagne" suggested that the wine was "Champagne from Spain," it was a lie. On the misleading point, the prosecution relied on a famous precedent in a case about "British Tarragona" and claimed that to argue that no one would be deceived was to assume too much knowledge on the part of the purchaser. In the British Tarragona case, it was argued by the sellers that the expression was a contradiction in terms, and that therefore it was absurd to suppose that anyone could be deceived into thinking that the wine came from Tarragona; but this argument failed because it was held that it assumed too great a degree of knowledge on the part of the purchaser.

The defence denied that "Spanish Champagne" was a lie. Champagne by itself no doubt meant what the prosecution said it meant; but when it was prefixed by the word "Spanish," it clearly meant a wine of champagne type made in Spain. Not only was it not a lie, but it deceived no one, and was a convenient expression both for trade and public. For years the British wine trade had used expressions of this kind; and Mr Gerald Gardiner gradually covered the very large table in the well of the court, used to receiving quite a different kind of criminal exhibit, with example after example of wines with mixed-up names ranging from Spanish Sauternes and Australian Burgundy to Palestinian Alicante and Chilean Barsac. If the practice is so widespread for other wines, he said, why can it not apply to Champagne, as it did, for instance, in America? The prosecution tried, but apparently in vain, to differentiate between Champagne and these other wines by calling evidence to show that the name "Champagne" had never, like those of other wines, been degraded by an alien, geographical adjective. The whole purpose of the prosecution, it was argued, was to prevent this degradation. Indeed, so far from being Champagne, Perelada was not even produced by the famous Champagne method of double fermentation in bottle. It was produced (and this was admitted) by the so-called tank method, whereby the second fermentation takes place in a huge glass-lined tank and the whole process, instead of taking years, is finished in a few weeks.

The judge's summing-up gave little comfort to the defence. He asked the jury to consider the meaning of Champagne in England only, and not to concern themselves with what it meant elsewhere.

He warned the jury against the defence's argument that the word "Spanish" made it perfectly clear that the wine was not Champagne in the limited sense but something different, and he referred the jury to a case about non-brewed vinegar. In this case, it was found that the essential feature of vinegar was that it was a natural product produced by fermentation. The product called "non-brewed vinegar," on the other hand, was a synthetic concoction. It was held that because vinegar is essentially a brewed product, to qualify the word "vinegar" with the word "non-brewed" was a false trade description. The judge observed that the case seemed to suggest that you cannot take a noun with a well-known meaning, add to it an adjective inconsistent with that meaning, and then say "well, taking the two together, they are not false; they are true."

Just before 3 o'clock, the jury retired, taking with them a bottle or two out of the many exhibits (for reflection rather than refreshment), and the opposing sides waited with such patience as they could muster for the verdict. At a quarter to four the jury returned and found the defendants not guilty. The judge said that it was a proper prosecution to bring and a proper case for enquiry, but made the prosecution pay the defendants' costs.

The case had attracted wide publicity in the English and Continental press; "Champagne v. Spain," *The Times* called it, and thus demonstrated a nice regard for the geographical significance of Champagne. The victors naturally took every means open to them to exploit their success. Indeed, so far as much of the English press was concerned, it appeared a popular win. The young English David had triumphed against the French Goliath. The common man and his common sense had routed the pedants and the wine snobs. (Nobody seemed to notice that the principal shareholder in the Costa Brava Wine Company was reputed to be one of the richest men in Spain or that the meaning of Champagne in England seemed unaccountably to have changed overnight.) But the more serious English dailies and weeklies found the verdict disquieting, and there were suggestions that it was time the wine trade put its house in order.

The French press uttered a roar of pained and indignant surprise. Anglo-French political relations were already at an unusually low ebb. The six Common Market countries, including France, were about to start operating in January, 1959, as an exclusive trading bloc; the United Kingdom was at the head of the rival European Free Trade Area. Guinea had just elected to withdraw from the French Community and link herself to Ghana, a member of the

British Commonwealth; and now "Spanish Champagne" was flooding into England, the most important foreign market for Champagne. Irritated as they already were with England and the devious ways of British politics, Frenchmen did not find it difficult to believe that somehow the British Government could have intervened in the Champagne case but deliberately chose not to as part of a general plan to embarrass France. Some bars in Paris refused for a time to sell Scotch Whisky; and a consignment of "Spanish Champagne" on its way to England was turned back by the French authorities on the Pyrenees frontier. In England questions were asked in the House of Commons by francophile M.P.s about the possibility of special protection for Champagne, but the answers were noncommittal and guarded.

Then, at least as far as British comment was concerned, public discussion was brought abruptly to an end by the announcement that twelve famous Champagne houses had issued a writ against the Costa Brava Wine Company in the Chancery Division of the High Court. The Champagne interests had been quick to realise that if nothing was done to repair the damage of the Old Bailey verdict, there might be an avalanche of spurious Champagnes on sale in England from wine-producing countries all over the world, and that Champagne might quickly become only a synonym for "sparkling wine" without any geographical significance at all. So again they went back to the law to see if a High Court judge would give them the remedy under the general common law of England which a jury had failed to give them under the criminal law.

The new action needed courage. Having chosen what appeared to have been the easier path via the Old Bailey and having failed to break through, the Champagne interests were now attempting the more ambitious step of obtaining an injunction to restrain the sale of "Spanish Champagne" on the ground that this was "passing off" as Champagne a wine which was not Champagne, and therefore amounted to unfair competition. Not unexpectedly Perelada met this attack by asserting that this kind of action was unknown in English law, and that even if everything which the Champagne interests said about Champagne was assumed in the plaintiffs' favour, no actionable wrong was disclosed. It was well known, they argued, that a trader could, and often did, bring successful proceedings to protect his own name from use by a rival trader because he could show he had the goodwill in that name. But this was not a case of Bollinger bringing an action against someone selling "Spanish Bollinger." That would be a normal passing-off action and would, at least, be properly constituted. This was an action brought by Bollinger and eleven other French houses, who claimed to represent all exporters of Champagne from France to England (and who were in fact the twelve houses exporting the greatest quantity of Champagne to England) to establish that collectively and exclusively they owned not the individual rights to their own names, but the right to the name "Champagne." The defendants maintained that this kind of collective right to a geographical name might hold water under some Continental legal systems, but did not exist in England; and they sought to have the case dismissed without looking further into the particular facts alleged by the plaintiffs.

The judge agreed to try this point of law separately as a preliminary issue, on the ground that, if Costa Brava were right, there was the end of the matter, the main case would never have to be heard, and much time and money would be saved. Accordingly a long legal battle took place in November 1959 before Mr Justice Danckwerts between Mr Richard Wilberforce Q.C. (now Mr Justice Wilberforce) for the Champagne houses and Sir Milner Holland Q.C. for Costa Brava. Champagne was scarcely mentioned throughout the five day hearing. It was an exceedingly specialised discussion on the nature of the actionable wrong of passing-off in English law and, not unnaturally, was scarcely noticed in the press. But it was in fact the hinge of the whole affair. Mr Wilberforce addressed the judge for two days, a dry, refined and brilliantly annotated address, reviewing a great range of cases and offering the judge a grain or two of argument from each to show that the English common law, looked at as a whole, did not exclude the kind of protection the Champagne interests were seeking, and that indeed it was no more than a logical extension of a principle which, in previous cases, had long been recognized. He capped his argument with a bold invitation to the judge to apply the reasoning in a recent American case concerned with Minnesota flour where a group of Minnesota flour manufacturers had successfully restrained a miller outside the Minnesota District from calling his flour Minnesota flour. In spite of a tremendous (and even lengthier) attempt by the defendants to discredit this argument and the cases cited in support of it, the judge found that the Champagne interests had a right in law to protect the name "Champagne" as against anyone making wine outside the Champagne district; but he hastened to make it clear that this did not decide the case in favour of the plaintiffs as they still had to prove the facts that they were asserting about Champagne. In particular his decision had no effect on the question of whether "Spanish Champagne" was likely to deceive.

But though the law was now established, the facts were still not easy, and confidence in the Spanish camp remained high. It was not enough in the Chancery Division to say, "it is a lie." What had also now to be proved was that there was a reasonable chance of someone who bought a bottle called "Spanish Champagne" being deceived by this description into thinking he was buying Champagne. At this point, the Champagne houses turned again to Mr Geoffrey Lawrence. New witnesses were interviewed, new documentary evidence was prepared, researches were made into the files of I.N.A.O. and C.I.V.C. to see what abuses there had been in the past and what action had been taken; and a note was prepared of the history of the development of Champagne both as a geographical province of France and as a wine, to show the meticulous care with which the French protected the name not only against foreign users but against makers of sparkling wines in other districts of France.

By November 1960 the formal preliminary steps had all been completed. Both sides took their taxi-loads of papers to the court, booked themselves private rooms in the courts to accommodate these and their witnesses (a procedure reserved for long and what lawyers call "heavy cases") and dug themselves in for a long siege. The final struggle—the French press later described it a little fancifully as "the Second Battle of the Marne"—opened again before Mr Justice Danckwerts on November 29, 1960.

So, just two years after the Old Bailey trial, Mr Geoffrey Lawrence again opened for Champagne. The Champagne houses had to succeed in convincing the judge that Champagne had an exclusive and non-generic meaning and a high reputation; and that there was a real risk that, by describing their Spanish wine as Spanish Champagne, the defendants might mislead the more uninformed section of the public into thinking that Champagne could come from Spain. It was not difficult to prove the exclusive meaning or the high reputation but to prove likelihood of deception was far from easy.

As at the Old Bailey, the defendants argued from "Spanish Sauternes" and other names of this kind that this practice was convenient and not unknown even as applied to Champagne. Erskine Childers' famous novel *The Riddle of the Sands*, published early this century, mentioned "German Champagne"; and there were other examples of this in a few old advertisements; there had been many recent references in the press to "Russian Champagne" and one to "Persian Champagne." Even in France, a recent press report describing a wine served at a banquet had said "the Champagne was German." All these and other examples were patiently put to the plaintiffs' witnesses by Sir Milner Holland; newspaper after newspaper was produced—but no bottles, because no one could produce anything on sale in England and described as Champagne except Perelada and the wine from the Champagne province. Old arguments about Cheddar cheese (on the basis that "Canadian Cheddar" equals "Spanish Champagne"), which had been put to some effect at the old Bailey, were put again in cross-examination. Later on in the case, the judge gave his view of these. Cheese, he observed, seemed to be as different from wine as from chalk.

But a certain unease settled upon the plaintiffs under what was a very sustained and penetrating cross-examination; indeed in this kind of case cross-examination is easier and therefore tends to be more effective than the examination by a witness's own counsel. The leading and loaded question must be answered under cross-examination; in examination-in-chief no lead can be given to the witness and he must make his own way with questions which are necessarily not always easy.

After calling twenty-one witnesses, the plaintiffs ended their case, a little dented here and there, but largely intact and with a great weight of authoritative and frank answers to support their main contentions that never had this happened to Champagne before; that Champagne occupied a unique prestige position, but that many people, particularly those with new money and developing tastes did not know where it came from; that these people seeing the word "Spanish Champagne" would easily come to think that Champagne was made in Spain. Some answers were more uncompromising that others. "No geographical description is legitimately generic in character," said one witness, and the Frenchmen in court glowed with a kind of wistful pleasure at hearing an Englishman express an opinion so at variance with much of the practice of the English wine trade. But had the witnesses sufficiently established that the public was as ignorant as the plaintiffs said? Was it really a fact that a significant section of the public really did not know, not that Champagne came from a province in France historically called Champagne, but from France at all? At least one witness thought so beyond any doubt, and he came from industrial Wales. His customers knew it simply as "the stuff they throw against ships." But the cross-examination had been powerful. The practice in the English wine trade of abusing geographical names had been regretfully admitted by the plaintiffs' witnesses; and of course none of the expert witnesses (and they were all experts) was in any danger of himself being deceived. All they could say or suggest was that in general the public was not well informed about wine. It was a matter of argument whether this would result in deception.

Then it was the defendants' turn to call their evidence. A few—very few—opening questions from Sir Milner Holland; and then the defendants' witnesses were exposed to Mr Lawrence's cross-examination. In substance, the defendants' argument was based on the simple proposition that the word "Spanish" showed that the wine did not come from France, and so "Spanish Champagne" could not be mistaken for Champagne from France. There might be a few excessively ignorant persons who might be deceived, said the defendants, but if they existed at all, they were so few and so exceptional as to be insignificant.

Nevertheless the fact remained that Spanish Champagne was not "Champagne" and the defendants' own witnesses found themselves at once in the greatest difficulty when cross-examined on this point. One witness agreed that to call it "Champagne" rather than "White Sparkling Wine" made it more attractive to the public; another said it was called a "Champagne" because it had the same characteristics as the real Champagne. (This, of course, ran counter to the great weight of evidence which had been given that Champagne in England had not, until the appearance of Perelada, been used generically.) Another admitted that since the Old Bailey decision his wine list had omitted the word "Champagne" from the description of Perelada.

Then, when only four witnesses had been called, suddenly and unexpectedly the defendants' case came to an end and Sir Milner Holland was on his feet making his closing speech. No one had come forward for the Costa Brava Wine Company; the long procession of witnesses who had appeared at the Old Bailey had shrunk to four, and of these one lived in Scotland, and the judge did not appear disposed to consider his evidence anyhow.

The speech for the defendants lasted from the morning of December 5 until the afternoon of the following day. It developed the points already made in cross-examination and launched a powerful attack on the plaintiffs' point that a substantial section of the public could be deceived. The judge heard it with scarcely any interruption; and when at length Mr Lawrence rose to his feet for the last time, the match still looked fairly open.

The final speech started quietly; then all at once the judge seemed to be asking questions, almost for the first time in the case, and at first a little uncomfortably for the plaintiffs. "Am I right in thinking there is no evidence whatever of anyone having asked for Champagne and having been sold Spanish Champagne?" Perelada enjoyed hearing the reply. "Put that way I think your Lordship is right." Mr Lawrence then reminded the judge of certain wine lists where "Perelada Spanish Champagne" was listed among the Champagnes. But this was brushed aside. "How far," said the judge, "would the defendants be responsible for that." But then there was a further exchange which gave Mr Lawrence the unmistakable whiff of victory. The judge posed an imaginary situation where some ignorant person orders Champagne, but says to the waiter that it is rather expensive. If, said the judge, the waiter than offered Perelada, would he not add, "but of course that is not French Champagne." This was the heart of the case and Mr Lawrence saw and took his chance. "My Lord, if he said 'Not *French* Champagne,' he would mean 'it is not French Champagne it is Spanish Champagne, but whether you have French Champagne or Spanish it is still Champagne.' " Counsel took this further in his answer to the judge's next question: "Spanish Champagne," said Mr Lawrence, "is likely to deceive the uninformed section of the public into thinking not that they are drinking the plaintiffs' goods, because that is not this form of action, but that they are drinking *a* Champagne which can, contrary to their sort of vague ideas in the past, come from Spain." At last the corner had been turned. "I think," replied Mr Justice Danckwerts, "your argument is supported by the menu—" and he referred to a menu put in evidence where Perelada was described simply as "Champagne (Perelada)."

Mr Lawrence evidently decided it was now safe to hit about him with increasing vigour. He referred to the "utterly disastrous answers" of the defence witnesses. "I was at a party," said one witness, "and I supplied the Champagne." Plainly, in the context, commented counsel, this was Spanish Wine. "Yes," said the judge. He referred to the "generic argument" and to the strenuous attempts of the defendants to show that Champagne had previously been used in England in conjunction with an alien geographical adjective. But in spite of all their efforts, it was a very tiny mouse indeed that in the end appeared—a book in 1873, an advertisement in 1888, a novel in 1902 and a few "journalistic inaccuracies." The judge seemed disposed to agree. "And German Champagne is of course forbidden by treaty," he commented, "and 'Australian Champagne' seems to have been discontinued." In fact there had never been any clear evidence that anything called "Australian Champagne" had ever been sold in England: but Mr Lawrence presumably thought that he had the judge sufficiently with him to pass to his last and most telling point.

Perelada had published a brochure, tricked out in pink and blue, and called "Giving a Champagne Party." This contained the plaintiffs' best evidence of the tendency to drop the adjective and concentrate on the noun, and so of the tendency to deceive; Mr Lawrence had put it briefly to two witnesses, and he now let none of it escape. If he needed any encouragement, he quickly got it. "On its face," said the judge, after a few preliminary comments by counsel, "it is quite plainly intended to cash in on the reputation of Champagne." Mr Lawrence respectfully agreed and did a little underlining. "A more wicked piece of propaganda, in the sense that it cuts into the plaintiffs' goodwill, it would be difficult to imagine. Attention is focused on what is the mischievous, deceptive and misleading part of the defendants' description. This is a document which patently and blatantly sets out to pass off the defendants' product as and for Champagne. Furthermore not only does the pamphlet tempt retailers (as the defendants' own evidence had shown) to sell Perelada as and for Champagne, but it tempts the public to buy it for Champagne occasions."

Having delivered this final broadside, Mr Lawrence sat down and there were probably few who did not think that the Perelada ship was sunk. The long hearing was over, after seven days of evidence and argument; the French returned to Paris and Epernay, and the case remained suspended for a fortnight while the judge composed his judgment.

On the December 16, 1960, Mr Justice Danckwerts read his judgment. He granted the Champagne houses their injunction restraining the Costa Brava Wine Company from selling Perelada under any name which included the word Champagne. He found that what the company had done had been dishonest trading, and he ordered them to change all their labels within 48 hours so as to obliterate all mention of the word Champagne. No appeal was entered against the judgment.

Champagne thus achieved a unique position in England. Not only was this victory a great commercial success for Champagne, but its repercussions in the wine trade were considerable. Many hoped that this judgment would give encouragement to those in the newer wine producing countries to establish their own goodwill with their own regional names. Certainly to the Champenois, those stouthearted Frenchmen, and their French and English friends and colleagues, the British wine trade owed a considerable debt.

The corks popped loud in celebration and the *mousse* was the *mousse* of Champagne.

An Aged and a Great Wine

GEORGE MEREDITH

Sir Willoughby advanced, appearing in a cordial mood.

"I need not ask you whether you are better," he said to Clara, sparkled to Lætitia, and raised a key to the level of Dr. Middleton's breast, remarking, "I am going down to my inner cellar."

"An inner cellar!" exclaimed the doctor.

"Sacred from the butler. It is interdicted to Stoneman. Shall I offer myself as guide to you? My cellars are worth a visit."

"Cellars are not catacombs. They are, if rightly constructed, rightly considered, cloisters, where the bottle meditates on joys to bestow, not on dust misused! Have you anything great?"

"A wine aged ninety."

"Is it associated with your pedigree, that you pronounce the age with such assurance?"

"My grandfather inherited it."

"Your grandfather, Sir Willoughby, had meritorious offspring, not to speak of generous progenitors. What would have happened had it fallen into the female line! I shall be glad to accompany you. Port? Hermitage?"

"Port."

"Ah! We are in England!"

"There will just be time," said Sir Willoughby, inducing Dr. Middleton to step out.

A chirrup was in the Rev. Doctor's tone: "Hocks, too, have compassed age. I have tasted senior Hocks. Their flavours are as a brook of many voices; they have depth also. Senatorial Port! we say. We cannot say that of any other wine. Port is deep-sea deep. It is in its flavour deep; mark the difference. It is like a classic tragedy, organic in conception. An ancient Hermitage has the light of the antique; the merit that it can grow to an extreme old age; a merit. Neither of Hermitage nor of Hock can you say that it is the blood of those long years, retaining the strength of youth with the wisdom of age. To Port for that! Port is our noblest legacy! Observe, I do not compare the wines; I distinguish the qualities. Let them live together for our enrichment; they are not rivals like the Idæan Three. Were they rivals, a fourth would challenge them. Burgundy has great genius. It does wonders within its period; it does all except to keep up in the race; it is short-lived. An aged Burgundy runs with a beardless Port. I cherish the fancy that Port speaks the sentences of wisdom, Burgundy sings the inspired Ode. Or put it, that Port is the Homeric hexameter, Burgundy the Pindaric dithyramb. What do you say?"

"The comparison is excellent, sir."

"The distinction, you would remark. Pindar astounds. But his elder brings us the more sustaining cup. One is a fountain of prodigious ascent. One is the unsounded purple sea of marching billows."

"A very fine distinction."

"I conceive you to be now commending the similes. They pertain to the time of the first critics of those poets. Touch the Greeks, and you can nothing new: all has been said: 'Graiis, . . . præter laudem, nullius avaris.' Genius dedicated to Fame is immortal. We, sir, dedicate genius to the cloacaline floods. We do not address the unforgetting Gods, but the popular stomach."

Sir Willoughby was patient. He was about as accordantly coupled with Dr. Middleton in discourse as a drum duetting with a bass-viol; and when he struck in he received correction from the paedagogue-instrument. If he thumped affirmative or negative, he was wrong. However, he knew scholars to be an unmannered species; and the Doctor's learnedness would be a subject to dilate on.

In the cellar, it was the turn for the drum. Dr. Middleton was tongue-tied there. Sir Willoughby gave the history of his wine in heads of chapters; whence it came to the family originally, and how it had come down to him in the quantity to be seen. "Curiously, my grandfather, who inherited it, was a water-drinker. My father died early."

"Indeed! Dear me!" the Doctor ejaculated in astonishment and condolence. The former glanced at the contrariety of man, the latter embraced his melancholy destiny.

He was impressed with respect for the family. This cool vaulted cellar, and the central square block, or enceinte, where the thick darkness was not penetrated by the intruding lamp, but rather took it as an eye, bore witness to forethoughtful practical solidity in the man who had built the house on such foundations. A house having a great wine stored below, lives in our imaginations as a joyful house fast and splendidly rooted in the soil. And imagination has a place for the heir of the house. His grandfather a water-drinker, his father dying early, present circumstances to us arguing predestination to an illustrious heirship and career. Dr. Middleton's musings were coloured by the friendly vision of glasses of the great wine; his mind was festive; it pleased him, and he chose to indulge in his whimsical-robustious, grandiose-airy style of thinking: from which the festive mind will sometimes take a certain print that we cannot obliterate immediately. Expectation is grateful, you know; in the mood of gratitude we are waxen. And he was a self-humouring gentleman.

He liked Sir Willoughby's tone in ordering the servant at his heels to take up "those two bottles": it prescribed, without overdoing it, a proper amount of caution, and it named an agreeable number.

Watching the man's hand keenly, he said,—

"But here is the misfortune of a thing super-excellent:—not more than one in twenty will do it justice."

Sir Willoughby replied: "Very true, sir, and I think we may pass over the nineteen."

"Women, for example: and most men."

"This wine would be a sealed book to them."

"I believe it would. It would be a grievous waste."

"Vernon is a claret-man: and so is Horace De Craye. They are both below the mark of this wine. They will join the ladies. Perhaps you and I, sir, might remain together."

"With the utmost good will on my part."

"I am anxious for your verdict, sir."

"You shall have it, sir, and not out of harmony with the chorus preceding me, I can predict. Cool, not frigid." Dr. Middleton summed the attributes of the cellar on quitting it: "North side and South. No musty damp. A pure air! Everything requisite. One might lie down oneself and keep sweet here."

Of all our venerable British of the two Isles professing a suckling attachment to an ancient port-wine, lawyer, doctor, squire, rosy admiral, city merchant, the classic scholar is he whose blood is most nuptial to the webbed bottle. The reason must be, that he is full of the old poets. He has their spirit to sing with, and the best that Time has done on earth to feed it. He may also perceive a resemblance in the wine to the studious mind, which is the obverse of our mortality, and throws off acids and crusty particles in the piling of the years, until it is fulgent by clarity. Port hymns to his conservatism. It is magical: at one sip he is off swimming in the purple flood of the ever-youthful antique.

By comparison, then, the enjoyment of others is brutish; they have not the soul for it; but he is worthy of the wine, as are poets of Beauty. In truth, these should be severally apportioned to them, scholar and poet, as his own good thing. Let it be so.

Meanwhile Dr. Middleton sipped.

After the departure of the ladies, Sir Willoughby had practised a studied curtness upon Vernon and Horace.

"You drink claret," he remarked to them, passing it round. "Port, I think, Dr. Middleton? The wine before you may serve for a preface. We shall have *your* wine in five minutes."

The claret jug empty, Sir Willoughby offered to send for more. De Craye was languid over the question. Vernon rose from the table.

"We have a bottle of Dr. Middleton's Port coming in," Willoughby said to him.

"Mine, you call it?" cried the Rev. Doctor.

"It's a royal wine, that won't suffer sharing," said Vernon.

"We'll be with you, if you go into the billiard-room, Vernon."

"I shall hurry my drinking of good wine for no man," said the Rev. Doctor.

"Horace?"

"I'm beneath it, ephemeral, Willoughby. I am going to the ladies."

Vernon and De Craye retired upon the arrival of the wine; and Dr. Middleton sipped. He sipped and looked at the owner of it.

"Some thirty dozen?" he said.

"Fifty."

The Doctor nodded humbly.

"I shall remember, sir," his host addressed him, "whenever I have the honour of entertaining you, I am cellarer of that wine."

The Rev. Doctor set down his glass. "You have, sir, in some sense, an enviable post. It is a responsible one, if that be a blessing. On you it devolves to retard the day of the last dozen."

"Your opinion of the wine is favourable, sir?"

"I will say this:—shallow souls run to rhapsody:—I will say, that I am consoled for not having lived ninety years back, or at any period but the present, by this one glass of your ancestral wine."

"I am careful of it," Sir Willoughby said modestly; "still its natural destination is to those who can appreciate it. You do, sir."

"Still, my good friend, still! It is a charge: it is a possession, but part in trusteeship. Though we cannot declare it an entailed estate, our consciences are in some sort pledged that it shall be a succession not too considerably diminished."

"You will not object to drink it, sir, to the health of your grandchildren. And may you live to toast them in it on their marriage-day!"

"You colour the idea of a prolonged existence in seductive hues. Ha! It is a wine for Tithonus. This wine would speed him to the rosy Morning—aha!"

"I will undertake to sit you through it up to morning," said Sir Willoughby, innocent of the Bacchic nuptiality of the allusion.

Dr. Middleton eyed the decanter. There is a grief in gladness, for a premonition of our mortal state. The amount of wine in the decanter did not promise to sustain the starry roof of night and greet the dawn. "Old wine, my friend, denies us the full bottle!"

"Another bottle is to follow."

"No!"

"It is ordered."

"I protest."

"It is uncorked."

"I entreat."

"It is decanted."

"I submit. But, mark, it must be honest partnership. You are my worthy host, sir, on that stipulation. Note the superiority of wine over Venus!—I may say, the magnanimity of wine; our jealousy turns on him that will not share! But the corks, Willoughby. The corks excite my amazement."

"The corking is examined at regular intervals. I remember the occurrence in my father's time. I have seen to it once."

"It must be perilous as an operation for tracheotomy; which I should assume it to resemble in surgical skill and firmness of hand, not to mention the imminent gasp of the patient."

A fresh decanter was placed before the doctor.

He said: "I have but a girl to give!" He was melted.

Sir Willoughby replied: "I take her for the highest prize this world affords."

from The Egoist

What You Always Wanted
to Ask About Wine *

RUSSELL BAKER

Many readers have urged me to divulge my wisdom about wine, and I do so gladly, for wine is a noble thing, being much slower than the martini (known in bibulous circles as the quick blow to the back of the head) and much harder than differential calculus.

* But were afraid Baker would tell you.

The most common wines are Chablis (rhymes with "wobbly") and Beaujolais (bo-joe-lay). These are excellent wines for beginners because they are easy to pronounce. Neither should be drunk, of course, unless the label bears the words *"appellation contrôlee"* (meaning "apples under control") and *"mis au domaine,"* which means "put at the domain."

These phrases are the buyer's guarantee that the wine has been made from grapes, with no apples mixed in, and sent to a good domain to acquire breeding, bouquet, good nose, smooth finish and skill at equitation.

Bottles whose labels bear these phrases are, unfortunately, so expensive that no one can afford to drink them except on a 25th anniversary, and since neither wine will keep for 25 years there is really no point in buying either, especially since, if you are right up on top of the 25th anniversary you would probably rather have three martinis and go to sleep.

Some labels will bear the words *"mis en bouteille dans nos caves,"* which means "bottled in our caves." This wine is made from fermented moss and must always be served at cave temperature. It is the perfect complement to ferns *en brochette.*

In ordering wine at a restaurant, a knowledgeable banter with the wine waiter helps establish one's *savoir-faire.* To avoid humiliation at the outset, the best wine to order is Châteauneuf-du-Pape, since it is relatively easy to pronounce (shot-oh-nuf-dew-pop).

An authoritative question or two creates a forceful impression. "This shot-oh-nuf-dew-pop," you might say, "has it been put at the domain?" or, "Whose caves was it bottled in?"

When the waiter hands you the cork, pass it to your dinner partner and ask him, or her, to squeeze it, then return it to the waiter and ask him to have it chopped very fine and put in the salad. In tasting the wine, roll a small quantity across the palate, then let it settle in the bottom of the mouth and gargle a quantity of air across it and into the lungs, while making loud snoring sounds. Tell the waiter to taste some after objecting that in this particular wine the apples have not been very well controlled.

Having mastered French wines, drinkers will find German wine even more expensive. This is because there is so little of it. The persistent story that Hermann Göring drank it all after the collapse of the Russian front is probably a canard, but it has gone someplace and will not come back for less than $40 or $50 a bottle. It goes beautifully with red cabbage and a Swiss bank account.

For value, the best buys are California and New York wines, but many uninformed sophisticates view them with contempt because they can understand the labels. I have solved this problem with a supply of empty French wine bottles and a funnel. Now my California Cabernet always comes to the table as a *"premier cru"* ("first crew") from Bordeaux.

In the East, unfortunately, the beginner will have to struggle with the wine dealer to get California wine, and this brings us to the crucial subject. Getting one's way at the wine shop.

There are in France huge, underground factories which make a drink compounded of banana skins, random acids, brown sugar and broken shoe strings. Dyed red and bottled, this is shipped to gullible American wine dealers, who sell it as "French country wine."

Merchants with crates of it threatening to eat their way through the cellar floor stalk wine shops on the lookout for innocents, who are always recognizable by the dismay on their faces as they gaze at the price of German wine or wrestle with the distinction between a Côte de Beaune ("Side of bone") and a Côtes du Rhône ("Sides of Rona Barrett").

When the merchant pounces, offering his irresistible bargain in rare French country wine, do not blanch, tremble, yield or buy. Tell him firmly, "Get me a jug of American wine and a half-dozen French empties." It should come to no more than about $4, and, best of all, it will be made from grapes.

Taste

ROALD DAHL

There were six of us to dinner that night at Mike Schofield's house in London: Mike and his wife and daughter, my wife and I, and a man called Richard Pratt.

Richard Pratt was a famous gourmet. He was president of a small society known as the Epicures, and each month he circulated privately to its members a pamphlet on food and wines. He organized dinners where sumptuous dishes and rare wines were served. He refused to smoke for fear of harming his palate, and when discussing a wine, he had a curious, rather droll habit of referring to it as through it were a living being. "A prudent wine," he would say, "rather diffident and evasive, but quite prudent." Or, "a good-humored wine, benevolent and cheerful—slightly obscene, perhaps, but nonetheless good-humored."

I had been to dinner at Mike's twice before when Richard Pratt was there, and on each occasion Mike and his wife had gone out of their way to produce a special meal for the famous gourmet. And this one, clearly, was to be no exception. The moment we entered the dining room, I could see that the table was laid for a feast. The tall candles, the yellow roses, the quantity of shining silver, the three wineglasses to each person, and above all, the faint scent of roasting meat from the kitchen brought the first warm oozings of saliva to my mouth.

As we sat down, I remembered that on both Richard Pratt's previous visits Mike had played a little betting game with him over the claret, challenging him to name its breed and its vintage. Pratt had replied that that should not be too difficult provided it was one of the great years. Mike had then bet him a case of the wine in question that he could not do it. Pratt had accepted, and had won both times. Tonight I felt sure that the little game would be played over again, for Mike was quite willing to lose the bet in order to prove that his wine was good enough to be recognized, and Pratt, for his part, seemed to take a grave, restrained pleasure in displaying his knowledge.

The meal began with a plate of whitebait, fried very crisp in butter, and to go with it there was a Moselle. Mike got up and poured the wine himself, and when he sat down again, I could see that he was watching Richard Pratt. He had set the bottle in front of me so that I could read the label. It said, "Geierslay Ohligsberg, 1945." He leaned over and whispered to me that Geierslay was a tiny village in the Moselle, almost unknown outside Germany. He said that this wine we were drinking was something unusual, that the output of the vineyard was so small that it was almost impossible for a stranger to get any of it. He had visited Geierslay personally the previous summer in order to obtain the few dozen bottles that they had finally allowed him to have.

"I doubt anyone else in the country has any of it at the moment," he said. I saw him glance again at Richard Pratt. "Great thing about Moselle," he continued, raising his voice, "it's the perfect wine to serve before a claret. A lot of people serve a Rhine wine instead, but that's because they don't know any better. A Rhine wine will kill a delicate claret, you know that? It's barbaric to serve a Rhine before a claret. But a Moselle—ah!—a Moselle is exactly right."

Mike Schofield was an amiable, middle-aged man. But he was a stockbroker. To be precise, he was a jobber in the stock market, and like a number of his kind, he seemed to be somewhat embarrassed, almost ashamed to find that he had made so much money with so slight a talent. In his heart he knew that he was not really much more than a bookmaker—an unctuous, infinitely respectable, secretly unscrupulous bookmaker—and he knew that his friends knew it, too. So he was seeking now to become a man of culture, to cultivate a literary and aesthetic taste, to collect paintings, music, books, and all the rest of it. His little sermon about Rhine wine and Moselle was a part of this thing, this culture that he sought.

"A charming little wine, don't you think?" he said. He was still watching Richard Pratt. I could see him give a rapid furtive glance down the table each time he dropped his head to take a mouthful of whitebait. I could almost *feel* him waiting for the moment when Pratt would take his first sip, and look up from his glass with a smile of pleasure, of astonishment, perhaps even of wonder, and then there would be a discussion and Mike would tell him about the village of Geierslay.

But Richard Pratt did not taste his wine. He was completely engrossed in conversation with Mike's eighteen-year-old daughter, Louise. He was half turned toward her, smiling at her, telling her, so far as I could gather, some story about a chef in a Paris restaurant. As he spoke, he leaned closer and closer to her, seeming in his eagerness almost to impinge upon her, and the poor girl leaned as far as she could away from him, nodding politely, rather desperately, and looking not at his face but at the topmost button of his dinner jacket.

We finished our fish, and the maid came around removing the plates. When she came to Pratt, she saw that he had not yet touched his food, so she hesitated, and Pratt noticed her. He waved her away, broke off his conversation, and quickly began to eat, popping the little crisp brown fish quickly into his mouth with rapid jabbing movements of his fork. Then, when he had finished, he reached for his glass, and in two short swallows he tipped the wine down his throat and turned immediately to resume his conversation with Louise Schofield.

Mike saw it all. I was conscious of him sitting there, very still, containing himself, looking at his guest. His round jovial face seemed to loosen slightly and to sag, but he contained himself and was still and said nothing.

Soon the maid came forward with the second course. This was a large roast of beef. She placed it on the table in front of Mike who stood up and carved it, cutting the slices very thin, laying them gently on the plates for the maid to take around. When he had served everyone, including himself, he put down the carving knife and leaned forward with both hands on the edge of the table.

"Now," he said, speaking to all of us but looking at Richard Pratt. "Now for the claret. I must go and fetch the claret, if you'll excuse me."

"You go and fetch it, Mike?" I said. "Where is it?"

"In my study, with the cork out—breathing."

"Why the study?"

"Acquiring room temperature, of course. It's been there twenty-four hours."

"But why the study?"

"It's the best place in the house. Richard helped me choose it last time he was here."

At the sound of his name, Pratt looked around.

"That's right, isn't it?" Mike said.

"Yes," Pratt answered, nodding gravely. "That's right."

"On top of the green filing cabinet in my study," Mike said. "That's the place we chose. A good draft-free spot in a room with an even temperature. Excuse me now, will you, while I fetch it."

The thought of another wine to play with had restored his humor, and he hurried out the door, to return a minute later more slowly, walking softly, holding in both hands a wine basket in which a dark bottle lay. The label was out of sight, facing downward. "Now!" he cried as he came toward the table. "What about this one, Richard? You'll never name this one!"

Richard Pratt turned slowly and looked up at Mike; than his eyes traveled down to the bottle nesting in its small wicker basket, and he raised his eyebrows, a slight, supercilious arching of the brows, and with it a pushing outward of the wet lower lip, suddenly imperious and ugly.

"You'll never get it," Mike said. "Not in a hundred years."

"A claret?" Richard Pratt asked, condescending.

"Of course."

"I assume, then, that it's from one of the smaller vineyards?"

"Maybe it is, Richard. And then again, maybe it isn't."

"But it's a good year? One of the great years?"

"Yes, I guarantee that."

"Then it shouldn't be too difficult," Richard Pratt said, drawling his words, looking exceedingly bored. Except that, to me, there was something strange about his drawling and his boredom: between the eyes a shadow of something evil, and in his bearing an intentness that gave me a faint sense of uneasiness as I watched him.

"This one is really rather difficult," Mike said, "I won't force you to bet on this one."

"Indeed. And why not?" Again the slow arching of the brows, the cool, intent look.

"Because it's difficult."

"That's not very complimentary to me, you know."

"My dear man," Mike said, "I'll bet you with pleasure, if that's what you wish."

"It shouldn't be too hard to name it."

"You mean you want to bet?"

"I'm perfectly willing to bet," Richard Pratt said.

"All right, then, we'll have the usual. A case of the wine itself."

"You don't think I'll be able to name it, do you?"

"As a matter of fact, and with all due respect, I don't," Mike said. He was making some effort to remain polite, but Pratt was not bothering overmuch to conceal his contempt for the whole proceeding. And yet, curiously, his next question seemed to betray a certain interest.

"You like to increase the bet?"

"No, Richard. A case is plenty."

"Would you like to bet fifty cases?"

"That would be silly."

Mike stood very still behind his chair at the head of the table, carefully holding the bottle in its ridiculous wicker basket. There was a trace of whiteness around his nostrils now, and his mouth was shut very tight.

Pratt was lolling back in his chair, looking up at him, the eyebrows raised, the eyes half closed, a little smile touching the corners of his lips. And again I saw, or thought I saw, something distinctly disturbing about the man's face, that shadow of intentness between the eyes, and in his eyes themselves, right in their centers where it was black, a small slow spark of shrewdness, hiding.

"So you don't want to increase the bet?"

"As far as I'm concerned, old man, I don't give a damn," Mike said. "I'll bet you anything you like."

The three women and I sat quietly, watching the two men. Mike's wife was becoming annoyed; her mouth had gone sour and I felt that at any moment she was going to interrupt. Our roast beef lay before us on our plates, slowly steaming.

"So you'll bet me anything I like?"

"That's what I told you. I'll bet you anything you damn well please, if you want to make an issue out of it."

"Even ten thousand pounds?"

"Certainly I will, if that's the way you want it." Mike was more confident now. He knew quite well that he could call any sum Pratt cared to mention.

"So you say I can name the bet?" Pratt asked again.

"That's what I said."

There was a pause while Pratt looked slowly around the table, first at me, then at the three women, each in turn. He appeared to be reminding us that we were witness to the offer.

"Mike!" Mrs. Schofield said. "Mike, why don't we stop this nonsense and eat our food. It's getting cold."

"But it isn't nonsense," Pratt told her evenly. "We're making a little bet."

I noticed the maid standing in the background holding a dish of vegetables, wondering whether to come forward with them or not.

"All right, then," Pratt said. "I'll tell you what I want you to bet."

"Come on, then," Mike said, rather reckless. "I don't give a damn what it is—you're on."

Pratt nodded, and again the little smile moved the corners of his lips, and then, quite slowly, looking at Mike all the time, he said, "I want you to bet me the hand of your daughter in marriage."

Louise Schofield gave a jump. "Hey!" she cried. "No! That's not funny! Look here, Daddy, that's not funny at all."

"No, dear," her mother said. "They're only joking."

"I'm not joking," Richard Pratt said.

"It's ridiculous," Mike said. He was off balance again now.

"You said you'd bet anything I liked."

"I meant money."

"You didn't *say* money."

"That's what I meant."

"Then it's a pity you didn't say it. But anyway, if you wish to go back on your offer, that's quite all right with me."

"It's not a question of going back on my offer, old man. It's a no-bet anyway, because you can't match the stake. You yourself don't happen to have a daughter to put up against mine in case you lose. And if you had, I wouldn't want to marry her."

"I'm glad of that, dear," his wife said.

"I'll put up anything you like," Pratt announced. "My house, for example. How about my house?"

"Which one?" Mike asked, joking now.

"The country one."

"Why not the other one as well?"

"All right then, if you wish it. Both my houses."

At that point I saw Mike pause. He took a step forward and placed the bottle in its basket gently down on the table. He moved the saltcellar to one side, then the pepper, and then he picked up his knife, studied the blade thoughtfully for a moment, and put it down again. His daughter, too, had seen him pause.

"Now, Daddy!" she cried. "Don't be *absurd!* It's *too* silly for words. I refuse to be betted on like this."

"Quite right, dear," her mother said. "Stop it at once, Mike, and sit down and eat your food."

Mike ignored her. He looked over at his daughter and he smiled, a slow, fatherly, protective smile. But in his eyes, suddenly, there glimmered a little triumph. "You know," he said, smiling as he spoke. "You know, Louise, we ought to think about this a bit."

"Now, stop it, Daddy! I refuse even to listen to you! Why, I've never heard anything so ridiculous in my life!"

"No, seriously, my dear. Just wait a moment and hear what I have to say."

"But I don't *want* to hear it."

"Louise! Please! It's like this. Richard, here, has offered us a serious bet. He is the one who wants to make it, not me. And if he loses, he will have to hand over a considerable amount of property. Now, wait a minute, my dear, don't interrupt. The point is this. *He cannot possibly win.*"

"He seems to think he can."

"Now listen to me, because I know what I'm talking about. The expert, when tasting a claret—so long as it is not one of the famous great wines like Lafite or Latour—can only get a certain way toward naming the vineyard. He can, of course, tell you the Bordeaux district from which the wine comes, whether it is from St. Emilion, Pomerol, Graves, or Médoc. But then each district has several communes, little counties, and each county has many, many small vineyards. It is impossible for a man to differentiate between them all by taste and smell alone. I don't mind telling you that this one I've got here is a wine from a small vineyard that is surrounded by many other small vineyards, and he'll never get it. It's impossible."

"You can't be sure of that," his daughter said.

"I'm telling you I can. Though I say it myself, I understand quite a bit about this wine business, you know. And anyway, heavens alive, girl, I'm your father and you don't think I'd let you in for—for something you didn't want, do you? I'm trying to make you some money."

"Mike!" his wife said sharply. "Stop it now, Mike, please!"

Again he ignored her. "If you will take this bet," he said to his daughter, "in ten minutes you will be the owner of two large houses."

"But I don't want two large houses, Daddy."

"Then sell them. Sell them back to him on the spot. I'll arrange all that for you. And then, just think of it, my dear, you'll be rich! You'll be independent for the rest of your life!"

"Oh, Daddy, I don't like it. I think it's silly."

"So do I," the mother said. She jerked her head briskly up and down as she spoke, like a hen. "You ought to be ashamed of yourself, Michael, even suggesting such a thing! Your own daughter too!"

Mike didn't even look at her. "Take it!" he said eagerly, staring hard at the girl. "Take it, quick! I'll guarantee you won't lose."

"But I don't like it, Daddy."

"Come on, girl. Take it!"

Mike was pushing her hard. He was leaning toward her, fixing her with two hard bright eyes, and it was not easy for the daughter to resist him.

"But what if I lose?"

"I keep telling you, you can't lose. I'll guarantee it."

"Oh, Daddy, must I?"

"I'm making you a fortune. So come on now. What do you say, Louise? All right?"

For the last time, she hesitated. Then she gave a helpless little shrug of the shoulders and said, "Oh, all right, then. Just so long as you swear there's no danger of losing."

"Good!" Mike cried. "That's fine! Then it's a bet!"

"Yes," Richard Pratt said, looking at the girl. "It's a bet.

Immediately, Mike picked up the wine, tipped the first thimbleful into his own glass, then skipped excitedly around the table filling up the others. Now everyone was watching Richard Pratt, watching his face as he reached slowly for his glass with his right hand and lifted it to his nose. The man was about fifty years old and he did not have a pleasant face. Somehow, it was all mouth—mouth and lips—the full, wet lips of the professional gourmet, the lower lip hanging downward in the center, a pendulous, permanently open taster's lip, shaped open to receive the rim of a glass or a morsel of food. Like a keyhole, I thought, watching it; his mouth is like a large wet keyhole.

Slowly he lifted the glass to his nose. The point of the nose entered the glass and moved over the surface of the wine, delicately sniffing. He swirled the wine gently around in the glass to receive the bouquet. His concentration was intense. He had closed his eyes, and now the whole top half of his body, the head and neck and chest, seemed to become a kind of huge sensitive smelling-machine, receiving, filtering, analyzing the message from the sniffing nose.

Mike, I noticed, was lounging in his chair, apparently unconcerned, but he was watching every move. Mrs. Schofield, the wife, sat prim and upright at the other end of the table, looking straight ahead, her face tight with disapproval. The daughter, Louise, had shifted her chair away a little, and sidewise, facing the gourmet, and she, like her father, was watching closely.

For at least a minute, the smelling process continued; then, without opening his eyes or moving his head, Pratt lowered the glass to his mouth and tipped in almost half the contents. He paused, his mouth full of wine, getting the first taste; then he permitted some of it to trickle down his throat and I saw his Adam's apple move as it passed by. But most of it he retained in his mouth. And now, without swallowing again, he drew in through his lips a thin breath of air which mingled with the fumes of the wine in his mouth and passed on down into his lungs. He held the breath, blew it out through his nose, and finally began to roll the wine around under the tongue, and chewed it, actually chewed it with his teeth as though it were bread.

It was a solemn, impressive performance and I must say he did it well.

"Um," he said, putting down the glass, running a pink tongue over his lips. "Um—yes. A very interesting little wine—gentle and gracious, almost feminine in the aftertaste."

There was an excess of saliva in his mouth, and as he spoke he spat an occasional bright speck of it onto the table.

"Now we can start to eliminate," he said. "You will pardon me for doing this carefully, but there is much at stake. Normally I would perhaps take a bit of a chance, leaping forward quickly and landing right in the middle of the vineyard of my choice. But I must move cautiously this time, must I not?" He looked up at Mike and he smiled, a thick-lipped, wet-lipped smile. Mike did not smile back.

"First, then, which district in Bordeaux does this wine come from? That is not too difficult to guess. It is far too light in the body to be from either St. Emilion or Graves. It is obviously a Médoc. There's no doubt about *that*.

"Now—from which commune in Médoc does it come? That

also, by elimination, should not be too difficult to decide. Margaux? No. It cannot be Margaux. It has not the violent bouquet of a Margaux. Pauillac? It cannot be Pauillac, either. It is too tender, too gentle and wistful for a Pauillac. The wine of Pauillac has a character that is almost imperious in its taste. And also to me, a Pauillac contains just a little pith, a curious dusty, pithy flavor that the grape acquires from the soil of the district. No, no. This—this is a very gentle wine, demure and bashful in the first taste, emerging shyly but quite graciously in the second. A little arch, perhaps, in the second taste, and a little naughty also, teasing the tongue with a trace, just a trace, of tannin. Then, in the aftertaste, delightful— consoling and feminine, with a certain blithely generous quality that one associates only with the wines of the commune of St. Julien. Unmistakably this is a St. Julien."

He leaned back in his chair, held his hands up level with his chest, and placed the fingertips carefully together. He was becoming ridiculously pompous, but I thought that some of it was deliberate, simply to mock his host. I found myself waiting rather tensely for him to go on. The girl Louise was lighting a cigarette. Pratt heard the match strike and he turned on her, flaring suddenly with real anger. "Please!" he said. "Please don't do that! It's a disgusting habit, to smoke at table!"

She looked up at him, still holding the burning match in one hand, the big slow eyes settling on his face, resting there a moment, moving away again, slow and contemptuous. She bent her head and blew out the match, but continued to hold the unlighted cigarette in her fingers.

"I'm sorry, my dear," Pratt said, "but I simply cannot have smoking at table."

She didn't look at him again.

"Now, let me see—where were we?" he said. "Ah, yes. This wine is from Bordeaux, from the commune of St. Julien, in the district of Médoc. So far, so good. But now we came to the more difficult part—the name of the vineyard itself. For in St. Julien there are many vineyards, and as our host so rightly remarked earlier on, there is often not much difference between the wine of one and the wine of another. But we shall see."

He paused again, closing his eyes. "I am trying to establish the 'growth,' " he said. "If I can do that, it will be half the battle. Now, let me see. This wine is obviously not from a first-growth vineyard—nor even a second. It is not a great wine. The quality, the—the—what do you call it?—the radiance, the power, is lacking. But a third growth—that it could be. And yet I doubt it. We know it is a good year—our host has said so—and this is probably flattering it a little bit. I must be careful. I must be very careful here."

He picked up his glass and took another small sip.

"Yes," he said, sucking his lips, "I was right. It is a fourth growth. Now I am sure of it. A fourth growth from a very good year—from a great year, in fact. And that's what made it taste for a moment like a third—or even a second-growth wine. Good! That's better! Now we are closing in! What are the fourth-growth vineyards in the commune of St. Julien?"

Again he paused, took up his glass, and held the rim against that sagging, pendulous lower lip of his. Then I saw the tongue shoot out, pink and narrow, the tip of it dipping into the wine, withdrawing swiftly again—a repulsive sight. When he lowered the glass, his eyes remained closed, the face concentrated, only the lips moving, sliding over each other like two pieces of wet, spongy rubber.

"There it is again!" he cried. "Tannin in the middle taste, and the quick astringent squeeze upon the tongue. Yes, yes, of course! Now I have it! This wine comes from one of those small vineyards around Beychevelle. I remember now. The Beychevelle district, and the river and the little harbor that has silted up so the wine ships can no longer use it. Beychevelle . . . could it actually be a Beychevelle itself? No, I don't think so. Not quite. But it is somewhere very close. Château Talbot? Could it be Talbot? Yes, it could. Wait one moment."

He sipped the wine again, and out of the side of my eye I noticed Mike Schofield and how he was leaning farther and farther forward over the table, his mouth slightly open, his small eyes fixed upon Richard Pratt.

"No. I was wrong. It was not a Talbot. A Talbot comes forward to you just a little quicker than this one; the fruit is nearer to the surface. If it is a '34, which I believe it is, then it couldn't be Talbot. Well, well. Let me think. It is not a Beychevelle and it is not a Talbot, and yet—yet it is so close to both of them, so close, that the vineyard must be almost in between. Now, which could that be?"

He hesitated, and we waited, watching his face. Everyone, even Mike's wife, was watching him now. I heard the maid put down the dish of vegetables on the sideboard behind me, gently, so as not to disturb the silence.

"Ah!" he cried. "I have it! Yes, I think I have it!"

For the last time, he sipped the wine. Then, still holding the glass up near his mouth, he turned to Mike and he smiled, a slow, silky smile, and he said, "You know what this is? This is the little Château Branaire-Ducru."

Mike sat tight, not moving.

"And the year, 1934."

We all looked at Mike, waiting for him to turn the bottle around in its basket and show the label.

"Is that your final answer?" Mike said.

"Yes, I think so."

"Well, is it or isn't it?"

"Yes, it is."

"What was the name again?"

"Château Branaire-Ducru. Pretty little vineyard. Lovely old château. Know it quite well. Can't think why I didn't recognize it at once."

"Come on, Daddy," the girl said. "Turn it round and let's have a peek. I want my two houses."

"Just a minute," Mike said. "Wait just a minute." He was sitting very quiet, bewildered-looking, and his face was becoming puffy and pale, as though all the force was draining slowly out of him.

"Michael!" his wife called sharply from the other end of the table. "What's the matter?"

"Keep out of this, Margaret, will you please."

Richard Pratt was looking at Mike, smiling with his mouth, his eyes small and bright. Mike was not looking at anyone.

"Daddy!" the daughter cried, agonized. "But, Daddy, you don't mean to say he's guessed it right!"

"Now, stop worrying, my dear," Mike said. "There's nothing to worry about."

I think it was more to get away from his family than anything else that Mike then turned to Richard Pratt and said, "I'll tell you what, Richard. I think you and I better slip off into the next room and have a little chat?"

"I don't want a little chat," Pratt said. "All I want is to see the label on that bottle." He knew he was a winner now; he had the bearing, the quiet arrogance of a winner, and I could see that he was prepared to become thoroughly nasty if there was any trouble. "What are you waiting for?" he said to Mike. "Go on and turn it round."

Then this happened: The maid, the tiny, erect figure of the maid in her black-and-white uniform, was standing beside Richard

Pratt, holding something out in her hand. "I believe these are yours, sir," she said.

Pratt glanced around, saw the pair of thin horn-rimmed spectacles that she held out to him, and for a moment he hesitated. "Are they? Perhaps they are. I don't know."

"Yes sir, they're yours." The maid was an elderly woman—nearer seventy than sixty—a faithful family retainer of many years standing. She put the spectacles down on the table beside him.

Without thanking her, Pratt took them up and slipped them into his top pocket, behind the white handkerchief.

But the maid didn't go away. She remained standing beside and slightly behind Richard Pratt, and there was something so unusual in her manner and in the way she stood there, small, motionless, and erect, that I for one found myself watching her with a sudden apprehension. Her old gray face had a frosty, determined look, the lips were compressed, the little chin was out, and the hands were clasped together tight before her. The curious cap on her head and the flesh of white down the front of her uniform made her seem like some tiny, ruffled, white-breasted bird.

"You left them in Mr. Schofield's study," she said. Her voice was unnaturally, deliberately polite. "On top of the green filing cabinet in his study, sir, when you happened to go in there by yourself before dinner."

It took a few moments for the full meaning of her words to penetrate, and in the silence that followed I became aware of Mike and how he was slowly drawing himself up in his chair, and the color coming to his face, and the eyes opening wide, and the curl of the mouth, and the dangerous little patch of whiteness beginning to spread around the area of the nostrils.

"Now, Michael!" his wife said. "Keep calm now, Michael, dear! Keep calm!"

Acknowledgments

Associated Book Publishers Ltd.: from *Reminiscences of a Vintner* by I. M. Campbell, published by Chapman and Hall.

Atheneum Publishers, Inc.: "For a Thirtieth Birthday" by John Hollander. From *Movie Going and Other Poems* by John Hollander. Copyright © 1962 by John Hollander. Reprinted by permission of Atheneum Publishers.

Janice Biala: from *Provence* by Ford Madox Ford. Copyright 1935 by Ford Madox Ford. Copyright © renewed 1962 by Janice Biala. Reprinted by permission.

The Bodley Head and Editions Gallimard: "The Wine of Paris" from *Across Paris* by Marcel Aymé, translated by Norman Denny. Published by The Bodley Head. Copyright © 1947 Editions Gallimard.

Michael Broadbent: from *Wine Tasting* by Michael Broadbent. Copyright © 1975 by Michael Broadbent.

Art Buchwald: "It Puckers Your Mouth" by Art Buchwald. Copyright © 1958, 1959, 1960 Art Buchwald.

Chatto and Windus Ltd.: from *The Grand Babylon Hotel* by Arnold Bennett. Reprinted by permission of Mrs. Cheston Bennett and Chatto and Windus Ltd.

Charles M. Clegg, Jr.: from "Uncle Ned's Wine Preferences" by Lucius Beebe. Reprinted by permission.

The Condé Nast Publications Ltd.: excerpts by Evelyn Waugh and Philippe de Rothschild from *The Pan Book of Wine*. Copyright © 1954–1959 The Condé Nast Publications Ltd.

Constable & Co. Ltd.: from *Tables of Content* by André L. Simon. From *A Miscellany of Wine* by Charles Walter Berry. From *Claret* by Maurice Healy. "Ten Little Bottle Boys" from *Viniana* by Charles Walter Berry. Reprinted by permission of Constable & Co. Ltd.

Derek Cooper: from an article on wine tasting. Reprinted by permission of the author.

Coward-McCann & Geoghegan, Inc.: from *Wine and Wine Lands of the World* by Frank Hedges Butler.

Crown Publishers, Inc.: from *The Eiger Sanction* by Trevanian. Copyright © 1972 by Trevanian. Used by permission of Crown Publishers, Inc.

Curtis Brown, Ltd.: "The Last Bottle in the World" by Stanley Ellin. Copyright

Everett Crosby. Copyright © 1973 by Everett Crosby. Reprinted by permission of Harper & Row, Publishers, Inc.

Harper & Row, Inc., and A. Watkins, Inc.: from *Busman's Honeymoon* by Dorothy L. Sayers. Copyright 1937 by Dorothy Leigh Sayers Fleming; copyright © renewed 1965 by Anthony Fleming. Reprinted by permission of Harper & Row, Publishers, Inc., and A. Watkins, Inc.

Harvard University Press: from *Essays* by Michel de Montaigne, translated by George B. Ives. Copyright 1925 by Harvard University Press; copyright renewed 1953 by Frederick M. Ives. From *On Agriculture* by Columella, translated by E. S. Forster and E. H. Heffner. Copyright © 1955, 1968. From *On Agriculture* by Cato, translated by William Davis Hooper. Copyright 1936. From "Symposium" by Xenophon, translated by O. J. Todd. Copyright 1922.

Hawthorn Books, Inc.: from *Mister Jelly Roll* by Alan Lomax, published by Duell, Sloane & Pearce. Copyright 1950 Alan Lomax. From *The Vineyard* by Idwal Jones. Copyright 1942 by Idwal Jones. Reprinted by permission of Hawthorn Books, Inc. All rights reserved.

David Higham Associates Ltd.: from *Colonel Lawrence* by Basil Liddell Hart, published by Dodd, Mead & Co. Reprinted by permission of David Higham Associates Ltd.

Merlin Holland: from *Time Remembered* by Vyvyan Holland. Copyright © 1964, 1968 the Estate of Vyvyan Holland. Reprinted by permission of Mrs. Thelma Holland. From "Sardines and Sauternes" by Vyvyan Holland. Copyright © 1964 the Estate of Vyvyan Holland and John Harveys & Sons Ltd.

John Hollander: "Thanks" by John Hollander. Copyright © 1975 by John Hollander. By permission of the author and *Thames Poetry*, London.

Holt, Rinehart and Winston and Harold Matson Company, Inc.: "Winesmanship" from *One-Upmanship* by Stephen Potter. Copyright 1951, 1952 by Stephen Potter. Reprinted by permission of Holt, Rinehart and Winston, Publishers, and Harold Matson Company, Inc.

P. M. Hubbard: "To Thea, at the Year's End, with a Bottle of Gewürztraminer" by P. M. Hubbard. Copyright © 1965 P. M. Hubbard.

Michael Joseph Ltd., London: from *Stay Me with Flagons* by Maurice Healy. From *Vintagewise* by André L. Simon. From *In the Twilight* by André L. Simon. Reprinted by permission.

Alfred A. Knopf, Inc.: "Taste" by Roald Dahl. Copyright 1951 by Roald Dahl. Reprinted from *Someone Like You* by Roald Dahl. This story first appeared in *The New Yorker*. From *Table Topics* by Julian Street. Copyright © 1959 by A. I. M. S. Street. From *A Mencken Chrestomathy* by H. L. Mencken. Copyright 1922 by Alfred A. Knopf, Inc.; copyright renewed 1950 by H. L. Mencken. From *Traps* by Friedrich Duerrenmatt, translated by Richard and Clara Winston. Copyright © 1960 by Alfred A. Knopf, Inc. From *My Young Years* by Arthur Rubinstein. Copyright © 1973 by Antela Rubinstein, Eva Rubinstein Coffin, Alina Rubinstein and John Arthur Rubinstein. From *The Letters of Wallace Stevens*, edited by Holly Stevens. Copyright © 1966 by Holly Stevens. All reprinted by permission of Alfred A. Knopf, Inc.

Bernard Levin: from "They Call It Hospitality" by Bernard Levin. Copyright © Bernard Levin.

J. B. Lippincott Company: from *The Romany Stain* by Christopher Morley. Copyright 1926, renewed 1954 by Christopher Morley. Reprinted by permission of J. B. Lippincott Company.

Little, Brown and Co.: from *The Autobiography of Bertrand Russell*, by Bertrand Russell. Reprinted by permission of Little, Brown and Co. in association with the Atlantic Monthly Press.

Little Brown and Co. and A. D. Peters & Co. Ltd.: from *Brideshead Revisited* by Evelyn Waugh. Copyright 1944, 1945 by Evelyn Waugh. Reprinted by permission of Little, Brown and Co. and A. D. Peters & Co. Ltd.

Liveright Publishing Corporation: from *The Travels of Marco Polo*, edited by Manuel Komroff. Copyright 1926 by Boni & Liveright, Inc. Copyright 1930 by Horace

Oliver Postgate: from "Oinoposiai" by Raymond Postgate. Reprinted by permission.

Punch: "My Cellar Book" by L. W. Desbrow. From "Bordeaux '73—A *Great Scandal?*" by Miles Kington. From "Water Works Wonders" by Barry Took. From "Champagne with Everything" by William Davis. From "The Wine Tasters" by Patrick Ryan. Reprinted by permission of *Punch*.

Quadrangle Books: "A Lucullan Fantasy" from *Diary of a Winetaster* by Harry Waugh. Copyright © 1972 by Quadrangle Books in conjunction with Wine and Spirit Publications, Ltd. Reprinted by permission of Quadrangle Books.

George Rainbird Ltd.: "The 'Spanish Champagne' Case" by Robert Keeling from *Champagne* by André L. Simon. Copyright © 1962 George Rainbird Ltd. Published by Octopus Books Ltd.

Random House, Inc.: from *The Knights* by Aristophanes, in *The Complete Greek Drama,* edited by Whitney J. Oates and Eugene O'Neill, Jr. Copyright 1938; copyright © renewed 1966 by Random House, Inc.

Routledge & Kegan Paul Ltd.: from *The Beverage Report* by Derek Cooper. Copyright © 1970 Derek Cooper.

Russell & Volkening, Inc.: from *Between Meals* by A. J. Liebling. Copyright © 1959 by A. J. Liebling.

The Estate of Frank Schoonmaker: from *Come with Me Through France* by Frank Schoonmaker. Copyright by the Estate of Frank Schoonmaker.

Charles Scribner's Sons: from *Of Time and the River* by Thomas Wolfe. Copyright 1935 Charles Scribner's Sons; copyright renewed © 1963 Paul Gitlin, Administrator C.T.A. From *The Sun Also Rises* by Ernest Hemingway. Copyright 1926 Charles Scribner's Sons. From "Champagne" in *Stories of Russian Life* by Anton Chekhov, translated by Marian Fell. Copyright 1914 Charles Scribner's Sons. From *The Masters* by C. P. Snow. Copyright 1951 by C. P. Snow. From *The Forsyte Saga* by John Galsworthy. Copyright 1918, 1920, 1921, 1922 by Charles Scribner's Sons. Copyright 1906 William Heinemann. Copyright 1918, 1920 by The International Magazine Co. From *Death in the Afternoon* by Ernest Hemingway. Copyright 1932 Charles Scribner's Sons. All reprinted by permission of Charles Scribner's Sons.

Sidgwick and Jackson Ltd.: from *The Wine of the Douro* by Hector Bolitho. Copyright © 1956 by Hector Bolitho. Reprinted by permission of Sidgwick and Jackson Ltd.

Simon & Schuster, Inc.: from *Zorba the Greek* by Nikos Kazantzakis, translated by Carl Wildman. Copyright 1952 by Simon & Schuster, Inc. From *Wine* by Hugh Johnson. Copyright © 1966, 1974 Hugh Johnson. From *The Final Days* by Bob Woodward and Carl Bernstein. Copyright © 1976 by Bob Woodward and Carl Bernstein. All reprinted by permission of Simon & Schuster, Inc.

The Society of Authors: from *Candida* by George Bernard Shaw. Reprinted by permission of The Society of Authors on behalf of the Bernard Shaw Estate.

Mrs. P. A. Spielman: "Red Wine" by Justin Richardson. Reprinted by permission of Mrs. P. A. Spielman, Literary Executor of Justin Richardson.

The University of Chicago Press: from *The Bacchae* by Euripedes, translated by William Arrowsmith, in *The Complete Greek Tragedies.* Copyright © 1959 The University of Chicago Press.

The Viking Press, Inc.: from *The Odes of Horace* translated by James Michie. Copyright © 1963 by James Michie. From *Travels in the South of France* by Stendhal, translated by Elisabeth Abbott. Copyright © 1970 by Elisabeth Abbott. Both reprinted by permission of Grossman Publishers. From "Grapes" in *The Complete Poems of D. H. Lawrence,* copyright © 1964, 1971 by Angelo Ravagli and C. M. Weekley, executors of the Estate of Frieda Lawrence Ravagli.

G. M. Watkins: "For a Wine Festival" by Vernon Watkins. Copyright © G. M. Watkins.

A. P. Watt & Son: from *The Prisoner in the Opal* by A. E. W. Mason. Reprinted by permission of Trinity College, Oxford and Hodder & Stoughton Ltd. From *The Vineyards of France* by J. M. Scott. Reprinted by permission of J. M. Scott. From *A*

Index of Authors

Campbell, I. M., 181, 245
Carew, Thomas, 91
Carroll, Lewis, 215
Cato, 298
Chaucer, Geoffrey, 169–170
Chekhov, Anton, 309–310
Chilman, Eric, 88–89
Chin P'ing Mei, 21
Clough, Arthur Hugh, 41
Colette, 249, 348
Columella, 81
Condon, Richard, 63–65, 245
Connolly, Cyril, 270–272
Cooper, Derek, 106, 300–302
Cooper, Duff, 21
Cowley, Abraham, 31–32, 87
Crabbe, George, 165
Crosby, Everett, 70–71, 80

Dahl, Roald, 421
Davis, William, 286–287
Defoe, Daniel, 57
De Quincey, Thomas, 171–173
Desbrow, L. W., 106–108
Dickens, Charles, 151–152, 333
Dickinson, Peter, 194, 231,
    315–316, 322
Disraeli, Benjamin, 289
Doran, John, 61, 291, 294–295
Druitt, Robert, 293–294, 313,
    326
Duerrenmatt, Friedrich, 214
d'Urfey, Tom, 88
Durrell, Lawrence, 227–228

Ellin, Stanley, 385
Ellmann, Richard, 235
Emerson, Ralph Waldo, 40
Etherege, Sir George, 92, 311
Eugenius, 169

Euripides, 36

Flagg, William J., 42, 278
Flanders, Michael, 191–193
Flower, Desmond, 272–273
Forbes, Patrick, 311
Ford, Ford Madox, 247, 252–
    254
Ford, Richard, 76, 259–260
Forrester, Joseph James, 53–54
Franklin, Benjamin, 219–220
Frayn, Michael, 119–120
Frazer, James G., 152

Galsworthy, John, 33, 187–188
Gittings, Robert, 222
Glover, C. Gordon, 104
Goodman, Ezra, 197
Greene, Gael, 28–30
Gronow, Rees Howell, 151,
    156, 316–318

Hamilton, Gerald, 339
Harris, Frank, 108–109
Hart, Liddell, 239
Hawthorne, Nathaniel, 75,
    201–204, 269–270
Healy, Maurice, 127–130, 180
Hemingway, Ernest, 25–26, 38,
    259, 308–309
Henderson, Alexander, 114–
    115, 167–168, 173, 241, 292
Henley, William Ernest, 41–42
Herbert, George, 167
Herrick, Robert, 69, 85
Holland, Vyvyan, 228–229,
    241–242, 289–290
Hollander, John, 208–209, 327
Homer, 69, 213, 265–266

Woodward, Bob, 199

Xenophon, 170

Young, B. A., 121–123, 248–249
Yüan Chen, 155